BUILDING KNOWLEDGE IN HIGHER EDUCATION

From pressures to become economically efficient to calls to act as an agent of progressive social change, higher education is facing a series of challenges. There is an urgent need for a rigorous and sophisticated research base to support the informed development of practices. Yet studies of educational practices in higher education remain theoretically underdeveloped and segmented by discipline and country. *Building Knowledge in Higher Education* illustrates how Legitimation Code Theory is bringing research together from across the disciplinary map and enabling practical change in a rigorously theorized way.

The volume addresses both students and educators. Part I explores ways of supporting student achievement from STEM to the arts, from introductory courses to doctoral training, and from using new digital media to reflective writing. Part II focuses on academic staff development in higher education, reaching from curriculum design to pedagogic practices. All chapters focus on issues of contemporary relevance to higher education, showing how Legitimation Code Theory enables these issues to be understood and practices improved.

Building Knowledge in Higher Education brings together internationally renowned scholars in higher education studies, academic development, academic literacies, and sociology, with some of the brightest new researchers. The volume significantly extends understandings of teaching and learning in changing higher education contexts and so contributes to educational research and practice. It will be essential reading not only to scholars and students in these fields but also to scholars and educators in higher education more generally.

Christine Winberg is a leading scholar in work-integrated learning, in which she holds a South African Research Chair.

Sioux McKenna is a renowned scholar in higher education studies.

Kirstin Wilmot is an emerging scholar in the field of doctoral education.

All three are associate members of the LCT Centre for Knowledge-Building.

Legitimation Code Theory
Knowledge-building in research and practice
Series editor: Karl Maton
LCT Centre for Knowledge-Building

This series comprises research and practice into knowledge-building in education and beyond. It focuses on Legitimation Code Theory or 'LCT', a cutting-edge approach rapidly being adopted by scholars and educators across the disciplinary map to understand, change and improve their practice. LCT builds on sociological ideas from Pierre Bourdieu and Basil Bernstein and integrates insights from such diverse fields as linguistics, philosophy, literary criticism, physics and anthropology. The framework reveals the otherwise hidden principles embodied by knowledge practices, their different forms, and their effects. By making these 'codes' visible to be learned or changed, work using LCT is making a real difference, from supporting social justice in education to improving design processes. Books in this series will focus on both cutting-edge developments in theory and research and developing new forms of educational practice. Books will explore topics across the institutional and disciplinary maps of education, from physics to ballet, from pre-school to university, as well as other social fields, such as politics and law.

Other volumes in this series include:

Accessing Academic Discourse
Systemic Functional Linguistic and Legitimation Code Theory
Edited by J. R. Martin, Karl Maton and Y. J. Doran

Studying Science
Knowledge, Language, Pedagogy
Edited by Karl Maton, J. R. Martin and Y. J. Doran

Turning Access into Success
Improving University Education with Legitimation Code Theory
Sherran Clarence

For a full list of titles in this series, please visit: www.routledge.com/Legitimation-Code-Theory/book-series/LMCT

BUILDING KNOWLEDGE IN HIGHER EDUCATION

Enhancing Teaching and Learning with Legitimation Code Theory

Edited by
Christine Winberg,
Sioux McKenna and
Kirstin Wilmot

LONDON AND NEW YORK

First published 2021
by Routledge
2 Park Square, Milton Park, Abingdon, Oxon OX14 4RN

and by Routledge
52 Vanderbilt Avenue, New York, NY 10017

Routledge is an imprint of the Taylor & Francis Group, an informa business

© 2021 selection and editorial matter, Christine Winberg, Sioux McKenna and Kirstin Wilmot; individual chapters, the contributors

The right of Christine Winberg, Sioux McKenna and Kirstin Wilmot to be identified as the authors of the editorial material, and of the authors for their individual chapters, has been asserted in accordance with sections 77 and 78 of the Copyright, Designs and Patents Act 1988.

All rights reserved. No part of this book may be reprinted or reproduced or utilized in any form or by any electronic, mechanical, or other means, now known or hereafter invented, including photocopying and recording, or in any information storage or retrieval system, without permission in writing from the publishers.

Trademark notice: Product or corporate names may be trademarks or registered trademarks, and are used only for identification and explanation without intent to infringe.

British Library Cataloguing-in-Publication Data
A catalogue record for this book is available from the British Library

Library of Congress Cataloging-in-Publication Data
Names: Winberg, Christine, editor. | McKenna, Sioux, editor. | Wilmot, Kirstin, editor.
Title: Building knowledge in higher education : enhancing teaching and learning with legitimation code theory / Edited by Christine Winberg, Sioux McKenna and Kirstin Wilmot.
Description: Abingdon, Oxon ; New York : Routledge, 2020. | Series: Legitmation code theory: knowledge-building in research and practice | Includes bibliographical references and index. | Summary: – Provided by publisher.
Identifiers: LCCN 2020008472 (print) | LCCN 2020008473 (ebook) | ISBN 9780367463328 (hardback) | ISBN 9780367463335 (paperback) | ISBN 9781003028215 (ebook)
Subjects: LCSH: Education, Higher–Aims and objectives. | Knowledge, Theory of. | College teaching.
Classification: LCC LB2322.2 .B85 2020 (print) | LCC LB2322.2 (ebook) | DDC 378/.01–dc23
LC record available at https://lccn.loc.gov/2020008472
LC ebook record available at https://lccn.loc.gov/2020008473

ISBN: 978-0-367-46332-8 (hbk)
ISBN: 978-0-367-46333-5 (pbk)
ISBN: 978-1-003-02821-5 (ebk)

Typeset in Bembo
by Wearset Ltd, Boldon, Tyne and Wear

CONTENTS

List of figures viii
List of tables xi
Notes on contributors xiii

1 'Nothing so practical as good theory': Legitimation Code
  Theory in higher education 1
  Christine Winberg, Sioux McKenna and Kirstin Wilmot

PART I
Student learning across the disciplinary map 17

2 Demystifying reflective writing in teacher education with
  semantic gravity 19
  Lucy Macnaught

3 Making waves in teacher education: scaffolding students'
  disciplinary understandings by 'doing' analysis 37
  Anna-Vera Meidell Sigsgaard

4 New assessment forms in higher education: a study of student
  generated digital media products in the health sciences 55
  Helen Georgiou and Wendy Nielsen

5 Misalignments in assessments: using Semantics to reveal
  weaknesses 76
  Ilse Rootman-le Grange and Margaret A.L. Blackie

6 Supporting the academic success of students through making knowledge-building visible 90
Lee Rusznyak

7 (Un)critical reflection: uncovering disciplinary values in Social Work and Business reflective writing assignments 105
Namala Tilakaratna and Eszter Szenes

8 Learning how to theorize in doctoral writing: a tool for teaching and learning 126
Kirstin Wilmot

PART II
Professional learning in higher education 143

9 Changing curriculum and teaching practice: a practical theory for academic staff development 145
Sherran Clarence and Martina van Heerden

10 A Semantics analysis of first-year physics teaching: developing students' use of representations in problem-solving 162
Honjiswa Conana, Delia Marshall and Jennifer Case

11 From principle to practice: enabling theory–practice bridging in engineering education 180
Karin Wolff

12 Building the knowledge base of blended learning: implications for educational technology and academic development 198
J.P. Bosman and Sonja Strydom

13 Legitimate participation in programme renewal: the role of academic development units 220
Gert Young and Cecilia Jacobs

14 Decolonizing the science curriculum: when good intentions are not enough 237
Hanelie Adendorff and Margaret A.L. Blackie

15 The role of assessment in preparing academic developers
   for professional practice   255
   Lynn Quinn

16 Academic development: autonomy pathways towards
   gaining legitimacy   272
   Jo-Anne Vorster

Index   290

FIGURES

1.1	The specialization plane	3
1.2	The semantic plane	5
1.3	Semantic profiles	6
1.4	The autonomy plane	8
2.1	Scaffolding strategies for teaching students how to identify and create shifts in the relative strength of semantic gravity	26
2.2	Framing the assessment task in relation to degrees of context-dependence	26
2.3	Text profiling	27
2.4	Exemplification of a full wave	28
2.5	A text annotation of a full wave	29
2.6	Sentences starters for signalling a shift in strength of semantic gravity	30
2.7	Relating assignment feedback to degrees of context-dependence	31
2.8	Planning relative shifts in degrees of context-dependence	32
3.1	Generic semantic wave	41
3.2	Students plotted their (different) versions of the semantic profile of a chosen KMP on the chalkboard for comparison	46
3.3	Generic profile identified by consensus	47
3.4	Three levels along the semantic gravity scale	48
3.5	Semantic profile corresponding with the analysed paragraph in Figure 3.5	49
3.6	Two groups' versions of a semantic profile for the same section of text from a successful KMP	50
4.1	Example image semantic density categories: Scientific complex image from MS (left), Scientific simple image from Malaria (right)	64

4.2	Relative strengths of semantic density per clause for Malaria and MS	65
4.3	Duration (as a proportion of total) of each type of image in Malaria and MS	66
4.4	Clause and image(s) present at Point A1 (Malaria text)	67
4.5	Clause and image(s) present at Point A2 (Malaria text)	68
4.6	Clause and image(s) present at Point A3 (Malaria text)	68
4.7	Images as part of a seven-clause sequence which builds up diagram of plasmodium processes (Malaria text)	69
4.8	Clause and image(s) present at Point B1 (MS text)	69
5.1	The semantic plane	79
5.2	Summary of analysis of the 83 questions with the two translation devices	86
6.1	Stars grouped as a cluster, then connected to form a constellation, to represent an image of Orion the Hunter (Southern Hemisphere view)	91
6.2	Images of the Orion Nebula and the Trapezium Open Star Cluster, taken by the Hubble Telescope	92
6.3	The constellation of Sagittarius depicted as a centaur (left) and in a competing constellation, as a teapot (right)	94
6.4	A representation of the epistemological constellations for understanding structure, diversity and agency in the Sociology course	98
6.5	Two of the competing constellations about King Shaka	101
6.6	Simplified representations of the opposing constellations of pre-colonized Africa and the impact of colonialism	102
7.1	An example of a negatively charged cluster	108
7.2	An example of a positively charged cluster in business	113
7.3	The construction of a positively charged constellation in Business Studies	113
7.4	A positively charged cluster of the social worker as powerful	117
7.5	A negatively charged cluster of the client	117
7.6	Oppositionally charged clusters in Social Work theory: 'social worker as powerful' and 'client as powerless'	118
7.7	Oppositionally charged clusters contrasting the student social worker with her client	119
7.8	A partial constellation of Social Work values	120
8.1	Strengths of semantic gravity informing the translation device	130
8.2	Generic semantic gravity profile	131
8.3	Semantic gravity profile of draft text	134
8.4	Semantic gravity profile of final text	138
9.1	A generic semantic wave	149
9.2	The semantic plane	150
9.3	Possible semantic wave across both courses	154

9.4	Plotting out feedback on the semantic plane	157
10.1	An illustration of the different representations needed to solve a Mechanics problem	165
10.2	Semantic profile of lecture in mainstream course	169
10.3	Semantic profile of lecture in foundation course	170
10.4	Pictorial representation – sketch of the problem scenario	171
10.5	Physical representation – force diagram of the problem scenario	172
10.6	Mathematical representation of problem scenario	173
10.7	Semantic profile of students tackling a task in the mainstream course	173
10.8	Semantic profile of students tackling a task in the foundation course	174
11.1	Annotated epistemic plane	185
11.2	Epistemic plane mapping of the AD case studies	187
11.3	Engineering problem-solving in the Oil & Gas sector	188
11.4	Group A1 Unit conversion code shifting	190
11.5	Lecturer A2 supporting Programming learning using the epistemic plane	191
11.6	Lecturer B1 Mathematical code shifting	193
11.7	Group B2 discussion on curriculum purpose	195
12.1	The specialization plane	202
12.2	All voices: The specialization plane for the knowledge base of blended learning from the perspective of all teachers' voices analysed as a unit	211
12.3	Voice A, B and C: Specialization planes for the knowledge base of blended learning when analysed separately for three main teaching voices	211
13.1	The specialization plane	227
14.1	The specialization plane	239
14.2	The autonomy plane	244
14.3	The autonomy plane: decolonizing science	247
14.4	Additional autonomy codes in decolonizing science	250
14.5	Winberg and Winberg's (2017) scenarios for decolonizing Engineering represented on the autonomy plane	251
15.1	Illustrative semantic profiles and semantic ranges	258
15.2	Semantic gravity scale for assessments	260
16.1	The autonomy plane	275

TABLES

4.1	Characteristics of three 'case' texts, with comparisons to wider sample	59
4.2	Characterization of two sample texts, including profiles (of resources used) and screenshots	61
4.3	Annotation and coding for wording type and subtype	62
4.4	Coded excerpts for each sample with annotation	63
4.5	Image categorization with semantic density (SD)	65
4.6	Assessment criteria for Malaria and MS 'principles of pharmacology' task (relevant criteria italicized)	71
5.1	Translation device for semantic gravity analysis of introductory Chemistry test paper	83
5.2	Translation device for semantic density analysis of introductory Chemistry test paper	85
7.1	An example of positive evaluation	111
7.2	A repeated pattern of positive evaluation of Australian values	112
7.3	A pattern of positive charging of the professional social worker	116
7.4	A pattern of negative charging of the client	117
7.5	A pattern of negative charging of the client's power	119
8.1	Coding key for analysis	132
10.1	Semantic gravity and semantic density in relation to representations in mechanics problem-solving	167
12.1	Broad themes/concepts from the data with ER or SR affinities	204
12.2	External language of description for epistemic relations	206
12.3	External language of description for social relations	208
12.4	Blended learning: translation device for specialization codes (ER+/−, SR+/−)	209
12.5	Quotes from the data that show examples of each of the four specialization codes	210

12.6	Percentages of the different specialization codes in terms of facilitator voices	210
12.7	Examples from the data indicating the code matches and clashes between Voices A, B and C	212
13.1	Translation device	226
14.1	Translation device for decolonizing science	245
16.1	Translation device that guided analysis of data	279

CONTRIBUTORS

Hanelie Adendorff is a Senior Advisor in the Centre for Teaching and Learning at Stellenbosch University. She has a PhD in Chemistry, but has been working in Professional Development since 2002. Her career in Professional Development started with an interest in blended learning, but has since included work in the areas of assessment, facilitation of collaborative learning, natural scientists' struggles with access to SoTL type work, and more recently the decolonization of science. As a member of the Science Faculty's teaching and learning hub, she works with the Vice-Dean (Teaching and Learning) to enhance the status of teaching in the Faculty.

Margaret A.L. Blackie is a Senior Lecturer in the Department of Chemistry and Polymer Science at Stellenbosch University. She has research interests in synthetic chemistry, science education and spirituality. Her major interest in science education is the development of the human person through science curricula. She uses LCT to critique and improve the teaching of chemistry at tertiary level.

J.P. Bosman is Director of the Centre for Learning Technologies (CLT) at Stellenbosch University, South Africa. He trained and taught in the field of Theology before becoming involved in academic development work. After working at the Centre for Teaching and Learning as well as a start-up educational software company, he became head and later Director of the CLT, which spearheads and supports strategies for the use of ICT in Learning and Teaching. His research interests are around blended and hybrid learning, m-learning literacy and graduate attributes. He currently lives in Cape Town with his wife and two children.

Jennifer Case is Professor and Head of the Department of Engineering Education at Virginia Tech in the USA. Prior to her appointment in this post she was a Professor in the Department of Chemical Engineering at the University of

Cape Town, where she retains an honorary appointment. She completed postgraduate studies in the UK, Australia and South Africa. Having done more than two decades of undergraduate teaching and curriculum reform work, she is also a renowned researcher in engineering education and higher education. Her work on the student experience of learning as well as on teaching and curriculum has been widely published. She was the founding president of the South African Society for Engineering Education (SASEE). She is a coordinating editor for the international journal *Higher Education* and a co-editor for the Routledge/SRHE series Research into Higher Education.

Sherran Clarence is an Honorary Research Associate in the Centre for Postgraduate Studies at Rhodes University. She was previously the coordinator of the Writing Centre at the University of the Western Cape, where she focused on tutor development, academic writing development with students and staff, and pedagogy in the disciplines. Her practical work revolves around academic writing at postgraduate and postdoctoral level, and developing theorized practical approaches to helping students make sense of the 'rules of the game' to produce more successful written texts. Her research looks at how teaching and learning, and student success, can be enhanced through theorizing pedagogic practice using the work of Basil Bernstein, Academic Literacies theory, and Legitimation Code Theory.

Honjiswa Conana is a Teaching and Learning Specialist in the Faculty of Natural Sciences at the University of the Western Cape. Her role is to support teaching and learning initiatives in the Faculty. Her research interests lie in physics education and academic literacies.

Helen Georgiou is a Lecturer of Science Education at the University of Wollongong. She holds an undergraduate degree in physics and a Diploma of Education, previously working as a high school physics teacher. Her PhD was awarded by The University of Sydney and focused on Physics Education, specifically, students' understanding of thermodynamics. Her research aims to understand the issues in science education, including students' conceptual difficulties, through studying the literacy practices and social aspects of the discipline. She is currently studying students' multimodal representations of scientific knowledge using Legitimation Code Theory.

Cecilia Jacobs is an Associate Professor in Higher Education at the Centre for Health Professions Education at the University of Stellenbosch. Prior to that she was the director of the Centre for Teaching and Learning at the University of Stellenbosch. Her field of expertise is Higher Education Studies, and she has worked predominantly in the area of the professionalization of academics for their teaching role. Her work has been of a transdisciplinary nature and she has always conducted research at the intersection of her field and other disciplines, such as Engineering and Health Sciences. Her research interests are in disciplinary literacies and how knowledge is communicated through discipline-specific language. Her current research focuses on the question of knowledge and the importance of its centrality in debates on higher education teaching and learning.

Lucy Macnaught is a Learning Advisor for academic writing development at Auckland University of Technology. She collaborates with the Graduate Research School and faculty staff to integrate and teach academic literacies across undergraduate and postgraduate programmes. Her research projects, including completed doctoral studies, focus on the development of theory and its repurposing for pedagogic purposes. Key research interests include academic literacy, classroom discourse, and the use of metalanguage in teaching practices. She is currently undertaking User Experience research to investigate how students interact with online resources for academic writing development.

Delia Marshall is a Professor in the Physics Department at the University of the Western Cape. She researches physics education, higher education and academic development. She teaches in the undergraduate programme in Physics and has also played a key role in the design and delivery of the extended programme.

Sioux McKenna is a Professor in Higher Education in the Centre for Higher Education Research, Teaching and Learning and is the Director of the Centre for Postgraduate Studies at Rhodes University. Her research reflects a concern with who gets access to higher education and how the norms and values of universities and their disciplines emerge as literacy practices. She is the project manager of a number of international projects and has supervised a variety of postgraduate studies, many of which have used Legitimation Code Theory to ask questions about the form and function of higher education.

Anna-Vera Meidell Sigsgaard is an Associate Professor in Danish as a Second Language in the Department of Education at the University College of Copenhagen, Denmark. She teaches pre- and in-service teachers in the areas of second language education, literacy development, and language teaching pedagogy. She also teachers courses in academic writing for non-native English PhD students. Her research interests include exploring connections between language, knowledge and teaching/learning, as well as developing language-based (second language education) pedagogy in mainstream classes. Her work has drawn on elements from both Legitimation Code Theory and systemic functional linguistics in order to support student teachers in writing academic texts, while exploring how analytical tools from both these theoretical frameworks complement each other in an academic writing context.

Wendy Nielsen is an Associate Professor of Science Education in the School of Education at the University of Wollongong. Her undergraduate work was in biology and she was a high school science and mathematics teacher for many years before undertaking Masters and PhD work at the University of British Columbia in Canada. Her research interests revolve around pre-service teacher education and conceptual understanding in science. Current work is investigating the quality of learning as university science students generate digital explanations.

Lynn Quinn is an Associate Professor in the Centre for Higher Education Research, Teaching and Learning at Rhodes University. She has been involved in the field of academic development since 1995. She was integral to the development of a Postgraduate Diploma in Higher Education for lecturers and for academic developers. Her research interests include academic staff development and developers, curriculum, assessment, and quality. She supervises higher education studies doctoral and master's students.

Ilse Rootman-le Grange is an Instructional Designer in the Faculty of Science at Stellenbosch University, where she supports Science lecturers in developing teaching practices with a focus on learning technologies. She has a PhD in Chemistry and previously held a position as Chemistry lecturer at this same institution. Her research in undergraduate science education focuses on modes of teaching, mitigating the articulation gap, and the role of multidisciplinary collaborations in science education. She also has a keen interest in the professional development of undergraduate Science lecturers.

Lee Rusznyak is an Associate Professor at the School of Education, University of the Witwatersrand, South Africa. Her research draws on LCT to analyse knowledge-building in teaching, learning, and teacher education. She has published widely on topics including assessing teacher knowledge, pre-service teacher education, the teaching practicum, and understanding the grounds of teacher professionalism. She is a forum member of the UNESCO Chair in Teacher Education for Diversity and Development.

Sonja Strydom is a Senior Academic Developer at the Centre for Learning Technologies at Stellenbosch University, where she is also a research fellow at the Centre for Higher and Adult Education. She recently completed a second PhD in Education focusing on the underlying structural and agentic factors associated with higher education technology-enhanced curriculum development. Her research interests include psychological aspects associated with technology integration, multi-method research methodologies in the field of educational technology, and digital wellness.

Eszter Szenes is a post-doctoral researcher at the Research Collegium for Language in Changing Society (RECLAS), Department of Language and Communication Studies at the University of Jyväskylä in Finland. Prior to this, she was based at The University of Sydney, where she worked in the Department of Linguistics, the Business School and the Learning Centre. Eszter completed her PhD at the University of Sydney. Her work (both research and pedagogical) primarily draws on the theoretical foundations and methodologies of Systemic Functional Linguistics and Legitimation Code Theory in the sociology of education. Her research interests include disciplinary and professional literacy development, the knowledge practices of critical reflection, and radicalization and far-right extremism.

Namala Tilakaratna is a Lecturer at the Centre for English Language Communication, National University of Singapore (NUS). Her PhD thesis in linguistics was awarded at the University of Sydney. Her research interests include national identity formation and academic literacy drawing on Systemic Functional Linguistics and Legitimation Code Theory. She is the principal investigator of an interdisciplinary project on clinical nursing practice and critical reflection, in collaboration with the Alice Lee Centre for Nursing Studies, funded by an NUS Teaching Enhancement Grant.

Martina van Heerden is a Lecturer and Tutor in the English for Educational Development Programme at the University of the Western Cape. Her research interests include feedback and academic development. She completed her PhD, titled *What lies beneath tutors' feedback? Examining the role of feedback in developing 'knowers' in English Studies*, in 2018 and still isn't quite used to being called 'Doctor'. She is currently working on a research project with tutors in English Studies, extending her PhD work. When not teaching, she enjoys playing videogames, cross-stitching, and reading.

Jo-Anne Vorster is Associate Professor and Head of the Centre for Higher Education Research, Teaching and Learning (CHERTL) at Rhodes University. She has worked in the field of academic development since 1993. With colleague, Lynn Quinn, she has designed and facilitated the first formal programme for inducting academic developers into the field. Her research interests include knowledge, curricula, and pedagogies in academic staff development programmes and for advancing the field of academic development.

Kirstin Wilmot is a lecturer in the Centre for Higher Education Research, Teaching and Learning (CHERTL) at Rhodes University. She received her PhD, *Enacting knowledge in dissertations: An exploratory analysis of doctoral writing using Legitimation Code Theory* in 2019 from the LCT Centre for Knowledge-Building, University of Sydney, under the supervision of Professor Karl Maton. She is passionate about research related to academic writing, particularly doctoral writing, doctoral supervision, and disciplinary literacy practices. Her research is aimed at finding ways to make elusive academic literacy practices explicit and demonstrable to a greater number of students.

Christine Winberg holds the South African National Research Foundation Chair in Work-integrated Learning and leads the Professional Education Research Institute at the Cape Peninsula University of Technology in Cape Town, South Africa.

Her research focus is professional and vocational education (with a particular focus on engineering education), the professional development of university teachers, and technical communication.

Karin Wolff has worked in Higher Education teaching, curriculum, learning support, staff development, and research at four South African universities. Her doctoral research looked at the relationship between engineering disciplinary theory and practice in complex industrial problem-solving. She draws on social realism, notably Legitimation Code Theory's epistemic relations, to improve theory–practice bridging in professional engineering education. She has been a collaborator on a number of education capacity development projects. She is currently leading the establishment of the STADIO Multiversity engineering faculty, and is senior education advisor and researcher to Stellenbosch University's engineering faculty.

Gert Young is a Senior Advisor in Higher Education in the Centre for Teaching and Learning at Stellenbosch University. His work in academic development focuses on the professionalization of the teaching role in higher education and the strategic advancement of teaching in the commercial sciences. This work is advanced through a research interest in the role of professional identities in teaching and learning, specifically as defined by Social Identity Theory. He holds a PhD in Political Science and researches both the fields of academic development and political science.

1
'NOTHING SO PRACTICAL AS GOOD THEORY'

Legitimation Code Theory in higher education

Christine Winberg, Sioux McKenna and Kirstin Wilmot

Introduction to higher education studies

The earliest universities served the dual aims of knowledge production and social reproduction. They ensured that an elite group were inducted into their roles at the apex of society's stratification and they were spaces for knowledge to be advanced and disseminated within this group. The aims of higher education institutions have become far more complex over a number of centuries, and the pace of complexity has accelerated exponentially since the last decades of the twentieth century with no signs of slowing. The early aims of social reproduction and knowledge production have been dramatically reframed in this era of supercomplexity. Widening participation in higher education has shaken the social reproduction aim and the emergence of the knowledge economy has shifted the ways in which knowledge is produced and disseminated.

As universities have broadened access beyond the elite, so the approach to teaching and to what gets taught has changed. The purpose of higher education has increasingly come to be the preparation of young people across society to take on highly skilled positions in industry. As Trow (1973) points out, massification is about much more than having to accommodate greater numbers in the system, it is about changing the basic nature of the institution. Many of the assumptions underpinning the more homogenous predecessors to the modern university have proven problematic when the student body brings with it a varied spectrum of languages, literacy practices, cultures, beliefs, values, prior education experiences, and so on. The inability of universities to adjust to such variation is most evident in the strong correlation between social class and student success across the world (Mettler, 2014; Case, Marshall, McKenna and Mogashana, 2018). Despite claims of being a meritocracy whereby it is on the basis of individual intelligence, skills and work ethic that students fail or succeed, universities often continue to play their earlier role of social reproduction. This has become a central concern for those who see the modern university as a space for social justice.

The notion that knowledge drives the economy has meant that a university education is highly desirable as a means of both individual social mobility and national economic growth. Technological advances and breakthroughs in multiple fields have led to rapid changes in curricula. Alongside these changes in content have come changes in understandings as to the role of the university, with demands that our institutions become more efficient and be more closely managed towards this end. This has led to the emergence of the administrative university where the collation of metrics occupies a great deal of time alongside the other practices expected of institutions.

Within this context, it is unsurprising that there has been an enormous growth in the field of higher education studies. Academics and postgraduate students have developed research projects and published thousands of articles looking at who gets access to higher education and who gets to succeed within it (Harland, 2009; Tight, 2014). Much of this research has a strong ideological intention and often focuses on classroom practice and assessment; however, it often lacks strong theory (Clegg, 2009a, 2009b; Shay, 2012) which makes it susceptible to common-sense conclusions underpinned by unexplored assumptions (Hlengwa, McKenna and Njovane, 2018; Boughey and McKenna, 2016). Furthermore, it has been noted that the concern with how higher education often serves to reproduce social inequalities rather than dismantle them has led to a curious blind spot in much of the research – that of knowledge itself. In looking at how curricula are structured and what happens in our lecture theatres, many studies have failed to consider how it is that certain knowledges are legitimated and others are not, and how it is that each discipline structures its knowledge and determines the kind of knowers who are deemed worthy of disciplinary membership.

This book brings together a rich collection of studies that uses a common framework, Legitimation Code Theory, to attend to these concerns about higher education studies. The framework acts as conceptual lenses, analytical tools and as teaching resources to open conversations about how it is we come to know and what it is that is deemed worth knowing.

An introduction to Legitimation Code Theory

Legitimation Code Theory or 'LCT' is a sociological framework motivated by issues of social justice and knowledge-building. It was developed from the late 1990s by Karl Maton and builds primarily on the sociological frameworks of Pierre Bourdieu and Basil Bernstein, as well as critical realist and critical rationalist philosophies (see Maton, 2014, 2018). The framework is multi-dimensional, offering a variety of concepts and tools to analyse practices. Three of these dimensions – Specialization, Semantics and Autonomy – are pertinent to this book. Each dimension explores a set of organizing principles of dispositions, practices and fields, conceptualized in LCT as different species of *legitimation codes*. An analysis of legitimation codes explores 'what is possible for whom, when, where and how, and who is able to define these possibilities, when, where and how' (Maton, 2014, p. 18).

LCT is increasingly being used as a primary framework to analyse the legitimation codes that enable or constrain knowledge-building in education contexts. In this sense it is able to reveal the 'rules of the game' by making the basis of success of any practice explicit. This has major implications for social justice in higher education, as these 'rules' can then be taught and learned more explicitly and they can be challenged and changed. This section provides a brief introduction to the LCT concepts used in this volume. For a fuller explanation of the framework and concepts, see Maton (2014, 2016a, 2016b, 2020) and Maton and Howard (2018).

Specialization

Specialization explores the basis of achievement underlying practices, dispositions and contexts (Maton, 2016a, p. 13). It begins from the simple premise that all practices are about or oriented towards something and by someone. One can, therefore, analytically distinguish: *epistemic relations* between practices and their object (that part of the world towards which they are oriented); and *social relations* between practices and their subject (who or what is enacting the practices). For knowledge claims, these are realized as: *epistemic relations* between knowledge and its proclaimed objects of study; and *social relations* between knowledge and its authors, actors or subjects. These relations highlight questions of: *what* can be legitimately described as knowledge (epistemic relations); and *who* can claim to be a legitimate knower (social relations).

Practices will always have *both* epistemic relations *and* social relations – there are always knowledge and knowers. Each of these relations may be more strongly (+) or weakly (−) emphasized and the two strengths together generate *specialization codes* (ER+/−, SR+/−). As shown in Figure 1.1, these strengths are visualized on the *specialization plane*, a topological space of infinite positions but with four principal modalities:

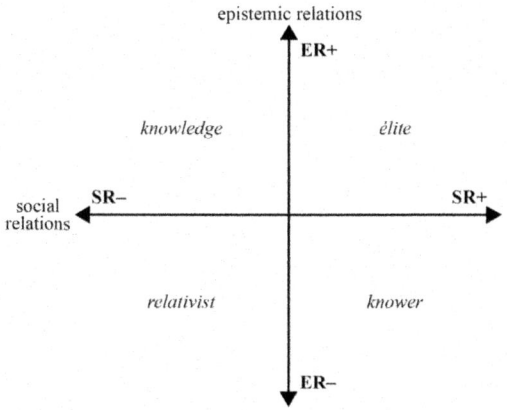

FIGURE 1.1 The specialization plane

Source: Maton, 2014, p. 30

- *knowledge codes* (ER+, SR−), where possession of specialized knowledges, principles or procedures concerning specific objects of study is emphasized as the basis of achievement, and the attributes of actors are downplayed;
- *knower codes* (ER−, SR+), where specialized knowledge and objects are downplayed and the attributes of actors are emphasized as measures of achievement, whether viewed as born (e.g. 'natural talent'), cultivated (e.g. 'taste') or social (e.g. feminist standpoint theory);
- *élite codes* (ER+, SR+), where legitimacy is based on both possessing specialist knowledge and being the right kind of knower; and
- *relativist codes* (ER−, SR−), where legitimacy is determined by neither specialist knowledge nor knower attributes – 'anything goes'.

In brief, knowledge codes emphasize what you know, knower codes emphasize the kind of knower you are, élite codes emphasize both what you know and who you are, and relativist codes emphasize neither (Maton, 2016a, p. 13). One specific kind of code can come to dominate as the basis of achievement or codes can shift over time. Analysing specialization codes is useful because they are not always transparent and universal and they are often contested. They also frequently result in 'code matches' and 'code clashes' in practices. A 'code match' is when two sets of practices or actors share the same basis of success and thus work harmoniously together towards shared goals. A 'code clash' occurs when conflicting codes work against each other (Maton 2016a, p. 13). Chapter 13 (this volume), for example, uses specialization codes to look at programme renewals in a South African university context. The authors show how programme renewal is conceptualized by academic staff in terms of both epistemic relations which distinguish between different specialized knowledges (e.g. disciplinary content, curriculum design etc.) underpinning the practice of programme renewal in universities, and in terms of social relations between the different dispositions of actors (e.g. personal experience, attitude) involved in the renewal process. This enables the authors to analyse competing claims to legitimacy in this context.

Semantics

Semantics explores the context-dependence and complexity of practices (Maton, 2016a, 2020). The central code concepts in Semantics are *semantic gravity* and *semantic density*. Semantic gravity (SG) refers to the degree to which meaning relates to a context: the stronger the semantic gravity, the more context-dependent meanings and practices; the weaker the semantic gravity, the more context-independent the meanings and practices. Semantic density (SD) relates to complexity of meanings. The stronger the semantic density, the more complex the meanings – typically as a result of condensing many meanings into instances of practice. The weaker the semantic density, the less complex meanings. When varying strengths of semantic gravity and semantic density are combined on a *semantic plane*, four principal *semantic codes* are generated. These are illustrated in Figure 1.2.

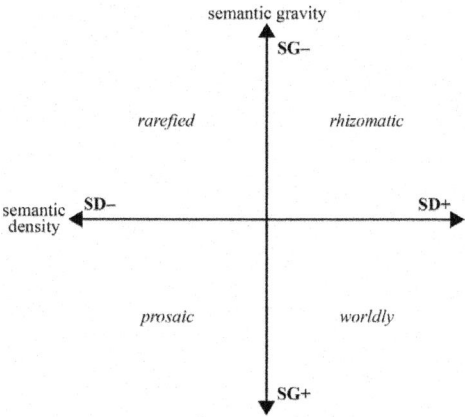

FIGURE 1.2 The semantic plane
Source: Maton, 2014, p. 131

Maton (2016a, p. 16) summarizes these principal modalities as follows:

- *rhizomatic codes* (SG−, SD+), where the basis of achievement comprises relatively context-independent and complex stances;
- *prosaic codes* (SG+, SD−), where legitimacy accrues to relatively context-dependent and simpler stances;
- *rarefied codes* (SG−, SD−), where legitimacy is based on relatively context-independent stances that condense fewer meanings; and
- *worldly codes* (SG+, SD+), where legitimacy is accorded to relatively context-dependent stances that condense manifold meanings.

Semantic codes complement specialization codes in that they illuminate a further set of organizing principles of practices. Once these codes have been revealed through analysis, changes in knowledge practices can be mapped using *semantic profiles* (see Figure 1.3). Profiling is a useful analytical tool because it is able to show shifts in practices over time.

Mapping semantic codes over time allows for different profiles to be revealed. Educational research (see Maton 2020) has shown that flat-lines (either high flat-lines such as profile A, or low flat-lines such as profile B) limit the potential for knowledge-building as the knowledge enacted is confined to a relatively small range of semantic gravity and semantic density. In contrast, the formation of *semantic waves*, as illustrated in profile C, has been shown to be one tool for cumulative knowledge-building in classrooms in that it enables a greater semantic range for students and teachers to draw on (e.g. Clarence, 2016; Wolff and Luckett, 2013). The specific shape of a wave is not important here; rather, the ability to traverse the full semantic range is what is key. Chapter 15 (this volume) for example, uses Semantics to analyse assessment portfolios from a postgraduate diploma in higher

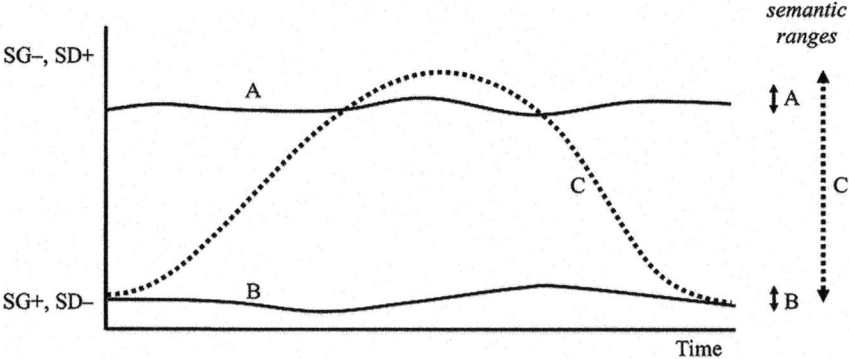

FIGURE 1.3 Semantic profiles
Source: Maton, 2014, p. 143

education for academic developers. The author uses the concepts of semantic gravity and semantic density to show how successful portfolios are able to traverse the full range of the semantic scale in their practices. This is shown to enable students to engage with complex theoretical concepts to formulate solutions for the challenges they confront in their everyday practice as academic developers.

Cosmologies

A *cosmology* is 'the logic of the belief system or vision of the world embodied by activities within a social field' (Maton, 2014, p. 152). Cosmologies provide the constitutive features of social fields that underlie the ways actors and practices are differentially characterized and valued – i.e. all fields have specific worldviews, logic or belief systems that legitimize particular ways of being and doing (Maton, 2014, p. 152). LCT analytically distinguishes between two principal dimensions in cosmological analyses: internal relations within practices and external relations of practices. Internal relations involve processes of *clustering* and *constellating*, while external relations involve processes of *condensing* and *charging*.

In terms of internal relations, *clustering* involves the grouping of ideas, practices, beliefs and attributes through their association with similar stances, and in contrast to other stances. These clusters of stances come to form relatively weakly or strongly bound *constellations* over time, distinguishable from other constellations in the field. How they are arranged (i.e. which stances get included and which are excluded), as well as how strongly or weakly they are bound from other constellations, varies according to different actors involved. These arrangements and boundaries can also shift and change over time and are often the site of struggles for legitimacy (Maton, 2014, p. 152).

External relations involve processes whereby cosmologies come to imbue whole constellations with meaning through *condensation* and *charging*. *Condensation* is a process whereby the *semantic density* (see Semantics, above) of stances is increased by adding meanings. Drawing on Specialization, Maton (2014, p. 153) explains how this can take different forms, including:

- *epistemological condensation*, where the condensing of meanings (from other concepts or empirical referents) emphasizes epistemic relations; and
- *axiological condensation*, where the condensing of meanings (from affective, aesthetic, ethical, political and moral stances) emphasizes social relations.

However, given the relational nature of LCT, it is possible for both kinds of condensation to occur in practices, as well as for neither to occur. The two types of condensation can also occur at infinite gradations along the spectrum. Once condensation has occurred, meanings can also be *charged* in varying ways, such as being portrayed relatively positively, neutrally or negatively in comparison to other meanings (Maton, 2014, p. 153).

Chapter 7 (this volume) uses these concepts to show the basis of achievement in high-achieving Business and Social Work assignments. In particular, the authors reveal how academic disciplines form constellations of meanings that are then condensed with particular axiological meanings and various kinds of charging. In effect, disciplines come to legitimate a 'right' kind of value system. Through their analysis the authors show how students are required to align with and reflect the 'right' kind of value system in their writing in order to achieve success.

Autonomy

The dimension of Autonomy begins from the simple premise that 'any set of practices comprises constituents that are related together in particular ways' (Maton and Howard, 2018, p. 6). These different constituents can take many different forms – for example, they can be actors, ideas, artefacts, institutions, body movements and so forth. They way in which they are related together may also take many different forms; for example, constituents can be related through explicit procedures, tacit conventions, explicitly stated aims, unstated orthodoxies, and so forth (Maton and Howard, 2018, p. 6). *Autonomy codes* therefore distinguish between and analyse the boundaries that practices create around their constituents and how these constituents are related together through the concepts of *positional autonomy* and *relational autonomy*. Maton and Howard (2018, p. 6) define these concepts as follows:

- *positional autonomy* (PA) between constituents positioned within a context or category and those positioned in other contexts or categories; and
- *relational autonomy* (RA) between relations among constituents of a context or category and relations among constituents of other contexts or categories.

As with the other tools in LCT, these concepts can be strengthened and weakened along a continuum and can be represented on an autonomy plane, illustrated in Figure 1.4.

8 Christine Winberg *et al.*

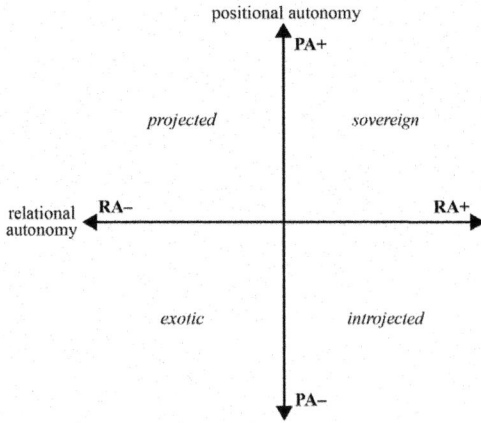

FIGURE 1.4 The autonomy plane
Source: Maton and Howard, 2018, p. 6

While the relative strengths of positional autonomy (PA) and relational autonomy (RA) have indefinite gradations along the continuum, when combined on the autonomy plane, four principal autonomy codes are revealed. Maton and Howard (in press, 2021) describe these as:

- *sovereign codes* (PA+, RA+) of strongly insulated positions and autonomous principles, where constituents are associated with the context or category and act according to its specific ways of working;
- *exotic codes* (PA−, RA−) of weakly insulated positions and heteronomous principles, where constituents are associated with other contexts or categories and act according to ways of working from other contexts or categories;
- *introjected codes* (PA−, RA+) of weakly insulated positions and autonomous principles, where constituents associated with other contexts or categories are oriented towards ways of working emanating from within the specific context or category; and
- *projected codes* (PA+, RA−) of strongly insulated positions and heteronomous principles, where constituents associated with the specific context or category are oriented towards ways of working from elsewhere.

In simple (hypothetical) terms, consider a teacher whose target is to teach her secondary school students about political revolutions in history and who draws on YouTube videos in her teaching. If she uses a video designed for the purpose of teaching revolutions to secondary school learners to teach her students about revolutions, she is working within a *sovereign code* (target content for target purposes). If the teacher uses a video of, say, the movie *Doctor Zhivago* to teach her class about revolutions, she is operating in an *introjected code* (non-target content for target purposes). If the teacher shows her class the first video in order to teach the students about kinds of music played in videos, she would be operating within a *projected code* (target content for non-target purposes). Lastly, if she showed her students the movie *The Lion King* for their entertainment, she would be operating within an *exotic code* (non-target content for non-target purposes).

Changes over time in practices can also be captured through an analysis of *autonomy pathways* or movements between different codes. Maton and Howard (2018, p. 8) highlight several key pathways:

- *stays* – practices that remain within one code;
- *return trips* – practices that move back and forth between two codes;
- *one-way trips* – practices that begin in one code and conclude in a second code; and
- *tours* – practices that begin in one code, move through one or more codes, and return to where they began.

Each of these pathways have important effects on the ability to integrate different forms of knowledge. They also enable examination of the different roles actors adopt and how this can have positive or negative effects on practices and identities. Chapter 16 (this volume), for example, uses Autonomy to analyse how academic staff developers at higher education institutions are assigned varying degrees of status depending on how their role is perceived by fellow academic staff, and the effect this has on their scholarly identity.

Having briefly overviewed the main LCT tools used by the authors of the chapters in this book, in the next sub-section we introduce the structure and content of the chapters, as well as the LCT tools used in different higher education contexts.

Introduction to 'building knowledge in higher education'

The chapters in this volume address two key issues in higher education studies, firstly the issue of supporting student learning towards academic success, and secondly, the issue of supporting academic staff engaged in professional learning to develop new ways of teaching and assessing their students. In Part I 'Student Learning across the Disciplinary Map', the authors explore ways of understanding and supporting student achievement across different disciplinary contexts – from STEM disciplines and fields to the Arts and Humanities – and at different levels – from introductory higher education courses to doctoral-level studies. Part II, 'Professional Learning in Higher Education', takes an in-depth look at academic staff development in higher education. Each chapter in the book focuses on pertinent issues in higher education practice, from how to support an increasingly diverse student body, to how to support university teachers in contexts of rapid change and growth. While there is some overlap across Parts I and II, in Part I, the authors show how a number of key challenges in higher education teaching, learning and assessment were addressed through the appropriate use of LCT tools. From teaching students to become reflective practitioners in professional programmes, to helping first years develop key disciplinary concepts and practices, the authors draw on a range of LCT tools for teaching and assessing students, as well as for interrogating their own practices as university teachers.

An underlying assumption in professional degrees is that engagement with theory will inform and improve students' future professional practice, consequently 'reflection' as a pedagogy towards enhancing professional knowledge has become a mainstay of many professional education programmes. Assessment tasks typically expect students to connect concrete events and personal experiences to theoretical concepts, and thus demonstrate their understanding of professional practice. In Chapter 2, Lucy Macnaught draws on *semantic gravity* (context-dependence) to show variance in academic reflection and to interrogate the principles informing teaching and learning materials intended to promote such reflection. She finds that there is little explicit guidance for students on the processes of reflection, because university teachers tend to assume that students can connect theory and practice. Drawing on the idea of the semantic gravity 'wave' (moves between context-dependence and context-independence across a programme of learning), Macnaught reveals a productive approach for teaching students how they might connect theory and practice in different ways.

In Chapter 3 Anna-Vera Meidell Sigsgaard's focus is bilingual students' understanding of theoretical and practical knowledge in assessment tasks, and how students can be supported in developing strategies towards achieving shifts between the practical and the theoretical. Meidell Sigsgaard uses both *semantic gravity* (contextual-dependence) and *semantic density* (complexity) to uncover, and make explicit, the basis of achievement in a high-stakes assessment task. The chapter reveals how gradual shifts between context-dependent, simpler meanings towards abstracted, more complex meanings, can help scaffold students' understanding of the course content, while preparing them for a final assessment.

In Chapter 4 Helen Georgiou and Wendy Nielsen draw on *semantic density* to explore the complexity of digital artefacts and the challenges they pose for professional communication. Communicating important health information to a lay public, and the public communication of science more generally, has entered many STEM-based professional programmes. Georgiou and Nielsen ask how students might be supported in an assessment task that draws on a wide variety of digital media to help students develop competence in the public communication of health information. Georgiou and Nielsen develop what is called in LCT 'a translation device' or means for explicitly showing the ways in which a concept is realized within data (Maton and Chen 2016; Maton 2016b). Using their translation device, they show how communicating health information to the general public needs to achieve an appropriate level of semantic density for accuracy, while too high a level of semantic density would not be understood by the lay public. This is highly relevant to all professional communication courses.

With Chapter 5 we move to the pure sciences, in this case an introductory Chemistry course. Ilse Rootman-le Grange and Margaret A.L. Blackie draw on *semantic gravity* and *semantic density* to reveal whether teachers are in fact assessing what they think they are assessing. Their analysis shows how an introductory course that strengthened its semantic gravity in order to make Chemistry accessible to students, also made it possible for students to pass the course without having developed the ability to abstract the principles of their chemistry embedded context to apply it in other related contexts. The authors propose ways of developing chemistry assessments in support of more effective cumulative learning to prepare students for university Chemistry studies.

In Chapter 6 Lee Rusznyak draws on *constellations* to show how students with very different kinds of prior knowledge pose challenges to university teachers who might make assumptions about their existing knowledge. Rusznyak finds that in using the concept of constellations, she is able to understand differences in her students' initial understandings of core concepts. When students encountered unfamiliar concepts, their understanding was tentative, but when students were already familiar with the subject, their conceptions tended to be more bounded and stable. Rusznyak thus argues that when students hold potentially constraining ideas, a process of making these preconceptions explicit is necessary before effective learning can happen.

In Chapter 7 Namala Tilakaratna and Eszter Szenes return to the role of reflection in professional writing and the assumptions that are made about the teaching of reflection. While Macnaught and Meidell Sigsgaard drew on Semantics to propose a pedagogy for academic reflection, Tilakaratna and Szenes draw on *axiological cosmologies* to unpack the hidden assumptions and values embedded in reflective writing assignments. Like Rusznyak, they use *constellations*, but to explore how various ideas and practices cluster around implicit values in high-achieving reflective essays and journals. By making these constellations visible, Tilakaratna and Szenes reveal how successful students reflect the values privileged by their professions.

In Chapter 8 Kirstin Wilmot examines doctoral writing, drawing on a translation device for semantic gravity to unpack the process of writing a doctoral thesis. Specifically, the chapter focuses on how empirical data and theoretical concepts are woven together in thesis writing. Wilmot makes the process of doctoral writing explicit and demonstrable to both doctoral candidates and their supervisors.

While the studies in Part I traverse the disciplinary map and address teaching and learning in higher education across a range of levels, they have relevance for university teachers beyond the specific disciplines, fields and ranges that are used as examples by the authors. All university teachers are in the business of teaching students who have diverse abilities and whose academic success is more likely when the 'rules of the game' are made more explicit. That is the contribution that these studies offer to university teachers who, regardless of discipline or level of teaching, are developing programmes, designing teaching and learning materials and activities, using multimedia artefacts, or inducting students into the valued practices of the profession. Theorizing teaching and learning with LCT concepts enables university teachers to develop a deeper understanding of the ways in which programmes, teaching, and assessment could be better structured for the purposes of enhancing students' knowledge and, ultimately, contributing to their academic success.

The authors of Part II turn their attention to how university teachers might be supported in their own professional learning about higher education pedagogy. Many studies show that students' learning is better supported when the academics who teach them are pedagogically competent to do so, but less is known about how to engage academic staff in professional learning. Part II covers pertinent issues in academic staff development from curriculum development and classroom pedagogies, to the appropriate inclusion of educational technologies in academic programmes.

In Chapter 9 Sherran Clarence and Martina van Heerden examine how academics learn to change their curricular and teaching practices. They show how a theorized way of talking about teaching and learning can stimulate productive conversations between academic developers and academic lecturers. Using short vignettes, the authors explore such interactions, focusing on the ways in which lecturers have responded to LCT concepts in relation to their own teaching. Clarence and van Heerden argue that LCT offers lecturers an accessible way of 'seeing' what they are teaching, thus enabling them to adapt their teaching to better facilitate successful student learning.

In Chapter 10 Honjiswa Conana, Delia Marshall and Jenni Case offer a Semantics analysis of first-year physics teaching, with a particular focus on how university teachers can draw on LCT in developing students' abilities. Modelling is key to Physics problem-solving, yet many students struggle to master the representational formats used in modelling. The authors show how the concepts of *semantic gravity* and *semantic density* provide a framework for characterizing movements between the abstract principles and concrete contexts that are required for solving problems in Physics. The authors argue that these LCT concepts enable undergraduate Physics lecturers to develop pedagogic approaches in support of enhanced student learning.

In Chapter 11 Karin Wolff studies engineering education, using the LCT concept of *epistemic relations*. Engineering education has been criticized for failing to produce students who are able to apply the knowledge that they learned in higher education to industry work practice, despite the increasing emphasis in applied and practical knowledge across engineering programmes. Wolff studies both real-world and curricular instances of problem-solving to reveal that, contrary to assumptions embedded in the curriculum, natural, mathematical and engineering sciences are underpinned by different kinds of knowledge. Her analysis considers what the focus of a knowledge claim is, and how the practitioner makes that claim across stages of the problem-solving process. Wolff reveals how successful learning entails shifting practices to be responsive both to the form of knowledge and the contexts in which problems occur. Drawing on epistemic relations enables educators to 'see' these differences and thus enhance the teaching of technology-based subjects.

Blended learning is increasing important in higher education, yet remains a largely under-researched and under-theorized area of pedagogy. In Chapter 12 J.P.

Bosman and Sonja Strydom present their research on blended learning in diverse higher education contexts in order to better understand its relevance and use. Focusing on a short course for academic staff, the chapter draws on Specialization to unpack the researchers' own knowledge practices in blended learning pedagogy. Bosman and Strydom find that they draw on different knowledge bases and knowledge practices at different times, such as when training academic staff in educational technologies, or when engaging academic staff in understanding the pedagogic implications of educational technologies.

In Chapter 13 Gert Young and Cecilia Jacobs explore the role of academic development units in curriculum development, usually regarded as the domain of academic departments, but becoming a more contested terrain. Academic development units and academic departments and faculties have different roles and contributions to offer, and the authors delve into the practice of curriculum transformation as a potential area of conflict, drawing on Specialization to explore the basis for achieving successful curriculum transformation from the perspectives of the different role players.

Universities across the world are facing the need to transform themselves as access is opened up and student cohorts diversify. In South Africa, for example, students and many academics are calling for higher education curricula to be 'decolonized'. In Chapter 14 Hanelie Adendorff and Margaret A.L. Blackie draw on Specialization, with a particular focus on 'gazes', to understand the basis of legitimacy in a Science programme. They also draw on Autonomy to explore the relations between the actors, ideas and objects in the field of Science to reveal what is at stake and what needs to be addressed. The chapter shows how different LCT concepts can reveal what a complex construct such as a decolonized Science curriculum might look like in practice, as well as why current attempts at decolonization might be perceived as perpetuating past injustices.

Chapters 15 and 16 focus on training-the-trainer, that is, supporting the academic developers who are tasked with supporting institutions and academic staff in times of change. Key to preparing academic developers for professional practice is enabling them to integrate their existing knowledge with new knowledge, and apply their understandings to new contexts. In Chapter 15 Lynn Quinn focuses on the summative assessment processes and products of a course specifically for academic developers to show how cumulative knowledge-building can be achieved in both course design and pedagogy. She draws on *semantic gravity* and *semantic density* to analyse high-achieving portfolios in the course. The analysis indicates that movements between knowledge that is relatively abstract, decontextualized and complex and knowledge that is relatively concrete, context-dependent and simpler, represents a key characteristic of cumulative learning for professional practice courses.

In Chapter 16, Jo-Anne Vorster explores how academic staff development practitioners at three universities seek and gain legitimacy among department academics. Drawing on Autonomy, Vorster analyses practices in terms of the fields from which they come and the purpose to which they are directed, and demonstrates how academic developers tend to occupy a difficult position that straddles academic and support work. Vorster finds that the basis of legitimacy underpinning successful academic development is being able to work collaboratively.

The chapters in Part II cover a wide range of academic staff development areas and practices; what unites them is how they use LCT tools to demonstrate how effective pedagogies draw on different kinds of knowledge, in different ways and at different times, and in different contexts. While the studies cover a range of professional development activities and programmes, from those that occur at the nexus of education, subject knowledge, and technology, to those that deal with institutional transformation in more or less extreme conditions, all are able to offer generalizable principles applicable to staff development in times of change. The chapters of both Parts I and II demonstrate how LCT can reveal the tacit 'rules' for success both student development and staff development, as well as pedagogical changes, interventions or strategies that can be designed to achieve the desired changes.

References

Boughey, C. and McKenna, S. (2016). Academic Literacy and the decontextualized learner. *Critical Studies in Teaching and Learning, 4*(2), 1–9.

Case, J., Marshall, D., McKenna, S. and Mogashana, D. (2018). *Going to university: The influence of higher education on the lives of young South Africans*. Cape Town: African Minds.

Clarence, S. (2016). Exploring the nature of disciplinary teaching and learning using Legitimation Code Theory Semantics. *Teaching in Higher Education, 2*(2), 123–137.

Clegg, S. (2009a). Forms of knowing and academic development practice. *Studies in Higher Education, 34*(4), 403–416.

Clegg, S. (2009b). Histories and institutional change: understanding academic development practices in the global 'north' and 'south'. *International Studies in Sociology of Education, 19*(1), 53–65.

Harland, T. (2009). People who study higher education. *Teaching in Higher Education, 14*(5), 579–582.

Hlengwa, A., McKenna, S. and Njovane, T. (2018). The lenses we use to research student experience. In P. Ashwin and J.M. Case (Eds), *Pathways to the public good: Access, experiences and outcomes of South African undergraduate education* (pp. 149–192). Cape Town: African Minds.

Maton, K. (2014). *Knowledge and knowers: Towards a realist sociology of education*. London: Routledge.

Maton, K. (2016a). Legitimation Code Theory: Building knowledge about knowledge-building. In K. Maton, S. Hood and S. Shay (Eds), *Knowledge-building: Educational studies in Legitimation Code Theory* (pp. 1–24). London: Routledge.

Maton, K. (2016b). Starting points: Resources and architectural glossary. In K. Maton, S. Hood and S. Shay (Eds), *Knowledge-building: Educational studies in Legitimation Code Theory* (pp. 233–243). London: Routledge.

Maton, K. (2018). Thinking like Bourdieu: Completing the mental revolution with Legitimation Code Theory. In J. Albright, D. Hartman and J. Widin (Eds), *Bourdieu's field theory and the social sciences* (pp. 249–268). London: Springer.

Maton, K. (2020). Semantic waves: Context, complexity and academic discourse. In J.R. Martin, K. Maton and Y.J. Doran (Eds), *Accessing academic discourse: Systemic functional linguistics and Legitimation Code Theory* (pp. 59–85). London: Routledge.

Maton, K. and Chen, R.T-H. (2016). LCT in qualitative research: Creating a translation device for studying constructivist pedagogy. In K. Maton, S. Hood and S. Shay (Eds), *Knowledge-building: Educational studies in Legitimation Code Theory* (pp. 27–48). London: Routledge.

Maton, K. and Howard, S.K. (2018). Taking autonomy tours: A key to integrative knowledge-building. *LCT Centre Occasional Paper, 1*, 1–35.

Maton, K. and Howard, S.K. (in press, 2021) Targeting science: Successfully integrating mathematics into science teaching In K. Maton, J.R. Martin and Y.J. Doran (Eds), *Studying science: Knowledge, language, pedagogy*. London: Routledge.

Mettler, S. (2014). *Degrees of inequality: How the politics of higher education sabotaged the American dream*. New York: Basic Books.

Shay, S. (2012). Educational development as a field: are we there yet? *Higher Education Research and Development, 31*(3), 311–323.

Tight, M. (2014). Discipline and theory in higher education research. *Research Papers in Education, 29*(1), 93–110.

Trow, M. (1973). *Problems in the transition from elite to mass higher education*. Berkeley: Carnegie Commission on Higher Education.

Wolff, K. and Luckett, K. (2013). Integrating multidisciplinary engineering knowledge. *Teaching in Higher Education, 18*(1), 78–92.

PART I
Student learning across the disciplinary map

2
DEMYSTIFYING REFLECTIVE WRITING IN TEACHER EDUCATION WITH SEMANTIC GRAVITY

Lucy Macnaught

Introduction

Reflective writing is a well-established form of assessment in higher education. It is usually taken to mean a task (or part of a task) where students are expected to demonstrate learning and growth in their professional knowledge (Carl and Strydom, 2017). High pedagogic value associated with reflective writing practices is particularly evident in the teaching and learning of health and social sciences (e.g. Craft, 2005; Rai, 2006). In fields such as teacher education, for example, reflective engagement with theory and research is seen as vital to both pre-service training and the lifelong development of teachers. These values are often explicitly stated in standards and codes for graduating teachers (e.g. in Department for Education [England], 2013).

What constitutes reflective writing practice, however, varies considerably (Calderhead, 1989; Hatton and Smith, 1995; Rogers, 2001; Ryan and Ryan, 2013). As Rogers (2001) reviews, terminology and definitions of reflective writing practices include a focus on the timing of reflection in relation to events, such as, anticipatory reflection (Loughran, 1996) or reflection-in-action (Schön, 1983, 1987). Additionally, terms such as critical reflection may encompass specific processes that students are expected to do, such as students 'paying critical attention to the practical values and the theories which inform everyday actions' (Bolton, 2010: xix). This kind of scope and variation means that assessment descriptors which include 'reflection' may carry different expectations, and these may not be intuitively understood by students (Ryan and Ryan, 2013).

One particular area of unfamiliarity is the extent to which reflective writing should involve specific connections between theory and experience (Stevenson *et al.*, 2018). In this regard, the distinction between personal reflection and academic reflection is particularly useful for students new to tertiary study. While personal reflection includes descriptions of experiences, the term academic reflection (after Moon, 2006; Ryan, 2011, 2012) highlights that students need to show evidence of learning through creating interconnections between personal experience and the 'academic' content of their subject areas, such as specific theories and theoretical constructs from their lectures and readings.

This chapter focuses on the design of teaching and learning materials for teaching academic reflections to students who are beginning a Bachelor of Education programme. The goal of these materials is to demystify what students are expected to do in academic reflections, and to identify features that contribute to the writing being awarded a high grade. More specifically, this chapter illustrates how the concept of *semantic gravity* (Maton, 2013, 2014a, 2020) is used in the design of pedagogic materials. In the theoretical framework of Legitimation Code Theory (hereafter LCT), this concept theorizes the extent to which knowledge is context-dependent. In this study, context-dependence is related to what first year students are expected to write about in their academic reflections. Discussion focuses on the challenge students face in learning how to deliberately increase and decrease the relative strength of semantic gravity as they craft their texts. The overall aim is to explore the affordances of semantic gravity as a concept with which to teach and critique key elements that contribute to 'successful' academic reflections.

Academic reflections in teacher education

The end goal of personal transformation or change is often seen as a desired outcome of reflection in professional training and development, including teacher education (Calderhead, 1989). For instance, frameworks for teaching reflective writing, such as the 5Rs Framework for Reflection (Bain *et al.*, 2002), associate future action plans or resolutions for future practice (Janssen *et al.*, 2008) as indicators of higher level or 'deep' reflection. This is compared with lower level superficial reflections, where students mostly recount descriptions from experiences (Orland-Barak, 2005). Such hierarchical classification of levels (or layers) of reflection is a common way to conceptualize the ideal outcome of reflective practices.

This focus on personal change and future action is also evident in popular online learning resources for tertiary students. Readily accessible resources, such as YouTube videos created by academic language and learning teams within universities, advise students to explain their thoughts and feelings, and state how they will act or think differently in the future (e.g. Skills Team, University of Hull, 2014; Academic Skills, The University of Melbourne, 2017; University of South Australia, 2017). In such instructional materials, the interpersonal aspects of reflection appear to be privileged over ideational content, that is, the discipline-specific knowledge with which students need to engage. However, as Calderhead (1989) discusses, teaching reflective writing to student teachers also needs to include specification of the knowledge that students are expected to draw upon in their reflections. In other words, while changes to personal feelings, values and beliefs are core to reflective writing, so too is the discipline-specific knowledge that may be the impetus for change.

While the importance of writing about both discipline-specific knowledge and personal experience in academic reflections is acknowledged by some teacher educators (e.g. Carl and Strydom, 2017; Cohen-Sayag and Fischl, 2012), there is currently little research on how student writers can appropriately achieve the desired integration (Stevenson *et al.*, 2018). A further issue is that academic reflections are associated with a wide range of texts, where text structure is typically not standardized (Shum *et al.*, 2017). For students, this means that the expected structure of reflections can change from one assessment task to another, and, even within one task, there may be a number of different ways to successfully organize and create connections between theory and experience.

In light of these issues, teacher educators and researchers stress the importance of explicit, writing instruction prior to the assessment of academic reflections. The modelling and analysis of examples of reflective writing, for instance, is seen as a key strategy for teaching students what is expected and valued (Moon, 2006; Ryan and Ryan, 2013; Ulsusoy, 2016). A central argument in support of explicit methods of instruction is not only related to the unfamiliarity of academic reflections, but also that assessment task descriptions, rubrics and learning outcomes are always open to varied interpretation by students. This may occur in spite of extensive efforts to make assessment standards clear (O'Donovan *et al.*, 2004). Students, therefore, are likely to benefit from seeing examples and engaging in assessment-related activities that make expectations clear, and which prepare them for specific kinds of reflective writing (Stevenson *et al.*, 2018).

Although the necessity of explicit instruction is well argued, there is currently little research on systematic, integrated and programme-wide pedagogic interventions to teach academic reflections (Ryan and Ryan, 2013). For instance, there has been little research into how the reflective writing of student teachers may change over an entire three-year undergraduate programme, nor how teaching and learning materials may gradually prepare students to create more complex and/or more 'in-depth' reflections. Initial steps towards such longitudinal studies include analysing the representations of knowledge that are valued in specific fields of study. Studies that draw on the dimension of Semantics from LCT, for example, have started to identify what is valued in student writing in fields as varied as Social Work, Business Studies (Szenes *et al.* 2015), History, and English (Maton, 2013, 2014a, 2014b). Semantics has also been used to inform teaching practices, such as teaching Chemistry (Blackie, 2014), Biology (Macnaught *et al.*, 2013), Political Science (Clarence, 2016), and English for Academic Purposes (Ingold and O'Sullivan, 2017). As yet, however, few published studies have discussed the use of Semantics to design a sequence of teaching and learning activities, including the documentation of how original LCT terms may be adapted and repurposed.

Research context

This study involves embedding academic literacies in a Bachelor of Education programme. The term *embedded* or *integrated* means that teaching is part of the curriculum and relevant to specific assessment tasks (Veitch et al., 2016); the term academic literacies (as proposed by Lea and Street, 1998) includes teaching academic writing. This approach contrasts with teaching about academic writing that is adjunct or external to the core curriculum, such as generic workshops that are conducted outside of regular class time. Currently, at Auckland University of Technology (AUT), embedded academic literacy is primarily taught by Learning Advisors (often referred to as Academic Language and Learning practitioners, or Learning Development Advisors, in literature) in collaboration with faculty staff. In the context of a Bachelor of Education programme, Learning Advisors are invited to design and deliver teaching materials to prepare students for assessment before the submission date. Typically, 30 to 60 minutes of lecture or tutorial time is allocated to Learning Advisors per assessment task. Lecturers provide further assignment support during tutorials, and also through learning management systems, such as Blackboard.

In the past, the Learning Advisor team at AUT has tended to focus on generic, widely applicable characteristics of academic writing. They have, for instance, designed materials related to analysing assignment questions, referencing systems and essay structure. However, in recent years, there has been a shift towards closer collaboration with faculty staff. This shift acknowledges the importance of instruction that anticipates student needs, and which targets specific assignments.

Within the Bachelor of Education program, all assessment tasks align with standards and codes for graduating teachers. The importance of learning how to relate theory to experience is prominent in standards related to 'professional learning' and 'design for teaching' (Education Council New Zealand, 2017). The teaching materials in this chapter relate to assessment tasks in students' very first semester of study. At this point in their studies, students are typically asked to add or integrate reflections into writing tasks, such as annotated bibliographies and autobiographical essays. In such tasks, students need to relate specific educational theories and theoretical constructs to the concrete particulars of their own experience, to the experience of family members, or to the details provided in case studies.

Theoretical frameworks

The teaching and learning materials that are illustrated and discussed in this chapter draw on concept of *semantic gravity* to explain how to organize and write academic reflections. Semantic gravity refers to varying degrees of context-dependency of practices (Maton, 2013, 2014a, 2014b, 2020). In this study, the relative strength of semantic gravity is related to what students are writing about. Relatively strong semantic gravity is related to parts of texts where students write about the concrete particulars of experiences. This knowledge includes events, social interactions and personal feelings at particular times, and in specific settings. Conversely, relatively weak semantic gravity is broadly related to parts of texts where students write about more abstract knowledge in the form of theories and theoretical constructs. This knowledge has been introduced to students in weekly lectures and readings. When compared to the details of experiences, theoretical knowledge is less bound to a particular context, and can, therefore, be flexibly related to a range of specific settings.

In this study, the concept of semantic gravity is specifically chosen for teaching students how to organize and write academic reflections, as it considers how more to less abstract representations of knowledge work together (Maton, 2020). In other words, it is not only useful for illuminating the varied knowledge that students are expected to include in an assignment, but also for identifying how and where student writers can purposefully shift between writing about their more concrete lived experiences, and also about the more abstract theoretical constructs that they encounter in lectures and course readings.

While semantic gravity informs explanations about how to create academic reflections, the sequencing of teaching materials follows the principle of *scaffolding*. Originally introduced by Wood, Bruner and Ross (1976), scaffolding describes instructional support where learners 'carry out new tasks while learning strategies and patterns that will eventually make it possible to carry out similar tasks without external support' (Applebee and Langer, 1983: 169). In the teaching and learning of academic literacy, scaffolding has often been aligned with Vygotskian theories of language development (1978), where social interaction is seen as vital to learning (Hammond and Gibbons, 2001, 2005). One influential scaffolding pedagogy for teaching academic writing is the Teaching and Learning Cycle (hereafter TLC) (Callaghan and Rothery, 1988; Martin, 1999; Rose and Martin, 2012). The design of the TLC follows the principle of scaffolding in that teaching gradually prepares students to write independently. Stages or steps in the TLC include the analysis and modelling of exemplar texts, guided practice to co-create texts with the support of the teacher, followed by students' independent construction of a text.

The design of the TLC is also strongly influenced by social-semiotic theories of language and language learning from within the tradition of Systemic Functional Linguistics or 'SFL' (Halliday, 1978; Halliday, 1993). SFL theorizes how we make meaning and learn to create new meanings through social interactions in specific contexts of language use. From this perspective, the sequence of teaching and learning activity in the TLC contributes to building a shared language for talking about meanings in texts and specific processes of text creation. This type of pedagogic goal is commonly referred to as developing students' knowledge about language, including a shared metalanguage with which to talk about language and writing practices (Schleppegrell, 2013). From an LCT perspective, the sequence of teaching and learning activity in the TLC can also be used to develop a shared metalanguage about the representation of knowledge in texts (e.g. Macnaught *et al.*, 2013). For the study of classroom activity where teachers and students talk about writing practices, it is important to differentiate original theoretical terminology from terms that teachers and students may adapt and repurpose. In this study, adaptations of terms are identified as part of 'classroom metalanguage' (Macnaught, 2018).

A focus on pedagogic frameworks for explicitly building shared knowledge about texts with students is particularly relevant to the cohort in this study. As the discussion of literature has highlighted, students new to tertiary studies may not yet understand the differences between personal and academic reflections. They may also not yet understand how reflective writing in one type of assessment task may be similar or different to another task. These students are, therefore, likely to benefit from teaching and learning materials that explicitly discuss what is valued in assessment, and which also explain how students can write successfully.

Methodology

The data for this study involve teaching and learning materials for the development of academic literacy, and, in particular, supporting students with writing academic reflections. The pedagogic materials were created specifically as teaching tools for Learning Advisors to use in the three core papers (courses) of the first semester. Assessment tasks in these papers included annotated bibliographies, essays and short pieces of writing, called reflective tasks. The pedagogic materials did not attempt to focus on explaining how to answer all aspects of these assessment tasks. Rather, given the constrained time available for teaching, they focused on one critical aspect common to all tasks, namely showing students how to connect theory and experience. These connections were adapted to the specific subject matter of each paper, such as theories of human development, and educational issues and trends in New Zealand.

The teaching materials were designed and delivered between 2016 and 2018. They comprise:

- PowerPoint slides
- Teacher notes under the PowerPoint slides
- A screencast/video (see: www.youtube.com/watch?v=P-NPNeNtr_8)
- A screencast script

These materials were either taught face to face in lecture time, and/or were made available to students through Blackboard – a Learning Management System.

The exemplification of these teaching materials in this publication includes several adjustments. Colour in the originals is changed to black and white, and colour differences are represented by changes in font. Slide annotations are also changed to static representations. However, apart from these changes, the examples very closely resemble the versions used in teaching.

The teaching materials have been primarily designed by the author with the incorporation of rigorous feedback from Learning Advisor colleagues and approval from faculty lecturers. These materials have subsequently been used in teaching by other Learning Advisor colleagues. For teaching purposes, one ethical consideration concerns the exemplification of student writing. For this study, example texts do not constitute samples of student writing. Instead, sample texts have been created by the author in response to discussions with faculty staff about student writing.

As a set of teaching tools, the data set aims to explicitly teach students how to connect theory with experience. In light of this pedagogic goal, the research question is:

- What strategies are used in teaching students to increase and decrease the relative strength of semantic gravity?

The data are analysed in relation to explicit methods of academic writing instruction that reoccur across the data. Comparisons are made between the teaching strategies in the data and the teaching strategies in well-known scaffolding pedagogies, such as the Teaching and Learning Cycle (Callaghan and Rothery, 1988; Martin, 1999; Rose and Martin, 2012). As the use of semantic gravity to design teaching materials happened gradually over several years and across different core papers, the analysis in this chapter represents a retrospective examination of how semantic gravity was used to teach writing. The findings are particularly relevant to practitioners who may be considering how to use the concept of semantic gravity to design and deliver assignment-specific academic writing resources for students.

Findings and discussion

Findings show four reoccurring scaffolding strategies for explaining how to increase and decrease the relative strength of semantic gravity in academic reflections. These include: *framing*, which uses assessment documents to identify the representations of knowledge that are valued in a specific assessment task; *modelling*, which analyses exemplar texts and creates a shared metalanguage for talking about writing practices; *self-evaluating*, where students use classroom metalanguage to examine representations of knowledge in their own writing; and *guided preparing*, where teachers support students to practise creating specific connections between theory and experience in preparation for writing their next assessment task. These scaffolding strategies are represented in Figure 2.1 and will now be exemplified and discussed in turn.

Framing

The scaffolding strategy of framing draws on assessment documents to interpret and identify the representations of knowledge that are valued in specific assessment tasks. Learning Advisors directed students to specific learning outcomes and corresponding marking criteria. These descriptions formed the basis of a diagram to illustrate the knowledge that students are expected to draw upon in their academic reflections. An example diagram appears in Figure 2.2. This diagram identifies that both theory/theoretical constructs and concrete experiences are valued in academic reflections. The relative strengths of semantic gravity are represented by the dotted double arrow – emphasizing that shifts are possible and expected. In specific papers/courses, such a diagram identifies particular theories and different kinds of experiences that are appropriate for the scope of the assessment task.

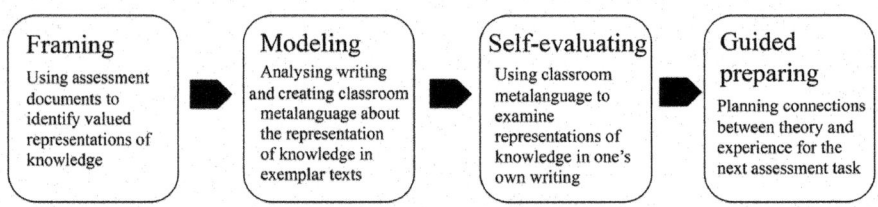

FIGURE 2.1 Scaffolding strategies for teaching students how to identify and create shifts in the relative strength of semantic gravity

The change between relatively strong or weak semantic gravity was also represented by the dotted double arrow – emphasizing that shifts are possible and expected.

The scaffolding strategy of framing corresponds to pedagogic frameworks with a 'deconstruction' stage or step. Typically, this stage engages students in the analysis of texts that are similar to the ones that students need to produce (Martin, 1999). In this study, the term framing is used to highlight one form of deconstruction, namely the analysis of assessment documents, and particularly the identification of knowledge that students are expected to draw upon. This scaffolding strategy acknowledges concerns by researchers that assessment task descriptions are prone to divergent interpretation from students (O'Donovan et al., 2004). It also acknowledges that differences between personal and academic reflections may not be readily understood by students (Moon, 2006; Ryan, 2011, 2012), and so teaching needs to explicitly identify theories that students are expected to use.

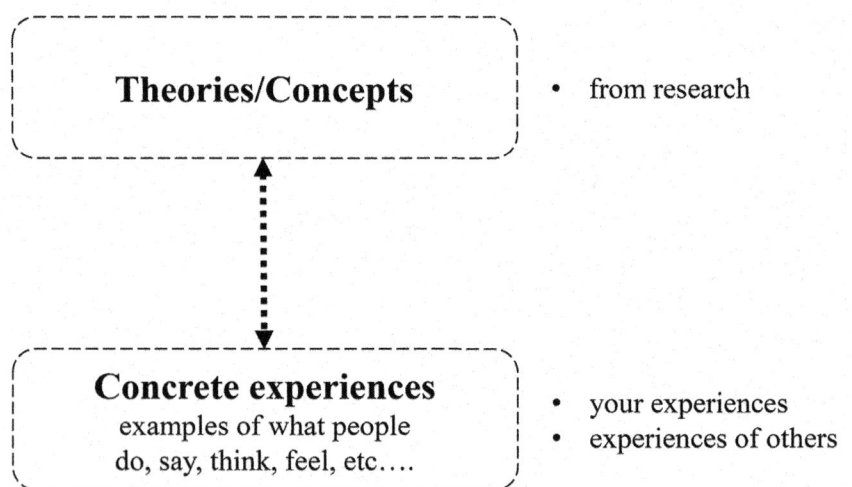

FIGURE 2.2 Framing the assessment task in relation to degrees of context-dependence

Modelling

The second scaffolding strategy of modelling focuses on the use of exemplar texts to analyse writing and create a shared classroom metalanguage for talking about texts (Feez, 1998/2006; Humphrey and Feez, 2016). In this study, three different types of modelling strategies were used to build understanding of how to create shifts in degrees of context-dependency: *text profiling*, *text annotation* and *sentence starters*. Each type is now discussed and illustrated with examples.

a Text profiling

The modelling strategy of text profiling draws directly on the concept of *semantic profiles* (Maton, 2013, 2014a, 2014b, 2020). A semantic profile provides a visual representation of where relative shifts in context-dependency occur in an unfolding text. In this study, findings show that various semantic profiles were taught to students. Descriptions followed Maton's notion of a *semantic wave* (2013, 2020). Using the wave metaphor, Learning Advisors referred to semantic profiles as *text profiles* or *wave shapes*, such as those illustrated in Figure 2.3. The *down wave* represented a shift to towards strengthening context-dependency, such as when writers start with theory and then relate theory to the details of an experience; the *up wave* represented a shift towards weakening context-dependency, such as when writers start with experience and then relate it to theory; and the *full wave* represented multiple shifts in the degrees of context-dependency, created by writing about theory, connecting it to experience, and then returning to theory.

These three 'wave shapes' were presented as successful ways to organize interconnections between theory and experience. Each option was further exemplified with content pertaining to the scope and length of a particular assessment task. For example, a 50-word reflection at the end of one annotated bibliography entry, can be effectively organized as a down wave. Alternately, when students are expected to show understanding of, and relationships between, multiple theories, such as in an autobiographical essay, then full waves are useful. An example of a full wave appears in Figure 2.4. In this example, a relative increase in the strength of semantic gravity is created when Erikson's psychosocial theory is related to events and feelings

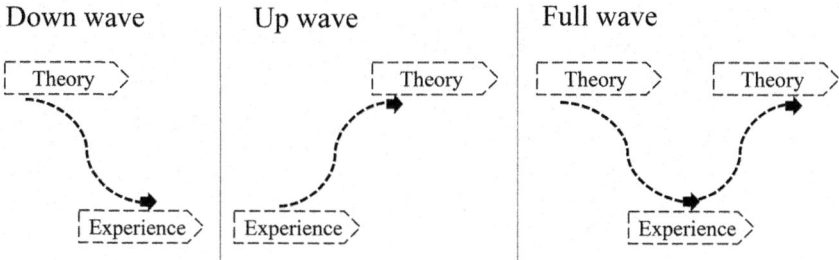

FIGURE 2.3 Text profiling

Full wave

FIGURE 2.4 Exemplification of a full wave

about joining a primary school football team, and then a weakening of semantic gravity is created when these details are further related to Kohlberg's theory of morality development. Such text profiling can be readily adapted to the precise content of different academic reflections. In this study, the naming of different semantic profiles (up wave, down wave, full wave) provided a shared classroom metalanguage between Learning Advisors and students for talking about the representation of knowledge in academic reflections.

b Text annotation

The second modelling strategy of text annotation involves the analysis and labelling of exemplar texts. For instance, Figure 2.5 shows the semantic profile that the teacher and students referred to as a full wave. In this annotation, the same colours were used – as per the framing strategy – to represent relative differences in the strength of context-dependency: blue for theory and green for experience. (These colours have been replaced by normal and bold fonts respectively.) Italics also represented text parts, called 'linking sentences', or just 'links', which overtly signal a relative shift between more to less abstract representations of knowledge. An example from Figure 2.5 is: *Issues related to approval and acceptance are illustrated in my experience of school sports as a 10 year old.* Here, the less context-dependent concepts of approval and acceptance (from previously introduced theory) are connected to an instance of a personal experience about playing school sport. The concrete details of that experience follow. Conversely, this text example also shows a link from the details of the experience to a new theory: *This experience of emotional conflict also relates to Kohlberg's (1984) theory of morality development.* This kind of text annotation aimed to identify where broad shifts in context-dependency occur, and how

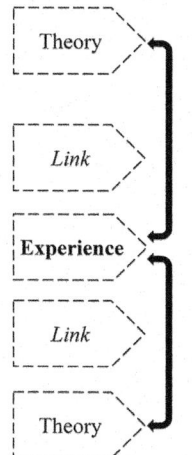

... In terms of Erikson's (1968) Psychosocial Theory, children in the middle years life stage begin to contend with the crisis of Industry verses Inferiority. This crisis involves conflict in relation to emotional development, and, in particular, the development of a child's self-confidence as they strive for approval from others (Erikson, 1968). *Issues related to approval and acceptance are illustrated in my experience of school sport as a 10 year old.* **I joined my primary school's football team despite not personally enjoying the sport. I joined because my friends were passionate about football. They did not pressure me into playing, but I received approval from them when I did. Despite my feelings, I felt unable to stop playing football as I feared disapproval, and also viewed quitting as wrong.** *This experience of emotional conflict also relates to Kohlberg's (1984) theorization of morality development.* His research highlights how children in this age range base their actions on the responses of others, and...

FIGURE 2.5 A text annotation of a full wave

writers deliberately use language to signal them. Text annotation was also used for subsequent exemplar texts, where students undertook the text annotation themselves, and Learning Advisors asked guiding questions, such as: Where does the writer start to connect theory with experience in this text?

c Sentence starters

The third modelling strategy in the data is the use of sentence starters. While text annotation provided initial examples of explicit interconnections between theory and experience, sentence starters show further examples of alternate wording. For example, Figure 2.6 shows a range of language patterns for explicitly connecting theory with experience. Sentence starters, such as *X (concept) provides insight into my own experience of ...* were also accompanied by the silhouette of a surfer. (Other examples focused on the converse shift where writers may start with experience and then relate these concrete particulars to theoretical constructs.) In maintaining continuity with the metaphor of waves, the position of the surfboard represented a change in the degree of context-dependency: the surfboard pointing down represented a strengthening of semantic gravity; and the surfboard pointing up represented a weakening of semantic gravity. Such examples aimed to show students a range of language choices that signal a shift between more and less context-dependent representations of knowledge.

Collectively, these three modelling strategies correspond to scaffolding pedagogies that include the deconstruction of exemplar texts (see Callaghan and Rothery, 1988; Feez, 1998/2006; Humphrey and Feez, 2016). In particular, the use of text profiles, text annotation and sentence starters focused on showing students how more and less context-dependent representations of knowledge are valued in their

Language: Links between theory and experience

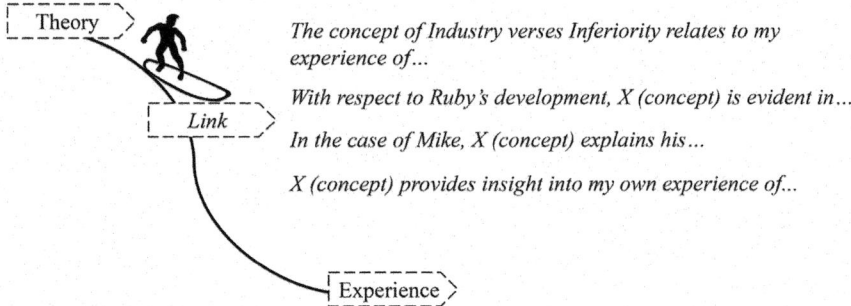

FIGURE 2.6 Sentences starters for signalling a shift in strength of semantic gravity

academic reflections. By showing more than one possible 'answer', the modelling strategies respond to research identifying flexibility in the structuring of academic reflections (Shum et al,. 2017). They also respond to concerns by faculty staff in the School of Education that students might be tempted to copy a single exemplar and would therefore benefit from seeing variation.

Self-evaluating

The third scaffolding strategy of self-evaluating involves students using the newly introduced classroom metalanguage about knowledge practices (such as the names for various wave shapes) to reflect on their past or current writing. Learning Advisors shared indicative lecturer feedback about academic reflections, such as 'use examples', 'problems with information flow', and 'too descriptive'. These types of comments were related to three additional text profiles: *a high flatline*, where students mostly write about theory; *a low flatline* where students mostly write about experiences (both these descriptions follow Maton, 2013); and *lonely islands*, where students write about both theory and experience, but in a fragmented way with few explicit connections – the text lacks what Maton (2013) terms 'semantic flow'. These text profiles and corresponding feedback from lecturers are illustrated in Figure 2.7. Following the discussion of feedback, students were asked to consider feedback that they received so far, and to critique and discuss the text profiles of own writing. Depending on the week of teaching, students examined a draft in progress, or work that had been previously submitted (for a similar assessment task).

The scaffolding strategy of self-evaluating is not always documented in pedagogic practices based on the principle of scaffolding. This is because many of these scaffolding pedagogies tend to focus on teaching that prepares students for tasks, rather than on repairing their initial attempts or drafts in progress (Martin, 1999).

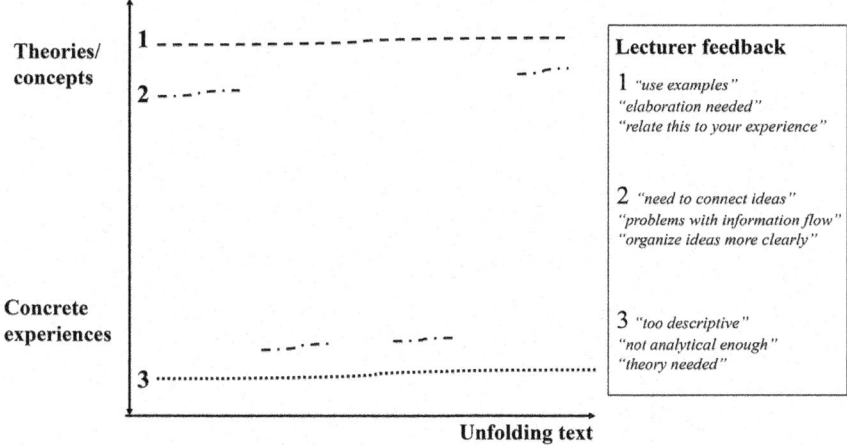

FIGURE 2.7 Relating assignment feedback to degrees of context-dependence

However, as Humphrey and Macnaught (2016) document, teachers may incorporate evaluation and feedback in cycles of explicit instruction. They may, for example, involve students in extended discussion to critique writing – their own and writing of others. For students in this study, self-evaluation was particularly useful for reflecting on the extent to which they were aware of and deliberately controlling the relative strength of context-dependency. Put simply, they could reflect on decisions about how much 'text time' they devoted to theory or experience, and whether or not they made connections between the two clear for their reader.

Guided preparing

The fourth and final scaffolding strategy is guided preparing. This strategy aligns with the principle of *guided practice* (Painter, 1986; Humphrey and Feez, 2016). A common manifestation of this principle involves teachers supporting students to try using new knowledge about writing practices before they continue to write independently. For example, teachers may lead the co-construction of a text before students write on their own (Macnaught, 2015; Rose and Martin, 2012). In this study, Learning Advisors drew on this principle to support students with planning deliberate shifts in the strengthening and weakening of semantic gravity. This pedagogic goal was described to students as planning the connection or 'the match' between theory and experience. Learning Advisors discussed an example relevant to the scope of a specific assessment task. For instance, in Figure 2.8, the assignment question centred on child development. In order to exemplify a relative shift in context-dependency, this broad topic was firstly narrowed down: from one domain of human development (e.g. the physical domain) to a specific theory (e.g. Gesell's theorization of maturation), and then, within this theory, one theoretical construct

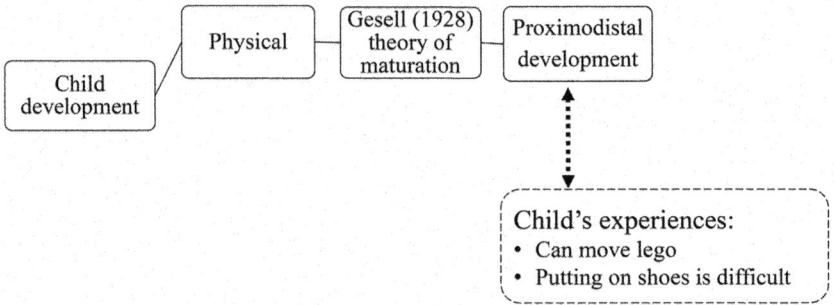

FIGURE 2.8 Planning relative shifts in degrees of context-dependence

was specified (e.g. proximodistal development). The planned connection occurs when this construct is related to examples of physical activity in a young child, such as the case where a little girl can move pieces of Lego, but she continues to have difficulty putting on shoes.

Following the presentation of such examples, students were then engaged in one or more activities to create and discuss 'matches' for their own writing. The faculty lecturer was available to listen as students talked through how they planned to connect a specific theoretical construct with a specific experience. Where needed, the faculty lecturers also gave students further guidance and direct feedback about the accuracy of their connections.

For writing academic reflections, guided preparation is particularly important, because crafting text into various 'wave shapes' will be of limited benefit if students create mismatches between theoretical constructs and their exemplification in the concrete particulars of experiences. As Shum and colleagues (2017: 78) warn, in creating academic reflections, it is still possible to create 'beautifully crafted nonsense', even when the 'right' rhetorical patterns are used. Guided preparation, thus, provides a crucial intermediate step between looking at examples and crafting academic reflections independently.

Conclusion

This chapter has illustrated how the concept of semantic gravity has been used in the design of pedagogic materials for teaching academic reflections. The central question has been concerned with identifying specific scaffolding strategies that were used to teach students how to increase and decrease the relative strength of semantic gravity. Across the data, four main strategies reoccurred. These were identified as framing, modelling, self-evaluating and guided preparing. Collectively, these strategies involved Learning Advisors engaging students in activities to identify and create connections between specific theoretical constructs and specific experiences. Analysis showed how these strategies closely align with scaffolding pedagogies that aim to explicitly teach students what is valued in academic writing, and how to create successful texts. More specifically, findings show that drawing on the concept of semantic gravity provided a shared classroom metalanguage for talking about representations of knowledge that are valued in academic reflections. For new Bachelor of Education students, this meant addressing the challenge of how to write 'academically', while also writing about one's own experiences or the experiences of others.

While this study has not attempted to address all facets of writing academic reflections, it has drawn attention to the knowledge that students are expected to integrate with their experiences. Arguably, this pedagogic focus is particularly important for new students who may have not yet experienced other dimensions or outcomes of reflective writing practices, such as shifts in personal values and beliefs. In other words, at this point in their studies, it is important for students to demonstrate their understanding of theoretical knowledge by making connections to concrete experiences, and they may not yet be expected to demonstrate personal transformation. As Szenes and Tilakaratna (2018) propose, examining both knowledge, and the beliefs and values associated with that knowledge, invites further inquiry and debate regarding the purpose of academic reflections in tertiary education. It raises questions, such as the extent to which student writing should focus on transferring knowledge to specific settings, and/or on demonstrating personal change. With such questions in mind, further research in Bachelor of Education programmes is needed, in order to gain a better understanding of the range of assessment tasks in which academic reflections manifest, and how assessment expectations may change as students progress in their studies.

The findings also invite further inquiry into how LCT theory is adapted and repurposed for use in discipline-specific academic writing instruction and classroom interactions with students. The analysis and exemplification of teaching materials in this study has revealed very little use of original theoretical terminology. Instead, Learning Advisors used simplified terms, colour, shapes and images to represent a relative weakening or strengthening of semantic gravity. As LCT continues to develop (e.g. see Maton and Doran, 2017 for developments in Semantics) educators have an expanding selection of theoretical knowledge that could be drawn upon in teaching. We must, therefore, make deliberate and careful choices in creating a shared classroom metalanguage about the representation of knowledge in texts, so that it is relevant and accessible to students.

Acknowledgements

The author would like to acknowledge the contribution of members of AUT's Learning Success team in the preparation of the teaching materials that have been analysed in this publication. Particular thanks to Robyn McWilliams for discussing, encouraging and critiquing my initial attempts to use early versions of these teaching materials, to Gema Carlson and Dr Quentin Allan for their critique around the accessibility of classroom metalanguage, and to Karen Margetts and Mark Bassett for being rigorous PowerPoint slide and screencast script editors.

References

Academic Skills, The University of Melbourne. (2017, June 1). *Reflective writing* [Video file]. Retrieved from www.youtube.com/watch?v=SntBj0FIApwandt=2s.

Applebee, A.N. and Langer, A.L. (1983). Instructional scaffolding: Reading and writing as natural language activities. *Language Arts, 60*(2), 168–175.

Bain, J.D., Ballantyne, R., Mills, C. and Lester, N.C. (2002). *Reflecting on practice: Student teachers' perspectives*. Flaxton: Post Press.

Blackie, M.A.L. (2014). Creating semantic waves: Using Legitimation Code Theory as a tool to aid the teaching of chemistry. *Chemistry Education Research and Practice, 15*(4), 462–469.

Bolton, G. (2010). *Reflective practice: Writing and professional development* (3rd ed.). London: Sage.

Calderhead, J. (1989). Reflective teaching and teacher education. *Teaching and Teacher Education, 5*(1), 43–51.

Callaghan, M. and Rothery, J. (1988). *Teaching factual writing: A genre based approach*. Sydney: Metropolitan East Disadvantaged Schools Program.

Carl, A. and Strydom, S. (2017). e-Portfolio as reflection tool during teaching practice: The interplay between contextual and dispositional variables. *South African Journal of Education, 37*(1), 1–10.

Clarence, S. (2016). Surfing the wave of learning: Enacting a Semantics analysis of teaching in a first-year law course. *Higher Education Research and Development, 36*(5), 920–933.

Cohen-Sayag, E. and Fischl, D. (2012). Reflective writing in pre-service teachers' teaching: What does it promote? *Australian Journal of Teacher Education, 37*(10), 20–36.

Craft, M. (2005). Reflective writing and nursing education. *Journal of Nursing Education, 44*(2), 53–57.

Department for Education. (2013). *Teachers standards: Guidance for school leaders, school staff and governing bodies*. Retrieved from https://assets.publishing.service.gov.uk/government/uploads/system/uploads/attachment_data/file/665520/Teachers__Standards.pdf.

Education Council of Aotearoa New Zealand. (2017). *Our code our standards: Code of professional responsibility and standards for the teaching profession*. Retrieved from www.teachingcouncil.nz/sites/default/files/Our%20Code%20Our%20Standards%20web%20booklet%20FINAL.pdf.

Feez, S. (1998/2006). *Text-based Syllabus Design*. Sydney, Australia: Macquarie University AMES, NSW NCELTR.

Halliday, M.A.K. (1978). *Language as a social semiotic: The social interpretation of language and meaning*. Baltimore, MD: University Park Press.

Halliday, M.A.K. (1993). Towards a language-based theory of learning. *Linguistics and Education, 5*, 93–116.

Hammond, J. and Gibbons, P. (2001). What is scaffolding? In J. Hammond (Ed.), *Scaffolding: Teaching and learning in language and literacy education* (pp. 1–14). Newtown, Australia: Primary English Teaching Association.

Hammond, J. and Gibbons, P. (2005). Putting scaffolding to work: The contribution of scaffolding in articulating ESL education. *Prospect, 20*(1), 6–30.

Hatton, N. and Smith, D. (1995). Reflections in teacher education: Towards definition and implementation. *Teaching and Teacher Education, 11*(1), 33–49.

Humphrey, S. and Feez, S. (2016). Direct instruction fit for purpose: Applying a metalinguistic toolkit to enhance creative writing in the early secondary years. *Australian Journal of Language and Literacy, 39*(3), 207–218.

Humphrey, S. and Macnaught, L. (2016). The effect of metalanguage on students' writing performance. *TESOL Quarterly, 50*(4), 792–816.

Ingold, R. and O'Sullivan, D. (2017). Riding the wave to academic success. *Modern English Teacher, 26*(2), 39–43.

Janssen, F., de Hullu, E. and Tigelaar, D. (2008). Positive experiences as input for reflection by student teachers. *Teachers and Teaching, 14*(2), 115–127.
Lea, M.R. and Street, B.V. (1998). Student writing in higher education: An academic literacies approach. *Studies in Higher Education, 23*(2), 157–172.
Loughran, J.J. (1996). *Developing reflective practice: Learning about teaching and learning through modeling.* Washington, DC: Falmer Press.
Macnaught, L. (2015). *Classroom talk and the negotiation of academic English: A linguistic analysis of collaborative text creation.* (Unpublished doctoral dissertation), University of Technology, Sydney.
Macnaught, L. (2018). Multimodal Metalanguage. In H. de Silva Joyce and S. Feez (Eds), *Multimodality across classrooms: Learning about and through different modalities* (pp. 144–160). Newcastle: Cambridge Scholars Publishing.
Macnaught, L., Maton, K., Martin, J.R. and Matruglio, E. (2013). Jointly constructing semantic waves: Implications for teacher training. *Linguistics and Education, 24*(1), 50–63.
Martin, J.R. (1999). Mentoring semogenesis: 'Genre-based' literacy pedagogy. In F. Christie (Ed.), *Pedagogy and the shaping of consciousness: Linguistic and social processes* (pp. 123–155). London: Continuum.
Maton, K. (2013). Making semantic waves: A key to cumulative knowledge-building. *Linguistics and Education, 24*(1), 8–22.
Maton, K. (2014a). *Knowledge and knowers: Towards a realist sociology of education.* London: Routledge.
Maton, K. (2014b). A TALL order? Legitimation Code Theory for academic language and learning. *Journal of Academic Language and Learning, 8*(3), 34–48.
Maton, K. (2020). Semantic waves: Context, complexity and academic discourse. In J.R. Martin, K. Maton and Y.J. Doran (Eds), *Accessing academic discourse: Systemic functional linguistics and Legitimation Code Theory* (pp. 59–85). London: Routledge.
Maton, K. and Doran, Y.J. (2017). Condensation: A translation device for revealing complexity of knowledge practices in discourse, part 2 – clausing and sequencing. *Onomázein*, 77–110.
Moon, J. (2006). *Learning Journals: A handbook of reflective practice and professional development.* London: Routledge.
O'Donovan, B., Price, M. and Rust, C. (2004). Know what I mean? Enhancing student understandings of assessment standards and criteria. *Teaching in Higher Education, 9*(3), 325–225.
Orland-Barak, L. (2005). Portfolios as evidence of reflective practice: What remains 'untold'. *Educational Researcher, 4*(1), 25–44.
Painter, C. (1986). Writing to mean: Teaching genres across the curriculum. *Applied Linguistics Association of Australia (Occasional Papers), 9,* 62–97.
Rai, L. (2006). Owning (up to) reflective writing in social work education. *Social Work Education, 25*(8), 785–797.
Rogers, R.R. (2001). Reflection in higher education: A concept analysis. *Innovation in Higher Education, 26*(1), 37–75.
Rose, D, and Martin, J.R. (2012). *Learning to write, reading to learn: Genre, knowledge and pedagogy in the Sydney school.* Sheffield: Equinox.
Ryan, M. (2011). Improving reflective writing in higher education: A social semiotic perspective. *Teaching in Higher Education, 16*(1), 99–111.
Ryan, M. (2012). Conceptualising and teaching discursive and performative reflection in higher education. *Studies in Continuing Education, 34*(2), 207–223.
Ryan, M. and Ryan, M. (2013). Theorising a model for teaching and assessing reflective learning in higher education. *Higher Education Research and Development, 32*(2), 207–223.

Schleppegrell, M. (2013). The role of meta-language in supporting academic language development. *Language Learning, 63*(1), 153–170.

Schön, D.A. (1983). *The reflective practitioner: How professionals think in action.* New York, NY: Basic Books.

Schön, D.A. (1987). *Educating the reflective practitioner: Toward a new design for teaching and learning in the professions.* San Francisco, CA: Jossey-Bass.

Shum, S., Sándor, A., Goldsmith, R., Bass, R. and McWilliams, M. (2017). Towards reflective writing analytics: Rationale, methodology and preliminary results. *Journal of Learning Analytics, 4*(1), 58–84.

Skills Team, University of Hull. (2014, March 3). *Reflective writing* [Video file]. Retrieved from www.youtube.com/watch?v=QoI67VeE3ds.

Stevenson, M., James, B., Harvey, A., Minkang, K. and Szenes, E. (2018). Reflective writing: A transitional space between theory and practice. In K. Spelman-Miller and M. Stevenson (Eds), *Transitions in writing, studies in writing.* Amsterdam, The Netherlands: Brill.

Szenes, E., Tilakaratna, N. and Maton, K. (2015). The knowledge practices of critical thinking. In Davies, M. and Barnett, R. (Eds), *The Palgrave handbook of critical thinking in higher education* (pp. 573–591). New York: Palgrave Macmillan.

Szenes, E. and Tilakaratna, N. (2018). *Towards a translation device for revealing axiological meanings: Hidden values in tertiary assignments.* Paper presented at the LCT Centre Roundtable, University of Sydney.

Ulusoy, M. (2016). Field experiences in teacher education: The perceptions and qualities of written reflections. *Teaching in Higher Education, 21*(5), 532–544.

University of South Australia. (2017, February 20). *Reflective writing* [Video file]. Retrieved from www.youtube.com/watch?v=Rj80Q_6xykg.

Veitch, S., Johnson, S. and Mansfield, C. (2016). Collaborating to embed the teaching and assessment of literacy in Education: A targeted unit approach. *Journal of Academic Language and Learning, 10*(2), 1–10.

Vygotsky, L.S. (1978). *Mind in society.* Cambridge, MA: Harvard University Press.

Wood, D., Bruner, J. and Ross, G. (1976). The role of tutoring in problem solving. *Journal of Child Psychology and Psychiatry, 17*, 89–100.

3

MAKING WAVES IN TEACHER EDUCATION

Scaffolding students' disciplinary understandings by 'doing' analysis

Anna-Vera Meidell Sigsgaard

Introduction

Supporting students in writing academic texts is a universal need in higher educational contexts, an assumption supported by the presence of learning and writing centres found at many colleges and universities (see e.g. Coffin and Donohue, 2012; Lillis *et al.*, 2015). This is also the case in undergraduate teacher-education programmes which require students to be able to present accumulated curriculum knowledge in written academic texts for evaluation. Through such texts students demonstrate their understandings by applying theoretical concepts to data (Lillis *et al.*, 2015; Lillis, 2001; Schmidt, 2001; Swales and Feak, 2005). Scaffolding students in higher education in developing their understanding of curriculum content by providing them with appropriate analytical tools allows them to become more cognizant of what counts as legitimate knowledge in their field of study (Clarence, 2016; Humphrey and Dreyfus, 2012; Kirk, 2017; Mahboob *et al.*, 2010). This chapter explores the above claim, showcasing an example from a pre-service teacher training degree programme in Denmark.

Like other vocational or technical degrees, teacher training programmes often focus on providing students with theoretical knowledge while also expecting them to demonstrate their ability to apply this theoretical understanding to real-life situations, for example, when completing practicum periods or observations in the field. This combination of theory and practice is meant to prepare them for their roles as professionals upon graduation. Accordingly, pre-service teacher training in Denmark introduces students to theories of human development and education such as those of Klafki (1983) and Illeris (2003) intended for understanding problematics of teaching and learning. Maintained as useful to understanding general principles of pedagogy such as planning, evaluation and implementation of educational courses or programmes, or for understanding broad problematics connected to the context of schools and school practices, students however often exhibit difficulty *applying* the theories to actual teaching/learning challenges.

Not unlike higher education students in other degree programmes, pre-service teachers in Denmark exhibit difficulty writing about practice in a theoretically informed way despite the presence of writing centres and other support centres at their places of study (Nielsen *et al.*, 2006). At the same time, research shows that isolating academic literacy support in English for Academic Purposes (EAP) centres provides only marginal development (Griffin, 1982), whereas incorporating writing support within the disciplines is known to be an effective way of supporting students' academic writing at all levels of study (see for example Coffin and Donohue, 2012; Lillis *et al.*, 2015; Macken-Horarik, 2006; Rose and Martin, 2012). The work reported on here is situated, specifically, in a language education module, providing a unique opportunity to support the students' written academic language development and, at the same time, modelling and reflecting the kind of scaffolding work students will be expected to provide for their future pupils[1] once they graduate as teachers.

This chapter is divided into two parts, where Part I provides the background and context for the example drawn upon here. It outlines the content and requirements that pre-service teachers must meet in a language education module in the teacher education degree programme. This section also introduces the analytical tools which students were introduced to, which also provide the analytical framework for this chapter. Part II of the chapter provides a further development of the scaffolding throughout the module. Using the analytical tools presented in Part I, Part II illustrates how students' writing was scaffolded while at the same time developing their understandings of the curriculum content. Finally, the conclusion highlights how scaffolding students' writing can be a means of developing their disciplinary understandings. The chosen analytical tools not only reveal the basis of achievement in students' own writing, but also equip them with the knowledge and know-how of how to teach these techniques to future pupils.

Part I

Like public school reforms, teacher education reform can be seen as a battleground for political and ideological positions. Determining the subjects pre-service teachers must complete and their curricular content has significant implications for the future of the public school system. Recent reforms in Danish teacher education have led to redesigning both the content and methodology of many of the offered modules. Consequently, teaching degree programmes have restructured their modules, providing an opportunity to incorporate academic writing support within the discipline. This section of the chapter presents one example of how higher education programmes strive to prepare students for their future professions, and constitutes the context for this chapter.

To become a K-9 teacher in Denmark, students must successfully pass a number of competency area assessments, including a core of knowledge and competency areas collectively known as *The teacher's basic professionalism*. This includes completing several modules and appurtenant assessments, one of which covers the competency area *Teaching bilingual pupils*. Like the final bachelor project for the teaching degree programme, this competency area requires students to apply relevant theory and knowledge from the fields of educational linguistics and second language pedagogy to one of their main teaching subjects, and based on this, make suggestions for pedagogical practice.

The 'teaching bilingual pupils' module: content and aims

Migration patterns and increased numbers of immigrants and refugees have added to (at least the visibility of) so-called 'bilinguals' (i.e. pupils with Danish as a second language) in the public school system (known as Folkeskolen). Dealing with the presence of these pupils in Folkeskolen has been a point of heated debate since Denmark opened its borders to migrant workers in the 1970s. Due to the need to integrate 'bilingual' pupils in the Folkeskolen, teacher education reform in 2007 introduced the elective teaching subject, 'Danish as a Second Language (DSL)', although the subject had existed in schools since 1995. In this way, schools were provided with (graduated) teachers specialized in supporting second language pupils in mainstream and specialized DSL classes.

The most recent reform in 2015, however, replaced DSL with a compulsory competency area known as *Teaching bilingual pupils*. Condensing DSL as a teaching subject into a competency area has resulted in a highly concentrated area of study. Arguably, *Teaching bilingual pupils* is the most concentrated module during the pre-service teacher training, covering a wide range of knowledge and competency objectives. The appurtenant 'competency area exam' (kompetencemålsprøven, or KMP), is the only exam in the current teaching degree programme which does not include an oral component. This means students' ability to communicate appropriately in writing within the genre is particularly important. The written-only aspect of this KMP is a source of anxiety for many students.

The aim of the KMP is for students to demonstrate that they are able to 'justifiably plan, implement, evaluate and develop the teaching of bilingual pupils in a linguistically diverse classroom' (Metropol, 2017, p. 17, own translation). The module is meant to prepare students to accommodate Folkeskolen's growing population of bilingual pupils to support both their second language and subject-knowledge development. Key in this module is the students' ability to integrate theory with practice and vice versa:

> Central to the module is the student's work with languages as a learning tool in the school's subjects, [...]. Thus, the student becomes prepared to integrate and theoretically justify second-language didactic reflections and approaches in the students' main teaching subjects.
>
> *(Metropol, 2017, p. 17, own translation)*

Students perceive the *Teaching bilingual pupils* module as high-stakes, since the resulting grade of the correlating KMP is shown on their final graduation certificate. At the same time, several challenges to performing well on the KMP apply, especially the ability to write clearly, demonstrating and understanding of theories of language development, and using these to analyse and justify implementations of pedagogic practices.

The KMP is a written assignment of a maximum length of ten pages, and students must:

> analyze an educational situation, a teaching unit and/or a teaching material from one of the student's major subject areas on the basis of relevant problematics of Danish as a second language within mainstream-subject instruction. In extension of the analysis, students provide suggestions for pedagogic practice based on second-language didactic reflections in order to accommodate bilingual pupils' learning in the relevant academic subject.
>
> *(Metropol, 2017, p. 34, own translation)*

The requirements in this module can be seen as universal for the higher education context, requiring students to demonstrate their understanding of relevant theory by applying it to practical examples from their fields of study. Because the KMP is a competency area exam (as opposed to a module's final exam), it sets relatively high standards for a relatively small competency area within the teaching degree. The nature of the requirements in the KMP means students have a vested interest in learning how to demonstrate their understanding of the curriculum knowledge and how to apply this knowledge to practice. The *Teaching bilingual pupils* module was designed with these challenging requirements in mind. To scaffold students' understanding and development of academic language, the dimension of Semantics from Legitimation Code Theory was introduced and implemented. This will be the focus of the following section.

Semantic gravity and semantic profiles

Semantics is a dimension of Legitimation Code Theory (LCT) that explores the context-dependence and complexity of meanings (see Maton 2013, 2014, 2016, 2020). Explicit training using Semantics has been shown to enable cumulative knowledge-building and more specialized 'academic' and discipline-specific meanings (e.g. Clarence, 2016; Macnaught *et al.*, 2013). Here I shall focus specifically on the concept of *semantic gravity*.

Semantic gravity describes the context-dependence of something, such as a concept or idea, an icon or a movement (Maton 2013, 2014, 2020). Semantic gravity conceptualizes how much understanding the meaning of a concept depends on the context to make sense: the stronger the semantic gravity (SG+), the more meaning is dependent on its context, and conversely, the weaker the semantic gravity (SG–), the less dependent meaning is on its context. By comparing semantic gravity at different points in time or different points throughout a text, it is possible to describe processes of *weakening* semantic gravity, i.e. moving from the concrete particulars towards generalizations and abstractions whose meanings are less dependent on that context; and *strengthening* semantic gravity, i.e. moving from abstract ideas towards concrete and delimited examples.

In the context of this chapter, the concept of semantic gravity was introduced to students of the *Teaching bilingual pupils* module as an analytical tool for understanding pedagogic challenges associated with teaching second language pupils in mainstream classrooms. Students read about a study that used semantic gravity to describe challenges in teaching bilingual pupils (Meidell Sigsgaard, 2013b, 2015), which followed a fifth grade history classroom learning about Denmark's history of the early 1900s, focusing on democracy. Weaker semantic gravity in this case was observed in both the teaching materials as task instructions to students such as 'use the word "evicted" in a sentence', and the teachers' questions to students such as 'When do we have democracy in Denmark?' These types of questions posed openly with no clear connection to the context of the unit of study (being a child 100 years ago) gave the observed pupils little opportunity to successfully answer these questions. Stronger semantic gravity, on the other hand, was observed in student answers, which were often repetitions of personal or shared experiences from the classroom, e.g. when the pupils voted to be allowed to stay indoors during recess.

The semantic gravity scale (the *y*-axis in Figure 3.1) and the notion of a *semantic wave* or recurrent movements between stronger and weaker semantic gravity (the plotted profile in Figure 3.1) were introduced in the study as a way of conceptualizing

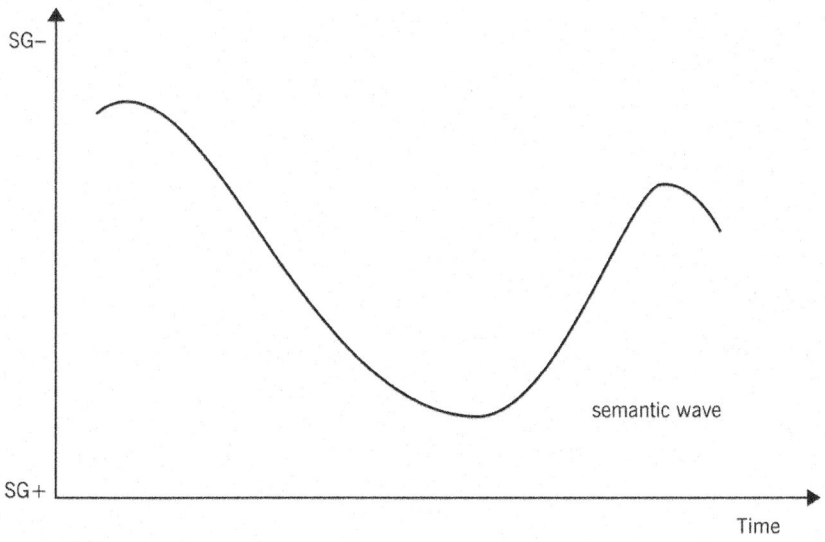

FIGURE 3.1 Generic semantic wave

Source: adapted from Maton (2013)

the challenges of making connections between teaching materials (which often have weaker semantic gravity) to pupils' own and shared experiences (stronger semantic gravity), and expected ways of answering correctly (higher up on the semantic gravity scale).

The movement from weaker semantic gravity to stronger semantic gravity (i.e. 'waving down'), was something the students of the *Teaching bilingual pupils* module recognized as a common feature of their own teaching experiences, as seen in their attempts to explain difficult concepts to pupils. The importance of 'waving up' (Macnaught et al., 2013; Maton, 2013, 2020), rather than only waving down through explanation, was highlighted in conjunction with the notion of *scaffolding* bilingual pupils' learning, i.e. supporting them in producing more generalized (and more 'correct') answers by teaching them about the language resources necessary for such answers. In this way scaffolding and waving up can be seen to build pupils' understanding of the subject being taught. On the other hand, not providing this scaffolding risks leaving confused pupils left to figure it out on their own (Meidell Sigsgaard, 2013a).

In the work reported on here, Semantics provides tools for analysing model texts. Stronger semantic gravity in the context of the KMP is associated with descriptions of teaching materials, cases, teaching plans, activity descriptions and/or excerpts of dialogue from the classroom. Weaker semantic gravity is associated with theories and models from the syllabus with which students work throughout the module, such as direct references to pedagogic and didactic models, theoretical terms from theories of language and literacy development, etc.

Applying semantic gravity to the KMP provided students with an immediate incentive for developing their understanding of this tool, and how it could be applied to producing a successful exam paper. This will be examined further in Part II. The following section describes the approach to scaffolding throughout the *Teaching bilingual pupils* module and how this approach is informed by the notion of semantic gravity.

Scaffolding throughout the module

Developing students' ability to appropriately scaffold instruction in their teaching subjects is an integral component in the *Teaching bilingual pupils* module, where scaffolding is defined as:

> not just any assistance which helps a learner accomplish a task. It is help which will enable a learner to accomplish a task which they would not have been able to manage on their own, and it is help which is intended to bring the learner closer to a state of competence which will enable them eventually to complete such a task on their own.
>
> *(Maybin et al., 1992, p. 188)*

Central to the notion of scaffolding is an environment of high intellectual challenge and simultaneously high support (Mariani, 1997). As described above, the *Teaching bilingual pupils* module provides the 'high challenge' aspect because of the condensed competency area and the high-stakes written KMP. Applying Semantics provides the 'high support' aspect, giving students tools for both understanding the challenges of their future practices as teachers, and for supporting them in their own academic success.

Because of the combination of a short amount of teaching time and the high-stakes KMP following the module, the participation requirements for the module as taught at the Metropolitan University College where this study takes place have been adapted to support the process of writing a successful KMP. The participation requirements for the module, which must be completed before signing up for the KMP, include handing in a five-page written assignment as well as giving a brief oral presentation, and providing feedback on another student's presentation.

The written assignment can be seen as a process document aimed at supporting the students' writing the KMP, as it is a draft including at least notes or ideas for the following KMP sections:

- a description of their area of interest, and a problematic;
- descriptions of chosen data (i.e. an educational situation, a teaching unit and/or a teaching material from one of the student's major subject areas);
- ideas for relevant theories for analysing the data and initial ideas for analysis; and
- suggestions for pedagogic practice.

Students are encouraged to highlight questions and difficulties they may be having in their draft. This draft then provides the student with the point of departure for the presentation, while other students, together with the instructor of the module, provide feedback aimed at helping the presenter in completing a successful KMP.

Instruction in the *Teaching bilingual pupils* module was designed to progressively decrease semantic gravity for the students throughout the module, starting with examples of successful KMPs from previous years, comparing these with the suggested (generic) structure of a KMP in this competency area, and discussing the purpose of the different sections in the suggested KMP structure. Using the concept of semantic gravity to discuss where each section might be placed along the profile and how this relates to the purpose of that section in the KMP more generally is a weakening of the semantic gravity. Together with the process of completing the participation requirements, students were scaffolded both in their understanding of the content knowledge of the competency area, and towards successful completion of their KMP.

Pushing students from novices towards 'experts' through jigsaw reading

Students in the *Teaching bilingual pupils* module were introduced to the notion of semantic gravity early in the semester, through reading an article on second language education in Denmark. This introduction used LCT as a theoretical framework along with systemic functional linguistics (Meidell Sigsgaard, 2015). Thus, students were introduced to the concepts of semantic gravity and the semantic wave from within their future context of professional practice, making the relevance of these notions pertinent. Together with three other readings which highlight the importance of explicit, language-sensitive instruction, students prepared for the lesson through an adaptation of a 'jigsaw reading' activity inspired by Gibbons (2015), as one way of scaffolding their understandings. In jigsaw reading students are assigned to groups of four. Each student reads a different article advancing the theme of the day. On the day when LCT was introduced, the themes were the implications of implicit pedagogies for (unsupported) second language development, and examples of explicit pedagogy demonstrating the strengths of, for example, 'Sydney School' genre pedagogy (Martin and Rose, 2012; Rothery, 1986) especially for second language learners.

In jigsaw reading, students participate in an authentic communication situation both in terms of speaking and in terms of listening, as they summarize and explain the content of each article to the other members of their 'home group' (Gibbons, 2015). To support their reading from home, students in the *Teaching bilingual pupils* module were given questions to guide their reading.[2] Each student in a 'home group' has read a different article approaching a common theme from different or complementary perspectives.

The exercise starts with students meeting with students from the other groups who have read and prepared notes for the same articles as themselves. Here the aim is to clarify misconceptions, and identify the main contribution of the article to the day's theme. Students are helped in this stage to gain more confidence in their understandings and can ask the instructor for help if needed as well.

In the second stage of the jigsaw reading, students re-join their home group and present each of their articles in turn. In presenting the main points of their article, each student is placed in a role of authority as a *primary knower*, meaning they have the information from the article they have read, while other students in the group do not (Martin and Rose, 2007, 2008). At the same time, the listening students have an authentic reason to listen, as *secondary knowers* (ibid.). Questions can be directed towards the content of the article, as well as interpretations of how this article relates to earlier readings or the other readings for the day.

The next step asks the group to discuss central questions, which requires them to apply their combined understandings and perspectives from the articles. This pushes students further in their understandings, requiring them to move from referencing the read articles, to discussing questions of pedagogy, implicitness and explicitness, and perhaps draw on examples from their own practice experiences, or view and analyse a video clip of a teaching situation. At the end of the session, students have up to 15 minutes of quiet time where they are prompted to consolidate their understanding of what the main theme of the day is, pull out key quotes or specific references from the readings, and relate their understandings of these.

Jigsaw reading is an organizational structure which supports students in using more academic spoken language by having them take part in substantive conversations (Gibbons, 2009). It is an activity students in the *Teaching bilingual pupils* module read about as an example of an activity which supports language development by moving students through a series of progressively and linguistically more challenging situations: from oral language use and high support at the start (where they, together with other readers of the same article define key points and definitions), through gradually more challenging language-use situations requiring more and more understanding, comparison and cross-referencing between articles, to finally writing summary notes which could be incorporated in their KMPs. Similarly, semantic gravity is weakened through the progression of the activity, as students move from a situation of relatively stronger semantic gravity when referencing key notions from the read articles to relatively weaker semantic gravity when they apply these notions to their own experiences from practice: they themselves are participants in the activity they are learning about.

Adapting jigsaw reading for tertiary students allows them to experience both how the activity works and how their own academic language use is supported. They also experience being 'pushed' toward taking on more responsibility and authority as they, through the activity, actively gain understanding and competency in how scaffolding pupils' language and understandings can look. Reminding them of this at the end of the class and coupling this experience to LCT Semantics gives them a direct understanding of this theoretical concept, which otherwise risks remaining detached from practical understanding and application. Asking students to use the terms *semantic gravity* and *semantic wave* in their discussions during such a reflection session resulted in developing a common metalanguage while also consolidating their understanding of how these concepts can be applied to different pedagogic contexts. Providing this metalanguage and returning to its use regularly throughout the module was an important aspect to the scaffolding of students' understandings and disciplinary development and will be further explored in Part II.

Part II

Having introduced students to the concepts from Semantics, the context was changed to scaffold students' work more explicitly. Next, the concepts of semantic gravity and the semantic wave were applied to students' own learning experiences from within the *Teaching bilingual pupils* module. Applying these concepts to previous students' successful KMPs allowed the students to better their understanding of the requirements they needed to meet in their final assignment, the KMP.

Understanding the structure of the exam paper and its component sections

Semantic gravity and the semantic wave were concepts reiterated throughout the *Teaching bilingual pupils* module. After being introduced to *semantic gravity* as both a way of understanding the challenges of bilingual pupils as presented in their literature, and applying the notion of semantic gravity to their experience of doing jigsaw reading, students were then re-introduced to these concepts in conjunction with their own KMP, inspired by Szenes, Tilakaratna and Maton, (2015).

The generic semantic wave profile (Figure 3.1) provided a point of departure for discussing semantic profiles produced by mapping semantic gravity changes over time, where the generic wave was one such example. Students were asked to apply the notion of semantic gravity to the suggested structure for a KMP: (1) introduction, ending in (2) a problematic for investigation, (3) theory and key concepts, (4) data, (5) analysis, (6) results, (7) suggestions for practice and (8) discussion/conclusion. They then discussed in groups where they would expect each section of the KMP paper to be placed on the semantic gravity continuum. This resulted in different semantic profiles, which then were drawn (overlapping) on the chalkboard.

The differences in semantic profiles (Figure 3.2) sparked a whole-class discussion about the purpose of each of the stages in the assignment and how they differ. For example, nearly all the groups agreed that the section of the KMP which presents the data (4 in Figure 3.2) would be lower on the semantic gravity scale when compared to the theory section (3 in Figure 3.2), but were not as unified in where the analysis section (5 in Figure 3.2) should be placed.

One group had the analysis section very low on semantic gravity scale while another group suggested the section would exhibit a (slow) ascent in approaching the results section. When asked to justify their placements, the group which had placed the analysis near the bottom of the semantic scale pointed out that an analysis has to be based on the practice being analysed. The group who had placed the analysis much higher on the scale argued that it is necessary to use the theory presented in the analysis. Another group had drawn waves on the top half of the semantic scale in the analysis section, arguing that theory should be connected to practice in this part of the KMP.

Upon further consideration, and with discussions led by the instructor, students came to agree that the purpose of the analysis section is to tease apart the data, using

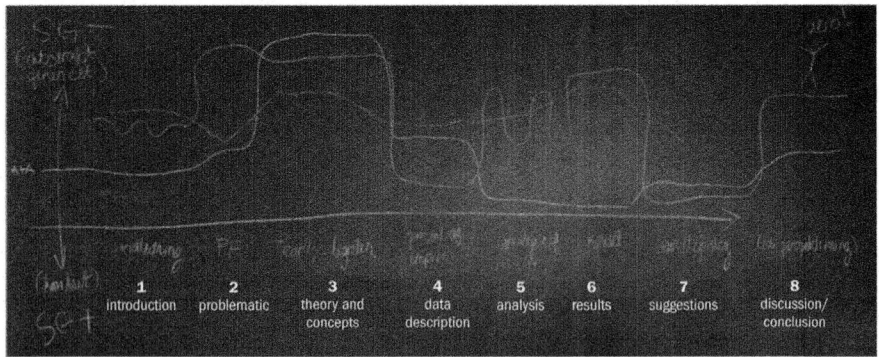

FIGURE 3.2 Students plotted their (different) versions of the semantic profile of a chosen KMP on the chalkboard for comparison

theoretical concepts to understand the data. This would result in several waves and 'dips' in the waves that are quite low on the semantic gravity scale. Similarly, the instructor pointed out that suggestions for practice tend to be most successful when students are very concrete in their suggestions for activities, justifying these by applying relevant theoretical concepts. This resulted in a new generic profile for the KMP – see Figure 3.3.

Students were highly engaged in discussing their different versions of the semantic profile for the KMP. Semantic gravity gave them a tool for approaching these discussions in a more principled way. It is the analysis (5 in Figure 3.3, the very wavy part in the middle) and the suggestions for pedagogic practice (the last few waves) that are important to a successful exam, as these are the sections where students can demonstrate their understanding of theoretical concepts and their application to practice and conversely, demonstrate their ability to generalize their practical experiences from a more theoretical perspective. Consequently, later classes in the *Teaching bilingual pupils* module focused more closely on analysis sections in both student texts (earlier KMPs) and in their readings.

In this way, the concepts are shown to be powerful analytical tools useful both in students' immediate contexts, but also when applied to other teaching tasks and contexts. Students were quickly able to grasp the notion of the semantic wave and how the 'waving' represents connecting theoretical concepts from their syllabus with concrete examples from their field of practice. This expands their understandings of what constitutes a successful academic written assignment beyond the structural template they are familiar with. The notion of the semantic wave enables an understanding of how to 'do' an analysis. This, along with examples of stronger and weaker semantic gravity in the KMP will be expanded upon in the following sections.

Practicing analysis: flipped learning and in-class application

In following lessons, semantic gravity and the semantic wave were revisited. Students were asked to watch an eight-minute 'flipped learning' video, where the instructor shows how to do a semantic gravity analysis on a section of text from one of the

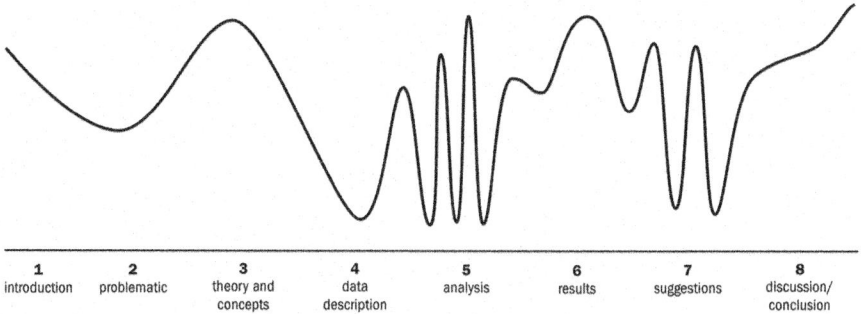

FIGURE 3.3 Generic profile identified by consensus

students' syllabus readings. The video introduces the heuristic of the semantic gravity scale, inspired by Kirk (2017), distinguishing three levels from stronger semantic gravity at the bottom to weaker semantic gravity at the top, as shown in Figure 3.4.

In this heuristic, stronger semantic gravity is associated with concrete experiences and examples, while weaker semantic gravity is seen in the abstracted and theoretical. The middle range of the semantic gravity scale is where patterns and generalizations occur. The video then demonstrates how to do a semantic gravity analysis (SG analysis) by identifying the three levels in a paragraph from a text in their syllabus. In the excerpt below **bold** text denotes stronger semantic gravity (SG+), *italicized* text are examples of theoretical terms with the weakest semantic gravity (SG–), while underlined text exemplifies generalization:

> Thus **children began by carrying out experiments in groups. Then each group of children reported what they had learned to the rest of the class.** One important aspect of the classroom organization was that each group had carried out a different experiment relating to magnetism, so that in

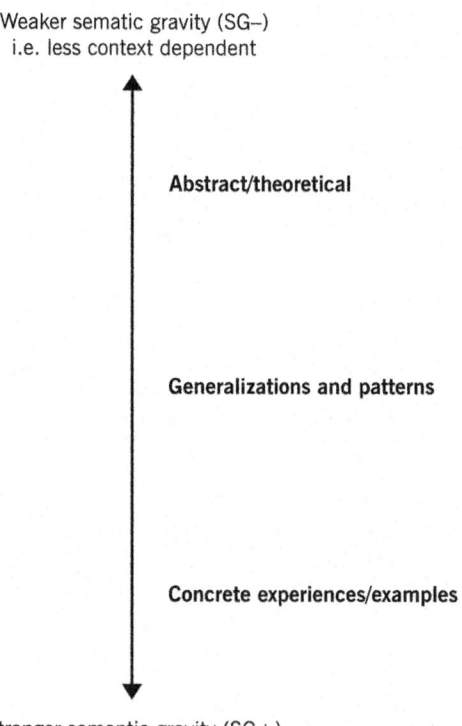

FIGURE 3.4 Three levels along the semantic gravity scale

Source: adapted from Kirk (2017)

the reporting-back session there was an authentic reason to talk about what they had learned. I refer to this activity as *teacher-guided reporting*, since the children were not expected to talk alone; instead **the teacher interacted with them as they reported what they had done to the class**. *She scaffolded new language*, **asked questions and clarified with the children the meanings they were attempting to share**. At this time she also *built up generalisations* with the children, **based on what all the experiments showed in common. In the final part of the sequence, the children wrote about their learning in their science journals.**

(Gibbons, 2005, p. 14)

This paragraph was chosen as it clearly shows what students are expected to do in their own analyses: successfully connect theoretical and central concepts (here: *teacher-guided reporting*, *scaffolded* and *built up generalisations* marked in *italics* in the text excerpt) with practical examples from an educational setting (here, what pupils and the teacher were doing in class: began by carrying out experiments, the teacher asked questions and clarified with the children, the children wrote about their learning in their science journals, marked in **bold**). The generalization in the text excerpt is underlined. A semantic profile from this short passage based on this analysis could generate a semantic wave as shown in Figure 3.5.

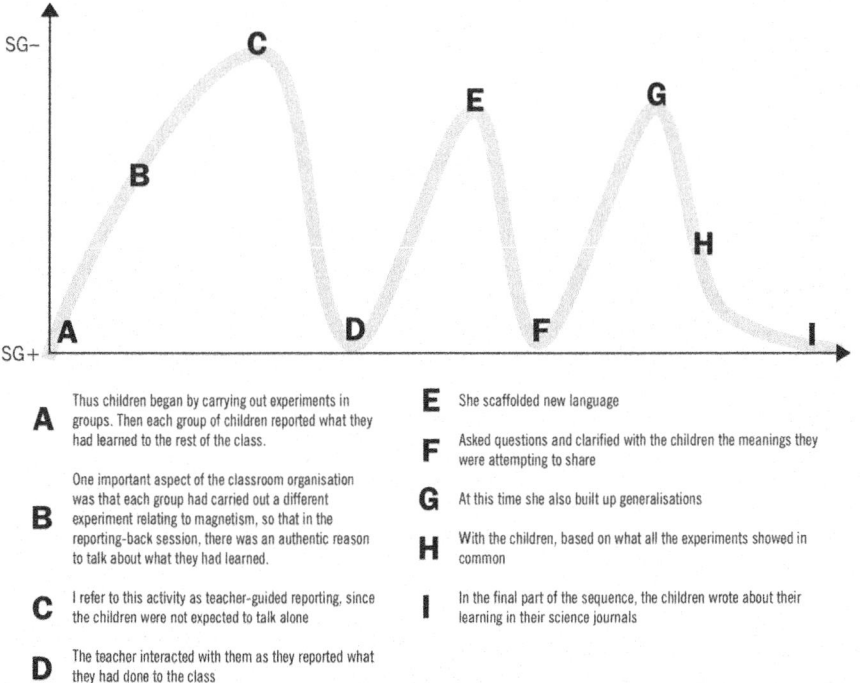

A Thus children began by carrying out experiments in groups. Then each group of children reported what they had learned to the rest of the class.

B One important aspect of the classroom organisation was that each group had carried out a different experiment relating to magnetism, so that in the reporting-back session, there was an authentic reason to talk about what they had learned.

C I refer to this activity as teacher-guided reporting, since the children were not expected to talk alone

D The teacher interacted with them as they reported what they had done to the class

E She scaffolded new language

F Asked questions and clarified with the children the meanings they were attempting to share

G At this time she also built up generalisations

H With the children, based on what all the experiments showed in common

I In the final part of the sequence, the children wrote about their learning in their science journals

FIGURE 3.5 Semantic profile corresponding with the analysed paragraph in Figure 3.5

After watching the video, students were asked to apply this type of analysis to an analysis section from a selection of three successful KMPs from the previous year. In groups of two or three, students selected a KMP to read and a section[3] from within the KMPs analysis section. The groups then attempted to do an SG analysis, discussing how and why they would draw the profile for that section, resulting in several drafts of semantic profiles. At the end of the activity, groups presented their analyses to the applied sections, showing their semantic profiles and presenting orally their reasons for drawing them as they did (see Figures 3.6a and 3.6b).

Figure 3.6a (left) illustrates the group's internal disagreements as to how the profile should be drawn. This group presented two semantic profiles, depending on how each member had understood the text. It is interesting to point out that despite these discrepancies, both versions broadly correspond with the profile drawn by a different group of students (Figure 3.6b, right). This instigated a discussion of how to actually *do* the SG analysis, and choosing appropriate units of meaning (i.e. individual words or word groups vs. clauses). Asking students to practice doing the SG analysis in groups in class provided a rich learning environment, where students were engaged with the theory. The activity and following discussions also gave students a clear understanding of how this sort of engagement with a (disciplinary) model text at the word/clause level scaffolds their academic development.

When asked to evaluate the lesson, students were generally very positive in terms of having worked with actual examples of KMPs. In other words, looking at KMP previously submitted rather than just talking about KMPs or written assignments more generally was an important aspect in their view. Incorporating actual examples of successful KMPs, and collaborating in applying the notion of semantic gravity to these, brought students 'far down' on the semantic gravity scale, they noted. Practicing applying semantic gravity to analysis sections of KMPs both strengthened their perception of how different analyses could look, while enabling an understanding of how a successful analysis is constructed.

Applying the same analytical tool to several different examples and different sections of KMPs gave students a way of deriving principles of what a successful analysis section accomplishes: applying key theoretical concepts to concrete examples of data to interpret data. In this way students in the class gained a clearer

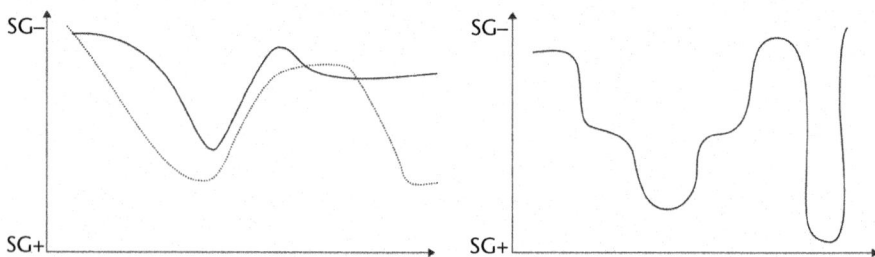

FIGURE 3.6 Two groups' versions of a semantic profile for the same section of text from a successful KMP

understanding of how they might do something similar in their own KMPs and other written assignments in the future. One student exclaimed in exasperation at the end of the lesson, 'Why haven't we been taught this before?!' pointing to the fact that they had often encountered templates intended to help students structure such assignments, but without actually looking more closely at how each section accomplishes its purpose.

Strengths and limitations of heuristics and models

This chapter demonstrates the utility and effectiveness of introducing and applying the concepts of *semantic gravity* and *semantic wave* to a group of undergraduate students needing to pass a high-stakes written exam. Introducing pre-service teacher students to LCT and especially concepts from the Semantics dimension provides students with analytical tools useful for understanding challenges in the context of developing pupils' learning and cumulative knowledge-building. Making visible these challenges accentuates the need for explicit teaching oriented towards how pupils can express their understandings in school subjects. Anchoring Semantics within students' own writing assignment works as a way of modelling a scaffolding approach as to how to express appropriate academic knowledge in a specific context.

Throughout the example drawn upon here, instruction was consistently doublesided: many of the types of language-scaffolding activities that students were introduced to (which are understood as integral to pedagogic models for supporting second language learners in mainstream classrooms) were also activities in which students participated during instruction throughout the module (such as jigsaw reading). The LCT concepts have been shown to provide students with accessible yet powerful analytical tools applicable to both students' current and future practices. These notions provided students and the instructor with a tool for 'meta'-talk, easily enabling them either to 'step back' during class and highlight where on the semantic gravity scale a current discussion or activity could be placed, and how this corresponds to, for example, a particular section in a written assignment. This type of scaffolding is particularly important in an obligatory module such as the one reported on here, since not all students are necessarily language-oriented (i.e. students who chose Mathematics and the Sciences as their teaching subjects) and can have difficulty understanding the requirements of the written exam genre.

Having semantic gravity as a shared concept also makes the comparison of different examples or analyses more efficient. In the case illustrated here, this was true for discussions of readings, in analysing video clips of classroom practice, and in activities throughout the module. Applying semantic gravity to different contexts, similar to those students might encounter once they graduate as teachers, also highlighted one of the principal aspects of the module's competency area – the importance of explicit instruction and use of model texts. While applying it to their own learning context as students, the notion of semantic gravity also helped to consolidate students' understandings, building bridges from their (shared) experiences to the knowledge and practices being taught.

Employing semantic gravity as an analytical tool for looking at successful examples of earlier exams reinforced students' understanding of the concept and provided them with an opportunity to apply it in practicing how to 'do' analysis. In this way, working on doing an SG analysis together enabled students to gain greater understanding of what academic analysis is – an aspect of their studies which they all recognize as important but often have difficulty demonstrating, let alone explaining. Through doing these analyses, students thus experienced support in developing their own academic writing, bringing them closer to a state of competence in producing their KMP, which for many students is a challenging and obscure genre. In this way, semantic gravity and the semantic wave provided powerful yet comprehensible tools for scaffolding students' ability to demonstrate their own understandings as expected in their programme of study.

The work highlighted in this chapter is ongoing, with an interest in continuing the explicit instruction in the curriculum content students are expected to demonstrate through written language. More specifically, further research will explore the language resources successful students leverage in order to demonstrate their understandings of theoretical concepts and how they apply these to practice while developing successful arguments throughout their written analyses. This research will build on work additionally informed by a systemic functional model of language such as that of Christie's analysis (2016) of written assignments in secondary school English literacy studies, and Hood's work (2010, 2016) on academic writing within the humanities in higher education studies. In line with these studies, future work in the context of academic writing in teacher education will be complemented by systemic functional linguistics, which can provide insights into the use of language resources in academic writing for a range of functions: for example, positioning theories and actors, expressing levels of agreement and generalization as well as opening up space for different positions and voices. Connecting such findings with scaffolding work informed by the notions of semantic gravity and the semantic wave can provide students and educators with simple yet powerful analytical tools for making explicit disciplinary requirements.

Notes

1. For the sake of readability, 'students' in this text refers to pre-service teacher students enrolled in the BA programme at a Danish University College to become teachers. 'Pupils' are students in the public school, grades K-9/10 and the target group/context of the BA students' readings and future work.
2. Example questions: What is the author's main point in this article? Find and define key notions. Choose 1–2 central quotes from the article and summarize their importance. If the author makes suggestions for pedagogic practice: what are these, and why are they important for second language learners?
3. Students decided in their group what denoted 'a cohesive section' from within the analysis section of the chosen KMP (from as little as a single paragraph up to several paragraphs).

References

Christie, F. (2016). Secondary school English literacy studies: cultivating a knower code. In K. Maton, S. Hood, and S. Shay (Eds), *Knowledge-building: Educational studies in Legitimation Code Theory* (pp. 138–157). Abingdon: Routledge.
Clarence, S. (2016). Exploring the nature of disciplinary teaching and learning using Legitimation Code Theory Semantics. *Teaching in Higher Education, 2*(2), 123–137.
Coffin, C. and Donohue, J.P. (2012). Academic literacies and systemic functional linguistics: How do they relate? *Journal of English for Academic Purposes, 11*(1), 64–75. https://doi.org/10.1016/j.jeap.2011.11.004.
Gibbons, P. (2005). Mediating learning through talk: Teacher-student interactions with second language learners. In I. Lindberg and K. Sandwall (Eds), *Språket Och Kunskapen. Att Lära På Sitt Andraspråk i Skola Och Högskola* (pp. 7–26). Göteborg: Institutet för svenska som andraspråk. Retrieved from http://hdl.handle.net/2077/20797.
Gibbons, P. (2009). *English learners, academic literacy, and thinking: Learning in the challenge zone.* Portsmouth, NH: Heinemann.
Gibbons, P. (2015). *Scaffolding language, scaffolding learning: Teaching English language learners in the mainstream classroom* (2nd edn). Portsmouth, NH: Heinemann Publishing.
Griffin, C.W. (Ed.). (1982). *Teaching writing in all disciplines. New directions in teaching and learning, no. 12.* San Francisco, CA: Jossey-Bass.
Hood, S. (2010). *Appraising research: Evaluation in academic writing.* London: Palgrave Macmillan.
Hood, S. (2016). Ethnographies on the move, stories on the rise : Methods in the humanities. In K. Maton, S. Hood, and S. Shay (Eds), *Knowledge-building : Educational studies in Legitimation Code Theory* (pp. 117–137). Abingdon: Routledge.
Humphrey, S. and Dreyfus, S. (2012). Exploring the interpretive genre in applied linguistics. *Indonesian Journal of SFL, 1*(2), 156–174.
Illeris, K. (2003). Towards a contemporary and comprehensive theory of learning. *International Journal of Lifelong Education, 22*(4), 396–406. https://doi.org/10.1080/0260137032000094814.
Kirk, S. (2017). Waves of reflection: Seeing knowledges in academic writing. In J. Kemp (Ed.), *EAP in a rapidly changing landscape: Issues, challenges and solutions* (pp. 109–118). Proceedings of the 2015 BALEAP Conference. Reading: Garnet Publishing.
Klafki, W. (1983). *Kategoriel dannelse og kritisk konstruktiv pædagogik: udvalgte artikler* (Udvalgte a). København: Nyt Nordisk Forlag.
Lillis, T., Harrington, K., Lea, M.R. and Mitchell, S. (Eds). (2015). *Working with academic literacies: Case studies towards transformative practice. Uma ética para quantos?* (Vol. XXXIII). Anderson, SC: Parlor Press.
Lillis, T.M. (2001). *Student writing: Access, regulation, desire.* London: Routledge.
Macken-Horarik, M. (2006). Knowledge through 'know how': Systemic functional grammatics and the symbolic reading. *English Teaching: Practice and Critique, 5*(1), 102–121.
Macnaught, L., Maton, K., Martin, J.R. and Matruglio, E. (2013). Jointly constructing semantic waves: Implications for teacher training. *Linguistics and Education, 24*(1), 50–63.
Mahboob, A., Dreyfus, S., Humphrey, S. and Martin, J.R. (2010). Applable linguistics and English language teaching: The Scaffolding Literacy in Adult and Tertiary Environments (SLATE) project. In, A. Mahboob and N. Knight (Eds), *Appliable linguistics: Texts, contexts and meanings* (pp. 25–43). London: Continuum.
Mariani, L. (1997). Teacher support and teacher challenge in promoting learner autonomy. *Perspectives: A Journal of TESOL Italy, 23*(2), 5–19. Retrieved from www.learningpaths.org/papers/papersupport.htm.
Martin, J.R. and Rose, D. (2007). *Working with discourse: Meaning beyond the clause* (2nd edn). London: Continuum.

Martin, J.R. and Rose, D. (2008). *Genre relations: Mapping culture.* London: Equinox.
Martin, J.R. and Rose, D. (2012). *Learning to write, reading to learn: Genre, knowledge and pedagogy in the Sydney school.* Sheffield: Equinox.
Maton, K. (2013). Making semantic waves: A key to cumulative knowledge-building. *Linguistics and Education, 24*(1), 8–22. https://doi.org/10.1016/j.linged.2012.11.005.
Maton, K. (2014). *Knowledge and knowers: Towards a realist sociology of education.* London: Routledge.
Maton, K. (2016). Legitimation Code Theory: Building knowledge about knowledge-building, in K. Maton, S. Hood and S. Shay (Eds), *Knowledge-building: Educational studies in Legitimation Code Theory* (pp. 1–24). London: Routledge.
Maton, K. (2020). Semantic waves: Context, complexity and academic discourse. In J.R. Martin, K. Maton and Y.J. Doran (Eds) *Accessing academic discourse: Systemic functional linguistics and Legitimation Code Theory* (pp. 59–85). London: Routledge.
Maybin, J., Mercer, N. and Stierer, B. (1992). Scaffolding learning in the classroom. In K. Norman (Ed.), *Thinking voices: The work of the National Oracy Project* (pp. 186–195). Sevenoaks, Kent: Hodder and Stoughton.
Meidell Sigsgaard, A.-V. (2013a). 'Hvad skal jeg så skrive? – Det må du selv vide ...' Udvekslingsstrukturanalyse af samtaler mellem lærere og elever i dansk som andetsprog- og historieundervisning. *NordAnd, 8*(1), 61–92.
Meidell Sigsgaard, A.-V. (2013b). *Who knows what? The teaching of knowledge and knowers in a fifth grade Danish as a second language classroom.* Unpublished doctoral dissertation. University of Aarhus. Retrieved from www.legitimationcodetheory.com/publications.html.
Meidell Sigsgaard, A.-V. (2015). Demokrati og semantiske bølger i andetsprogsundervisningen. *Viden Om Literacy, 18*(På flere sprog), 12–25. Retrieved from www.videnomlaesning. dk/tidsskrifter/nr-18-flersprogede-borns-laesning-og-laering/.
Metropol. (2017). Studieordning 2017/18: Modulbeskrivelser and Kompetencemålsprøver, studieordningens del 3. København: Metropol. Retrieved from www.phmetropol.dk/ uddannelser/laerer/uddannelsen/studieordning.
Nielsen, B., Henningsen, C., Laursen, P.F. and Paulsen, J. (2006). *Teori og praksis i læreruddannelsen – En interviewundersøgelse.* Copenhagen: CVU København and Nordsjælland.
Rose, D. and Martin, J.R. (2012). *Learning to write, reading to learn: Genre, knowledge and pedagogy in the Sydney school.* Sheffield: Equinox.
Rothery, J. (1986). Teaching genre in primary School: A genre based approach to the development of writing abilities. In *Writing Projekt: Report 1986 ø8 Working Papers in Linguistics no. 4* (pp. 3–62). Sydney: Department of Linguistics, University of Sydney.
Schmidt, L.-H. (Ed.). (2001). *Det videnskabelige perspektiv.* København: Akademisk Forlag.
Swales, J. and Feak, C. (2005). *Academic writing for graduate students: Essential tasks and skills* (2nd edn). Ann Arbor, MI: University of Michigan Press.
Szenes, E., Tilakaratna, N. and Maton, K. (2015). The knowledge practices of 'critical' thinking. In M. Davies and R. Barnett (Eds), *Critical thinking in higher education* (pp. 573–591). London: Palgrave Macmillan.

4
NEW ASSESSMENT FORMS IN HIGHER EDUCATION

A study of student generated digital media products in the health sciences

Helen Georgiou and Wendy Nielsen

Background

Technology has drastically changed the nature of tertiary assessment, not simply in terms of efficiency or administration but also in terms of design (Bennett *et al.*, 2017). New assessment types, such as podcasts, video productions and wikis are slowly appearing in a growing number of tertiary science courses (Hoban *et al.*, 2016; Shute *et al.*, 2016). Though clearly prompted by advances in – and access to – new technologies, there are also other drivers. The nature of employment is changing and universities are more conscious of developing a wider set of skills in students, including communication (McComas, 2014). Research has established that in science, communication skills are not emphasized in courses and thus not well-developed in students, and this is particularly true for communication skills beyond the written forms (Chan, 2011; de la Harpe *et al.*, 2009).

A wider range of assessment forms offer new possibilities. Assessments, such as the multimodal texts[1] that will be discussed in this chapter show potential in achieving multiple aims, in particular, developing attributes such as communication as well as developing disciplinary knowledge (Hoban *et al.*, 2011). For example, in a study on primary school students, the use of multimodal assessment was demonstrated to facilitate their expression of scientific concepts, as well as extend their thinking and knowledge about the topic (O'Byrne, 2009). A similar positive finding has been discovered among ninth graders asked to explain the 'work–energy' concept (Tang *et al.*, 2011). In this study, students demonstrated a development of their conceptual understanding through a holistic approach to learning, including improvements in quantitative understanding as well as increased epistemological awareness. Perhaps in recognition of this potential, Australian curricula have explicitly prioritized the development of effective multimodal communication in students: students are *expected to* 'select and use suitable forms of digital, visual, written and/or oral forms of communication' (NESA, 2017). In tertiary science, though, there exists a paucity of research; researchers have linked the mastery of representational fluency to disciplinary achievement, implicating the importance of multimodal communication (Prain and Tytler, 2012; Sinatra and Pintrich, 2003).

Given that there are wide-ranging issues in terms of measurement even in the more traditional forms of assessments for more straightforward outcomes such as testing content knowledge in multiple-choice tests (Shute et al., 2016; Wallace and Bailey, 2010), assessment of communication using 'new' written forms, which might draw on a range of principles that not yet defined, need to be very carefully considered (Chan, 2011; Lea and Street, 1998). Without understanding what we are assessing and how, we will not be able to help students develop these communication skills and might also sacrifice the precision of our existing assessments (Watson, 2001). This is especially true in Science and especially true at this point in time, when general capabilities or skills are being promoted as the answer to the impending 'STEM crisis' (Australian Government, 2014; PwC, 2015).

Literature review

Scientists are increasingly expected to be able to communicate their science directly to lay audiences, a task which has generally been the responsibility of journalists or science communicators. This sharing of responsibility across groups with disparate philosophies and communicative aims, together with the increasing ease of communication across multimodalities, has focused attention on the how and why of science communication (e.g. Baram-Tsabari and Osborne, 2015; Davies, 2008). One key concern in scientific communication is how to deal with complexity, or a recognition that individuals with highly specialized knowledge need to be able to select and communicate relevant and interesting aspects of their work to non-specialized or general audiences (e.g. Hilgard and Li, 2017, p. 80). Complexity is a common theme across various strands of science education and literacy, and communication research. Some key threads are outlined below.

Research in representational use in science has shown that mastery or fluency across representational use provides students with epistemic access to disciplinary knowledge. Airey and Linder (2009) describe representations, together with activities and tools, as constituting many different modes, including (but not limited to) images, spoken and written language, mathematics and gesture. They identify how achieving fluency in a 'critical constellation of modes' is implicated in accessing 'disciplinary ways of knowledge'. That is, students that are able to interpret and use a variety of key modes are more likely to appreciate and gain access to disciplinary ways of thinking. Various studies have also shown that the act of representation *making* by the student can lead to improved conceptual understanding and higher levels of engagement (Ainsworth et al., 2011; Hubber et al., 2010; Prain and Tytler, 2012). Implicated in this is that 'representations do not simply transmit scientific information; they are integral to reasoning about scientific phenomena' (Klein and Kirkpatrick, 2010, p. 78). Airey and Linder identify that disciplinary ways of knowing can be 'more or less complex and/or more or less abstract' (2009, p. 44) and that both the number and affordances of modes play a role in determining and negotiating this complexity. Modes can be complex in their arrangement or their individual character and these reflect disciplinary complexity.

Studies from systemic functional linguistics (SFL) similarly reveal the important role of complexity in science education (Derewianka and Jones, 2016; Martin and Veel, 2005). With a focus on language, Fang, for example (2005), characterizes scientific writing as exhibiting four grammatical features which distinguish it from the everyday: informational density (number of 'content words'[2] per clause); abstraction (turning everyday experiences into abstract entities through nominalization); technicality (words with specialized meaning within the discipline of science, often reflecting physical quantities, processes and objects); and authoritativeness (being presented with objectivity and certainty).

Science is both multimodal and complex. Multimodality is a new and developing field and frameworks for analysis are still in their infancy (Bateman *et al.*, 2017). Characterizing complexity across different modes and, in particular, considering the interaction between the various resources, is an immense challenge. So too is considering how the analysis from a research perspective will feed back into practice.

Legitimation Code Theory (LCT) is a theoretical framework in which complexity is conceptualized by *semantic density* (Maton 2011, Maton and Doran 2017a, 2017b). Alongside the concept *semantic* gravity, which captures context-dependence, this concept forms part of the wider dimension of Semantics (Maton, 2014, 2016, 2020). Importantly, these 'qualities' of complexity and context-dependence have increasingly been implicated as being an important part of the teaching and learning of science. For example, in a state-wide compulsory test for junior high school students in Australia, scientific explanations (open-ended responses) are graded using the SOLO taxonomy, ranked by degree of complexity (McPhan, 2008). In tertiary physics, Georgiou *et al.* (2014) show how a focus on degree of context-dependence is able to reformulate how we think about conceptual change. Studies also suggest that systematic and sequenced shifts in the degrees of complexity is a key aspect of building knowledge in classroom practices (e.g. Macnaught *et al.*, 2013; Maton, 2013, 2014, 2020).

Method and results

We have been collecting examples of digital explanations created by tertiary science students as part of a larger research project to understand science learning, while generating these products (see Nielsen and Jones, 2016). Since these assessments are new, an outline of the contexts in which they appear is provided in the first part of this section. Following this, and in an effort to understand the negotiation of complexity in scientific knowledge, the close analysis of two texts using the LCT concept of semantic density is presented.

Multimodal assessments in science subjects

The data set that this chapter draws on includes: 43 media files from nutrition/dietetics, pharmacology, biology, engineering and pre-service science teaching methods for both primary and secondary level; 21 interviews with students; four interviews with subject instructors; subject outlines for each subject; and task descriptions and rubrics. Instructors also supplied a marks summary in the form of class mean and marks range. Since these tasks are still relatively new in the tertiary sector (see for example, Hoban *et al.*, 2016), sampling for the study aimed to capture a range of products from different science learning contexts. These data provide a picture of the nature of the products, justifications for the assessment, state of the assessment criteria/rubrics, as well as the perceptions of the tasks by students. Table 4.1 summarizes these characterizations by providing a description of three individual cases. Later in the chapter, excerpts from interviews from the pharmacology assessment will also be used for illustrative purposes.

Additionally, we also analysed the individual products in order to understand which resources students were using. The different resources used by students are outlined below and were corded to these categories in NVivo (examples in parenthesis):

- **Video:** Fast-moving images give real-life view of phenomenon; may be student-generated or imported (e.g. YouTube clip of people dancing).
- **Slowmation:** Still images uploaded to video production software and played slowly at two frames-per-second to give appearance of movement (e.g. Sequence of images where frog hops across lily pads on a pond).
- **Animation:** Generally created using specialized software; played at video replay speed so images appear to move, 'cartoonish' (e.g. Animated clip of Pokémon character emerging from an egg).
- **Still image:** Static image left on screen for longer than two seconds (e.g. Molecular diagram of ferroquine).
- **Narration:** Audio track of voiceover by the blended media creator (e.g. Voice-over highlighting red portion of ferroquine molecule).
- **Music:** Any continuous sound or piece of music appearing in the text (e.g. stock backing track/jingle running for the duration of a text).
- **Text-on-screen:** Words used to highlight or label other material (e.g. Text label 'Tavche Gravche' superimposed on image of the food).
- **External objects:** Digital object inserted wholesale from another source (e.g. Inserted clip of a titration simulation with existing narration).

We aimed to consistently identify resources as distinct categories based on our assumption that each resource carries some sort of meaning. This task was not necessarily straightforward. For example, we differentiated between 'text-on-screen' as added by the science student (and thus, intentional) and text that appeared in imported diagrams or images (coded as 'images'). We also added a code for

TABLE 4.1 Characteristics of three 'case' texts, with comparisons to wider sample

	Range in data set	Case 1: Malaria (Pharmacology)	Case 2: Macedonia (Nutrition/Dietetics)	Case 3: Lifecycles (Primary science)
Purpose of digital media task (from Subject Outline)	varies	Outline the topic of the technical literature review for non-specialist audience, up to 5 mins	Highlight staple foods, geographic influences, food customs, issues for achieving a healthy diet, dietary provisions for aged-care, up to 4 mins	Explain a concept from an allocated primary level learning outcome to children of that age, 2–3 mins
Subject	varies	Principles of Pharmacology (3rd Year–2015)	Food Service and Dietetics Management (3rd Year–2015)	Science in the Primary Curriculum (1st Year–2016)
Basic form of artefact	varies	Image + narration	Video	Slowmation
Task purpose (instructor quote)	varies	'If you've got to explain something to somebody it becomes much more powerful'	'getting students to understand more about other cultures and their food habits'	'to assess the students' abilities in putting together a teaching sequence or product'
Indiv. or group?	both	individual	Group of 3–4	individual
Task weighting	5% to 50%	5% (5/5)	10% (9/10)	40%
Mark earned	50–100%	100%	90%	85%
Duration	(2–3) to 6 mins	4:54 mins	4:30 mins	3:01 mins

'external object', which we defined as a digital object that, despite possibly containing one or more resources, was embedded in the digital artefact with minimal or no manipulation by the student. Following the categorization of semiotic resources, we generated a 'profile' using features in NVivo in order to better visualize the resources used by student creators. Examples of these profiles are presented in the next section (Table 4.2).

As expected, students used resources in different combinations and thus the products varied widely across the sample, both within and across the various tasks. This variety is one of the challenges in assessing these particular types of task.

Theorizing complexity

Sample and analysis

The theoretical approach to understand complexity was developed using a close analysis of two student-generated artefacts created as part of an assessment in a third-year Principles of Pharmacology subject in 2015. The products addressed different assessment questions and one was higher scoring. Table 4.2 depicts some characterizations drawn from the analysis process outlined above, including the profiles of resources used.

Various software programmes were used to analyse the data. First, the narration was transcribed and the transcript was structured by clause. The corresponding images were then split by individual frames, matched to each clause and exported into Excel, where the analysis of the narration and quantitative treatment took place. The analysis of the images with respect to semantic density occurred in NVivo, where durations could be calculated.

Analysis and results are presented in two main parts. Analysis of the two texts begins with semantic density analysis of the narration, followed by analysis of the images or visual component. In the final part of the results section, we offer a possible method for combining these analyses to make more holistic judgements about the texts.

To analyse the language portion of the texts (the narration as audio track), a coding structure developed by Maton and Doran (2017a) was implemented. This structure, known as a 'translation device', considers various units of meaning, from the individual word to the sequencing of longer stretches of discourse. The translation device looks at both discrete 'degrees' of *epistemic-semantic density* (the 'amount' of condensation of epistemic meanings in any one word) and *epistemological condensation* or how much that amount is increased through combining words. In this analysis, the epistemic-semantic density was determined through the use of the 'wording tool' of the translation device. That is, coding occurred with respect to the degree of complexity of the word only, and this was used to consider complexity across the text and between the text and image. This decision is consistent with Fang's (2005) consideration of 'information density' and 'technicality' within an SFL framework (Martin, 1993).

New assessment forms in higher education 61

TABLE 4.2 Characterization of two sample texts, including profiles (of resources used) and screenshots

Text	Details	Assessment	Audience	Basic form	Accuracy
Malaria	Length: 4:53 Subject: Principles of Pharmacology Year: 2015	Topic: Is Ferroquine an ingenious anti-malarial? Mark: 5/5	Non-specialist	95% Image-narration-text, 5% animation explanation, informational	High
Multiple Sclerosis (MS)	Length: 4:54 Subject: Principles of Pharmacology Year: 2015	Topic: What are the latest developments in therapeutics for the treatment of multiple sclerosis? Mark: 4/5	Non-specialist	100% slowmation explanation, informational	High

TABLE 4.3 Annotation and coding for wording type and subtype

SD	Type	Subtype	Examples
+	**Technical** (meanings are given by their location within a specialized domain of social practice)	**CONGLOMERATE** (comprise multiple distinct parts that each possess a technical meaning)	Monosaccharides Ferroquine Leukocytes
↑		Compact (comprise a single part with a technical meaning)	Force Parasite
↓	Everyday (meanings are given not by their location in specialized domains but rather through their usage in commonplace practices and contexts)	CONSOLIDATED (encode happenings or qualities as things) 'Happenings' are processes or events that are normally realized by verbs and 'things' are elements or items (physical or intangible) that are normally realized by nouns	Death Prevention Action
–		Common (leave happenings or qualities as qualities)	Moves Mosquito

Words were categorized into types and subtypes with the main division being that of 'technical' and 'everyday' with two subtypes in each category (Table 4.3). A technical term like 'force' belongs in this category because its meaning is given by its location within the specialized domain of physics. 'Mosquito' is an everyday term because its meaning is given through its usage in everyday practices and contexts. The two subtypes of technical words are 'conglomerate' and 'compact', which relate to whether words have multiple or single parts that have technical meanings, respectively. The two subtypes of everyday words are 'consolidated' and 'common'. Consolidated words are those which encode happenings as things. The term 'prevention', for example, is a nominalization of 'prevents'. 'Prevents' is a happening (and would thus belong to the 'everyday common' category), but 'prevention' is a thing. It has stronger semantic density because embedded in the term is the meaning that 'something is preventing something else'.

The analysis occurred over two cycles, with the researcher consulting specialists of SFL and an author of the original paper (Doran), to ensure reliability. The analysis employed the same annotation as Maton and Doran (2017a), also depicted in Table 4.3. For example, annotations included font changes, capitalizations or bold letters to indicate type and/or subtype in the wording tool. Table 4.4 shows an illustrative excerpt from each text that contains all four subtypes of word.

Given that the current research is making a judgement about how complexity is negotiated in the text, we quantified complexity as part of the analysis. The different word types were assigned a value, which represented different strengths of semantic density as shown in Table 4.3. A higher value represented stronger semantic density (more complex meaning) and a small value represented weaker semantic density (less complex meaning). The scale assumes a larger gap between the technical and everyday types than between the subtypes in each category. This assumption is already qualitatively supported by work in SFL, although work is continuing in this field (Hao, 2015; Martin, 1993). The quantitative assignments are therefore meaningful when considering relative values, but absolute values of differences are not meaningful.

The degree of semantic density (how technical the text is at this point) was measured relative to the clause. The clause is considered the unit onto which different kinds of meanings are mapped, according to Halliday and Matthiessen in SFL (Halliday and Matthiessen, 2014, p. 10). The quantitative measurement

TABLE 4.4 Coded excerpts for each sample with annotation

Text	Excerpt with coding
Malaria	This is attributed to the INABILITY of the transporter producing **CHLOROQUINE resistance** to remove **FERROQUINE** from a digestive vacuole
Multiple Sclerosis	inhibiting the MIGRATION of **LEUKOCYTES** into **Central Nervous System tissues**

therefore reflects relative strengths of semantic density of the narration per clause, across the text. Everyday words attracted zero value, everyday consolidated attracted 1, and so on. If multiple counts of the word subtype were present, they were added together. For example, in Malaria in Table 4.4 shows one everyday consolidated word type (inability), three technical compacts (resistance, digestive and vacuole) and two technical conglomerate (Ferroquine, Chloriquine). This would attract a quantitative assignment of 18.

In the first instance, the overall average degree of semantic density for both texts was calculated by adding the value for epistemic semantic density for each clause and diving by the total number of clauses (Eq. 1). This modest measure simply indicates that on average, MS had relatively stronger semantic density than Malaria.

$$SD_{AVE} = \frac{Sum\ SD\ values}{total\ no.\ of\ clauses}$$

Equation 1. Calculation of average semantic density of the two texts. $SD_{AVE} = 4.0$ for Malaria and $SD_{AVE} = 8.5$ for MS.

The quantitative assignments for the word subtypes were then displayed as a function of clause number to reflect the relative strength of epistemic semantic density across the narration for both texts, as shown in Figure 4.2 in the results section.

The concept of semantic density was also used to consider the images in these two texts. The two texts were primarily of the 'Image and Narration' form, which allowed the straightforward delineation. That is, the individual images could be isolated, as there were no 'film/video' or significant sections of 'animation', as were present in other texts from our sample (see Table 4.1). A distinction was made between 'technical' and 'everyday', with a further distinction within each category. The four levels were consistently identified and did not introduce any significant disputes. The categories and examples of image types are provided in Table 4.5.

Figure 4.1 shows two example images from the texts. One is a scientific complex image from the Multiple Sclerosis (MS) text. It is coded as such both because it

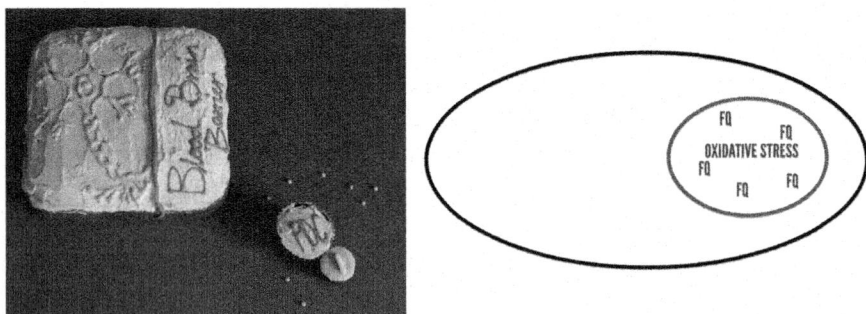

FIGURE 4.1 Example image semantic density categories: Scientific complex image from MS (left), Scientific simple image from Malaria (right)

TABLE 4.5 Image categorization with semantic density (SD)

SD	Image Type
+	**Scientific complex** i) Images that represent a scientific object(s) or representation in a traditional format. ii) Images that represent a scientific process. **Scientific simple** Images that represent a scientific object or representation in a simplified or 'non-traditional' format. **Everyday real** Single/isolated images that are photographs (or 'photoreal') of real objects **Everyday illustrative** Single/isolated images that are illustrative or stylistically (but not 'technical') representative of the 'natural' version (e.g. cartoon-like images) **Text image** Images that include text and symbols (including punctuation and not assigned a semantic density value).
−	Blank (blank screen)

contains multiple parts (neuron, blood–brain barrier and pharmacological process) and a complex representation of a neuron (as would appear in a science textbook or online resource). The second image is a scientific simple image from the Malaria text. It is assigned so due to its simplification of process and content. The other categories are not supported by way of example but are relatively self-explanatory.

Results

Figure 4.2 illustrates that the Malaria text exhibited a consistently weaker semantic density across the text, while MS had consistently stronger semantic density on average, with a small number of sections of relatively stronger semantic density manifesting as clear 'peaks'. These peaks are labelled as they inform our subsequent analysis, considering language/narration and image together.

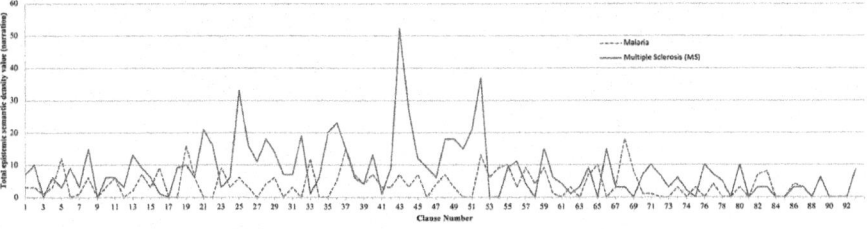

FIGURE 4.2 Relative strengths of semantic density per clause for Malaria and MS.

The key differences in the use of images for the two products were types used and relative durations (see Figure 4.3). Multiple Sclerosis used more of the 'Scientific Complex' type, easily the most prevalent choice in this text (accounting for 80 per cent of all images used). Malaria used a greater variety of image type, including a significant number of blank frames.

Combining image and narration; analysis and results

Though we began by coding language and 'image' separately, subsequently 'points of interest' (A1, A2, A3 and B1) were identified through our analysis as displayed in Figure 4.2. Since the focus in this chapter is on how the creators of these digital explanations negotiated the complexity of meaning through the text, points of interest constituted points where the narration or image contained a 'maximum value' of semantic density. Though the quantification of image is not shown as it is for narration in Figure 4.2 (for ease of readability), the identified maxima in Figure 4.2 remain the same even with the image assignments added. These points were then more closely examined to consider how the complex ideas were negotiated. For Malaria, three different points (A1-clause 5, A2-clause 19, A3-clause 68) were chosen from maxima in the combined text–image 'quantities'. Malaria was more varied than MS, so three points were necessary to represent the different 'points of interest'. For the MS text, only a single relevant maximum was found (B1-clause 43), as the patterns of semantic density were similar throughout the text. It should

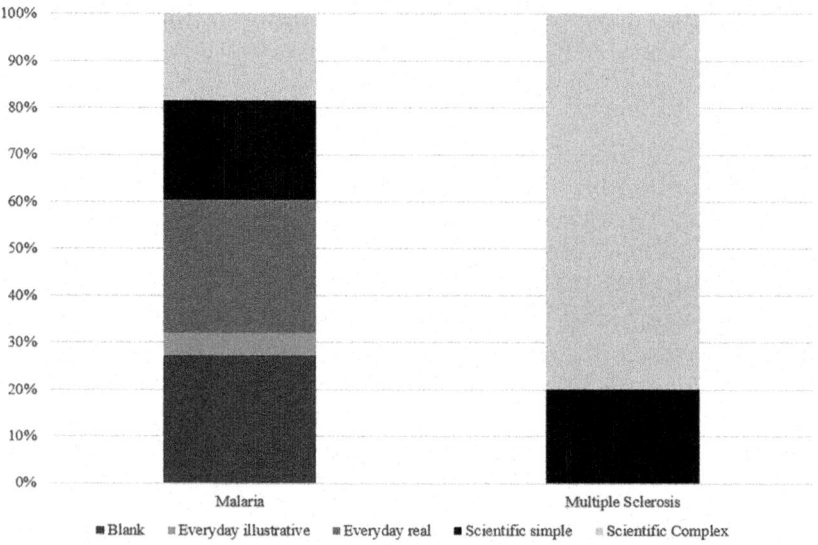

FIGURE 4.3 Duration (as a proportion of total) of each type of image in Malaria and MS

Note
Relative strengths of semantic density increase down the column

be noted that the three highest points on MS were each higher than any of the points from Malaria. Each point will be expanded on below.

At this point in the text (A1, which is the first point of interest in Malaria), the narration exhibits a relatively high value for the strength of semantic density. Four technical compact terms are used in the one clause, with three consecutive terms amassed at the end (Figure 4.4). To communicate this complexity, two distinct techniques are apparent. We call these techniques 'negotiation'. For example, considering point A1, a peak in semantic density, the narration in the next clause: 'and can cause fever, headaches, chills and vomiting in a patient', is relatively less complex; we observe no technical or everyday consolidated terms, which means the semantic density has changed from a relatively stronger to a relatively weaker value in the space of time of these two clauses. In terms of the relationship between the image and the narration, we see that the image which accompanies the technical narration 'protozoan parasite, plasmodium' is in fact an 'everyday real' image of a plasmodium. The image is also accompanied by the text on screen "plasmodium" (Figure 4.4). Together, the image and narration act to signal that the plasmodium is a 'thing' and this 'thing' can cause a range of familiar symptoms. Complexity has therefore been 'negotiated'; work has been done to create a placeholder for technical meaning. In addition, a shift to a section of lower semantic density follows. This technique is used repeatedly in this text, as demonstrated further by Point A2.

Point A2 represents the second highest peak in terms of the strength of semantic density for Malaria and is another illustration of the negotiation we explored at point A1. In terms of the image and narration shown in A2, we can see that three everyday real images of 'drugs' are presented (Figure 4.5), supporting the considerably technical terms used in the accompanying narration. Like the signalling of the 'plasmodium', here, the images of drugs are used as a placeholder for 'mefloquine, doxycycline and chloroquine'. In the clause immediately following this one: 'CHLOROQUINE is the most widely used among developing nations due to its EFFECTIVENESS and low cost of PRODUCTION', we see that two everyday consolidated ('effectiveness' and 'production') and one technical conglomerate ('chloroquine') words are used. In the two clauses that follow: 'If we've got so many drugs already'

PLASMODIUM

FIGURE 4.4 Clause and image(s) present at Point A1 (Malaria text)

Note
Accompanying narration: 'Malaria is a disease caused by the protozoa parasite, plasmodium'

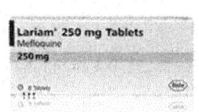 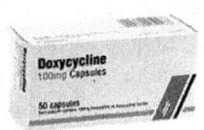 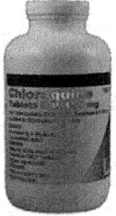

FIGURE 4.5 Clause and image(s) present at Point A2 (Malaria text)

Note
Accompanying narration: 'Current antimalarials include MEFLOQUINE, DOXYCYCLINE and CHLOROQUINE'

and 'why do we need another?' no semantically dense terms are used. Again, this reflects the arbitration of a stronger semantically dense section with weaker ones. Negotiation is again illustrated here therefore through the use of the 'placeholder' for 'drugs' and the use of sections lower in semantic density after a peak.

The peak at Point A3 exhibits the highest value for semantic density overall. It was also the point of highest value for semantic density in language per clause for the Malaria text. We see that this image is also semantically dense (at the second highest level according to the image categorization in Table 4.5). The image is coded as 'simple scientific' because aspects of the scientific diagram have been simplified to only display the process described in the narration (Figure 4.6).

At this point in the text, we do not see the tandem use of the two techniques outlined in Points A1 and A2. Instead, though the image used is not the most technical or complex, both image and language (narration) together make this point the most technical in the Malaria text (Figure 4.6). This point provides an example of 'building' and is extremely important, as it fundamentally answers the question

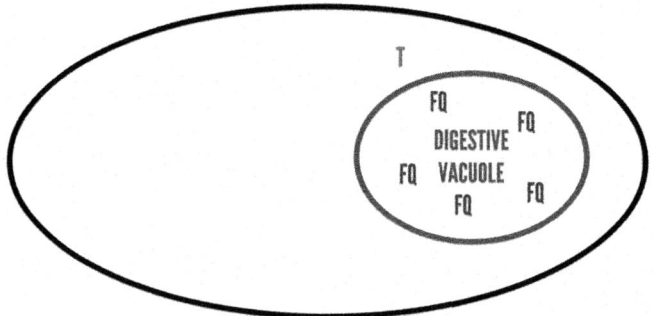

FIGURE 4.6 Clause and image(s) present at Point A3 (Malaria text).

Note
Accompanying narration: 'This is attributed to the INABILITY of the transporter producing CHLOROQUINE resistance to remove FERROQUINE from a digestive vacuole'

posed for the assessment (Is Ferroquine an ingenious anti-malarial?). The creator concludes that Ferroquine *is* ingenious because it is not as prone to resistance as compared to its main alternative, Chloroquine.

The key mechanism behind this statement was outlined in an earlier section of the resource: Ferroquine accumulating in the digestive vacuole and causing oxidative stress, killing the plasmodium. The building of the image from Point B3 was slowly created throughout the text, with sections added and the same diagram used multiple times (Figure 4.7), to show the different stages of the process. Simple scientific images were used and these act to highlight the important parts of the mechanism (rather than using the more 'textbook' style representations of this microbiological process). The image and narration work together to develop the explanation, building on themselves (across the text) and each other. This is the single example of such building in this text.

Point B1-MS

In this excerpt, from Multiple Sclerosis, the semantic density in the narration was well above any clause from Malaria. There are 15 technical compact terms and two everyday consolidated terms. Looking to the images used to support this narration, these are also coded the highest level of semantic density, both because they contain 'standard' scientific diagrams (the neuron – as would be represented in a textbook, for example) and multiple technical parts (depictions of immune cells, drugs and a structural depiction of the blood brain barrier) (Figure 4.8).

FIGURE 4.7 Images as part of a seven-clause sequence which builds up diagram of plasmodium processes (Malaria text)

FIGURE 4.8 Clause and image(s) present at Point B1 (MS text).

Note
Accompanying narration: 'and causes apoptosis; complement dependant cytotoxicity where a complement strand binds to the cell and causes cell DEATH; and antibody-dependent cell-mediated cytotoxicity where an antibody binds to the cell and causes cell DEATH'

In this example, we do not see the negotiation techniques illustrated at Points A1 and A2 in the Malaria text. In fact, the clauses preceding and following the clause shown in B1 are extremely technical. For example, the clause that follows this one is a segment that is similarly relatively semantically dense but unrelated in theme to the clause at Point B1: 'Daclizumab binds to the Tac epitope on the IL-2 receptor on the CD25 chain on T cells'. This results in an extended section of much stronger (relative) semantic density with no attempt at negotiating the complexity. None of the semantically dense terms in this clause have been described or explained elsewhere; their meaning is assumed and there is no placeholder for the non-specialized audience in the image.

This section does illustrate an example of 'building'. The images are in fact doing most of this building work; they demonstrate the process of cell death described in the narration. Two specific forms of cell death (apoptosis) are represented (represented by the first three and last two sample images in Figure 4.8). These images (used in a 'stop motion' approach) communicate the message that the drugs are used to contribute to cell death, which is important as the accumulation of white blood cells in the brain (left of the blood–brain barrier) causes the damage to the myelin sheath (responsible for symptoms of MS).

However, the accelerated growth of complexity within the images coupled with the lack of negotiation within the narration, makes this attempt at building knowledge less successful than those in the Malaria text. Furthermore, this text contains a significant number of 'building' moments, which are not related or built up to at any point in the text, clearly signalling this text is for an audience with significant expertise or background knowledge.

Discussion

The potential for multimodal texts as authentic and holistic assessment is being increasingly recognized. In our interview data, a student's comment on the task captures the essence of the extant research introduced in these studies: 'this sort of task ... I learn better by researching it and figuring it out myself than just being taught it because I have to get it, because if I don't, I don't get the marks'. However, there are several challenges in using multimodal assessment. In Science, it is generally understood that communication skills, particularly beyond the written form, are difficult to assess. As Shanahan and Shanahan (2008) state, communication skills become increasingly more complex throughout schooling at the same time that explicit instruction drastically decreases. In our sample of collected digital products, there is an extraordinary amount of variety present in the resources used. Different semiotic resources offer different meaning making potential, so making judgements, for example in terms of achieving assessment criteria, becomes extremely difficult (and there would be similar difficulties in instruction).

In the assessment criteria of this task, provided in Table 4.6, for example, the key outcomes associated with the communication of complex ideas are emphasized (italicized). Interviews with the creators of the two resources give a sense that what

New assessment forms in higher education **71**

TABLE 4.6 Assessment criteria for Malaria and MS 'principles of pharmacology' task (relevant criteria italicized)

- *Information is presented in a logical sequence.*
- Presentation appropriately cites sources.
- Introduction grabs attention and leads into the body of the presentation.
- *Technical terms are well-defined in language appropriate for a general audience.*
- *Content is accurate.*
- *Material is relevant and an appropriate amount is provided (balance of detail vs. general overview).*
- Speaker uses a clear, audible voice. Pace of speaking good.
- *Digital media is of a high quality and well aids in conveying pharmacological concepts to a general audience.*
- Length of presentation is within the assigned time limits.

is valued most is 'getting the science right' (content is accurate), at the expense of communication:

> if you are trying to teach students effective communication, we did not really get an assessment brief I did not really know what I was actually meant to be producing.
>
> If you are teaching these skills – in my experience they do try and teach communication skills but a lot of the time they do not mark towards the communication skills, they mark towards the content that is communicated. So even if it is communication poorly, you can still go okay.

LCT offers the concept of semantic density to more reliably assess quality of communication (how complex and how much condensation is appropriate for each audience). Analysing the multimodal texts in terms of the relative semantic density expressed in both the image and the narration revealed the two texts to have different overall 'quantities' of average semantic density as well as different ways in which semantic density was negotiated.

The considerable difference in the levels of semantic density in the two texts (as well as across the whole sample) demonstrates that judgement around the level of semantic density, or technicality, used in a text for a specific audience is inconsistent. These quantities could be used as a crude measure of the level of technicality for the students, calling on them to consider whether this was appropriate or not, for example when compared to other texts for the same audience or a model text provided by the instructor.

More importantly, two distinct techniques to negotiate complexity were apparent in both these texts: negotiation and building. They provide us with insight into *how* complexity is communicated effectively. In Malaria, these two techniques were used to great effect, as signalled by the full marks awarded for the assessment (Table 4.2). Negotiation involved 'place-holding': using common-sense language or images at points where technical terms or complex processes were introduced. When listing the names of the various drugs, for example, a picture of a pill box was shown. This idea is further explained by the creator of Malaria in response to a question about how they attended to audience:

> So a lot of the decisions I made was just because if you are an unspecialized audience you don't really care about the science behind it ... so it's not a detailed image, there's not information image: it's just more this is a mosquito, that's a mosquito, so I'm saying mosquito here's a picture of a mosquito.

This negotiation attempt acknowledges that the text is at a semantically dense section (in the section the creator is referring to, the term 'female anopheles mosquito' is used) and lowers the strength of semantic density by simplifying the message (mosquito). Negotiation also occurs when periods of relatively stronger semantic density. As Figure 4.2 and the discussion of Points A1 and A2 show, in the Malaria text, there are many of these examples of negotiation of complexity, and overall, they result in an accurate and accessible text.

Point A3 shows a period of sustained semantic density (across the narration and image), which is also related to an earlier section where the meaning was built to answer the question posed in the assessment. In this section, the building was necessary, negotiation was not possible or appropriate; a complex idea *needed* to be communicated and this required careful building across image and language. However, this only happened once in the text and as such, points of negotiation were intentional acts to climax to the 'building' activity that communicated the central message of the text.

In Multiple Sclerosis, we see evidence of multiple points of building but not negotiation of complexity. Point B1, for example, builds complexity in reflecting the process described in the narration in the imagery. However, the whole process is described in only two clauses (as stated in the previous section, this includes the clause in Point B1 and the previous clause). What is significant about this is that the text essentially consists of a series of such processes; very complex 'building' processes that are neither linked to each other nor negotiated in the narration or image. The text stays extremely semantically dense throughout; though this means the 'content' may be 'accurate', it is not clear that there are any attempts to, as the assessment criteria also state, define 'Technical terms', use 'language appropriate for a general audience', and ensure 'Material is relevant and an appropriate amount is provided (balance of detail vs. general overview)' (Table 4.6). The creator interview provided some insight into this assessment: When asked how the product would be different if it were for an expert (rather than non-expert audience), they stated: 'I'd just go like MS – you either know what it is or you don't ...'. However, the description of MS from this creator was: 'Multiple Sclerosis is a neurodegenerative disease whereby demyelination of neurons occurs due to an increase in the body's inflammatory response.' Given this assessment was still relatively high scoring, it is fair to say that successful communicative elements of the text were neither assessed clearly nor understood well by the creator.

Semantic density offers a language with which to communicate how complexity manifests across multimodal forms in science. This may facilitate the development of important and otherwise overlooked communication skills in Science courses, and help us better understand assessments that are both new and complicated. Beyond assessment, such insight is critical for education, especially at a time when Science is under the microscope and the outcomes of education are becoming more difficult to define.

Notes

1. These are introduced in a later section but represent dynamic, standalone products (that can be 'played' from beginning to end) that might take the form of PowerPoint or Prezi shows or videos.
2. Content words are any words that carry meaning: nouns, some verbs, some adverbs, some adjectives etc. (but not conjunctions, prepositions etc.).

References

Ainsworth, S., Prain, V. and Tytler, R. (2011). Drawing to learn in science. *Science, 333*(6046), 1096–1097.

Airey, J. and Linder, C. (2009). A disciplinary discourse perspective on university science learning: Achieving fluency in a critical constellation of modes. *Journal of Research in Science Teaching, 46*(1), 27–49.

Australian Government, Office of the Chief Scientist. (2014). *Science, Technology, Engineering and Mathematics: Australia's Future*.

Baram-Tsabari, A. and Osborne, J. (2015). Bridging science education and science communication research. *Journal of Research in Science Teaching, 52*(2), 135–144.

Bateman, J., Wildfeuer, J. and Hiippala, T. (Eds). (2017). *Multimodality: Foundations, research and analysis–A problem-oriented introduction*. Berlin, Germany: De Gruyter Mouton.

Bennett, S., Dawson, P., Bearman, M., Molloy, E. and Boud, D. (2017). How technology shapes assessment design: Findings from a study of university teachers. *British Journal of Educational Technology, 48*(2), 672–682.

Chan, V. (2011). Teaching oral communication in undergraduate science: Are we doing enough and doing it right? *Journal of Learning Design, 4*(3), 71–79.

Davies, S.R. (2008). Constructing communication: Talking to scientists about talking to the public. *Science Communication, 29*(4), 413–434.

de la Harpe, B., David, C., Dalton, H., Thomas, J., Grirardi, A., Radloff, A. and Lawson, A. (2009). *The B factor Project: Understanding academic staff beliefs about graduate attributes, final report*. Retrieved from www.olt.gov.au/project-b-factor-understanding-academic-cqu-2007.

Derewianka, B. and Jones, P. (2016). *Teaching language in context*. New York: Oxford University Press.

Fang, Z. (2005). Scientific literacy: A systemic functional linguistics perspective. *Science Education, 89*(2), 335–347.

Georgiou, H., Maton, K. and Sharma, M. (2014). Recovering knowledge for science education research: Exploring the "Icarus effect" in student work. *Canadian Journal of Science, Mathematics and Technology Education, 14*(3), 252–268.

Halliday, M. and Matthiessen, C. (2014). *An introduction to functional grammar*. London: Routledge.

Hao, J. (2015). *Construing biology: An ideational perspective.* (Unpublished doctoral thesis). University of Sydney, Sydney, Australia.

Hilgard, J., Li, N. (2017). A recap: the Science of Communicating Science. In K.H. Jamieson, D. Kahan and D.A. Scheufele (Eds), *The Oxford handbook of the science of science communication* (pp. 79–84). Oxford: Oxford University Press.

Hoban, G., Loughran, J. and Nielsen, W. (2011). Slowmation: Preservice elementary teachers representing science knowledge through creating multimodal digital animations. *Journal of Research in Science Teaching, 48*(9), 985–1009.

Hoban, G., Nielsen, W. and Shepherd, A. (2016). *Student-generated digital media in science education: Learning, explaining and communicating content.* London: Routledge.

Hubber, P., Tytler, R. and Haslam, F. (2010). Teaching and learning about force with a representational focus: Pedagogy and teacher change. *Research in Science Education, 40*(1), 5–28.

Klein, P.D. and Kirkpatrick, L.C. (2010). Multimodal literacies in science: Currency, coherence and focus. *Research in Science Education, 40*(1), 87–92.

Lea, M.R. and Street, B.V. (1998). Student writing in higher education: An academic literacies approach. *Studies in Higher Education, 23*(2), 157–172.

Macnaught, L., Maton, K., Martin, J.R. and Matruglio, E. (2013). Jointly constructing semantic waves: Implications for teacher training. *Linguistics and Education, 24*(1), 50–63.

Martin, J.R. (1993). Technicality and abstraction: Language for the creation of specialized texts. In M.A.K. Halliday and J.R. Martin (Eds), *Writing science: Literacy and discursive power* (pp. 203–220). Abingdon, Oxford: Routledge.

Martin, J.R. and Veel, R. (Eds). (2005). *Reading science: Critical and functional perspectives on discourses of science.* London: Routledge.

Maton, K. (2011). Knowledge-building: Analysing the cumulative development of ideas. In G. Ivinson, B. Davies and J. Fitz (Eds) *Knowledge and identity* (pp. 23–38). London: Routledge.

Maton, K. (2013). Making semantic waves: A key to cumulative knowledge-building. *Linguistics and Education, 24*(1), 8–22.

Maton, K. (2014). *Knowledge and knowers: Towards a realist sociology of education.* London: Routledge.

Maton, K. (2016). Legitimation Code Theory: Building knowledge about knowledge-building. In K. Maton, S. Hood and S. Shay (Eds), *Knowledge-building: Educational studies in Legitimation Code Theory.* London: Routledge, 1–24.

Maton, K. (2020). Semantic waves: Context, complexity and academic discourse. In Martin, J.R., Maton, K. and Doran, Y.J. (Eds), *Accessing academic discourse: Systemic functional linguistics and Legitimation Code Theory.* London: Routledge, 59–85.

Maton, K. and Doran, Y.J. (2017a). Semantic density: A translation device for revealing complexity of knowledge practices in discourse, part 1—wording. *Onomázein Special Issue*, March, 46–76.

Maton, K. and Doran, Y.J. (2017b). Condensation: A translation device for revealing complexity of knowledge practices in discourse, part 2 – clausing and sequencing, *Onomázein Special Issue*, March, 77–110.

McComas, W.F. (2014). 21st-century skills. In W.F. McComas (Ed.), *The language of science education* (p. 1). Rotterdam: Sense Publishers.

McPhan, G. (2008). Generalizing levels of students' understandings about conductivity: A SOLO analysis. *Teaching Science: The Journal of the Australian Science Teachers Association, 54*(4), 22–29.

NESA–New South Wales Education Standards Authority (2017). *Science and Technology K–6 Syllabus.* Retrieved from http://educationstandards.nsw.edu.au/wps/portal/nesa/k-10/learning-areas/science/science-and-technology-k-6-new-syllabus.

Nielsen, W. and Jones, P. (2016). The quality of learning as students create digital explanations of Science: DP160102926. Canberra: Australian Government.

O'Byrne, B. (2009). Knowing more than words can say: Using multimodal assessment tools to excavate and construct knowledge about wolves. *International Journal of Science Education, 31*(4), 523–539.

Prain, V. and Tytler, R. (2012). Learning through constructing representations in science: A framework of representational construction affordances. *International Journal of Science Education, 34*(17), 2751–2773.

PwC–Price Waterhouse Coopers. (2015). *A smart move*. Retrieved from www.pwc.com.au/pdf/a-smart-move-pwc-stem-report-april-2015.pdf.

Shanahan, T. and Shanahan, C. (2008). Teaching disciplinary literacy to adolescents: Rethinking content-area literacy. *Harvard Educational Review, 78*(1), 40–59.

Shute, V.J., Leighton, J.P., Jang, E.E. and Chu, M.W. (2016). Advances in the science of assessment. *Educational Assessment, 21*(1), 34–59.

Sinatra, G.M. and Pintrich, P.R. (Eds). (2003). *Intentional conceptual change*. London: Routledge.

Tang, K.S., Tan, S.C. and Yeo, J. (2011). Students' multimodal construction of the work-energy concept. *International Journal of Science Education, 33*(13), 1775–1804.

Wallace, C.S. and Bailey, J.M. (2010). Do concept inventories actually measure anything. *Astronomy Education Review, 9*(1), 010116.

Watson, D.M. (2001). Pedagogy before technology: Re-thinking the relationship between ICT and Teaching. *Education and Information Technologies, 6*(4), 251–266.

5

MISALIGNMENTS IN ASSESSMENTS

Using Semantics to reveal weaknesses

Ilse Rootman-le Grange and Margaret A.L. Blackie

Introduction

Across all faculties there are introductory courses which serve as a foundation for more specialized and advanced courses. Often these courses are 'service' courses, that is to say, the majority of students in the class have no intention of continuing with the specific subject, but entry to the more advanced courses requires that the student takes and passes the introductory course. For example, students wishing to major in Chemistry are required to take a year of Mathematics. Introductory Chemistry courses are mandatory for a wide variety of degrees in physical science, health science and some engineering degrees. All too often the complaint that students haven't been taught properly or don't know what they need to know reverberates around the offices of those who teach the courses for which introductory Chemistry is a prerequisite. And yet those who teach the introductory course will point to the curriculum and protest that the work is indeed covered. So what is the source of this gap? If there is no obvious problem with the curriculum, where might the problem lie?

The issue that is highlighted by this particular problem is not likely to be limited just to introductory Chemistry courses. The heart of the problem appears to be that students are not successful at transferring the key concepts and ideas of chemistry into other knowledge domains where chemical problems may emerge, albeit in a slightly different guise. This capacity to apply knowledge appropriately when it is framed in a new way is at the heart of the concept of 'powerful knowledge' (Wheelahan, 2007).

In a short chapter one cannot critically review all aspects of a course to ascertain where the disconnect might be, but an obvious place to start is the assessment. Could there be a systemic problem in this domain? Are we testing what we think we are testing? All through assessment literature variations on the theme that 'when students study for an examination, they attempt to understand the material in ways that they perceive will meet requirements,' (Biggs, 1996) are repeated in various guises. Nearly 40 years ago Elton and Laurillard (1979) stated that 'here is something approaching a law of learning behaviour for students: namely that the quickest way to change student learning is to change the assessment system'. And slightly more recently, Entwistle and Entwistle (1992) put forward the rather sobering argument that examinations are often a hurdle towards students developing a personal understanding of content, rather than an aid. Coupled with this is the reality that teaching large classes comes with all kinds of challenges, not least of which is creating meaningful assessment whether summative or formative (Broadbent et al., 2018; Mostert and Snowball, 2013).

Meaningful assessment is perhaps one of the greatest challenges in formal education. Coming from a background in science, the illustration which succinctly captures the issue was described by Mazur and co-workers in the early 2000s (Crouch and Mazur, 2001; Fagen et al., 2002). In these studies pre-med students in an undergraduate Physics class were asked to solve two different kinds of problems. The first, following classical introductory Physics courses, required the use of complex mathematical operators, and can be thought of as advanced 'story sums'. A complex scenario would be described and the student would have to figure out which mathematical operation would correctly solve the problem. The second set of problems involved the prediction of how a particular physical situation would respond given some simple changes to the environment, which would have an impact on the system. An example is to ask what would happen to the size of a hole in a metal plate if the plate was heated uniformly. No mathematical operation is required but a good grasp of the implications of what is actually occurring, in this case on a molecular level, is required. It was somewhat disconcerting to discover that students who could score consistently in the high 90s on the first kind of assessment would do very poorly on the second. Clearly, the ability to perform complex mathematical operations has no direct correlate to actually understanding physical phenomena. So why are the assessments in introductory Physics courses focusing on mathematical manipulation?

This example from undergraduate Physics is obviously just one particularly stark illustration of one of the ways in which assessment can be relatively meaningless. The question we want to explore in this chapter is whether we were making a similar mistake in introductory Chemistry courses. To this end we turned to Legitimation Code Theory (LCT), specifically concepts from the Semantics dimension (see Maton 2013, 2014, 2016, 2020).

LCT Semantics has been used to excellent effect in teaching and learning. It has caught the attention of educators across the spectrum of disciplines from biology to engineering, law and academic literacy (Clarence, 2017; Kelly-Laubscher and Luckett, 2016; Kirk, 2017; Wolff, 2017). There are two significant gains which the use of Semantics affords. First, Semantics raises questions at the heart of LCT: how do we educate in such a way that we truly open the doors of knowledge to all who desire to enter? How do we reveal the means through which outsiders have the possibility of becoming true contributors to a field? (Maton, 2014). If we fail to do this, education becomes another way in which social injustices are perpetuated. Second, Semantics gives us a way of mapping variations in context-dependence (*semantic gravity*) and complexity (*semantic density*). The distinction between complexity and context-dependence is profoundly useful as it can reveal some of the blind spots in traditional teaching. In the discipline of Chemistry in particular it is very easy to make the mistake of presuming that a good grasp of complexity (accurate use and interpretation of symbols, etc.) is a good indication of a student's capacity to transfer learning successfully from an existing context to a new one (a task which requires abstraction) (Blackie, 2014).

Semantics gives us a way to critique our teaching through the idea of semantic waves. For powerful knowledge to be accessed we need to facilitate cumulative learning. Pop psychology loves a clear dichotomy and happily divides us into two kinds of learners. Some people prefer the big picture first and then want it broken down, and others like the fragments to be presented first and then the tension resolved with the big picture 'reveal'. As educators we will unconsciously bias one position over the other depending on our own preference, and of course we will quietly dismiss the opposite approach as being not quite so good. The LCT notion of *semantic waves* puts paid to all of this: which happens first probably is a matter of personal preference, but both movements are necessary. Maton (2013, 2014, 2020) argues strongly for the importance of unpacking *and* repacking dense concepts, or packing and unpacking, depending on your style of teaching.

To date much of the work using the Semantics dimension of LCT has focused on semantic waves. This follows directly from Maton's conjecture that cumulative learning requires this wave approach to teaching. Examples from across the academic spectrum have been reported, and enthusiasm for semantic waves readily catches on wherever it is taught, even among those who veer towards scepticism with respect to education research methodology. While the contribution of semantic waves is substantial, and its importance should not be underestimated, we will focus here on the mechanism which Semantics provides to distinguish between complexity and context-dependence or abstraction. Semantic density gives a measure of complexity, where stronger semantic density indicates greater condensation of meaning in specialized terms. Semantic gravity gives a measure of abstraction. Weaker semantic gravity indicates a greater abstraction from context. In terms of both science and engineering education, this separation has the potential to be extremely powerful. Chemistry, in particular, is renowned for being somewhat obscure (Blackie, 2014). In terms of both complexity and abstraction it would appear from a fairly cursory analysis that the entire subject matter could arguably sits in upper right quadrant, a *rhizomatic code* (Figure 5.1). At least this appeared to be the case with the original definitions of semantic gravity varying between real-world examples (stronger semantic gravity or SG+) and abstract concepts (weaker semantic gravity or SG−), and semantic density as varying between common words used in their common understanding (weaker semantic density or SD−) and specific, specialized terms and symbols (stronger semantic density or SD+) (Maton, 2011).

Misalignments in assessments 79

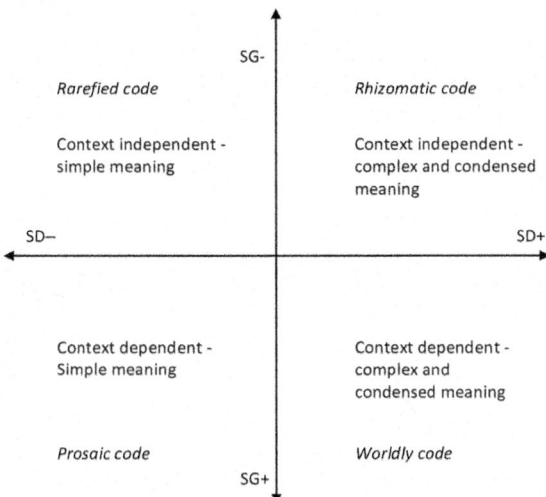

FIGURE 5.1 The semantic plane (Maton, 2014, p. 131)

Our purpose here is to explore the use of Semantics (Figure 5.1) to critique the quality of Chemistry assessments. The challenge is that the modules using content knowledge from the introductory Chemistry course may well be presenting Chemistry problems in quite a different format to that used in the introductory course. Only students who have successfully managed to grasp the broader concept, i.e. have successfully moved to a position of weaker semantic gravity, will be able to see the application of the concept in the new and unfamiliar context. Assessment can examine both the range of semantic gravity and semantic density. Therefore, the question that arises is whether we, as Chemistry lecturers, are sufficiently excavating the range of both of these dimensions.

Up until now one of the challenges of applying Semantics to STEM education has been a fairly plain reading of semantic gravity in terms of a variance from 'real world examples to abstract concepts' (Blackie, 2014). The challenge in Chemistry, and across most science and engineering disciplines is that the move to the 'real world' is in fact highly complex. From Engineering (Wolmarans, 2017) and Physics (Conana et al., 2016) the example of the problem based on a force diagram is substantially more simple that the problem based on a real-world situation where the force diagram must first be determined.

The immediate temptation is to simply invert the axes, to say real-world is more complicated therefore it has weaker semantic gravity. In Chemistry terms the equation on the page is a simpler beast than the reaction happening in the flask because the variables have been stripped away and the situation idealized for the equation on the page. However, these are simply two different specific contexts. That is to say both have relatively stronger semantic gravity. The weakening of the semantic gravity is the capacity to connect these two contexts with the more powerful concept of, for example, the 'Grignard reaction' (Grignard reaction is simply the name given to a specific class of reaction in organic chemistry). The equation of the reaction written on the page, and the physical reaction occurring on the flask are clearly quite different contexts, but the use of the term 'Grignard reaction' is entirely appropriate to both. Thus, the term 'Grignard reaction' has weaker semantic gravity.

One should note, though, that 'Grignard reaction' itself is also a particular context albeit at weaker semantic gravity, which can tie together two different but overlapping concepts of 'addition reactions of carbonyl compounds' and 'organometallic reagents'. Thus, one can develop a range of semantic gravity with different levels of precision depending on how much detail is useful. This is not an exhaustive description but hopefully highlights the general point that one must be extremely careful in the application of semantic gravity to a particular problem to ensure that the right question is being asked. In fact, the development of what is termed in LCT a 'translation device', a means of explicitly showing how concepts are realized in data, will quickly reveal if there are issues with how one is applying semantic gravity in a given situation. Nonetheless, scientists and engineers using the Semantics dimension as a tool should proceed with caution and be willing to rethink the framing.

The purpose of this chapter is to use Semantics as a tool to critique Chemistry assessments. The goal here is simply to show how Semantics can be used to good effect in this way. Semantics is not a tool which can be used in a 'cut and paste', one-size-fits-all manner. It requires the development of a *translation device* which is appropriate for the particular context (see Maton and Chen 2016; Maton and Howard 2016). Therefore, our goal here is to make explicit how we created our translation device, and how we then applied it. This is done with the hope that it will make Semantics accessible to educators, particularly in STEM fields.

Methodology

Context

For the purpose of this study we focused on a specific introductory level Chemistry course. It is a semester long course offered to students from the Faculty of Health Sciences. These students are enrolled for degree programmes in dietetics, medicine and physiotherapy. This course was chosen because no student who takes this course will continue with Chemistry per se. Therefore, the primary outcome should be that students will be able to recognize and solve a chemistry problem as a chemistry problem even when it emerges from an environment which is not labelled 'chemistry'.

The course curriculum was designed by the lecturers, who reside in the Faculty of Science, but staff from the Faculty of Health Sciences were consulted on the curriculum content. All topics were explicitly connected to future courses in the course outline. Despite the significant effort made to communicate to students how the content of the chemistry course related to their further studies, there were still concerns as to what extent cumulative learning was being encouraged, in particular how that was occurring in the teaching and assessment practices. Since the content and structure of assessments tends to be a deciding factor in how students approach their learning, we decided to analyse the format of the main summative assessment of this course, the final exam paper. The aim of the analysis was to determine what the typical range of semantic gravity and semantic density in these assessments looked like and whether it supported the development of cumulative learning.

For the purpose of this study, we analysed two final exam papers from this course. Each of these papers contained both multiple choice and written response-type questions. Questions with sub-sections were broken down and each subsection was coded separately. This resulted in a total of 83 questions. To analyse these questions two translation devices were designed, one for semantic gravity and the other for semantic density.

We will present here the translation devices as they were finally employed to analyse the two exams. It is important to recognize, though, that the development of the translation devices is an iterative process. We began with discussing what we thought constituted a variation in complexity and a variation in abstraction using particular examples. We then tried to apply the translation device to all the questions and found that certain modifications needed to be made to be able to use the translation device to code all questions. It took three iterations to finally settle on the translation devices as described below.

In addition, the translation devices are given now in language which should be understandable even to a non-chemist, but the initial translation device was described in fairly Chemistry-specific terms. For this reason a full description of the development of the translation device would require a lengthy explanation of the chemical terms which is simply not required in the application of the principle of this method to other knowledge areas.

Designing translation devices: semantic gravity

Designing an appropriate translation device for semantic gravity can be quite challenging and it is crucial to keep in mind the context in which it will be used. Chemistry is a hidden science. In essence

> it is a profoundly abstract subject. As a subject in its own right, it took far longer to emerge than the closely related disciplines of physics and biology. This is precisely because the molecular or atomic understanding of matter is neither intuitive nor obvious to the casual observer.
>
> (Blackie, 2014, p. 462)

Precisely because of this 'profoundly abstract' nature of the subject, students have no real life context, or frame of reference for Chemistry. Therefore, when designing the translation device for semantic gravity, we defined context as the course curriculum. Thus, stronger semantic gravity would refer to questions that were very clearly located in the curriculum, while weaker semantic gravity would refer to questions where the link to the curriculum was less explicit.

Another factor that guided the design of the translation device for semantic gravity was the structure of the course curriculum, which follows a natural weakening of semantic gravity, starting with a strong focus on basic chemistry principles, then moving towards applications in a purely chemistry context and finally broadening the context of application by introducing the chemistry of biological molecules.

Based on these guidelines, a translation device comprising of four levels was designed (Table 5.1). Starting from the strongest level of semantic gravity and moving towards greater degrees of abstraction, the first level (SG++) represents questions that require factual recall of definitions, equations or laws directly from the curriculum. The next level (SG+) represents questions that require the application of these fundamental principles, located in a specific topic of the curriculum, to well-defined, and deeply chemistry-embedded examples. The third level (SG–) represents questions that require the integration of principles from different sections in the curriculum to solve a problem. The fourth level (SG– –) represents questions that require the application of both chemistry principles and principles from everyday life to solve a problem.

Semantic density

In designing a translation device to analyse the semantic density of the exam papers we decided not to take the approach of a detailed word-by-word analysis, but rather to have a device that would enable us to allocate an average semantic density to each question. We argued that this would be more suited to the purpose of our analysis, as it would be easier to get an impression of the range of semantic density that is represented by the questions. Furthermore, we had to keep in mind that the language used, even at an introductory Chemistry level is very dense, due to the symbols and structures that are commonly used to represent the very abstract concepts. Thus, we were also wary of the fact that a word-by-word analysis would most likely only reiterate this, and not reveal anything new.

Our approach was thus to look at each question from a student's perspective and determine the amount of unpacking or manipulation of the given information they would need to do to get to the information required to answer the question. Thus, the focus was not on the number of condensed terms in a question, but rather on how much interpretation students needed to do around these terms, to answer it.

This meant that if a student could answer a question without having to understand any chemistry terms or interpreting any chemical structures, it was rated as the lowest level of semantic density (SD– –). This was typical of questions that required students to do mathematical manipulations of data that was framed in a chemistry context, without the context contributing to the solution of the problem. The next level of semantic density (SD–) was defined by questions that required students to know what a given chemical term meant, or what a given symbol represented to

TABLE 5.1 Translation device for semantic gravity analysis of introductory Chemistry test paper.

Semantic gravity	Coding used	Code description	Example from paper	Explanation
Weaker	SG– –	Concepts situated in the curriculum are integrated with general everyday knowledge to create meaning that is applicable in any type of context.	Why do you need to consume Group B Vitamins on a daily basis, whereas this is not the case with Vitamins A & E?	This requires to know the difference in solubility of these vitamins and what the physiological implications are. This question is not obviously a chemistry question unless one happens to be a chemist!
	SG–	The question requires concepts from different sections in the curriculum to be integrated to create a unified theory that is applicable to a broader context.	If 7.24 g of sodium pantothenate ($C_9H_{16}NO_5Na$) is added to 0.200 dm^3 a 0.100 M solution of pantothenic acid, calculate the pH of the resulting solution.	The molecule shown is an organic molecule which happens to be a weak acid. The question is one which requires knowledge of acids, acid strength and buffer solutions, but it is presented in the context of an organic chemistry question. Two different chapters or sections of work need to be drawn from to recognize the kind of question that is being asked and therefore what theory should be applied.
	SG+	The question requires application of Chemical concept(s) from one section of the curriculum to a specific example.	Carbon and oxygen can also react to form carbon monoxide. Draw the Lewis structure of this molecule.	It is the clear application of a concept (Lewis structure) to a particular problem (the structure of carbon monoxide. It is not likely that the student would have encountered this problem before.
Stronger	SG++	The question is located in a specific section of the curriculum and only requires recall of the concepts, definitions or rules.	The effective nuclear charge of an atom is less than the actual nuclear charge due to ____ Shielding Penetration Paramagnetism Electron-pair donation Relativity	The student could answer this question with rote learning. It is an essential building block in the development of an understanding of chemical reactivity and bonding.

Note

* There was no example of this level in the test papers. This is a proposed example from the authors.

answer the question. The third level of semantic density (SD+) was defined by questions that required students to do some manipulation or unpacking of the given information. In other words, if they were given the chemical name of a substance, but needed to draw the structure to answer the questions, this was seen as SD+. Finally, the highest level of semantic density (SD++) was defined by questions where students first needed to identify what the chemistry problem was, before they were able to answer it. This would typically be questions where the common name of a compound was used, instead of the chemical name. Thus, a student was required to first identify what the chemical compound in question was, before they could determine its structure and from there identify its chemical properties. Table 5.2 displays the translation device for semantic density, along with example questions for each defined level of the device.

Results

To delve deeper into how the analyses were conducted and how the translation devices were applied, let us discuss some of the analysed questions in more detail. The two questions chosen to illustrate the use of the translation devices are intentionally quite similar in content and structure so that the coding may be illustrative without use of exhaustive examples, which may not prove all that illuminating for an audience of non-chemists.

> Question 1: Vitamin B_5 (pantothenic acid) is shown below. This biologically active molecule is an optical isomer that behaves as a weak acid in water. Pantothenic acid partially dissociates to form pantothenate ions and hydrogen ions in aqueous solution. If the K_a value of pantothenic acid is 3.89×10^{-6}, calculate the pH of a 0.100 M solution of this vitamin.

> Question 2: If 7.24 g of sodium pantothenate ($C_9H_{16}NO_5Na$) is added to 0.200 dm³ of a 0.100 M solution of pantothenic acid, calculate the pH of the resulting solution.

TABLE 5.2 Translation device for semantic density analysis of introductory Chemistry test paper

Semantic gravity	Coding used	Code description	Example from paper	Explanation
Weaker	SG– –	No chemical terminology or concepts are required to answer the question.	A solution contains 150.8 grams of NaCl in 678.3 grams of water. Calculate the mass percentage of NaCl in the solution.	Whilst the question is framed around the chemical compound NaCl this information is entirely superfluous to the question. The problem can be solved with simple mathematics
	SG–	Only one term/structure/formula is given and needs to be interpreted in order to answer the question.	Consider the element Vanadium. Write its complete ground state electron configuration.	This question requires that the student knows the correct chemical symbol for Vanadium and can appropriately interpret the numbers given on the Periodic Table.
	SG+	The given information needs to be manipulated – unpacked before it can be interpreted.	Draw the Lewis structure of the formate ion (HCOO–) and use it to illustrate the concept of resonance.	The question, what is resonance, requires the appropriate drawing of a structure and the application of the concept of resonance to that structure.
Stronger	SG++	The chemical problem must first be identified before any interpretation or manipulation can be done in order to get to a solution/answer to the question. (multiple steps required)	Why do you need to consume Group B Vitamins on a daily basis, whereas this is not the case with Vitamins A&E?	This requires the student to have knowledge of the structures of the different vitamins and to be able to identify what structural difference will give rise to the difference in solubility which ultimately accounts for this dietary fact.

Question 1 was coded SG+ and SD+. In terms of semantic gravity the question is clearly and unambiguously located within the topic of acids and bases. It is a simple pH calculation. If this was the only topic the student had mastered they could solve this problem. With respect to semantic density there are several technical terms which the student must understand, some of which are crucial to understanding the question and some of which are extraneous. The student must be able to separate the crucial information from the rest. Furthermore, when these questions are presented in a clear acid, base, buffer solution format, an equation is usually given. Here the student must construct the equation for the chemical reaction before the problem can be solved.

Question 2 was coded as SG– and SD–. Again a pH calculation is asked for, but the student would have to recognize that this is in fact a buffer solution. It is highly likely that the student would never have seen pantothenic acid being used in this way, and therefore would have to make the mental connection. Hence the semantic gravity is weaker than that given in Question 1. With respect to semantic density there are fewer terms which require interpretation. The molecular formula of sodium pantothenate is given, and the structure of pantothenic acid is given in Question 1.

Figure 5.2 is a summary of the analysis of the 83 questions, presented on the semantic plane. As we assumed when we first elected to analyse two randomly selected papers, there was very little variation between the two papers. Therefore, the results were collated and are presented here on one semantic plane. This

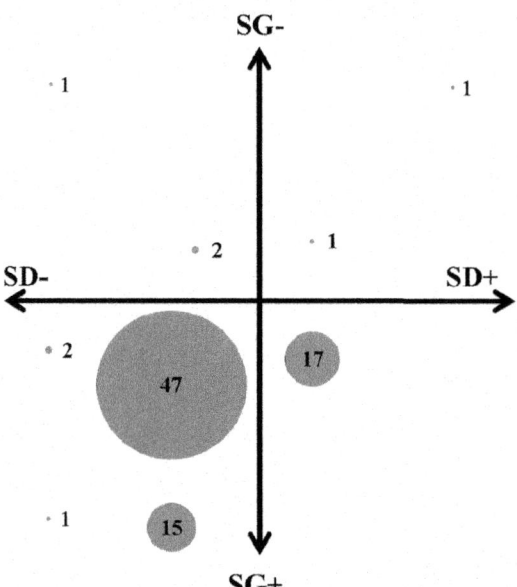

FIGURE 5.2 Summary of analysis of the 83 questions with the two translation devices

summary clearly highlights that the majority of questions have both stronger semantic gravity and semantic density, with slightly more variation along the semantic density axis than along the semantic gravity axis. By far the most questions (47) were allocated the codes SG+, SD−, with the second largest number of questions (17) being at the same level of semantic gravity (SG+), but having slightly stronger semantic density (SD+). An almost equal number of questions (15) were coded as SG++, SD−. The most noticeable results from this analysis is the revelation that there are only two questions at the weakest level of semantic gravity. This analysis thus revealed that the questions in these two papers are very strongly embedded in the context of the curriculum.

Discussion

It was surprising to discover the lack of variation in the semantic range of the questions. The relatively stronger semantic gravity was expected, but we anticipated greater variation in semantic density. There are several questions which arise from this analysis. Firstly, given the lack of variation with nearly 57% of questions showing up as in just one of the 16 possible combinations (namely SG+, SD−), does the problem sit with the translation device or with the assessment itself? There are two important points of consideration here, as all four levels of both SD and SG were observed in the data set, that is to say the full range of SG++ through to SG−−, and SD−− through to SD++. The total number of combinations of variation was 16. Not all combinations were observed but nine out of the 16 were evident. Furthermore, nine out of the 16 possible combinations of variation of SG and SD did show up in the analysis. These two factors suggest that spectrum afforded by the translation device is appropriate for this assessment. In other words, the problem is the more likely to be the assessment itself than the translation device. Only four out of the 83 questions showed relatively weaker semantic gravity, thus indicating that the assessment is failing to adequately test depth of conceptual understanding.

The second consideration is that the translation device as currently constructed may not be sufficiently granular. Could a more granular translation device be constructed which would reveal variation within the questions which now sit in just one of the 16 possible combinations (i.e. SG+, SD−)? This is certainly worth further exploration. However, we must keep in mind the ultimate goal of the study is not to create the perfectly constructed translation device but rather to create an assessment which will afford cumulative learning in this Chemistry course. Therefore, it would be better to put time into improving the assessment itself than improving the translation device. Although in time both will ideally happen.

Nonetheless, it is evident from this analysis that students will all be able to pass this module, without necessarily having developed the ability to abstract some of these principles from their strongly chemistry embedded context, to apply them in other related contexts. The complaints which emanate from those whose courses rely on this basic chemistry foundation seem to have a legitimate basis. Much more importantly though, if we take seriously the project of social justice to which education is an important contributor, this analysis of the assessment of this course suggests there is work to be done here. A more thorough analysis of the entire teaching environment and a more comprehensive study of curriculum as a whole would be well recommended.

Our aim was to demonstrate the power of Semantics in revealing the underlying nature of an assessment. The translation devices that we have created here could be relatively easily modified for use in other subjects. The chapter has focused on the application of Semantics in a STEM environment, and we hope that educators in these environments will make use of this as a departure point for their own work. Nonetheless, the model and method discussed can be used across the educational spectrum. The only substantial consideration will be to have a clear focus on what counts as 'context'.

References

Biggs, J. (1996). Assessing Learning Quality: Reconciling institutional, staff and educational demands. *Assessment and Evaluation in Higher Education, 21*(1), 5–16.

Blackie, M.A.L. (2014). Creating semantic waves: Using Legitimation Code Theory as a tool to aid the teaching of chemistry. *Chemistry Education Research and Practice, 15*(4), 462–469.

Broadbent, J., Panadero, E. and Boud, D. (2018). Implementing summative assessment with a formative flavour: A case study in a large class. *Assessment and Evaluation in Higher Education, 43*(2), 307–322.

Clarence, S. (2017). Surfing the waves of learning: Enacting a Semantics analysis of teaching in a first-year Law course. *Higher Education Research and Development, 36*(5), 920–933.

Conana, H., Marshall, D. and Case, J.M. (2016). Exploring pedagogical possibilities for transformative approaches to academic literacies in undergraduate physics. *Critical Studies in Teaching and Learning, 4*(2), 28–44.

Crouch, A.H. and Mazur, E. (2001). Peer instruction: Ten years of experience and results. *American Journal of Physics, 69*(9), 970–977.

Elton, L.R.B. and Laurillard, D.M. (1979). Trends in research on student learning. *Studies in Higher Education, 4*(1), 87–102.

Entwistle, A. and Entwistle, N. (1992). Experiences of understanding in revising for degree examinations. *Learning and Instruction, 2*(1), 1–22.

Fagen, A.P., Crouch, C.A. and Mazur, E. (2002). Peer instruction: Results from a range of classrooms. *The Physics Teacher, 40*(4), 206–209.

Kelly-Laubscher, R.F. and Luckett, K. (2016). Differences in curriculum structure between high school and university biology: The implications for epistemological access. *Journal of Biological Education, 50*(4), 425–441.

Kirk, S. (2017). Waves of reflection: Seeing knowledges in academic writing. In J. Kemp (Ed.), *EAP in a rapidly changing landscape: Issues, challenges and solutions* (pp. 109–118). Proceedings of the 2015 BALEAP Conference. Reading: Garnet Publishing.

Maton, K. (2011). Theories and things: The semantics of disciplinarity. In F. Christie and K. Maton (Eds), *Disciplinarity: Functional linguistic and sociological perspectives* (pp. 62–84). London: Continuum.

Maton, K. (2013). Making semantic waves: A key to cumulative knowledge-building. *Linguistics and Education, 24*(1): 8–22.

Maton, K. (2014). *Knowledge and knowers: Towards a realist sociology of education*. London: Routledge.
Maton, K. (2016). Legitimation Code Theory: Building knowledge about knowledge-building. In K. Maton, S. Hood, and S. Shay (Eds), *Knowledge-building: Educational studies in Legitimation Code Theory* (pp. 1–23). London: Routledge.
Maton, K. (2020). Semantic waves: Context, complexity and academic discourse. In J.R. Martin, K. Maton and Y.J. Doran (Eds), *Accessing academic discourse: Systemic functional linguistics and Legitimation Code Theory* (pp. 59–85). London: Routledge.
Maton, K. and Chen, R.T-H. (2016). LCT in qualitative research: Creating a translation device for studying constructivist pedagogy. In K. Maton, S. Hood and S. Shay (Eds), *Knowledge-building: Educational studies in Legitimation Code Theory* (pp. 27–48). London: Routledge.
Maton, K. and Howard, S.K. (2016). LCT in mixed-methods research: Evolving an instrument for quantitative data. In K. Maton, S. Hood and S. Shay (Eds), *Knowledge-building: Educational studies in Legitimation Code Theory* (pp. 49–71). London: Routledge.
Mostert, M. and Snowball, J.D. (2013). Where angels fear to tread: Online peer-assessment in a large first-year class. *Assessment and Evaluation in Higher Education, 38*(6), 674–686.
Wheelahan, L. (2007). How competency-based training locks the working class out of powerful knowledge: A modified Bernsteinian analysis. *British Journal of Sociology of Education, 28*(5), 637–651.
Wolff, K. (2017). Engineering problem-solving knowledge: The impact of context. *Journal of Education and Work, 30*(8), 840–853.
Wolmarans, N. (2017). *The nature of professional reasoning: An analysis of design in the engineering curriculum*. (Unpublished doctoral thesis). University of Cape Town, South Africa.

6
SUPPORTING THE ACADEMIC SUCCESS OF STUDENTS THROUGH MAKING KNOWLEDGE-BUILDING VISIBLE

Lee Rusznyak

Introduction

When relatively few school-leavers obtain entrance into higher education, high levels of student dropout are cause for alarm. In these contexts, a priority in higher education is finding ways to support the academic success of students. Proposed interventions abound. General courses in life skills, academic literacy and notetaking are included in some curricula (e.g. Walton, Bowman and Osman, 2015). Some lecturers seek to make students' transition easier by using teaching strategies similar to those used during their secondary schooling (e.g. Craig, 1996). In conditions of increasing class sizes and constrained resources, the use of accessible but generic 'large class pedagogies' is advocated (e.g. Hornsby *et al.*, 2013). Smaller-class tutorials are proposed as a means to provide students with social and emotional support (e.g. Underhill and McDonald, 2010). While these generic approaches to support may contribute to a supportive learning environment for students, they are essentially 'knowledge-blind' (Maton 2014, p. 7). As such, they do little to reveal to students how knowledge is structured across different courses, and how knowledge is used to develop a specialist gaze in that field. Knowledge-building processes differ vastly over courses. These differences have profound implications for how courses need to be taught, how achievement is recognized. The differences in knowledge-building between one course and another is not always visible to students. If lecturers want to support the academic success of students, they need to make explicit how knowledge is structured and built in their courses. In this chapter, I will show how the concept of *epistemological constellations* from Legitimation Code Theory (Maton, 2014; Maton and Doran, 2017; Doran, 2019) is useful in achieving these aims. Illustrative examples from introductory courses in History and Sociology will be offered hereunder to illustrate how lecturers need to work very differently with knowledge in order to achieve the purposes of their courses.

I will show how these two courses use epistemological constellations differently to build students' understanding of concepts central to a field of study.

Stellar and epistemological constellations

The concept of constellations draws an analogy between the grouping of stars into images, and groups of ideas that are associated together. Stellar constellations are made up of clusters of stars selected from a vast array of possible astronomical objects. Connections have been drawn between clusters of stars to form sets of recognizable images. An *epistemological constellation* is a collection of objects, ideas, practices and beliefs that are constructed as belonging together (Maton, 2014). They too are clustered and connected from a vast field of possible ideas and objects. Epistemological constellations can be regarded as a network of ideas that offer a way of interpreting an aspect of the social or natural world. The boundaries of an epistemological constellation may be compared to the boundaries that separate the stars that exist within a stellar constellation from those stars that lie outside of it. For example, a group of stars including Rigel, Betelgeuse, Bellatrix and Saiph were clustered together by the ancient Greeks to form an imaginary image of the mythological hunter, Orion (see Figure 6.1). This constellation has a boundary that excludes the nearby 'dog star' Sirius.

The objects and ideas in an epistemological constellation are understood to be connected to form a coherent and internally structured cluster, as seen from a particular stance. Ancient Southern Hemisphere communities used different sets of stars to form and name their own constellations. The same stars that form Orion's belt was constellated as an image of three zebras by the Nyae Nyae !Kung Bushmen (Fairall, 2006, p. 26). The stars that are grouped together in a constellation may be held together in close proximity by gravitational forces (such as those in the Pleiades' star cluster of Taurus). Alternatively, stars might be constellated together simply because they appear to be on a similar line of sight from Earth, while they are actually hundreds of light-years away from one another in space. If the same set of stars are viewed from another part of our Milky Way galaxy, the relative positioning of

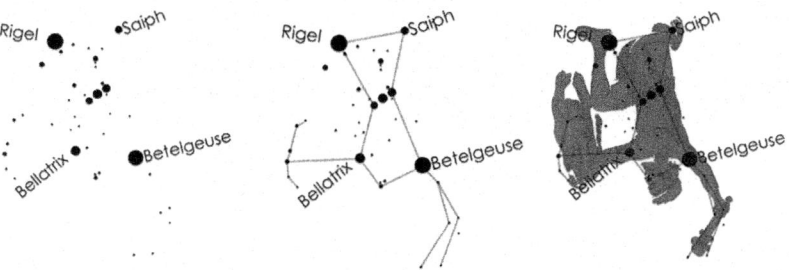

FIGURE 6.1 Stars grouped as a cluster, then connected to form a constellation, to represent an image of Orion the Hunter (Southern Hemisphere view)

stars would change, and they would not form the familiar images that were inherited from Greek mythology. Irrespective of their actual or apparent connections, stellar constellations are useful to skygazers because from the perspective of Earth, these images remain stable over time and have enabled navigation for centuries.

Epistemological constellations reveal a property called *semantic density*. Semantic density (SD) describes the degree of complexity of a symbol, term, concept or practice (Maton, 2014, p. 129). Each idea located within an epistemological constellation can have stronger semantic density (when they have greater degrees of internal complexity with many meanings), or weaker semantic density (when they are straightforward, with less internal complexity). The nature of semantic density of a concept may be illustrated by the stars that make up Orion's sword. With the naked eye, one simply sees three stars. There seems to be no difference between them, or complexity that resides therein. However, when viewed through a telescope, it becomes clear that the middle 'star' of Orion's sword is unlike the other two. It is not a star at all, but made up of a nebula of gas and dust. Looking inside the nebula, a trapezium of four newly formed stars can be identified. Much more detail of the structure of the Orion Nebula and the Trapezium open star cluster becomes discernible in the images taken by the Hubble Space Telescope (see Figure 6.2). In much the same way, concepts that have stronger semantic density are not as straightforward as they may first appear.

When an object or idea is positioned as part of a constellation, it is brought into relationship with other objects and ideas (Maton, 2014). Semantic density can also be used to describe complexity of the connections (or relationality) between ideas within an epistemological constellation (Maton and Doran, 2017). A constellation created from associated ideas with a dense network of connections between them therefore has stronger semantic density than simple ideas with few relations among them (Maton, 2013, 2020). To illustrate how semantic density works relationally

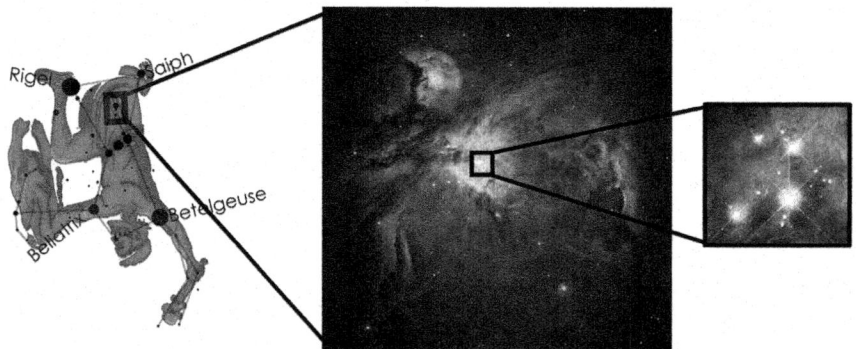

FIGURE 6.2 Images of the Orion Nebula and the Trapezium Open Star Cluster, taken by the Hubble Telescope (open access with acknowledgement to NASA, ESA, M. Robberto (Space Telescope Science Institute/ESA) and the Hubble Space Telescope Orion Treasury Project Team)

among objects within a constellation, consider the stars Betelgeuse and Rigel of the constellation Orion. Using a model of the lifecycle of stars, the colour of a star is connected to its chemical composition, size, temperature and age. Betelgeuse is a red supergiant whose attributes enable astronomers to deduce that Betelgeuse is a massive and cool star nearing the end of its stellar lifecycle. It is likely to become unstable and then collapse to form a planetary nebula and white dwarf star in its death throes. By way of contrast, Rigel is a massive, hot blue supergiant and is predicted to have a violent end as a supernova explosion. The two objects, though separate entities in a constellation, are associated through a classification system that allows their properties and their fates to be compared and contrasted. Similarly, when clusters of objects or ideas are brought together in a constellation of meaning, that may include, for example: dis/similar attributes that enable objects to be classified in a systematic way; the connections that may be parts-to-whole relationships of a system; cause-and-effect relations; processes or stages in which the object or concept is involved, or the manner in which some objects correlate in particular ways with others (Maton, 2014; Klein, 2011; Maton and Doran, 2017). In constructing constellations through these kinds of relationships, semantic density is revealed.

Constellations of meaning in everyday practices tend to be more 'transitory, mobile, shifting and flexible' than those associated with formalized bodies of knowledge which show greater levels of 'complexity, depth and stability' (Maton and Doran, 2017, p. 58). In established bodies of formal knowledge, the core concepts have often been the subject of rigorous and systematic study, and their interrelationships subjected to extensive scrutiny over time and in a wide range of contexts. The existence of stable, complex epistemological constellations within disciplinary subjects does not mean that the composition of constellations are uncontested. Knowledge production through research is often driven by the contestation of how constellations are constructed (Maton and Howard, 2018). Through research and innovation, constellations are often in a state of flux and may form, change shape, or size or have their boundaries altered as new knowledge or new insights are developed. As Maton explains,

> constellations may also be in motion: new stars may be added, new relations among stars drawn, old stars expunged, old relations changed or erased. Meanings may also be added or removed and subject to revaluation. Rather than static knowledge structures, cosmological analysis thus delineates a universe of movement and becoming in which the bases of constellations may be analysed
>
> *(2014, p. 154)*

It is also possible to form different images from the same set of stars. Generated in ancient Greece, the images comprise mythological figures. As seen from the Northern Hemisphere, these constellations are 'upright' but viewed from the Southern Hemisphere, the images are seen as being upside-down. Competing constellations can be visualized in much the same way as a part of the constellation Sagittarius is more frequently recognized in modern times through the image of a teapot, rather than the image of a centaur, as illustrated in Figure 6.3.

A set of associated ideas may sometimes be constellated in different ways to give competing interpretations. Epistemological constellations are therefore not necessarily neutral, and may be charged with values. From one stance, a constellation of ideas can be charged as being preferable and thus become valorized. A competing constellation of ideas seen from the same stance may be dismissed as being undesirable and any associated insight offered is simply rejected. Others, occupying a different stance, may very well regard the inherent value of the constellations differently. As will be demonstrated later in the chapter, exposing students to different constellations and then charging some positively and others negatively has important implications in how particular 'gazes' in the Humanities are cultivated (Doran, 2019).

Knowledge selection for university-based coursework

Introductory courses often acquaint beginner students with the widely accepted parts of epistemological constellation/s in a field of knowledge: an understanding of the central concepts; how and when to apply them within context-based realities; and understanding the grounds or evidence (beyond strong belief) for regarding the knowledge to be trustworthy and reliable (Winch, 2013). In addition, it is important that students come to understand how that body of knowledge is organized, and how new knowledge is created and verified through research. Students should also become aware of the contested constellations that form debates in the field. Becoming familiar with both the widely accepted and contested parts of the cosmology of an intellectual field is necessary if students are to enter into conversation with others in the field, and participate in extending and redefining its boundaries through research (Slonimsky and Shalem, 2006).

The target knowledge of a particular course may be thought of as an epistemological constellation of associated ideas, with actual or conceptual objects representing the

FIGURE 6.3 The constellation of Sagittarius depicted as a centaur (left) and in a competing constellation, as a teapot (right)

'stars' in a cluster. Without organizing principles for selecting knowledge, a course could merely be a disjointed collection of facts or ideas. Possibilities for cumulative knowledge-building would be reduced. The boundary of the constellation is determined by what ideas are selected as target knowledge within a course. Boundaries would separate target knowledge from associated ideas that may lie within the constellations of the intellectual field, but lie beyond the scope of the course. From the array of possible concepts and relationships in a field of knowledge or practice, lecturers need to select and sequence a target set of connected concepts for learning within the courses they teach. The selection of ideas for coursework is determined by the core concepts and the structure of knowledge in the intellectual field, as well as a consideration of the particular purpose of the qualification in which the course is located. A sociology course for prospective teachers, for example, may have different knowledge selection criteria to one designed for prospective social workers. A body of knowledge is presumably selected for coursework inclusion because it has inherent value in providing students with access to a system of meaning that is necessary for their development in an intellectual field or a set of intended practices. Lecturers may also need to consider the contextual realities and current debates that may need to be included for learning at a particular point in time.

Constellation analysis makes visible how courses work in building knowledge. In some courses, knowledge-building may introduce students to an epistemological constellation that is built up systematically with increasing complexity over time. Alternatively, students may be introduced to a range of competing or successive epistemological constellations which are compared and contrasted. In fields with hierarchical knowledge structures (like intellectual fields that make up the natural sciences), there tend to be greater degrees of consensus about the structure of dominant epistemological constellations, and a course may focus on the building of an elaborate and expansive epistemological constellation. As precise concepts are introduced and connected to a network of knowledge, so there is a strengthening of semantic density over time. In contrast, knowledge-building in many of the Humanities subjects often demand that students become familiar with a range of competing constellations that provide contrasting perspectives on understanding aspects of the social world (Maton, 2014; Doran, 2019). These may be introduced to students sequentially (if the purpose is to show how knowledge has shifted focus or developed over time), or simultaneously (if the purpose is to highlight the differences between competing, incompatible perspectives).

The symbols, concepts or terminology used to build up specialist knowledge necessarily have stronger semantic density than everyday words. Introducing students to specialist knowledge requires that they become acquainted with that internal complexity, and that lecturers do not assume it is self-evident to students. The process of building students' understanding of the semantic density of a technical term, an object or a concept may include, for example: introducing students to the constituent parts of an object or concept; ascribing attributes to it; exploring its sub-categories and the distinctions between them; helping them to understand its position within a classification system; the processes in which it is involved, and so on (Maton, 2013; Maton and Doran, 2017). Having access to the internal complexity of objects located in an epistemological constellation allows students to notice nuances and complexity that were not visible to them previously. For students to gain access to the internal structure and inner workings of the complex concepts, pedagogical processes could usefully include a process of weakening and strengthening of semantic density (Maton, 2013). In courses where students are introduced to a new idea or one superficially understood, the target concept would need to be elaborated upon to make it more understandable and its inner complexity revealed (pedagogically, this may require a weakening of its semantic density as technical terms are explained using more simple language). The knowledge-building process may then provide opportunities for students to work with the parts and the whole of the target knowledge (through their participation in reading of texts, discussions, tutorial or assessment tasks to name a few) and repack it into its condensed form (strengthening its semantic density again). Further knowledge-building of the epistemological constellation could then proceed, with the internal complexity of the concept being better understood by students.

Constellation analysis in action

To illustrate the way in which the analysis of epistemological constellations' knowledge can be useful for thinking through course design and the constellating processes demanded by coursework, I draw on a research study of the target knowledge in introductory courses in History and Sociology. These courses are studied by student teachers for 12 weeks in their first year of study, each with 5 hours of contact time per week. The first group of research participants were teams of subject specialists in History and Sociology who had conceptualized and given lectures in introductory courses situated in an initial teacher education programme. Focus group discussions explored the basis on which lecturers had selected target knowledge for their respective courses, how they conceptualized knowledge-building over the duration of the course, and how they anticipated they would need to work with students' pre-existing understandings of the subject and the target concepts. Course documentation (including syllabus entries and course outlines) was also consulted. These different datasets enabled the mapping of epistemological constellations in the target body of knowledge.

The second group of participants was drawn from a cohort of students who had just entered their first year of a teaching degree that would enable them to become secondary school History teachers. As part of their curriculum, participants were required to enrol for introductory courses in History and Sociology. Students were asked questions about their background and choice of history teaching as a career. At the start of the academic year and before attending any formal lectures, participants articulated their expectations of these two courses first in a questionnaire and thereafter in focus group discussions.

In the next section, illustrative examples show how the use of constellations is useful in considering how knowledge-building is enabled in coursework. The data suggests that students' initial understanding of the concepts may sometimes be nebulous, sometimes partially constellated, or misaligned with the targeted constellation/s for learning.

Introduction to sociology for teachers

In the Sociology course students are introduced to the concept of a sociological imagination and use it to explore the distinction and relation between public issues and personal troubles (Mills, 1959). They then consider how structures within society work to enable or restrict agency. Using a structural functionalist approach, students study why both macrological approaches (including economic, cultural and political dimensions) and micrological approaches (including aspects of diversity such as 'race', gender, dis/ability and class) are relevant in understanding how society and schooling reproduce privilege and inequality. Through interactionist approaches, students are introduced to the relationships between society and institutional structures, human consciousness and their agency. It is expected that the conceptual insights from the coursework will enable students to gain new insights into their experiences of schooling, and their future roles as teachers within the South African context.

Constellating in the sociology course

While most students participating in this study began their first year of study confident that they had a good understanding of the nature of History, none of them had previously studied Sociology. Students were much more tentative in their expectations, and they entered the Sociology course expecting to be introduced to unfamiliar ideas and perspectives. In describing what they thought they would learn about in Sociology several participants prefaced their responses with words like, 'I don't know much about Sociology, but I hope to learn …'. Some students seemed to conflate Sociology and Psychology as if they have the same constellations. Some expected to 'learn about how people think and develop' and 'learn about people's minds'. Other responses included objects that were far removed from the constellations of the intended sociological study: 'how to survive the environment'; 'how to communicate and listen to others'; how to make an 'investment in sustainable development'; and 'what the universe is made from'. Students were not yet able clearly to distinguish between objects that would fit into the constellations of a sociological study and those ideas better associated with coursework in other disciplines such the Geographical Sciences, Astronomy or Economics. While some of these concepts may be studied through a sociological lens, they are not a part of the target constellations for the course. Other participants indicated that they expected to learn about society, social interaction and diversity in the Sociology course. While many regarded these concepts as self-explanatory, some elaborated by stating that they expected to learn about the 'factors that make people to behave the way they do', about 'society at large and the people living within it' and about 'the social behaviour of people'. Their articulated understanding has weaker semantic density that does not (yet) incorporate social structures and power relations that impact on the lives of people.

Through the building up of epistemological constellations, students' initial understandings of society can be challenged and complexified. First a core concept (in this case, *social structure*) is introduced, defined and elaborated. The teaching team work with students' understanding of the world around them to link the concept of *social structures* to aspects of their social lives, including economics, politics, family, education, sports, media, military and religion. They extend the constellations further by adding examples of *institutions* (including parliament, the stock exchange, prisons, clubs, places of worship, universities and schools). The key relation that students are required to understand is that social structures and institutions act on people to enable and constrain social behaviour and interactions. These concepts, their relations and exemplars form an epistemological constellation. The epistemological constellation has stronger semantic density than students' initial understanding society as an amorphous collection of people.

The next constellation that the teaching team constructs is that of *human diversity* (see Figure 6.4). To enable students to access more extended and complex epistemological constellations, some of their assumptions about the nature of human diversity needed to be challenged by the teaching team. Prior to the Sociology course, students listed gender, dis/ability, age, class and 'race' as general aspects of human diversity. They did not distinguish between those aspects that are biologically

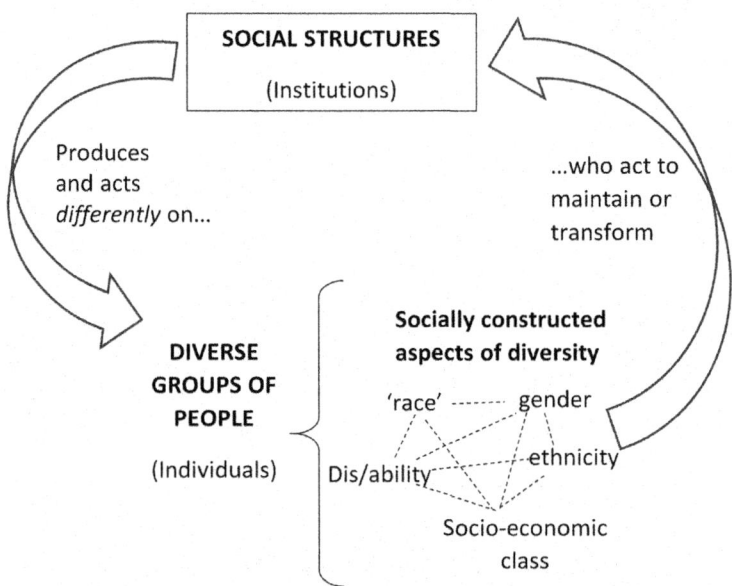

FIGURE 6.4 A representation of the epistemological constellations for understanding structure, diversity and agency in the Sociology course

determined and those that are socially constructed. The epistemological constellation is extended when the concepts of 'race', disability and gender as *socially constructed* (not biological) phenomena are introduced. And thus the semantic density of the epistemological constellation strengthens.

The epistemological constellation constructed during this course enables students to understand the basis of unequal power relations that are created and maintained between social groups. As much as they are subject to the social structures, they also have the capacity to act on the structures and transform them. The linking of the two constellations through the concept of agency enables students to access both explanatory and transformative power. The interaction of epistemological constellations of social structures and human diversity provides a basis for them to think about how structures within society (and schooling in particular) can act to privilege some students and disadvantage others. This is considered crucial knowledge for prospective teachers who could unwittingly perpetuate inequalities in their classroom spaces. It also provides the conceptual tools to consider themselves as potential agents who interact with social structures to maintain or transform them.

Introduction to history for teachers

In an introductory course on History, students are introduced to the fundamental idea that the ideological stances of historians influence their selection of evidence and how the evidence is interpreted (e.g. Carr, 2008; Munslow, 2012). This historiographical approach is introduced implicitly at first and then made explicit to students midway through the course. The teaching team emphasizes the importance of prospective teachers acquiring a historical gaze, which is different to the gaze that students would acquire were they to study similar topics as part of courses in Anthropology, International Relations or Archaeology. The teaching team argued that their specialist way of seeing the world with a command of historical inquiry skills, is crucial for prospective teachers who will one day be required to introduce others into disciplinary ways of knowing History.

Using historical accounts of key periods of change in ancient African civilizations students learn about the ways in which primary and secondary evidence is selected and interpreted to yield conflicting narratives about historical events and people. In the course, narratives about pre-colonial Africa are contrasted with evidence from complex societies in Egypt, Great Zimbabwe and Mapungubwe. In the second semester students are introduced to conflicting debates about Spanish and Dutch voyages of 'discovery' in the North and South Americas and in Africa. Students then study the impact of colonial settlements on indigenous societies.

Constellating in the history course

The History teaching team observed that 'the South African History school curriculum covers so many topics' and that the pressures of curriculum coverage influenced how students engaged with the subject during their own schooling. When asked what makes a study historical, participants in this study provided an array of topics that one could potentially learn as a part of History coursework. Their responses included: 'World War II', 'Apartheid and black people' and 'the French Revolution'. These participants' responses were portrayed as a cluster of discrete topics, but not as a networked body of knowledge with organizing principles and an associated intellectual gaze. If what constitutes a historical gaze is not intentionally designed into coursework and made explicit, it is probable that students will continue to regard History as a collection of discrete or related topics about things that happened in the past. This is likely to constrain their ability to construct opportunities for cumulative knowledge-building in the history lessons they teach.

As all participants in the study had taken History as a school subject, it was not surprising that most expressed confidence in what they *thought* they knew about historical ways of knowing. Nearly all the participants articulated a view that History involved learning about past events, and the way in which those events had shaped the present. Seven participants articulated a view that looking back on past events from the current perspective is important 'so that we understand how those events have shaped the world into what it is today' and that 'we don't repeat the mistakes of the past'. Before the course, almost all students articulated a belief that history provided an authoritative account of a single, truthful narrative. The confidence in their responses suggested that students were not expecting their assumptions about the nature of History to be challenged. Instead, they expected that new coursework in History would extend the range of topics that they had already learnt, with a study of a different selection of events or different time periods compared to what they had learnt at school.

Students' expectations of History as learning the accepted facts of a single narrative was not congruent with the conceptualization of History as understood by subject specialists on the teaching team. To challenge students' notion that some historical actors are 'good' who do 'right', while others are 'bad' who do 'wrong', the History team ensured that students were 'explicitly exposed to different sources, [and] the debates written by historians' who write competing interpretations from different stances. To build a legitimate gaze, lectures work within a historical period, and then expose the students to competing accounts/interpretations of significant events, historical figures and experiences of the marginalized.

Using constellations as a means of building a legitimate gaze helps the students to shift their understanding of historians: from those who provide rigorous, objective accounts of what happened to a view that the historian occupies a stance in space. School textbooks, especially those used during Apartheid, presented the eighteenth century Zulu King Shaka as a brutal, violent and cruel warrior who murdered his own people to further his power-hungry ambitions. This portrayal constructs a constellation of ideas that presents King Shaka as a villain. Historians who come from an African nationalist perspective portray King Shaka as an admirable and brilliant military leader, a brave and powerful king who was fearless against his enemies and as someone who brought unity of purpose to the Zulu people. These competing constellations may be represented in Figure 6.5.

Making knowledge-building visible **101**

Constellation of King Shaka as a historical leader from a colonial nationalist perspective		Constellation of King Shaka as a historical leader from an African nationalist perspective
Brutal, violent king Cruel tyrant and murderer Power-hungry and ambitious Unjust dictator to be neutralised VILLAIN	versus	Powerful, visionary king Brilliant, strategic military leader Fearless against enemies Inspiring leader who united his people HERO

FIGURE 6.5 Two of the competing constellations about King Shaka

Note
Constructed from interview data, and further refined by Maluleka's (2018) analysis of South African textbooks and students' views of the legacy of King Shaka

These two incompatible constellations produced from different stances are simultaneously presented to students during the history course. Both are axiologically charged, with one constellation presenting King Shaka as a historical leader to be despised (and therefore justify colonial attacks on him and his army); the other presenting him as a respected leader to be admired (and to use as a role model for defiance and resistance against colonial powers). Confronted by contradictory evidence and incompatible interpretations, students then reach a 'point of discomfort' with complexity in the evidence and its conflicting interpretations. They need to be able to simultaneously acknowledge the contradictory ways in which evidence is selected/concealed and foregrounded/backgrounded. According to the History teaching team, students typically come to a point where they say, 'I actually don't know who King Shaka is anymore'. This realization represents a crucial point where students and prompted to reconsider their understanding of History as a truthful, single narrative account of past events. This process not only challenges their views of Shaka, but also contributes to a process of reshaping their assumptions about the nature of history. The stance of the historian needs to be understood in order to make sense of their accounts and interpretation of historical figures and events.

To create opportunities for students to develop a historical gaze, lecturers insisted it was important to reveal to students competing stances whose interpretations of events are drawn from differently selected and connected evidence from primary and secondary sources. Knowledge-building in this course involves introducing students to epistemological constellations that stand in opposition to one another. Lecturers intentionally select topics where contrasting interpretations of evidence from competing perspectives constellate incompatible narratives. In the course, history lecturers used conflicting constellations of Africa as their starting point. Students are introduced to colonialist texts that portrayed pre-colonial Africa as a 'empty, unexplored land' until the so-called 'voyages of discovery' took place. This constellation of ideas about pre-colonized Africa is challenged as students are also introduced to opposing constellations, based on evidence that was omitted and concealed in the construction of the dominant colonial narrative. Sources revealing evidence of sophisticated kingdoms in Africa (see Figure 6.6) with established trade routes and centres of education provide evidence for an incompatible constellation about the nature of Africa in the fifteenth century. Authors of texts reveal their stances through charging the constellating with emotive and value-laden language. One dominant stance charges their preferred narrative with values such as stewardship and benevolence, another by resistance to invasion and oppression as right and just. Through the ongoing juxtapositioning of incompatible narratives, students became aware of the way in which evidence is selected and interpreted to reveal power relations within constellated ideas.

Historical ways of knowing require that as prospective teachers of History, students learn simultaneously to view historical events, societies or people from different perspectives or stances. The history teaching team do this implicitly at first and then introduce the students formally and more explicitly to the notion of historiography. By studying conflicting historical constellations from competing stances, the teaching team expect that students will no longer seek a simplified neutral 'truth about what happened in the past'. Through their studies over four years, students are prompted to continually ask, 'What position is this interpretation of events coming from?' and 'What is missing from the text, evidence or interpretation?' They are thus taught to actively question accounts that present a single narrative as truth, but to understand that there exist various interpretations. The teaching team also insist that for students to acquire the gaze of a historian, they need to learn 'to look at the past on its own terms' rather than from a stance in the present time. This is a crucial part of their professional preparation as prospective History teachers who would need to be critically aware of school textbooks that present a single, reductionist account of historical events and periods.

15th Century AFRICA as...	versus	15th Century AFRICA as...
• Empty		• Occupied, with great civilisations (including Egypt, Great Zimbabwe, Mali, Mapangubwe)
• Unexplored and wild		• Explored with established trade routes
• Ungodly		• Established religious orders
• Uneducated		• Educated, with scholars and established centres of education
Colonisation as...		**Colonisation as...**
• Stewardship		• Oppression
• Settlement on land by pioneers		• Invasion of land by settlers
• Religion as offering salvation		• Religion as indoctrination
• Industrialisation of people and resources		• Exploitation of people and plunder of resources
• Education as means to empower		• Education as a means to control and subjugate

FIGURE 6.6 Simplified representations of the opposing constellations of pre-colonized Africa and the impact of colonialism

Constellations for knowledge-building and knower-building

Students' transition into higher education is not simply about adjusting to an unfamiliar institution with unfamiliar pedagogies. General support initiatives or different pedagogies will not be enough to support student success if the knowledge-building work processes that operate in courses remains obscure. Although the Sociology and History courses are both considered as subjects in the Humanities, the constellation analysis revealed that their knowledge-building processes differed considerably. To students, Sociology was a completely unfamiliar field of study, and they were not sure what to expect. The course worked systematically to build up two separate epistemological constellations. These constellations required many students to interrogate their assumptions about concepts like 'race', gender and society. Knowledge-building continued by connecting the two into a more complex constellation through the concepts of interaction and agency. To succeed in the course, students needed to demonstrate a good understanding of the parts-to-whole relationships. In the case of History, students were initially confident that their existing knowledge would simply be extended through the coursework. Instead, students' understanding of the nature of History was challenged, and students were introduced to a very different constellation of historical knowledge. The knowledge-building worked through presenting them with conflicting constellations at the same time. To succeed in the course, students needed to demonstrate their understanding of how constellations are constructed from different stances. These differences in how courses work with epistemological constellations and what matters is significant for supporting student success. Initiatives for supporting the academic success of students will have limited impact if they neglect the central role of knowledge-building through coursework. Consideration of how epistemological constellations work over time in their courses, lecturers work more intentionally to make the conceptual moves clear in their teaching. They may also find themselves empowered to make knowledge-building processes more explicit to the students they teach.

Acknowledgements

My grateful thanks the editors of this volume, and Elizabeth Walton, Tebello Letseka and Elsie Cloete for feedback on earlier drafts of the chapter, and to Claire Flanagan for producing the astronomical diagrams used in this chapter. The astronomical images were produced using Stellarium open access software. This work is based on the research supported in part by the National Research Foundation of South Africa (Grant Numbers 109224).

References

Carr, E.H. (2008). *What is history?* New York: Penguin.
Craig, A.P. (1996). Education for all. *South African Journal of Higher Education*, 10(2), 47–55.
Doran, Y. (2019). *Knower-building: Developing axiological constellations in the Humanities*. Keynote address: Third International LCT Conference. 4 July 2019. Johannesburg.

Fairall, A. (2006). *Stargazing from game reserves in southern Africa*. Cape Town: Struik.

Hornsby, D., Osman, R. and de Matos-ala, J. (2013). Teaching large classes: Quality education despite the odds. In D. Hornsby, R. Osman, and J. de Matos-ala (Eds), *Large-Class Pedagogy* (pp. 7–11). Stellenbosch: Sun Press.

Klein, D.B. (2011). *Knowledge and coordination: A liberal interpretation*. London: Oxford University Press.

Maluleka, P. (2018). *The construction, interpretation and presentation of King Shaka: A case study of four in-service history educators in four Gauteng schools*. (Unpublished Masters in Education Research Report). University of the Witwatersrand: South Africa.

Maton, K. (2013). Making semantic waves: A key to cumulative knowledge-building. *Linguistics and Education*, 24(1), 8–22.

Maton, K. (2014). *Knowledge and knowers: Towards a realist sociology of education*. London: Routledge.

Maton, K. (2020). Semantic waves: Context, complexity and academic discourse. In J.R. Martin, K. Maton and Y.J. Doran (Eds), *Accessing academic discourse: Systemic functional linguistics and Legitimation Code Theory* (pp. 59–85). London: Routledge.

Maton, K. and Doran, Y.J. (2017). Semantic density: A translation device for revealing complexity of knowledge practices in discourse, part 1 – wording. *Onomázein* (2017), 46–76.

Maton, K. and Howard, S.K. (2018). Taking autonomy tours: A key to integrative knowledge-building, *LCT Centre Occasional Paper 1*: 1–35.

Mills, C. (1959). *The sociological imagination*. New York: Oxford University Press.

Munslow, A. (2007). *Narrative and history*. New York: Palgrave MacMillan.

Munslow, A. (2012). *A history of history*. New York: Routledge.

Slonimsky, L. and Shalem, Y. (2006). Pedagogic responsiveness for academic depth. *Journal of Education*, 40, 35–58.

Underhill, J. and McDonald, J. (2010). Collaborative tutor development: Enabling a transformative paradigm in a South African University. *Mentoring and tutoring: Partnership in learning*, 18(2), 91–106.

Walton, E., Osman, R. and Bowman, B. (2015). Promoting access to higher education in an unequal society. *South African Journal of Higher Education*, 29(1), 262–269.

Winch, C. (2013). Curriculum design and epistemic ascent. *Journal of Philosophy of Education*, 47(1), 128–146.

7

(UN)CRITICAL REFLECTION

Uncovering disciplinary values in Social Work and Business reflective writing assignments

Namala Tilakaratna and Eszter Szenes

Introduction

There has been a long-standing interest in critical reflection and reflective writing in higher education contexts, evidenced by the growing popularity of reflective assignments. Critical reflection for professional practice is also emphasized in university strategic plans as a necessary graduate attribute that tertiary students should acquire before entering the workforce. The ability to deal with emotionally challenging situations that students can expect to face in the workplace is considered a crucial component of critical reflection (Nesi and Gardner, 2012). Another requirement in reflective writing tasks is the ability to relate *subjective knowledge* to *objective knowledge*, such as linking personal experience and theoretical knowledge (Szenes *et al.*, 2015). However, students' engagement with subjective meanings is often invisible, under-valued and under-theorized in higher education pedagogy and assessment practices. This chapter will illustrate how subjective meanings and values in reflective writing can be uncovered by drawing on the concept of *axiological cosmologies* from Legitimation Code Theory (LCT).

We begin by reviewing the literature on critical reflection which explains why it is considered an important skill despite the challenges associated with its teaching, learning and assessment. Unlike learning traditional disciplinary content, critical reflection requires students to examine their actions, behaviour and feelings from a theoretical perspective. Students are also expected to challenge the 'status quo' by exploring alternative perspectives to those already established within their disciplines. However, there appears to be little consensus in the literature on what counts as *evidence* of successful critical reflection. In this paper we draw on LCT to show that high-achieving students demonstrate critical reflection by *aligning* with privileged disciplinary values in business and Social Work reflective assignments. In doing so, we illustrate the usefulness of LCT for unpacking axiological meanings in reflective writing. We conclude by discussing the importance of demonstrating alignment with disciplinary values and its implications for learning *critical* reflection.

Reflective writing: a review of the literature

In the context of higher education, critical reflection is assessed through assignments that are exclusively designed to evaluate the capacity of students to make 'judgements about whether professional activity is equitable, just and respectful of persons or not' by drawing on 'personal action' examined within wider socio-historical and politico-cultural contexts (Hatton and Smith, 1995, p. 35). Reflective types of assignments for assessing students' capacity for critical reflection include critical reflection essays, learning journals, reflective journals, critical reflection reports, case studies, teamwork and so on. These assignments are increasingly popular in applied disciplines such as nursing (Epp, 2008; Smith, 2011), teacher education (Blaise *et al.*, 2004; Hume, 2009; Mills, 2008; Otienoh, 2009), early childhood education (Cornish and Cantor, 2008), psychology (Sutton *et al.*, 2007), business and management education (Carson and Fisher, 2006; Fisher, 2003; Swan and Bailey, 2004), and Social Work and health sciences (Fook, 2002; Fook and Askeland 2007; Fook and Gardner, 2013).

Reflective assignments are defined as 'written documents that students create as they *think* about various concepts, events, or interactions over a period of time for the purposes of gaining insights into self-awareness and learning' (Thorpe, 2004, p. 328, as cited in O'Connell and Dyment, 2011, p. 47, emphasis added). Thus, these assignments are introspective in nature, requiring students to examine their own behaviour and reactions as the object of study. In contrast with the traditional understanding of learning as 'objective', 'theoretical' and 'rational' (Fook *et al.*, 2016, p. 527), reflective writing requires students to find a connection between 'personal and emotional concerns' and the theoretical content covered in the course material (Crème, 2008, p. 60). Typically, reflective assessment tasks require students to identify a personal and 'disorienting dilemma' (Mezirow, 2000), analyse problematic situations in field placements through applying the theoretical concepts of their discipline, and/or deconstruct dominant assumptions and challenge existing power structures and the status quo in institutional settings (see e.g. Brookfield, 2000; Crème, 2008; Fook, 2004; Fook and Morley, 2005).

Due to this focus on challenging the status quo, reflective writing assignments are often lauded for presenting students with an opportunity to externalize and investigate core values and power relations inherent in their roles as practitioners (Brookfield, 2001, p. 301). Research has suggested that the shift in focus from the 'objective' and 'theoretical' in traditional assignments to the 'subjective' and 'personal' in reflective assignments allows students to 'deconstruct ... personal assumptions' (Fook, 2002, pp. 98–100), engage in 'divergent and ambiguous thinking' (Fook *et al.*, 2016, p. 527), and 'call into question the power relations that [...]

promote one set of practices to be defined as technically effective' over others (Brookfield, 2016, p. 6).

Despite the 'emancipatory' claims of reflective writing (Mezirow, 2003), few examples are available in the literature that show evidence of *how* students construct and engage with dominant values in their texts. This is partly due to the fact that there appears to be considerable contention on how to analyse and identify what counts as critical reflection. In a recent publication, Fook *et al.* (2016) note that the plethora of research on critical reflection appears 'piecemeal' and 'relatively unrelated (sometimes even within one discipline), meaning that it is hard to be clear about exactly what we do know about critical reflection, *how it is practised* and what it can deliver' (p. 3, emphasis added). This means that while a prolific body of research has revealed that critical reflection consists of the subjective and personal, and is emancipatory and empowering in nature, there is little research that reveals *how* these subjective meanings and their use in deconstructing institutional values are operationalized in different disciplinary contexts. We draw on Legitimation Code Theory (LCT) to make visible subjective meanings and the forms they take in reflective writing to understand how successful students engage with the subjective in their assignments in the context of their disciplinary fields. To do so, we specifically draw on the LCT concept of *axiological cosmologies* to explore what axiological values are privileged within the disciplinary fields of Business and Social Work and how they are produced within reflective writing texts.

Theoretical foundations: Legitimation Code Theory and axiological cosmologies

This research draws on the concept of *axiological cosmologies* (Maton, 2014, pp. 148–170), a useful concept for exploring values in the fields of undergraduate business and Social Work. All fields have cosmologies, i.e. specific worldviews, logic or belief systems (Maton, 2014, p. 152), underlying not only the knowledge structures of the field but also its actors, social practices, activities, values and beliefs, i.e. its 'emotional, aesthetic, ethical, political and moral stances' (Maton, 2013, p. 20). Axiological meanings within the axiological cosmology of a field are often organized into *clusters* of meanings, i.e. recognizable and recurring patterns of meanings evaluated by positive or negative *charging*. Several clusters grouped together may form a larger unit termed an *axiological constellation*, which can reveal the nature of the practices generated by axiological cosmologies (Maton, 2014; Maton *et al.*, 2016). This chapter draws on these concepts to understand how high-achieving Business and Social Work students demonstrate their alignment with the 'right' kind of values legitimated in their fields of practice.

Research methods

To understand how students engage with axiological meanings, we investigated what kind of elements form *clusters* of axiological meanings in reflective assignments.

To understand subjective meanings and values in these texts, we drew on systemic functional linguistics, an approach that has often been enacted in tandem with LCT (Martin et al., 2020; Maton and Doran, 2017; Maton et al., 2016). Specifically, we analysed all instances of *evaluation*, often expressed as judgements about a person's behaviour (e.g. ethical) (Martin and White, 2005). As all evaluations are aimed at something, it is equally important to study *what* is being evaluated (Martin and White, 2005, p. 59), i.e. the *targets* of evaluation (e.g. *John* is ethical). In our analyses below, we will term instances that evaluate 'evaluation' and their targets 'evaluated' to illustrate their role in the construction of clusters in the disciplines of Social Work and Business Studies. Instances of '**evaluations**' will be coded in **bold** font and their targets (i.e. the 'evaluated') will be underlined. Their charging will be indicated by the signs '+' for positive and '−' for negative evaluation. Based on *repeated* instances of positive or negative evaluations of targets, we will generalize such *recurring* patterns as a positively or a negatively charged *cluster*, as shown in Figure 7.1.

This visual representation will be used in subsequent examples to capture the nature of axiological meanings clustered together in business and Social Work reflective writing texts.

The reflective assignments analysed for this study are drawn from the international multidisciplinary research project *Knowledge practices of critical thinking in higher education: Understanding the disciplinary requirements of undergraduate reflective writing* involving Szenes, Tilakaratna and Maton. Our data set includes high-scoring third-year undergraduate critical reflection essays (3,000 words) in the field of Social Work (Pockett and Giles, 2008) and high-scoring second-year undergraduate reflective journals from Business Studies (1,000 words).

The six Social Work essays analysed in this study were published as an edited collection of high-level critical reflection essays titled *Critical reflection: Generating theory from practice* (Pockett and Giles, 2008). The Business reflective journals were collected from a second-year undergraduate unit, *Business in the Global Environment*[1]

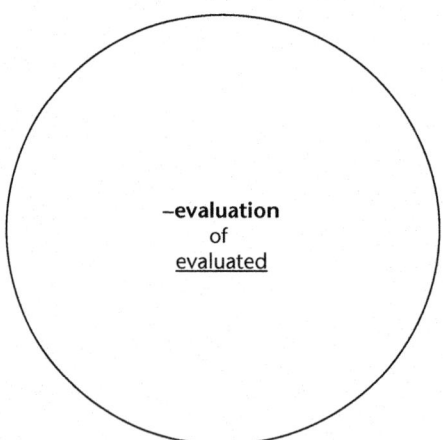

FIGURE 7.1 An example of a negatively charged cluster

(CISS2001), which was a core interdisciplinary unit within the business faculty at a large metropolitan Australian university. After gaining ethics approval for the project from the Human Research Ethics Committee, 64 students consented formally to their reflective journal assignments being collected and analysed. However, in order to study *successful* demonstrations of critical reflection, only High Distinction (HD) student assignments were chosen for the purposes of this research. All grades awarded to reflective journals were exported into an Excel spreadsheet and ordered from highest to lowest. The six highest scoring assignments were then chosen for analysis. In this chapter we only focus on identifying the recurring patterns of axiological meanings in student texts that demonstrate critical reflection (indicated by their high grades). For this reason, all identifying details of students were removed. The texts were then numbered as Text 1, 2, 3, and so on. In the following section we will show how high-achieving business and Social Work students build axiological constellations aligned with the axiological cosmologies underlying their disciplines to demonstrate successful critical reflection.

Axiological cosmology in high-achieving reflective journals in Business Studies

The reflective journal assignment in *Business in the Global Environment* was designed to develop students' critical thinking skills, reflective practice and intercultural competence, considered important graduate attributes in business school curricula and essential skills for working in multinational organizations (Solomon and Schell, 2009). Intercultural competence is defined in the Unit of Study Outline as 'a dynamic ongoing interactive *self-reflective learning* process that *transforms* attitudes, skills and knowledge for effective communication and interaction across cultures and contexts' (Freeman, 2009, p. 1; emphases added). To demonstrate their intercultural competency and reflective skills in reflective journals, students were required to critically reflect on their experience of multinational teamwork by analyzing both their visible behaviours and hidden values, beliefs and assumptions, drawing on key concepts from Solomon and Schell's (2009) intercultural competency framework (pp. 49–50). According to this framework, 'core elements of culture' such as *myth, folklore, heroes* and *history* influence 'on the surface' personal behaviour as well as 'below the surface' cultural values (e.g. egalitarianism, honesty, loyalty, etc.). The following questions were provided to guide students when structuring their reflective journals:

1. Choose one behaviour that you thought was a strength or weakness and identify the 'below the surface' value that underpins that behaviour.
2. Having identified the cultural value that you believe underpins your particular strength or weakness, now explain how and from where that cultural value developed using the 'core elements of culture' provided on page 50 of Solomon and Schell.
3. What does this teach you about the way you behave, and your expectations of others, when working in multinational teams?

4. How might you integrate this awareness into future team work, either at university or in the workplace?

The highest scoring business reflective journals analysed for this study were found to unfold through three distinct stages:

Excavation ^ Reflection ^ Transformation

In the Excavation stage of the journals, successful student writers discussed their personal experiences of working on a multinational team assignment and described their behaviour towards team-mates. Examples include the 'bad habit of shallow listening' to team-mates' opinions or judging non-English speaking background peers as 'free-loaders'. In this stage students also explored hidden 'below the surface' values that underpinned their behaviour, for instance, the values of integrity and egalitarianism. In the subsequent Reflection stage, student writers discussed how their hidden values uncovered in the previous stage of the journal led to their inappropriate and ignorant behaviours towards their peers. In the final Transformation stage, the student writers pledged that their newly acquired intercultural competence skills would guide their behaviours in future teamwork situations.

The following section will provide textual evidence of one successful student's engagement with subjective meanings to build a value-laden constellation in a business reflective journal. Specifically, the sections below will explore what kind of values construct clusters and how those clusters are then organized into a partial constellation to reflect the 'ideal knower' in Business Studies.

Reasons for inappropriate behaviour: uncovering 'hidden' values

The first stage (i.e. the Excavation stage) of the high-scoring business reflective journals typically describes the student writers' experiences concerning a multinational team assignment, specifically, their negative experiences of teamwork, including negative judgements of their peers. This stage also reveals the 'below the surface' values that underpin students' negative attitudes towards their team-mates. It is the construction of these 'hidden' values that this chapter focuses on.

To begin, we will first investigate the types of evaluations and their targets (i.e. the instances we term '<u>evaluated</u>' in this paper) in detail to understand how one of the high-scoring students explores the elements of Australian core culture that influenced her upbringing:

> I was taught about tales of the diggers of the gold rush, migrants working hard, wars in which <u>our soldiers</u> were **courageous** against imminent defeat, [...].

As shown in Table 7.1, an instance of positive judgement (**courageous**) is used to spread positive charging over its target, <u>our soldiers</u>:

TABLE 7.1 An example of positive evaluation

evaluated	evaluation	charging
our soldiers	**courageous**	positive

Further analysis of the Excavation stage has revealed other instances of positive evaluations in the text. The following extract will illustrate that certain choices of evaluation can dominate longer stretches of text (even when there are no further instances of explicit evaluation) by occupying a dominant position at the beginnings or endings of texts (Hood, 2010; Martin and White, 2005). If we look at the extract from Text 2 below, we can see examples of these dominating evaluations at the beginning (e.g. values) and end of the text (fair go, equality, honesty, etc.):

[Text 2] The core elements of culture according to (Solomon and Schell 2009) include, 'religious ideals, heroes, mythology, folklore, landscapes and history.' My **values** result little from religious ideals, as my family background is atheist. However, as an Australian born and bred, the history, heroes, mythology and folklore have impacted greatly upon my **values**, beliefs, morals and behaviour. Having been educated through the Australian schooling system I was taught about <u>tales of the diggers of the gold rush</u>, <u>migrants</u> **working hard**, <u>wars in which our soldiers were</u> **courageous** <u>against imminent defeat, drovers and their wives, the indigenous dreamtime stories, the tale of Ned Kelly</u>, <u>William Buckley</u>, <u>larrikins</u> and <u>mateship</u>, <u>convicts</u> and <u>'the sun burnt country'</u>. Even <u>the second verse of 'Advance Australia Fair'</u> states that <u>'for those who've come across the sea, we've boundless plains to share'</u>, <u>this notion of a</u> **'fair go'** and **equality**, <u>sharing</u>, **honesty**, **humor**, <u>comradery</u> and <u>'having a stab'</u> have been *deeply engrained* in me since birth, and hold *great emphasis* in my value system.

As shown in Table 7.2, there are few instances of explicit evaluation in this text. Instead, the instance **values** repeated twice functions to spread positive evaluation over several targets indicated by the underlined examples, which represent the student's Australian ideals (e.g. <u>the indigenous dreamtime stories, William Buckley</u> or <u>mateship</u>). Further, the instances *deeply engrained* and *hold great emphasis in my value system* at the end of the text provide positive implicit evaluation of the targets listed in the Table (e.g. <u>sharing</u>, **honesty**, etc.) Some of these targets can be further unpacked, for example, **honesty** can be unpacked as 'someone is **honest**' to make explicit the positive judgement it encodes (i.e. how truthful someone is). This reveals the positive evaluation encoded in these kinds of targets. By identifying these axiologically charged targets and the items that evaluate them we can thus retrieve what the student constructs as Australian values in the business reflective journal.

Further analysis of these targets reveals that the student is exploring the values underpinning her behaviour through the application of key theoretical concepts from Solomon and Schell's (2009) framework of intercultural competency,

TABLE 7.2 A repeated pattern of positive evaluation of Australian values

evaluated: Australian ideals	evaluation	charging
tales of the diggers of the gold rush migrants **working hard** wars in which our soldiers were **courageous** against imminent defeat drovers and their wives the indigenous dreamtime stories the tale of Ned Kelly William Buckley larrikins mateship convicts 'the sun burnt country'	my values	positive
the second verse of 'Advance Australia Fair': 'for those who've come across the sea, we've boundless plains to share' this notion of a '**fair** go' **equality** sharing **honesty** **humor** comradery 'having a stab'	*deeply engrained* and hold *great emphasis* in my *value system*	positive

especially focusing on the core elements of culture. Each of these key concepts is individually unpacked by the student writer through the examples shown above. For example, the targets <u>diggers of the gold rush</u>, <u>migrants working hard</u>, <u>wars</u> and <u>drovers and their wives</u> can be traced back to the concept of 'history', one of the core elements of culture in the theoretical framework students are required to apply in their reflective assignments. As Table 7.2 has shown, these targets are positively charged by the instance 'my **values**'. By tracing them back to the theoretical concept, we are able to retrieve the positive axiological charging of meanings within the concept of 'history' despite its lack of explicit evaluation in the text. We will generalize the construction of 'history' as an axiological value illustrated by Figure 7.2 as a positively charged stabilized cluster.

Further analysis of the data has also revealed that high-achieving students assign axiological values to other theoretical concepts applied to the analysis of their values. We will explore these values in the following section.

Building a constellation of values

As we show below, the positively charged history cluster unpacked above is not the only cluster that was constructed in the student's reflective journal. Similar to

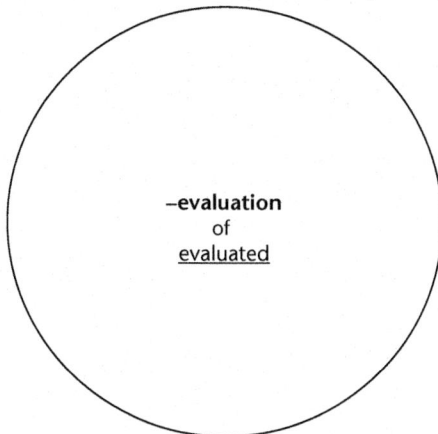

FIGURE 7.2 An example of a positively charged cluster in business

the construction of 'history' as an axiological value, for example, the term 'heroes' becomes associated with examples such as Ned Kelly and William Buckley; the concept 'folklore' can be unpacked as larrikins, mateship and the sun burnt country. Each of these concepts therefore represents a positively charged cluster. Together these clusters form a positively charged constellation of Australian values. The relationship between the clusters forming the constellation is visualized by Figure 7.3.

The construction of an axiological constellation through clusters of positively charged meanings allows student writers to omit explicit evaluation in subsequent

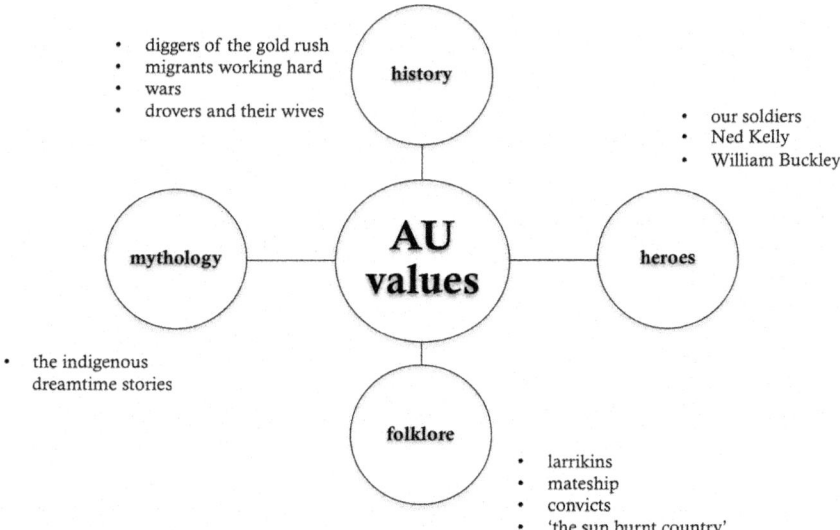

FIGURE 7.3 The construction of a positively charged constellation in Business Studies

mentions of the theoretical concepts from Solomon and Schell's (2009) framework of core elements of culture. By removing the explicit evaluations, the assumed positive charging of the concepts of history, folklore or heroes can now be taken for granted. In producing the constellation of Australian values, the student shows that her inappropriate behaviour towards her team-mates was influenced by a system of values that are not immediately visible to the reader. In doing so, she has aligned herself with the theoretical framework of 'intercultural competency', a skill highly valued in the context of business higher education, also considered essential for becoming a business practitioner capable of working in multinational environments.

While the business reflective journal above illustrated the construction of axiologically charged clusters which form a constellation of hidden values, the following section explores how such clusters and constellations are created in a Social Work reflective essay. The section below will show how one successful student demonstrates their capacity to align with the values that are privileged in the field of Social Work through the process of critical reflection.

Axiological cosmology in high-achieving critical reflection essays in Social Work

The high-achieving reflective essays in Social Work aim to prepare students to write for publication and focus on operationalizing critical reflection to 'derive clear theoretical and practice guidelines for further professional action' (Pockett and Giles, 2008, p. vii). Students were required to focus on 'their emerging identity as "new graduate social workers" about to enter the workplace' and were asked to '*select a critical incident* from their field education experience' (pp. 98–100). In order to help students 'maximise the learning they might make' and 'to interpret and guide the reflective process', they were provided with Fook's (2002) model of critical deconstruction and reconstruction (Pockett and Giles, 2008). The model consists of four stages:

1. *critical deconstruction* involves 'searching for contradictions, different perspectives and interpretations' (p. 92);
2. *resistance* involves 'refusing to accept or participate in aspects of dominant discourses which work to disempower, or perhaps render a situation unworkable because of this' (p. 95);
3. involves 'identification or labeling of both the existence and operation of discourses and that which is hidden, glossed over or assumed' (p. 96);
4. *reconstruction*, which 'involves formulating new discourses and structures' (p. 96).

The above overview of Fook's framework for critical reflection shows that students are expected to challenge the status quo and reinterpret their actions in light of disciplinary knowledge that they acquire over the course of their degree. Five distinct stages were identified in the Social Work reflective writing task (see also Szenes *et al.*, 2015; Tilakaratna and Szenes, 2017a). They are as follows:

Introduction^Critical Incident²^Excavation^Transformation^Coda

Due to the length of the individual Social Work texts (3,000 words), illustrative examples from one Social Work essay will be presented in this chapter. In this essay, following a brief introduction to the task, the student narrates a 'problematic incident' encountered during her field placement in the Critical Incident stage of the text (Wieczorek, 2008). The narrative focuses on an instance when, as a young female apprentice social worker, she was subjected to verbal sexual harassment by a young male client attending a drug and alcohol rehabilitation programme. In the Excavation section that follows, the student contrasts her initial reaction (to report the incident with resulting consequences for the male client) with her understanding of the incident as a result of critical self-reflection from a disciplinary perspective. To do this, she identifies three major themes that she will focus on in her essay: 'power', 'gender' and 'boundaries'. In this chapter we specifically focus on the student's analysis of 'power' by exploring how she presents this concept through reference to the theoretical frameworks relevant to Social Work.

The section below shows the development of two clusters that allows the student to explore the concept of 'power', its construction in the discipline of Social Work and its influence on relations between social worker and client. This relationship is construed via two clusters: a positively charged cluster constructing the social worker as powerful and a negatively charged cluster constructing the client as powerless. The section below will demonstrate that these two clusters constitute a partial constellation of the field of Social Work.

Power and powerlessness in Social Work: revealing disciplinary values

In the first stage of the text, the Critical Incident, the student narrates the incident in which a client verbally sexually harasses her during a field placement. In the final 'Transformation' stage, she explains how she would change her future behaviour following her reflection on the critical incident and her understanding of her role as a social worker. In this stage, the student draws on the Australian Association of Social Work Code of Ethics to illustrate her understanding of the roles assigned to the social worker and the client in Social Work practice. As highlighted in the example below, both social worker and client function as the targets evaluated in the text:

> According to the AASW Code of Ethics, social workers **have an obligation to work for social justice** and **to advocate with and on behalf of the disadvantaged and the marginalised**.

> Working from an anti-oppressive stance, **I could endeavour to work in partnership wherever possible to assist** clients **to gain more control over their lives** and **to overcome the obstacles in meeting their aspirations** and **to ensure that their voices are heard in decision-making**.
> *(Payne, 1997, p. 250) (Wieczorek, 2008, p. 27)*

The above analysis of the literature on the social worker/client relationship reveals a repeated pattern of positive evaluations of the professional social worker as powerful and in control as shown in Table 7.3.

As in the business text explored in the previous section, the repeated pattern of positive evaluation targeting 'social workers' in general and the student as a social worker ('I') results in the formation of a positively charged stabilized cluster of the *social worker as powerful* as shown in Figure 7.4.

In contrast to the position of power that social workers occupy, the literature negatively evaluates clients' capacity by highlighting their inability to act. Table 7.4 illustrates this recurring pattern of negative evaluations targeting the client, which indicates their lack of control or '*powerlessness*':

Similar to the cluster of social worker as *powerful*, the pattern results in the formation of a negatively charged stabilized cluster. This cluster, where the client is constructed as *powerless* within the discipline of Social Work, is illustrated in Figure 7.5.

A further significant pattern that emerges is that the positively charged cluster of the *professional social worker as powerful* enters into a symbiotic relationship with the negatively charged cluster of *the client as powerless*. These oppositionally charged clusters of *professional as powerful* and *client as powerless* are shown in Figure 7.6.

It needs noting that the oppositional clusters in Figure 7.6 do not refer to a *specific* social workers and client, but 'social workers' and 'clients' as groups of people

TABLE 7.3 A pattern of positive charging of the professional social worker

evaluated: the social worker/I	evaluation	charging
social workers	have an obligation to work for social justice	positive
[social workers]	to advocate with and on behalf of the disadvantaged and the marginalised	positive
[I]	working from an anti-oppressive stance	positive
I	could endeavour to work in partnership wherever possible	positive
[I]	to assist clients to gain more control over their lives	positive
[I]	to overcome the obstacles in meeting their aspirations	positive
[I]	to ensure that their voices are heard in decision-making	positive

(Un)critical reflection 117

FIGURE 7.4 A positively charged cluster of the social worker as powerful

FIGURE 7.5 A negatively charged cluster of the client

TABLE 7.4 A pattern of negative charging of the client

evaluated: clients	evaluation	charging
[clients]	**the disadvantaged and the marginalised**	negative
clients	**to gain more control over their lives**	negative
clients	**to overcome the obstacles in meeting their aspiration**	negative
[clients]	**to ensure that their voices are heard in decision-making**	negative

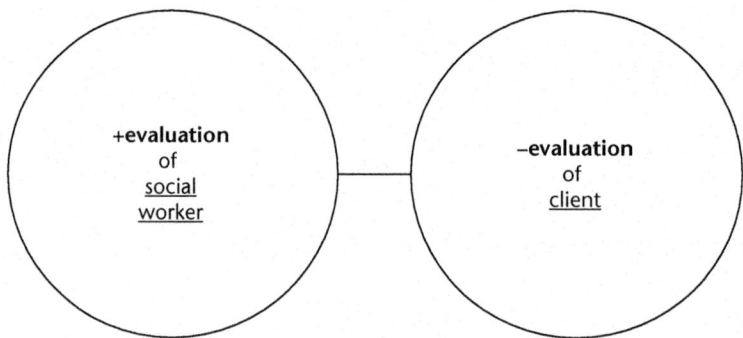

FIGURE 7.6 Oppositionally charged clusters in Social Work theory: 'social worker as powerful' and 'client as powerless'

who function *within the field of Social Work* with whom the student aligns herself. Significantly, these *generic* Social Work clusters (i.e. *social worker as powerful* and *client as powerless*) influence the student's interpretation of the relationship between her and the client, Jared, who verbally sexually harasses her in her field placement in the Excavation stage. In the final Transformation stage, the student presents her understanding of Social Work values in order to show why she interprets the critical incident in a specific and surprising way. Rather than finding Jared's behaviour unacceptable, the student explains that his response can be contextualized by the field of Social Work practice where power, inherent in her role as the professional social worker, remains in her hands. Further, she argues that Jared's inappropriate response must be interpreted as an attempt to 'subvert the power balance' (Wieczorek, 2008, p. 23), as giving him a 'voice' in an institutional context where the client is essentially powerless:

> On a structural level, it would be important to challenge policies and structures that serve to disempower young people, like Jared and strip them of choice … [t]he issues that would need to be explored relate to how social workers can work with involuntary clients to empower them to make decisions that lift them out of the state system into meaningful participation in society.

In the Transformation stage of the text the student reconstructs the disciplinary clusters illustrated in Figure 7.6 but this time with reference to the specific client, Jared, who was involved in this incident. This pattern of negative capacity of the client and his conflation with the generic role of the 'client' is shown in Table 7.5.

These instances can be contrasted against the social worker's role as represented by the student. She maintains that 'social workers' are clustered with the positive capacity to act to 'empower', 'make decisions' and 'lift [clients] out of the state

TABLE 7.5 A pattern of negative charging of the client's power

evaluated: client (Jared)	evaluation	charging
young people, like Jared	disempower	negative
them	strip ... of choice	negative
clients	involuntary	negative

system'. The student thus reinterprets Jared's verbal sexual harassment from an institutional perspective and essentially reproduces the same oppositional clusters seen in Figure 7.6, i.e. *social worker as powerful* and *client as powerless*, but in relation to a specific social worker (herself) and client (Jared). This second set of oppositional clusters informed by her disciplinary gaze is illustrated in Figure 7.7.

Based on the above analysis, we can surmise that uncovering stabilized clusters of axiological meanings reveals the student's understanding of disciplinary values. Drawing on the Australian Association of Social Workers (AASW) Code of Ethics in the field of Social Work, the student social worker creates two sets of oppositionally charged stabilized clusters of *social worker as powerful* and *client as powerless*. As visualized by Figure 7.8, these clusters constitute a partial constellation of the field of Social Work.

Notably, by reinterpreting the incident the student establishes the constellation of privileged Social Work values in order to demonstrate her ability to reflect the cultivated gaze of Social Work. The following section will discuss the implications of making explicit the basis of achievement in business and Social Work reflective assignments in relation to disciplinary values.

Discussion of findings

In the introduction we argued that the way students engage with axiological meanings is often under-theorized in higher education research. By using LCT to make

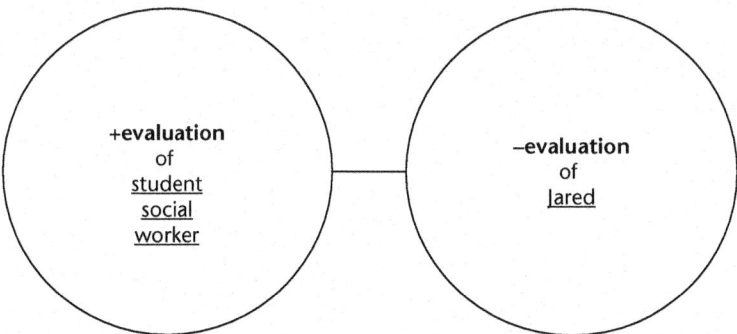

FIGURE 7.7 Oppositionally charged clusters contrasting the student social worker with her client

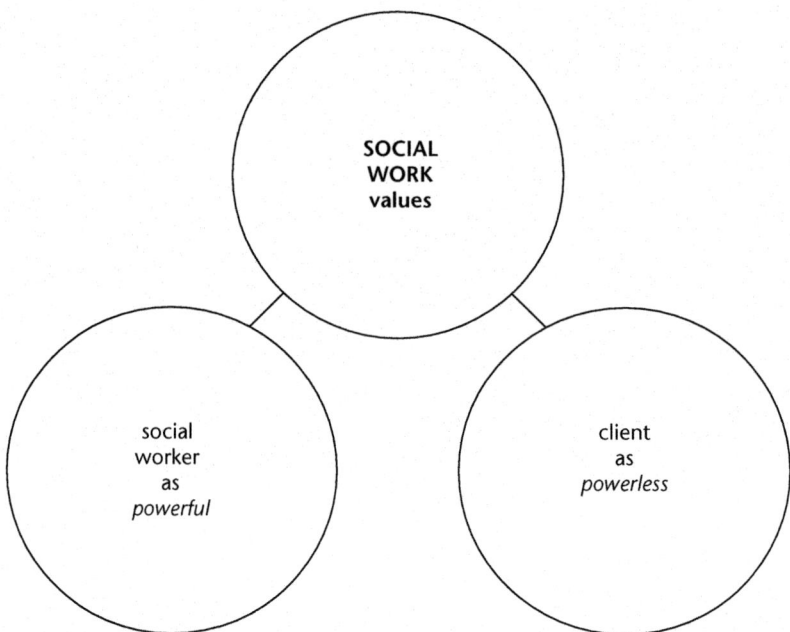

FIGURE 7.8 A partial constellation of Social Work values

these kinds of meanings visible we unpacked the axiological clusters that form partial constellations in two high-achieving students' reflective writing assignments from the fields of Business Studies and Social Work. In producing axiological constellations in their reflective writing, both students demonstrated their *alignment* with valorized disciplinary values in their respective fields.

This is a significant finding contrary to the arguments presented in the literature on critical reflection. Previous studies have emphasized the importance of critical reflection as a form of 'emancipatory education' (see Mezirow, 2003), which requires students to 'challenge the status quo' (see e.g. Brookfield, 2000; Crème, 2008; Fook, 2004; Fook and Morley, 2005). However, the findings of the current study do not support these emancipatory claims in previous research. For instance, in the Business reflective journal the student unquestioningly applied her internalized Australian values to justify her prejudices and negative judgement of her teammates during multinational teamwork. Similarly, the Social Work critical reflection essay drew on a range of literature to construct clusters of meaning that represent disciplinary Social Work values. These values were reflected in the student's analysis of the 'critical incident': despite the client's inappropriate comment, the student social worker maintained that even in an instance of clear vulnerability on her part, *the client was powerless* within the institutional and social structures of the field placement. In light of this, she argued that his comment was an attempt at 'regaining' power where he had none while she, as the social worker, remained in a position of power over the client. One aspect common to both texts is that they demonstrate mastery of constructing axiologically charged clusters of meaning, in other words, they *align* with the disciplinary values of Business and Social Work rather than questioning or challenging them.

From a pedagogic perspective, then, we argue that both Business and Social Work students need to learn, through the use of clusters of axiological meanings, the axiological cosmologies underlying their disciplines to be able to demonstrate their capacity for critical self-reflection. Students are expected to move from common-sense understandings of events and unprofessional behaviour to professional and ethical behaviour and values upheld by their disciplines. However, students are rarely taught *explicitly* the process by which they are expected to re-interpret and transform their behaviour to align with disciplinary values. Our findings are similar to those of other studies that have used LCT to explore axiological cosmologies of particular fields. A project on the teaching and learning of history discourse in Australian secondary school classrooms (Martin *et al.*, 2010), for instance, revealed that students are not only required to learn the abstract concepts and events of history through a focus on epistemological knowledge but also the systems of 'right values', i.e. the axiologically loaded and 'ideologically invested' gazes of various historical perspectives (p. 435). Similarly, a study by Martin, Zappavigna and Dwyer (2013) on youth justice conferencing revealed that young offenders in the proceeding are given a number of personae they can affiliate with, all of which require them to display self-discipline as a social subject (p. 40).

Previous research also reports that while teachers laud critical reflection, students are often resentful of reflective writing tasks. Reasons include the lack of explicit pedagogy, unclear assessment criteria, the requirement to share personal and private matters, and the perception among students that reflective tasks have little relevance to traditional learning that takes place at university (O'Connell and Dyment, 2011; Sinclair Penwarden, 2006). We propose an additional reason why critical reflection is often met with resistance by students. According to Maton (personal communication), displaying capacity for critical reflection is an issue of social justice: not all students are able to demonstrate the mastery of constructing axiologically charged clusters and constellations that pedagogic research suggests is so highly valued across many academic disciplines. This means that an assignment type that has long been praised for enabling 'transformative learning' (Mezirow, 2003), expected to result in students' 'empowerment' (Fook *et al.*, 2016), can, in fact, disadvantage students who lack the cultivated gaze of their disciplines.

Concluding remarks

In recent years, reflective writing tasks which test students' critical reflection skills have been gaining popularity in higher education. The importance of equipping students with critical reflection skills is also emphasized in higher education research and policy documents. Reflective assignments are especially valued in applied disciplines where students often face difficult or problematic incidents that may trigger an emotional and opinionated response. However, in higher education students are not explicitly taught how to engage with subjective meanings in their texts. Few studies explore how reflective writing tasks are designed to ensure that students can engage with subjective feelings by drawing on their understanding of theoretical frameworks from their individual disciplines. The ability to bring theory together with 'feelings' and 'opinions', we have argued elsewhere, is an important feature of reflective writing (Tilakaratna and Szenes, 2017a, 2017b). However, much less attention has been paid to the way students demonstrate their ability to move beyond merely expressing their emotions or opinions to relating these to privileged values in their disciplinary fields. By drawing on the concept of *axiological cosmologies* from LCT, we made visible the processes by which high-scoring students engage with subjective meanings in higher education assessment tasks. For reasons of space, we focused only on two illustrative texts from Business Studies and Social Work. We conclude by arguing that using a common descriptive framework for analyzing knowledge practices in individual disciplines allows us to make visible and *compare* valued reflective practices across two distinct disciplinary fields.

In this chapter we have argued that the construction of axiologically charged clusters of meanings that form a constellation of social and disciplinary values in the business and Social Work texts represents a *reproduction* of these values rather than a challenge to them. We have demonstrated that LCT offers a useful framework for making explicit the nature of these reproduced axiological cosmologies and their application to everyday experiences that allow students to demonstrate their capacity to align with discipline-specific values. If, as our analysis of these high-scoring texts appear to suggest, reproduction of these values is the basis for success in reflective writing tasks in these disciplines, then we need to also account for the implications of this research and the potential pedagogical interventions it could contribute to. In Maton's terms, students need to learn the axiological cosmologies of the field because:

> one's intellectual choices classify and they morally classify the classifier. They show whether your heart is in the right place, your aesthetic, ethical, moral or political affiliations correct, and so whether you are one of us or one of them
>
> *(2014, p. 163)*

Not only has using the LCT concept of axiological cosmologies for analyzing reflective assignments enabled us to challenge the *emancipatory* claims of critical reflection, it has also enabled us to uncover that successful critical reflection at undergraduate level appears to be a sophisticated form of *uncritical* reproduction.

Notes

1. In the old *Bachelor of Commerce* degree.
2. Throughout this chapter *Critical Incident* with initial letters capitalized will refer to the generic stage, while *critical incident* with lowercase letters will be used to refer to the actual event the student social worker discusses in her assignment.

References

Blaise, M., Dole, S., Latham, G., Malone, K., Faulkner, J. and Lang, J. (2004). Rethinking reflective journals in teacher education. Paper presented at the Australian Association of Researchers in Education (AARE) at Melbourne, Vic.
Brookfield, S. (2000). Transformative learning as ideology critique. In J. Mezirow (Ed.), *Learning as transformation* (pp. 125–149). San Francisco: Jossey-Bass.
Brookfield, S. (2001). The concept of critical reflection: Promises and contradictions. *European Journal of Social Work, 12*(3), 293–304.
Brookfield, S. (2016). So what exactly is critical about critical reflection? Critical reflection in management and organization studies. In J. Fook, V. Collington, R. Ross, G. Ruch and L. West (Eds), *Researching critical reflection: Multidisciplinary perspectives* (pp. 48–62). London: Routledge.
Carson, L. and Fisher, K. (2006). Raising the bar on criticality: Students' critical reflection in an internship program. *Journal of Management Education, 30*(5), 700–723.
Cornish, M.M. and Cantor, P.A. (2008). 'Thinking about thinking: It's not just for philosophers': Using metacognitive journals to teach and learn about constructivism. *Journal of Early Childhood Teacher Education, 29*(4), 326–339.
Crème, P. (2008). A space for academic play: Student learning journals as transitional writing. *Arts and Humanities in Higher Education, 7*(1), 49–51.
Epp, S. (2008). The value of reflective journaling in undergraduate nursing education: A literature review. *International Journal of Nursing Studies, 45*(9), 1379–1388.
Fisher, K. (2003). Demystifying critical reflection: Defining criteria for assessment. *Higher Education Research and Development, 22*(3), 313–325.
Fook, J. (2002). *Critical deconstruction and reconstruction.* London: Sage.
Fook, J. (2004). Critical reflection and transformative possibilities. In L. Davies and P. Leonard (Eds), *Social work in a corporate era: Practices of power and resistance* (pp. 16–30). Ashgate: Avebury.
Fook, J. and Askeland, G.A. (2007). Challenges of critical reflection: 'Nothing ventured, nothing gained'. *Social Work Education, 26*(5), 520–533.
Fook, J. and Gardner, F. (2013). *Critical reflection in context: Applications in health and social care.* Oxford: Routledge.
Fook, J. and Morley, C. (2005). Empowerment: A contextual perspective. In S. Hick, J. Fook and R. Pozzuto (Eds), *Social work: A critical turn* (pp. 67–86). Toronto: Thompson Education.
Fook, J., Collington, V., Ross, R., Ruch, G. and West, L. (2016). *Researching critical reflection: Multidisciplinary perspectives.* London: Routledge.
Freeman, M. (2009). *Embedding the development of intercultural competence in business education. Final Report CG6-37.* Australian Learning and Teaching Council.
Hatton, N. and Smith, D. (1995). Reflections in teacher education: Towards definition and implementation. *Teaching and Teacher Education, 11*(1), 33–49.
Hood, S. (2010). *Appraising research: Evaluation in academic writing.* London: Palgrave Macmillan.
Hume, A. (2009). Promoting higher levels of reflective writing in student journals. *Higher Education Research and Development, 28*(3), 247–260.
Martin, J.R., Maton, K. and Matruglio, E. (2010). Historical cosmologies: Epistemology and axiology in Australian secondary school history discourse. *Revista Signos, 43*(74), 433–463.
Martin, J.R. and White, P.R.R. (2005). *The language of evaluation: Appraisal in English.* New York: Palgrave Macmillan.

Martin, J.R., Maton, K. and Doran, Y.J. (Eds) (2020). *Accessing academic discourse: Systemic functional linguistic and Legitimation Code Theory*. London: Routledge.

Martin, J.R., Zappavigna, M. and Dwyer, P. (2013). Beyond redemption: Choice and consequence in youth justice conferencing. In F. Yan and J.J. Webster (Eds), *Developing systemic functional linguistics: Theory and application* (pp. 18–47). London: Equinox.

Maton, K. (2013). Making semantic waves: A key to cumulative knowledge-building. *Linguistics and Education, 24*(1), 8–22.

Maton, K. (2014). *Knowledge and knowers: Towards a realist sociology of education*. London: Routledge.

Maton, K. and Doran, Y.J. (2017). SFL and code theory. In T. Bartlett and G. O'Grady, (Eds), *The Routledge systemic functional linguistic handbook* (pp. 605–618). London: Routledge.

Maton, K., Hood, S. and Shay, S. (Eds). (2016). *Knowledge-building: Educational studies in Legitimation Code Theory*. Abingdon: Routledge.

Maton, K., Martin, J.R. and Matruglio, E. (2016). LCT and systemic functional linguistics: Enacting complementary theories for explanatory power. In K. Maton, S. Hood and S. Shay (Eds), *Knowledge-building: Educational studies in Legitimation Code Theory* (pp. 93–113). London: Routledge.

Mezirow, J. (2000). Learning to think like an adult: Core concepts of transformation theory. In J. Mezirow and Associates (Eds), *Learning as transformation: Critical perspectives on a theory in progress* (pp. 3–33). San Francisco: Jossey-Bass.

Mezirow, J. (2003). Transformative learning as discourse. *Journal of Transformative Education, 1*(1), 58–63.

Mills, R. (2008). 'It's just a nuisance': Improving college student reflective journal writing. *College Student Journal, 42*(2), 684–690.

Nesi, H. and Gardner, S. (2012). *Genre across the disciplines: Student writing in higher education*. Cambridge: Cambridge University Press.

O'Connell, T.S. and Dyment, J.E. (2011). The case of reflective journals: Is the jury still out? *Reflective Practice: International and Multidisciplinary Perspectives, 12*(1), 47–59.

Otienoh, R.O. (2009). Reflective practice: The challenge of journal writing. *Reflective Practice, 10*(4), 477–489.

Payne, M. (1997). *Modern social work theory* (2nd Edition). Abingdon: Oxford University Press.

Pockett, R. and Giles, R. (2008). *Critical reflection generating theory from practice: The graduating social work student experience*. Sydney: Darlington Press.

Sinclair Penwarden, A. (2006). Listen up: We should not be made to disclose our personal feelings in reflection assignments. *Nursing Times, 102*(37), 12.

Smith, E. (2011). Teaching critical reflection. *Teaching in Higher Education, 16*(2), 211–223.

Solomon, C.M. and Schell, M.S. (2009). *Managing across cultures – The seven keys to doing business with a global mindset*. New York: McGraw Hill.

Sutton, L., Townend, M. and Wright, J. (2007). The experiences of reflective learning journals by cognitive behavioural psychotherapy students. *Reflective Practice, 8*(3), 387–404.

Swan, E. and Bailey, A. (2004). Thinking with feeling: The emotions of reflection. In M. Reynolds and R. Vince (Eds), *Organizing reflection* (pp. 105–125). Aldershot: Ashgate.

Szenes, E., Tilakaratna, N. and Maton, K. (2015). The knowledge practices of 'critical' thinking. In M. Davies and R. Barnett (Eds), *Critical thinking in higher education* (pp. 573–591). London: Palgrave Macmillan.

Tilakaratna, N. and Szenes, E. (2017a). The linguistic construction of critical 'self reflection' in social work and business. In P. Chapell. and J. Knox (Eds), *Transforming contexts: Papers from the 44th International Systemic Functional Congress* (pp. 61–66). Wollongong: ISFC.

Tilakaratna, N. and Szenes, E. (2017b). Axiological cosmologies for writing about 'self-reflective' praxis. Paper presented at the *2nd International Legitimation Code Theory Conference* (LCTC2), Sydney, Australia.

Wieczorek, J. (2008). Crossing invisible lines: Professional boundaries, gender and power in social work. In R. Pockett and R. Giles (Eds), *Critical reflection generating theory from practice: The graduating social work student experience* (pp. 15–29). Sydney: Darlington Press.

8
LEARNING HOW TO THEORIZE IN DOCTORAL WRITING

A tool for teaching and learning

Kirstin Wilmot

Introduction

Higher education internationally is undergoing major transformations as universities widen access to a greater number and a more diverse cohort of students. Part of the reality of a more diverse cohort of students is that universities are no longer dealing with homogenous groups of students who share the same educational and socio-cultural background. The contact time between lecturers/supervisors and students is also diminishing, given the demands being made on academic staff as universities continue to massify. As a result, not all students will necessarily acquire tacit academic practices in the same manner or at the same speed. Doctoral writing is one such practice. Despite research showing that doctoral writing is a social practice that students learn over time through the supervisory socialization process, many supervisors still assume that it is a neutral skill that students should already possess when commencing their doctoral studies (Starke-Meyerring, 2014). Given the changes in higher education, together with some supervisor attitudes towards writing, we can no longer assume that learning to write through socialization processes will occur in equivalent ways, or with similar results. What is needed, therefore, is more explicit teaching of doctoral writing.

Doctoral writing pedagogy

Research on doctoral writing pedagogy remains 'shrouded in silence and marginalised' (Starke-Meyerring, 2014, p. 140), with common-sense assumptions abounding. For example, supervisors often conceptualize writing as somewhat divorced from other research practices – assuming that students 'do' research and then 'write up' at the end of their candidature (Kamler and Thomson, 2007). This assumption treats writing as separate from the rest of the disciplinary knowledge-building process of research; as a transparent 'vehicle' for thought (Christie, 1985, p. 298) instead of being the means to construct such thought in the first instance (Kamler and Thomson, 2006). Such an assumption is further reinforced in the many 'self-help' thesis writing handbooks available in most university libraries which prioritize other aspects of the research process while offering very little practical advice and strategies for the writing of the actual dissertation (Kamler and Thomson, 2008).

Furthermore, the assumption that students 'think' and then 'write' – i.e. that the first draft is the final or complete draft in need of only minor editorial polishing – abounds in academia (Kamler and Thomson, 2006). Such an assumption obscures the iterative drafting process that is crucial for doctoral writing. Instead of language, and subsequently writing, being seen as a 'resource' (Christie, 1985, p. 299) that is 'centrally involved in the ways in which information, thought, feeling, attitude, are established' (Christie, 1990, p. 9), supervision practices often treat writing as a neutral conveyer of already established thought. Research has shown, however, that by adopting a writing-in-process pedagogical approach in supervision practices, writing can be used in a number of ways to enhance and develop student learning (Lee and Murray, 2015). This process approach encourages the iterative process of drafting, creating more space to develop, refine and build disciplinary knowledge.

Essential to the development of meaning-making is feedback from those who know disciplinary knowledge-building practices best – supervisors. Research such as Lee and Murray's (2015, p. 560) paper on supervising writing has shown, however, that the practical teaching of doctoral writing is often negatively regarded by supervisors who find the process 'painful', 'tedious', 'frustrating' and 'time-consuming'. Feelings of apprehension or inadequacy to supervise writing often stem from the fact that not all supervisors possess the same knowledge and skills to deal with the demands of writing, with the large majority having never received training to learn how to develop a metalanguage to talk about their practices (Paré, 2011). Paré (2011), drawing on Bazerman (2009, p. 289), explains that not all supervisors have the 'reflective ability' to understand how their disciplinary practices work – i.e. they lack the ability to explicitly unpack and engage with the writing practices that they have come to internalize through years of socialization in their discipline. Therefore, although supervisors are typically well adept at writing themselves, they often lack the means or confidence to teach this craft to their students effectively.

This chapter argues that what is needed to address this problem is a way to better understand doctoral writing so that we may then begin to find ways to teach it more effectively. This calls for a new way to analyse doctoral writing itself – one that can offer practical insights and tools for supervisors to use to identify and teach successful features of writing. The remainder of this chapter describes one such tool for learning how to apply theory to data.

Practical tools for analyzing the theorizing process

Scholars working in teaching and learning in higher education agree that the craft of *theorizing* is an important part of research; however, it is an issue that is often side-lined due to a favoured focus on *theory* (Swedberg, 2012). Those who have considered what it means to theorize claim that data should drive the process (Swedberg, 2012); however, research has also shown that moving between theory and data and back again is a particularly complex and difficult process (Clegg, 2012). In an attempt to teach students how to move between abstract and concrete knowledge, Paré (2011, p. 66) notes that supervisors commonly use metaphors such as 'bridge', 'zigzag', 'maps' and 'mosaics' in their feedback on writing. These metaphors, according to Paré (2011, p. 65), are used to signify the 'conceptual structure' of a text, or what Giltrow (2002, p. 77) refers to as the 'high altitudes of generality' and the 'deep valleys of detail'.

Using metaphors is a useful starting point to explain to students that a text needs to include varying levels of abstraction and concreteness. They are limited, however, in that they are not fully able to engage with the kinds of knowledge that give rise to these movements, nor are they able to identify strategies to help students achieve this in their own writing. Paré (2011) argues that supervisors come to rely on these figures of speech because they lack the ability to unpack how their disciplinary practices work. To help supervisors bridge this gap, as well as provide students with practical strategies to use in their own learning, a new tool for analyzing and understanding the theorizing process is presented. The remainder of this chapter demonstrates how the concept of *semantic gravity* from Legitimation Code Theory (LCT) can provide both a conceptual understanding of the different forms the knowledge takes when theorizing data, as well as a practical scaffolding tool for supervisors and students of how this craft can be achieved in doctoral dissertations.

Theoretical framework and methodology

The analysis presented in this chapter traces the development of one doctoral student's writing practices as she learns how to apply theory to her data. The aim of the analysis is to show how the development of this craft is reflected in the iterative process of drafting chapters. The selected data for the analysis is taken from an Australian doctoral student's PhD dissertation in the social sciences that explores the general public's views on climate change. The analysis focuses on a section of one of the student's data chapters that looked at a discussion of 'the solutions' to climate change, as proposed by a Rotary focus group. In this section the student is using interview data gathered through focus groups and the theory she is applying to that data is Legitimation Code Theory. To better understand how the craft of theorizing develops over time, two versions of the student's chapter are analysed here. The first text, 'draft text', is taken from a draft version of the chapter, written approximately a year before submission. The second text, 'final text', is taken from the final (successful) version of the thesis. By analyzing both versions of the chapter, the process involved in theorizing and how this craft develops over time can be revealed. In addition, the analysis can identify what successful theorizing looks like in writing, in practical terms.

The analysis makes use of the concept of *semantic gravity* from the Semantics dimension of LCT to analyse the process of theorizing data (see Maton 2013, 2014, 2020). Semantic gravity refers to varying degrees of context-dependence in practices (Maton, 2014, p. 110). It is always defined relationally, according to the object of study. Its relational characteristic means that it is always represented on a continuum: practices cannot be said to have a fixed quality of 'strong' semantic gravity or 'weak' semantic gravity. Rather, they will always be relatively *stronger* or *weaker* in relation to the strengths of something else. In doctoral writing, these different strengths are seen in moves between detailed description of specific instances of data from a context of study (stronger semantic gravity) and more general and abstract interpretations of the data (weaker semantic gravity). For example, moving from a particular experience of one student in one context, 'Being part of the Tuesday reading group helped develop my thinking' to a more general and abstracted interpretation that could account for multiple students across multiple contexts, 'Communities of practice play an important role in students' learning in higher education'. A semantic gravity analysis enables an understanding of the forms the knowledge takes, and how this changes over time as the student develops her writing craft.

The semantic gravity analysis presented in this paper was undertaken using what is termed in LCT a *translation device* (see Maton and Chen, 2016; Maton and Howard, 2016). A translation device is a tool that is created from the data at hand and in simplest terms, provides an explicit bridge between theoretical concepts and real instances of data. In this way it acts as a kind of 'mediating tool' in that it reveals how the theory has been used to interpret instances of data. By using a translation device, the method of analysis is made more transparent: it enables greater potential for reproducibility of the study and it ensures greater consistency in the analysis. To create the translation device the data was first thematically coded to ascertain the strengths of semantic gravity (concrete to abstract knowledge) in the two texts. At the most concrete level were quotes from the interview data itself and at the most abstract level were theoretical codings of data. Between these two ends of the semantic gravity spectrum identified in the data, a further three strengths of semantic gravity were revealed. The total of five strengths of semantic gravity that made up the translation device are illustrated in Figure 8.1.

Referring to Figure 8.1, the coding categories are defined and exemplified below, with the relevant coded part of the example highlighted in *italics*:

- **Quoted data**, the relatively strongest level of semantic gravity where knowledge is concrete and dependent on its context for meaning. Includes quotations of raw data, e.g. 'it was a *"very money-focussed conversation"'*.
- **Descriptions of data**, a relatively stronger level of semantic gravity where knowledge is relatively context-dependent. Includes summarizing descriptions or paraphrasing of the data, e.g. '*Several of the participants spoke of the need to reduce pollution*'.

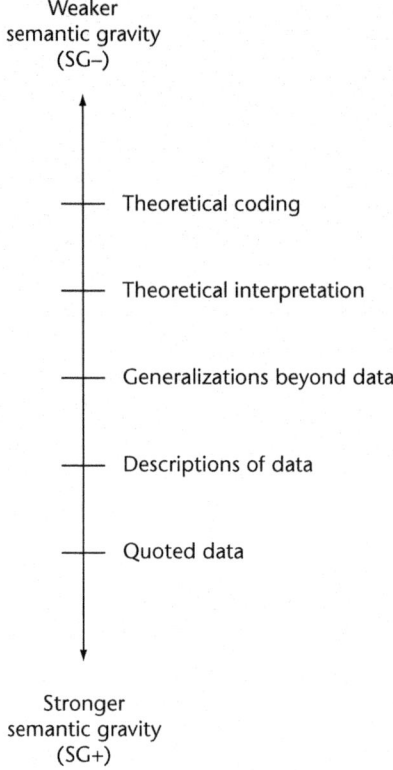

FIGURE 8.1 Strengths of semantic gravity informing the translation device

- **Generalizations beyond data**, a mid-level strength of semantic gravity where knowledge is relatively context-independent. Includes a-theoretical interpretations of data, e.g. '*Participants constructed the climate change issue as a duel between opposing interests*'.
- **Theoretical interpretation**, a relatively weaker level of semantic gravity where knowledge is relatively context-independent and abstract. Includes theoretical interpretations of data, e.g. '*The carbon tax became emptied of its technical and evidential aspects, reflecting weaker epistemic relations*'.
- **Theoretical coding**, the relatively weakest level of semantic gravity where knowledge is abstract and generalizable. Includes a theoretical coding of interpretations, e.g. '*The focus on personalities and their motives and character traits reflects stronger social relations (SR+)*'.

These categories were used to code and analyse the varying strengths of semantic gravity being enacted in the two texts. What are called 'specific translation devices' are always developed and defined according to the data at hand, and are, as such, data-specific (see Maton and Howard, 2018). Thus, the categories as well as the examples provided all relate to the specific climate change study that used LCT as the theoretical framework. While the implications of this specific translation device will reach beyond this data to other social science dissertations that use theory in similar ways, the device may need to be adjusted depending on what kind of knowledge the new data contains.

Once data has been analysed using a translation device, the results of that analysis can be graphically illustrated to reveal how the knowledge moves between the varying strengths of semantic gravity over a whole text. This is achieved by plotting the various moves between stronger and weaker semantic gravity (i.e. between concrete instances of data and abstract theory) onto a semantic profile (see Figure 8.2). The *semantic profile* comprises two axes: the *y*-axis represents the different strengths of semantic gravity (as identified in the translation device) and the *x*-axis represents the unfolding of the text in number of words. By plotting the results a 'semantic profile' is produced. Figure 8.2 provides an example of a generic semantic gravity profile to exemplify this explanation.

The profiling of texts has been shown to be an effective modelling tool for students in classrooms (Ingold and O'Sullivan, 2017), and is argued here to be applicable to doctoral writing pedagogy as well. Profiles provide a useful visual of how knowledge is being built in a text and are a useful tool for gaining an overall impression of texts, as well as comparing the structure of knowledge in different texts. Tracking the movements between concrete and abstract knowledge in doctoral writing, as well as making these moves explicit to students, is valuable, as research (see, for example, Hammond, 2018) shows that this is not an easy aspect of writing. Furthermore, it is an aspect that doctoral students need to learn as it enables the insights they gain from one research context to be generalized across contexts.

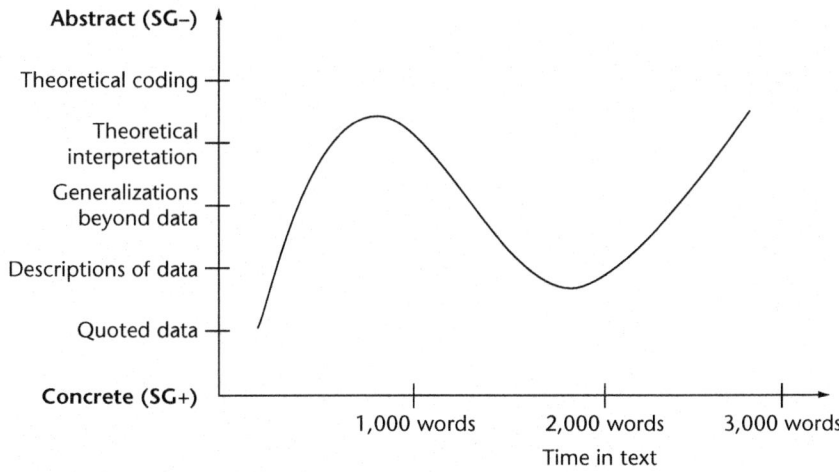

FIGURE 8.2 Generic semantic gravity profile

To illustrate the different strengths of semantic gravity at work in the student's writing in the analysis section below, the examples used to exemplify are marked up using **bold**, *italics* and underline. Table 8.1 provides a key for this allocation.

Analysis

Using the identified coding categories outlined in Table 8.1, the analysis of the two texts is now presented.

Draft text

In the draft text, the student spends a large proportion of time working at a very descriptive level. This is evident in how she provides rich description of the data, including frequent use of quotes from the interviews. The following extract provides an example of how the student describes the participants' views on the inability of humans to reduce climate change, and the reasons behind this. The extract starts with a summarizing description of the participants' viewpoints (indicated in *italics*), before the student draws on quotes from the data itself to substantiate the description (evident in her use of quotation marks):

> *Several participants expressed that humans, either individually or collectively, are unable to mitigate climate change. For example, in response to David's question about whether they should take some action, Geoff said* 'It's too late for us mate. You've got more time than me, but um. I haven't got any of that time.' *At the collective level, Joe said* 'We got no control on climate change, no matter what they tell us. If we, if we take off, most of the carbon which we'll spend millions and billions we still won't have only a drop in an ocean …'.

TABLE 8.1 Coding key for analysis

Semantic gravity range	*Indication in text*	*Example*
Theoretical coding	**bold**	The focus on personalities and their motives and character traits reflects stronger social relations (**SR+**)
Theoretical interpretation	***bold italics***	***The carbon tax became emptied of its technical and evidential aspects, reflecting weaker epistemic relations***
Generalizations beyond data	underlined *italics*	*Participants constructed the climate change issue as a duel between opposing interests*
Descriptions of data	*italics*	*Several of the participants spoke of the need to reduce pollution*
Quoted data	'quotation marks'	it was a 'very money-focussed conversation'

The pattern of moving between summarizing description and quotes from the data occurs for much of the first part of the text. As a result, the rich description generated by these two semantic gravity strengths means that the majority of the knowledge expressed in the draft text is relatively context-dependent and concrete: it refers to specific viewpoints from a specific research context. This results in the knowledge staying at relatively stronger semantic gravity, in that its meaning is dependent on the research context from which the data was generated.

When the student does start to incorporate theory into the discussion, she makes an attempt to move towards the abstract by first including a-theoretical interpretations of the data. In the extract below the student is generalizing beyond the specifics of the data and interpreting the participants' proposed solutions to climate change as being simple, concrete solutions that could be enacted in their local contexts. These simple solutions to concrete problems are then compared to the broader effects and impacts of climate change (such as the damage to the ozone layer), which the participants felt was the domain of climate scientists, not the individual. This generalizing beyond the data is indicated in <u>*underlined italics*</u>:

> <u>*Ditto all the conversations about waste, littering, landfills – material, tangible. Prioritize action on other issues such as starvation and plastic rubbish floating in the ocean: both material – in contrast to climate change – indirect and can only be observed by climate scientists. Similarly, as pointed out by Ted the recovery of the ozone layer is not directly perceptible by lay people.*</u>

Following this a-theoretical interpretation (a mid-level strength of semantic gravity identified in the translation device), the student moves back to summarizing description, drawing on key quotes from the data to illustrate the point being put forward, before moving back to a more generalized a-theoretical interpretation of this description:

> *The types of actions that participants identified for 'do the right thing', (recycle, compost, don't litter, pick up others' litter, turn off the lights, plant trees, keep the backyard mown and tidy, get smoky car emissions fixed at the mechanic)* <u>*are all very local, tangible, specific solutions....*</u>

Following this description and a-theoretical interpretation, the student then assigns a theoretical coding to the interpretation that has been made. This is evident in the following extract where the student has used '(SG+, SD–)' – a theoretical coding from LCT – the theory the student is using to analyse her data. The theoretical coding is indicated in **bold** and the generalization beyond data is indicated in <u>*underlined italics*</u>:

> <u>*are all very local, tangible, specific solutions*</u> **(SG+, SD-)**. <u>*Several times participants spoke of the need to reduce 'pollution', meaning air pollutants*</u> *(visible: particulates, smog, 'dark green cloud' over China)* <u>*rather than greenhouse gases which are invisible.*</u>

The assignment of a theoretical coding in this example indicates a marked jump in the text from a mid-level strength of semantic gravity (generalizing beyond data) to the relatively weakest level of semantic gravity identified in the translation device (theoretical coding). Once the theoretical coding of '(SG+, SD–)' has been assigned, the student immediately proceeds with a generalization of another aspect of the data. As such, the slightly stronger level of semantic gravity (seen in the generalization beyond data) is used to make sense of the *next* data point; it is not used to explain the theoretical coding which has just been made.

When considering the semantic gravity profile of the draft text (Figure 8.3), it is evident how much of the text stays at a relatively descriptive level, where knowledge is closely dependent on its context. This can be seen in the relatively 'low flatline' (Maton, 2013) represented on the profile, indicating smaller movements between the first two strengths of relatively stronger semantic gravity ('quoted data' and 'summarizing descriptions of data' from the translation device). It is also evident that theory is only incorporated towards the end of the text – seen in the move towards weaker semantic gravity at the end of the profile.

The profile in Figure 8.3 highlights the somewhat disjointed use of theory alluded to in the analysis of the extract above. It is evident here how the student often makes big jumps to theory, or a theoretical coding might appear without much build up to it and with little explanation of it. Furthermore, the profile shows how rich descriptions of data are often treated separately to abstract theoretical interpretations or coding – i.e. the two kinds of knowledge are, to a large extent, dealt with in discrete stages in the text, without much integration between them. This is evident in the jumps between the relatively strongest and weakest levels of semantic gravity in the profile instead of moving incrementally

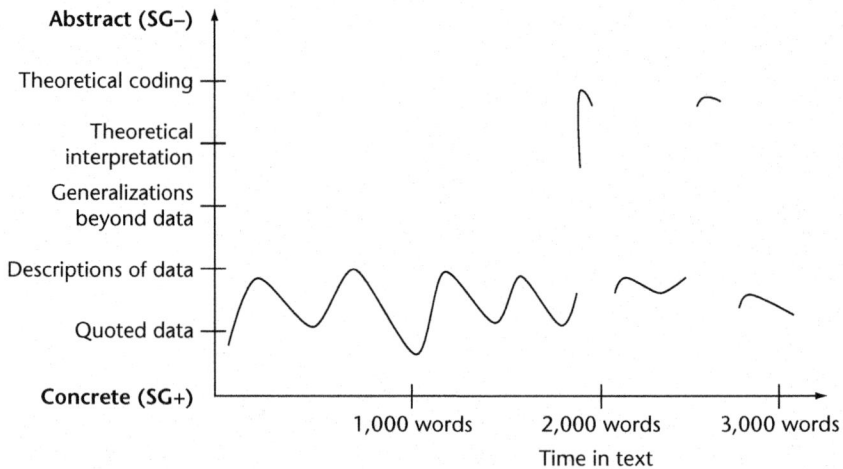

FIGURE 8.3 Semantic gravity profile of draft text

through the different strengths. The disjointedness caused by these jumps in semantic gravity often gives the impression that theory has been imposed onto data, instead of gradually incorporating theoretical knowledge to concrete instances of data as the text unfolds.

Final text

In the final text, the student engages with more strengths of semantic gravity from the beginning of the text. While she still provides rich description, she consistently moves between and integrates more levels of semantic gravity, allowing her to incorporate generalizations beyond the data from the start. In doing so, the student can start lifting the interpretation of the data beyond specific instances to more general patterns earlier in the text. This movement is repeated in the beginning stages of the text, forming a kind of 'wave' formation as she moves up and down from the relatively strongest level of semantic gravity to the mid-point strength of semantic gravity identified in the translation device. Thus, the student builds to abstraction more gradually, progressively weakening the semantic gravity towards theory.

This movement can be seen in the following set of extracts. The student starts by making an a-theoretical interpretation of the data. She has generalized the participants' reactions to possible solutions to climate change into 'us' and 'them' groups (between community-based, grassroots solutions versus government-led responses) and is now making a generalized interpretation of how the participants judge these solutions to be fair or not:

> <u>Further to the division into 'us' and 'them' groups, participants judged climate responses to be fair or unfair based on whether the parties involved were said to be fulfilling their responsibilities or not.</u> *There was a sentiment that governments, industries and countries have moral responsibilities to 'play fairly' and a duty to ensure that solutions are fair and equitable.*

<u>So</u>, the student is able to generalize beyond the specifics of the data at hand. She then locks this generalization onto the data by including a summarizing description of the data, as well as a quote from the data itself to illustrate her point:

> *The carbon tax was seen as being unfair because* 'they've let the biggest polluters off!'
>
> (Shann)

By moving between these three levels, the student is able to incorporate rich description without being confined to this relatively stronger semantic gravity. The movement between the first three relatively stronger semantic gravity strengths is evident throughout much of the text, as can be seen in the following ('generalization beyond data' indicated in <u>underlined italics</u>, 'summarizing descriptions' in *italics*, and 'quoted data' shown in quotation marks):

> *There was also a perception that Australia,* 'the cleanest country in the world' (Joe) *should not be required to take action on climate change and that this responsibility falls to more polluting countries, primarily China and India. Australia was said to be shouldering an unfair burden by acting alone to our detriment:* 'it increases all our energy prices and makes us less competitive, and we don't know anyone else around the world who's doing it.' (Jock). *It represents double standards in that China and India do not have to pay a carbon tax*: 'we export coal to China and they can do what they bloody like with it!' (Joe) *and* 'it's alright for them to do it and not pay a tax on it' (Ted). *These assessments are based on judgments of fairness and responsibility of different groups of people.*

When the student starts to build towards theory, she gradually increases the use of generalizations beyond the data, frequently connecting these interpretations to the data by drawing on key quotes and summarizing descriptions to illustrate the point she is making.

When theory is introduced, the student establishes more explicit connections between the data and the theoretical interpretation in her writing. In this sense, she steps the reader through the theorizing process more explicitly. This is evident in the following extracts, which show how the student moves between progressively weaker strengths of semantic gravity. The author starts by generalizing the data by providing an a-theoretical interpretation (seen in *underlined italics*):

> *Section 4.2.3 described participants' binary world in which people were assigned to an 'us' or 'them' group. Accordingly, climate change solutions were associated with one or the other group. As a general pattern, participants positively judged solutions that were associated with the 'us' group and negatively judged those associated with 'them'.*

Next, the student applies concepts from her theory, including 'epistemic relations', 'ER−', 'social relations' and 'SR+'. In the first instance, the student generates a theoretical interpretation of the generalization that has just come before (see previous extract). The student uses the theoretical concept of 'epistemic relations' to interpret the participants' evaluations of the proposed solutions to climate change. She then assigns the theoretical coding of '(ER−)' to this interpretation, which codes this interpretation in notation form. The theoretical interpretation is evident in **bolded italics** and the theoretical coding is represented by **bold**:

> ***The fact that evaluations were not made on the basis of evidential points such as the technical feasibility of solutions or their emission abatement potentials means that epistemic relations were downplayed.* (ER−)**

The student then repeats this process, including the theoretical concepts of 'social relations' and the theoretical coding of 'SR+' to the interpretation:

> *The focus on solutions resting on people's attributes and servicing their needs, and the value judgments of solutions on the basis of their association with an 'us' or 'them' group, are indicative of stronger social relations.* **(SR+)**

She then brings these two theoretical interpretations (***bold italics***) and codings (**bold**) together to form a further theoretical coding of the interpretation that has been made, seen in the application of the concept of a 'knower code'. The student also shows how this coding can be expressed in notation form as '(ER−, SR+)'.

> *Together the weaker epistemic relations* **(ER−)** *and stronger social relations* **(SR+)** *indicate a* **knower code (ER−, SR+).**

The student has thus moved between and integrated different levels of progressively weaker strengths of semantic gravity before an abstract theoretical coding has been applied to the data. By doing this, the student has made her interpretation process more explicit to the reader, rather than jumping straight from the data to theory.

The student also manages to make the connections between the abstract and concrete knowledge explicit when she incorporates theory. This is seen when theory is introduced, in how the knowledge does not stay fixed at a relatively weaker level of semantic gravity. Instead, the student establishes connections between the theory and the data by incorporating and integrating stronger levels of semantic gravity when making a theoretical interpretation. This is apparent in the following extract where quotes from the data (shown in quotation marks) and generalizations of the data (indicated in <u>*underlined italics*</u>) are used in the same space where the student starts applying a theoretical interpretation (shown in ***bolded italics***) as well as a theoretical coding (indicated in **bold**):

> ***In relation to the LCT dimension of Semantics, at least some of the sentiments about climate change being unproblematic appeared to stem from viewing climate change as daily changes of the weather*** ('[climate] changes from day to day. So what? What effect does it have on us?'). <u>*To the extent that climate change was seen as being problematic, it was portrayed as a 'tame' problem with simple and painless solutions.*</u> ***The tangible, current, concrete, local, everyday nature of the 'do your bit' solutions that participants favoured means that they are more strongly context dependent, that is, they exhibit stronger semantic gravity.*** **(SG+)**

The student strategically uses key quotes (the relatively strongest level of semantic gravity) to lock the theoretical interpretation and coding (both relatively weaker levels of semantic gravity) onto instances of data. This explicitly shows the connections the student has made in her thinking and better integrates the interpretation, rather than working only at an abstract level.

When considering the overall semantic gravity profile of the final text (Figure 8.4), it is evident how the knowledge-building practices have developed from the draft text.

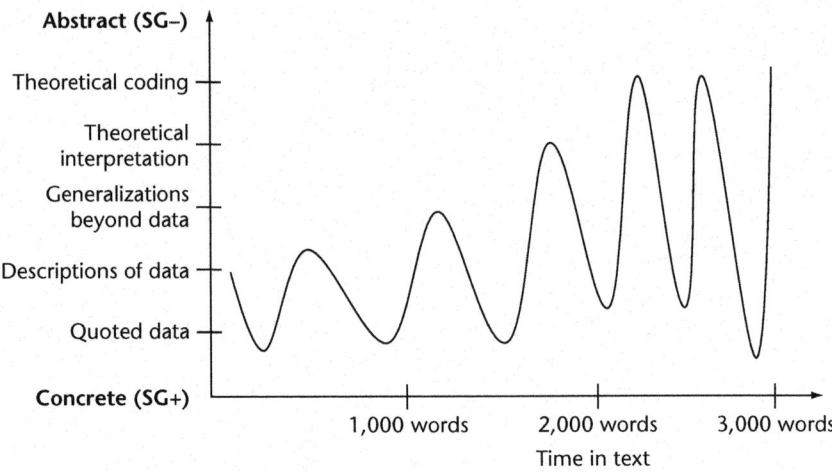

FIGURE 8.4 Semantic gravity profile of final text

In particular, the final text profile (Figure 8.4) shows how the movements between the varying strengths of semantic gravity are more integrated and smooth, indicating how the student has weaved these different strengths together more fluidly. The time spent in the text at these different strengths also creates greater flow between the different forms of knowledge, which helps mitigate the disjointed feel apparent in the draft text. The profile also reveals how the student is able to gradually work towards a theoretical interpretation by progressively weakening the semantic gravity. However, when theory is introduced, it is not confined to weaker semantic gravity. Instead, the student incorporates key quotes and descriptions at this stage (strengthening semantic gravity) which helps make the logic of the theorizing process explicit to the reader. The movements on the profile also show how rich description of data and abstract theory are not treated in two distinct stages. While there is a move towards more abstract knowledge towards the end of the chapter, its integration is much more gradual. This has been achieved by weaving between the different strengths of semantic gravity throughout the text.

The profile of the final text (Figure 8.4) also reveals how the student ends the text at relatively weaker strengths of semantic gravity (i.e. at an abstract level). This allows the implications of the findings to be interpreted at a more abstract level, meaning that they are no longer locked onto specific data from a specific research context. Rather, the abstract knowledge generated from the data can now be extrapolated beyond the immediate context and can be applied elsewhere in the field.

Discussion and conclusion

This chapter has identified and analysed one aspect of doctoral writing that students often struggle to learn and supervisors struggle to teach: applying theory to data.

Using the concept of semantic gravity from LCT, the analysis has revealed how this tool can make this learning process more explicit. Through the use of a semantic gravity translation device, the analysis revealed five main strengths of semantic gravity that enabled this student to move between context-dependent rich description of data to abstract and generalizable interpretations of the data that are applicable to the field more broadly. Such movements have been shown in research (such as in the field of higher education studies) to be valued by examiners (McKenna *et al.*, 2018). Using the concept of 'semantic gravity' from LCT and working from examples of real texts presents an opportunity to start to make this process explicit.

A key finding from the analysis is that although moving between data and theory can initially seem like a straightforward process, it is seldom one that students successfully achieve on their first attempt. The analysis presented here, particularly the use of profiling, provides evidence for the need to supervise the writing of dissertations as a process. Literature reviewed at the beginning of this chapter — such as Kamler and Thomson (2006) and Lee and Murray (2015) — discusses the need for writing-centred supervision models that enable space for students to develop their knowledge-building practices through increased writing and drafting opportunities. The findings of this analysis show how through multiple draft versions, the student is able to develop her theorizing craft over time, revealing that a more fully theorized text is able to move across the full range of the semantic gravity continuum.

With regards to the craft of theorizing, the analysis also suggests that texts which provide a more gradual climb towards theory — working from (and moving between) raw data description to explanation, followed by a more abstract theoretical interpretation — are more highly regarded. The analysis also suggests that making links between abstract knowledge (the theory) and concrete knowledge (the data) is a valued feature of theorizing, in that it helps to make the logic of the interpretation explicit. This suggests that a 'high flatline' (Maton, 2013) — i.e. working solely at a theoretical level) is not held in the same esteem as showing how you can move between the semantic gravity strengths. In this case, successful theorizing is not only about working at an abstract level, it is about showing how that abstract knowledge has been generated. Ending a text on an abstract level also appears to be a rewarded feature in this example. By doing this, the student is able to show how the findings can be generalized beyond the confines of the study, and can be applied to (and have relevance for) the broader field.

The lengths of the two texts analysed in this chapter suggest that successful theorizing does not necessarily require additional text space (i.e. word count) to occur. As seen in the final text — which is approximately 1,000 words shorter than the draft version — the student is able to move between more strengths of semantic gravity more often, and is able to build towards theory more effectively in a shorter space of time than the draft text. In effect, the student has done more knowledge work in the final text, in less time. Again, this provides evidence for the need to understand writing as an iterative process whereby meaning is developed and refined over time.

An important point to emphasize is that the semantic gravity profiles presented in this chapter are by no means the 'ideal' profile for all theorizing across all disciplinary contexts. Some disciplines may require students to start theoretical and then gradually unpack the abstract knowledge to show how it connects to concrete experience. Other disciplines may require more abstract knowledge overall, while others may favour more descriptive, context-dependent knowledge. The point here is that the concept of semantic gravity affords us a tool to make these different expectations, requirements or preferences explicit in any text, from any discipline. A semantic gravity analysis not only unpacks the process in explicit terms (i.e. it plays a valuable role as an analytical tool), but through the development of the translation device, it can be used as a pedagogic tool that can provide a scaffold for students on how to bring theory and data into a genuine dialogue by stepping through the different semantic gravity strengths. Furthermore, it can be used as a shared metalanguage in the supervision space; as a way for supervisors to explain what is needed in a text, as well as provide more explicit feedback on the strengths and weaknesses of a student's work. This shared metalanguage provides a practical and meaningful alternative to nebulous metaphors by providing an explicit scaffolding framework for supervisors and students to work with, without being prescriptive.

While focusing on only one aspect of doctoral writing from one student, in one discipline, the findings presented in this chapter show how tools from LCT can provide the necessary means to analyse and understand aspects of doctoral writing more effectively. The framework provides an alternate perspective to most approaches to writing in that it maintains a focus on the knowledge being expressed through the writing, rather than delving into the more surface textual features of the text. By exploring different aspects of doctoral writing in this way, LCT provides a lens through which this elusive practice can be made explicit and be better understood. In this sense it affords a useful starting point to better understand what knowledge-building features make some texts more legitimate than others. Understanding these features is a necessary first step before conceptualizing effective pedagogical solutions for future doctoral students.

References

Bazerman, C. (2009). Genre and cognitive development: Beyond writing to learn. In C. Bazerman, D. Figueiredo, and A. Bonini (Eds), *Genre in a changing world* (pp. 279–94). Fort Collins, Colorado: The WAC Clearinghouse.

Christie, F. (1985). *Language education*. Victoria: Deakin University Press.

Christie, F. (1990). The changing face of literacy. In F. Christie (Ed.), *Literacy for a changing world* (pp. 1–25). Victoria: The Australian Council for Educational Research Ltd.

Clegg, S. (2012). On the problem of theorising: An insider account of research practice. *Higher Education Research and Development*, 31(3), 407–418.

Giltrow, J. (2002). Academic writing: Writing and reading in the disciplines (3rd edn). Peterborough: Broadview.

Hammond, M. (2018). 'An interesting paper but not sufficiently theoretical': What does theorising in social research look like? *Methodological Innovations*, 11(2), 1–10.

Ingold, R. and O'Sullivan, D. (2017). Riding the waves to academic success. *Modern English Teacher, 26*(2), 39–43.

Kamler, B. and Thomson, P. (2006). *Helping doctoral students write: Pedagogies for supervision.* Abingdon: Routledge.

Kamler, B. and Thomson, P. (2007). Rethinking doctoral work as text work and identity work. In B. Somekh and T.A. Schwandt (Eds), *Knowledge production: Research in interesting times* (pp. 166–179). London: Routledge.

Kamler, B. and Thomson, P. (2008). The failure of dissertation advice books: Toward alternative pedagogies for doctoral writing. *Educational Researcher, 37*(8), 507–14.

Lee, A. and Murray, R. (2015). Supervising writing: Helping postgraduate students develop as researchers. *Innovations in Education and Teaching International, 52*(5), 558–70.

Maton, K. (2013). Making semantic waves: A key to cumulative knowledge-building, *Linguistics and Education,* 24(1): 8–22.

Maton, K. (2014). *Knowledge and knowers: Towards a realist sociology of education.* London: Routledge.

Maton, K. (2020). Semantic waves: Context, complexity and academic discourse. In J.R. Martin, K. Maton and Y.J. Doran (Eds), *Accessing academic discourse: Systemic functional linguistics and Legitimation Code Theory* (pp. 59–85). London: Routledge.

Maton, K. and Chen, R.T.-H. (2016). LCT in qualitative research: Creating a translation device for studying constructivist pedagogy. In K. Maton, S. Hood and S. Shay (Eds), *Knowledge-building: Educational studies in Legitimation Code Theory* (pp. 27–48). London: Routledge.

Maton, K. and Howard, S.K. (2016). LCT in mixed-methods research: Evolving an instrument for quantitative data, in K. Maton, S. Hood and S. Shay (Eds), *Knowledge-building: Educational studies in Legitimation Code Theory* (pp. 49–71). London: Routledge.

Maton, K. and Howard, S.K. (2018). Taking autonomy tours: A key to integrative knowledge-building*, LCT Centre Occasional Paper 1:* 1–35.

McKenna, S., Quinn, L. and Vorster, J. (2018). Mapping the field of higher education research using PhD examination reports. *Higher Education Research and Development, 37*(3), 579–592.

Paré, A. (2011). Speaking of writing: Supervisory feedback and the dissertation. In D. Starke-Meyerring, A. Pare, N. Artemeva, M. Horne, and L. Yousoubova (Eds), *Writing in knowledge societies* (pp. 59–73). Fort Collins, Colorado: WAC Clearinghouse.

Starke-Meyerring, D. (2014). Writing groups as critical spaces for engaging normalized institutional cultures of writing in doctoral education. In C. Aitchison and C. Guerin (Eds), *Writing groups for doctoral education and beyond: Innovations in practice and theory* (pp. 137–65). Abingdon: Routledge.

Swedberg, R. (2012). Theorizing in sociology and social science: Turning to the context of discovery. *Theory and Society, 41*(1), 1–40.

PART II
Professional learning in higher education

9
CHANGING CURRICULUM AND TEACHING PRACTICE

A practical theory for academic staff development

Sherran Clarence and Martina van Heerden

Introduction

Academic staff development work in higher education is typically understood as practical, focused on connecting academic support staff with specialization in teaching, learning and assessment approaches and theory with academic teaching staff to enable the latter to 'diagnose' and address difficulties in teaching and learning. For example, a lecturer who is struggling to engage students in class might consult an academic developer who could observe the teaching, talk to students and the lecturer, and help the lecturer address the problem through practical action.

An important, though often underdeveloped, aspect of this type of academic development work is the use of theory to both understand current practice and provide a way to inform future practice. Yet, the term 'theory' can put lecturers on guard, especially theory coming from unfamiliar fields outside of one's own. Theory can be alienating, and difficult to connect with lived practice unless carefully used. Thus, the term itself needs to be used cautiously in engagement between academic developers and lecturers. The emphasis in this chapter will be on how an accessible, useful theory can be used in real-world teaching and learning situations. Legitimation Code Theory (LCT) tools drawn from the dimension of Semantics will be applied to two 'vignettes' drawn from enacted staff development practice in two different academic departments: English Studies and Political Studies. Through this exercise, the chapter will demonstrate the value of academic development work in supporting staff with, as well as illustrating the value of, LCT as a strong example of 'practical theory' that can be put to use effectively in enhancing and changing pedagogy in higher education.

Academic development as a field

Academic development is a growing field of research and practice globally (Manathunga, 2006; Quinn, 2003, 2012); yet there is often much uncertainty about what academic development staff and units do in tertiary institutions (Staniforth and Harland, 2003; Bath and Smith, 2004). Academic development (also called educational development in the UK and Antipodes) refers to 'a range of developmental and research practices aimed at the professionalization of teaching and learning in higher education' (Shay, 2012, p. 311). Academic development therefore aims to improve teaching and learning practices of disciplinary staff. This suggests a (false) dichotomy between academic development work and disciplinary work, which may translate into generic approaches to teaching and learning or, rather than and, discipline- or field-specific approaches.

However, recent research in South Africa, Australia and the UK has begun to look more closely at the convergences and divergences between generic and discipline-specific approaches to teaching, learning, curriculum and assessment (Carter and Laurs, 2014; Bharuthram and Clarence, 2015; Kirk, 2017). The research suggests that rather than focusing on creating either more or less generic approaches to teaching and learning, university lecturers – assisted by academic development staff – should be more focused on creating scholarly, or research-led 'praxis' that is fit for purpose. Praxis, in essence, refers to 'embedding theory within practice' (Maton et al., 2016, p. 72). Thus, academic development needs to task itself with facilitating greater awareness of teaching, learning and knowledge, and connect these with academics' concerns about their own teaching, assessment, and their students' successes and struggles. A key concern for academic development work is to encourage theorized thinking about learning and teaching, and a 'both/and' (Maton, 2016) approach to the generic skills/disciplinary content debate. This is important if we are to avoid a situation where students who fail to meet expectations are 'blamed' for not possessing the rights kinds of prior knowledge, skills or motivation (Boughey and McKenna, 2016), or a situation where we veer too far into one side of the binary over the other, potentially shortchanging meaningful student learning and opportunities for success.

Ultimately, therefore, academic development work is not merely geared towards engaging academic staff only for the sake of improving their teaching; instead what underpins academic development is how it may enhance student learning and success. In fact, academic development work has largely emerged as a field in responses to changes in the university structure, such as increased student numbers and increased diversity of students (Clegg, 2009). In the South African context, for instance, Boughey and McKenna (2017) have shown that academic development is motivated to better enable transformation, success and access at higher education. As such, academic development work aims to enable students' engagement with disciplinary knowledge and knowing, so that they may, in turn, understand, reproduce and create new disciplinary knowledge.

If academic developers are to provide practical and useful ways of improving teaching and learning, and as a result, student learning and engagement, it becomes imperative for them to have both conceptual and practical tools at their disposal to better enable educators to unpack the ways in which they teach and provide possible alternatives to improve current practices (Quinn, 2003; Jacobs, 2007). That is to say, academic development practitioners will have to work from within their positions as 'knowers' or specialists in the academic development field, to enable educators to make explicit the discourses and practices of a discipline for students to have more successful learning experiences (Case, 2013). The focus should therefore be on having academic development staff and disciplinary lecturers working in collaboration with one another. Jacobs (2007), for instance, draws on the work of James Paul Gee to show that disciplinary educators seem to be principally concerned with educating students within specific disciplinary traditions, canons or ways of knowing. But, over time, these ways of knowing and doing may become common-sense knowledge and as such increasingly difficult to see as strange or new. This can mean that many educators within the disciplines find it difficult to see their discipline as a novice student might, and adapt their pedagogy to scaffold and support students' learning so that they come to know consciously and successfully over time (Jacobs, 2007). However, working as they do from outside the disciplines, and coming from disciplinary backgrounds that may be different to those of the educators they work with (Manathunga, 2006), academic development practitioners can do their most valuable work in helping these educators to see their disciplines in new, more naïve ways through questioning closely what students are learning, how and why. But, how we ask these questions, and what questions to ask then becomes a very important consideration. A practical language, rooted in theory, is needed to assist educators and academic developers, to guide these kinds of questions.

There is a gap in the field when it comes to academic developers using theory to create a practical language with which to talk to lecturers about their discipline and their teaching within the discipline, and not just to analyse teaching practices. This chapter contributes to closing this gap by analyzing two encounters with academic lecturers and peer tutors, created from data generated through academic development-based workshops, using the Semantics dimension of LCT. These analyses show how academic developers can assist with improving teaching and learning practices (in this instance, specifically curriculum development and enhancing feedback-giving practices) through using the language and tools offered by Semantics. These can offer lecturers a language with which to think analytically, and creatively, about their teaching and assessment practices. The examples, or 'vignettes', show how academic developers can use theory to understand and unpack practices, which in turn, could be used to theorize practice, and lead to meaningful change.

Framework for the analysis

Semantics is a dimension of LCT concerned with meaning-making practices, such as building knowledge and understanding over time (see Maton, 2013, 2014, 2020). In this chapter, we are using the concepts of *semantic gravity* and *semantic density* to analyse *semantic waves* (Vignette A) and the *semantic plane* (Vignette B). These cases show what can be accomplished by applying these tools to curriculum and assessment respectively to enact meaningful change in how students, and lecturers, create appropriate meanings in their teaching and learning.

Semantic gravity (SG) refers to the context-dependence of meanings (Maton, 2013). In teaching this often refers to students being able to take more abstracted meanings, for example the concept of power, and use these to analyse and discuss a range of different problems that implicate this concept, and related concepts. *Semantic density* (SD) refers to the relative complexity of meanings, such as the condensation of meanings within a concept (Maton, 2013). In teaching, this is often enacted as students developing more complex understandings of, and greater ability to use, concepts and meanings in their own course work. As students 'wave' between more and less abstracted meanings and problem-scenarios in their learning, they can build deeper and broader understandings of the interrelations between concepts and applications, and develop an enhanced ability to write, read and engage effectively in discussion, over time.

For example, in Political Science, students learn about power, authority and citizenship in the first year, and return to and build on these concepts in each course, but with different problems and applications across the rest of the undergraduate degree. Initially, the meanings and problems are fairly simple (e.g. apply Galbraith's concept of power to an understanding of your own life and how you engage with people around you – first year). But these become more difficult over time (e.g. using selected aspects of Galbraith and Lukes on power, analyse the current situation in parliament where political parties are vying for control over debates on tax reform – third year). The build from first to third year is slow, and the semantic waves begin as relatively 'shallow', meaning moving from simpler abstractions and relatively small amounts of meaning condensation to simpler applications with relatively 'thin' understandings of concepts, and back (see Figure 9.1). Over time, the waves become 'steeper', meaning that the meanings become more condensed, and the problems more layered and multi-dimensional, requiring greater knowledge and skill to solve. Unpacking is a term that refers to a downward move in the wave, from greater condensation (abstraction) to lesser condensation (contextualization) in meaning (SG−, SD+ to SG+, SD−), often achieved in practice through explanation and exemplification. Repacking refers to consolidating understanding, and building incrementally more condensation as the meanings are developed through their use in the application or examples (SG+, SD− to SG−, SD+). Semantic waves can be a useful theoretical tool in talking with academic teachers about the articulation of courses within the curriculum, within and across year levels, especially when similar concepts are invoked and developed throughout a coherent degree programme (see Clarence, 2014). Vignette A will explore this in more detail.

The *semantic plane*, the second tool this chapter will use, provides a different picture of intended or expected learning, and an alternative way of conceptualizing learning and teaching. It helps to provide an overview of larger contexts, such as a whole assessment programme, or a whole degree programme, but can also be used to map smaller contexts, such as the progression from the first to the final assignment across one semester or one year of teaching (see Vignette B). There are four

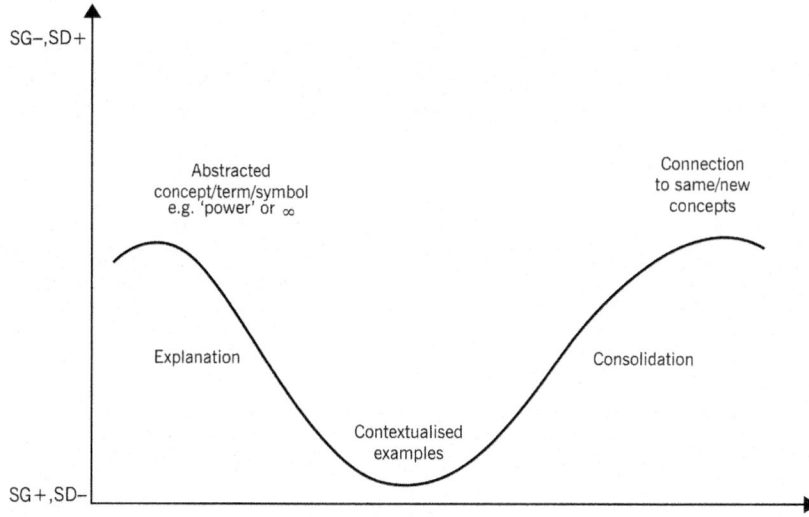

FIGURE 9.1 A generic semantic wave
Source: adapted from Maton 2013

principal code modalities depicted in the plane, created by combining relative strengths of semantic gravity and semantic density (see Maton, 2016, 2020):

- *Rarefied codes* (SG–, SD–) are characterized by stances that are relatively independent of particular contexts (weaker semantic gravity) and that have fewer meanings condensed within a concept (weaker semantic density). An example may be students using abstract concepts and terms in their writing, without necessarily having the depth of understanding to use them effectively or to create complex meanings of their own, such as referring to 'feminist orientations to social engagement' without being able to explain or show what that means in the rest of the text; the terms are there but not integrated fully into meaning-making.
- *Rhizomatic codes* (SG–, SD+) comprise stances that are similarly relatively independent of contexts (weaker semantic gravity), but which have more complex meanings condensed within a concept (stronger semantic density). An example might be a disciplinary field, such as English Studies, which aims to build complex, but relatively abstracted meanings to enable application to a range of as-yet unknown problems scenarios. Think here of building an understanding of feminism and patriarchy through reading Margaret Atwood, Simone de Beauvoir and Rebecca Solnit, with the aim of being able to read any other books or papers, and engage in any other discussions, and be able to use and build further on that understanding.
- *Prosaic codes* (SG+, SD–), on the other hand, are characterized by stances that are relatively dependent on particular contexts (stronger semantic gravity), but

which have fewer meanings condensed with concepts (weaker semantic density). This calls to mind subjects or learning that depends on context for meaning, and is enacted in relatively simple ways, for example many undergraduate writing or 'literacy' courses tend towards prosaic codes as they aim to make academic writing relatively context-dependent and accessible to novice students.

- Lastly, *worldly codes* (SG+, SD+) similarly are characterized by stances that are relatively dependent on particular contexts (stronger semantic gravity), and that have concepts in which manifold meanings are condensed (stronger semantic density). This code can be representative of professional fields, such a Law or Medicine, where the problems are always context-dependent, but the meanings or tools used to solve them are complex, such as using statutory and case law to assist a client in a divorce and custody case, or treating a patient with multiple injuries or illnesses.

It is important to note that this section accounts for the semantic plane and semantic waves in their theoretical form. How they are enacted, or realized, in practice does depend to an extent on the context, the actors, and the purposes for which the tools are being used. In these vignettes, there is a blend of research and practice in the enactment of the Semantics tools, as is the case in much academic development work, where research – one's own or published – informs praxis in context.

Curriculum and assessment can be heuristically mapped onto the plane to delve into expected or intended compared to actual outcomes of assessment, as Vignette B will discuss, and explore possible ways of closing problematic gaps, for example.

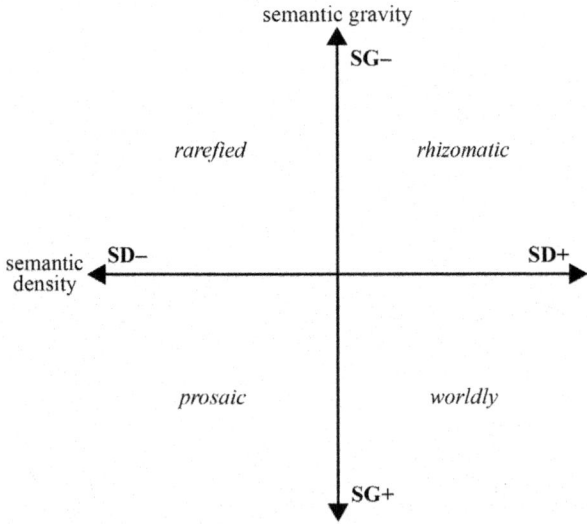

FIGURE 9.2 The semantic plane

Source: Maton, 2014, p. 131

In other words, if you are working in a field or discipline that will require students to solve increasingly complex, but context-dependent problems with increasingly complex tools and meanings, such as a doctor would across their basic medical training and into their residency, you would be referencing a worldly code as an endpoint. But, if many assignments seem to be directed to students producing a prosaic or rhizomatic code in their responses, it will be challenging for them to achieve this endpoint, which may jeopardize their professional becoming, and also the field itself. The semantic plane, then, can provide a useful mapping tool in an instance like this, to see where assessment, curriculum and teaching seem to be located, and where students need to end up.

The data

The data used in the following sections as the basis for analysis and discussion is drawn from notes and transcripts of workshops with lecturers (A) and peer tutors (B), facilitated by the authors. Rather than presenting the data in its raw form, which would be lengthy, the data has been transformed into 'vignettes' that capture the nature of the engagement reflected in the generated data. Both sets of data were generated during the course of larger, qualitative studies that used LCT to unpack, analyse and understand classroom pedagogy and assessment in new ways (see Clarence, 2014; van Heerden, 2018).

Vignettes and analysis

Vignette A: Teaching research methodology in Political Studies

Two Political Studies lecturers, Jan and Claire (pseudonyms), are teaching research methodology in the International Relations (IR) programme, at a South African university. IR studies use both qualitative and quantitative research methodologies, thus the courses they are designing need to include input and exercises on both so that students have adequate opportunities to learn about the appropriate methodology for their own research projects. One course is for final-year undergraduate students (third year), and the other is taught in the first postgraduate year (Honours). A chief concern, leading to the creation of the third year course, is students' lack of confidence and knowledge in designing and conducting the small-scale research projects required in the Honours year. As the third year course has been enacted to give students a basic introduction to, and practice in, doing a small research project, it should articulate with the Honours course that the postgraduate students will take in the following year.

This is where the two lecturers sought input from the first author, in her role as an academic developer. Their concerns were twofold: first, they did not want students to learn methodology 'rote' style; they wanted them to learn both the 'theory' and 'practice' of doing research through practical application and practice. Second, they wanted students to feel more confident in understanding, choosing and employing methodological tools that would fit their chosen research projects; they wanted students to become more independent researchers. Behind these concerns is a larger concern about the skill and confidence levels of researchers at Masters and PhD level, thus getting things right at these more introductory levels will have significant consequences for building student research capacity throughout the postgraduate programme.

The first author decided to begin with the first concern, as the second was connected, and would hopefully result from more integrated, contextualized teaching of research methodology and practice. The first step in the conversation was to unpack the connection between the expectations of the two courses, particularly as the final-year undergraduate course is designed to lay a foundation for the postgraduate course. Key questions that were asked and explored in the conversation were:

- What are the key research concepts and ideas that students need to have a working knowledge of?
- What 'tools' for doing research will they most likely need to learn to use?
- What are the main ways in which these have been taught prior to now?
- What were the problems, or gaps in knowledge and practice, that emerged from prior modes of teaching?

Answers to these questions were then used as a starting point for looking at connecting the curriculum and teaching of the two courses, the assessment and the tasks that students would be expected to complete in the process of designing their own research projects. Once the expectations embedded in the outcomes of both courses, some tacitly so, were better articulated and made visible, the group could begin to critically examine, and change, the structure, pedagogy and assessment in both courses to better align the proposed outcomes, and terminology and use of concepts, and the guided in-class and assessment problems and tasks.

In Semantics terms, the undergraduate course needs to have stronger semantic gravity and weaker semantic density in terms of the meanings embedded in the key methods, research concepts (such as 'qualitative' and 'quantitative' data), and the tasks students will complete. But, it must push students towards and stronger semantic density so that the postgraduate course can pick up and build on this the following year. Pitching a 'theoretical' course, packed with a long list of concepts and methods to learn about will not help these students eventually do a research project in this or the following year. This is because we learn to do research by actually putting these concepts and methods into action, making errors, learning from these through feedback and reflection, and developing our knowledge, skills and practices as researchers. Thus, the learning must be practically gained, but it must enact and use more generalized and abstracted understanding of research so that future research practice can build on and advance this learning. In other words, there must be a more overt, visible and learnable connection between generalized learning and knowledge about how to do research, and students' own research practice and projects.

The group determined that a practical way to address this concern was to 'map' the current concepts and how they were taught or used in terms of their relative semantic gravity and semantic density. This was done very simply with a blank semantic profile (see Figure 9.1, minus the wave). The lecturers, in discussion, each created a basic map of their own course, indicating where on the profile (higher or lower/SG–, SD+, SG+, SD–) their teaching of the concepts or generalized understandings of research currently fitted. We also drew very rough waves for their courses as a whole, based on their impressions of how students seemed to receive the teaching and learning, visible in their assignments and research projects. What this showed us was that too much of the learning was weaker than necessary in semantic gravity, and stronger than necessary in semantic density. In other words, there was too much focus on generalized, 'textbook'-type knowledge on, for example, what case studies are, how to conduct interviews, why small-scale projects should use qualitative rather than quantitative research designs and so on. There was then a gap – a leap for students to make – between this knowledge and learning, and its enactment or application in their own research projects. Their sense of the students' experiences of both courses was that doing research successfully and in a way that gave the lecturers confidence in promoting students to higher levels of study was compromised by the current curriculum, and teaching.

Their conclusion was that they needed, in both years, to make the waves connected (rather than jumping from generalized knowledge to applied research projects), and to build more consciously an understanding of the why and how of research in more intertwined ways. For example, 'We do qualitative research to enable the generation of XYZ data, and this is useful in ABC instances. *Here are examples of these kinds of studies.* Who of you are thinking of doing something similar? **What kinds of projects are you planning? What kind of data might you generate**, and why would it be "qualitative"?' The italics indicate a basic unpacking process, of moving from more abstracted knowledge about qualitative research, to examples of published studies that exemplify the lecturer's claims, to thinking about students' own projects. Repacking (in bold) might then take them through a process of connecting their own study with others in the field, towards explaining, with reference to more generalized understandings, how their study exemplifies a particular kind of qualitative research design. In a nutshell, this is what lecturers wanted students to be able to do: to follow the unpacking that largely occurred in lectures, with work on their own that showed an ability, through their writing and oral presentations on their projects, to repack and build greater semantic density around their understanding of the whys, whats and hows or research in IR, and Political Studies more generally.

This 'wave' of unpacking and repacking would be repeated over and over throughout each course: unpacking and consciously repacking learning about research through repeated waves – between moving 'down' the wave from abstracted learning and heuristic examples to students' own research projects, and then repacking, often through students' own writing and oral presentations on their projects, from their own work, through related studies in their field, to a consolidation of the conceptual understanding. This ability to understand, use and

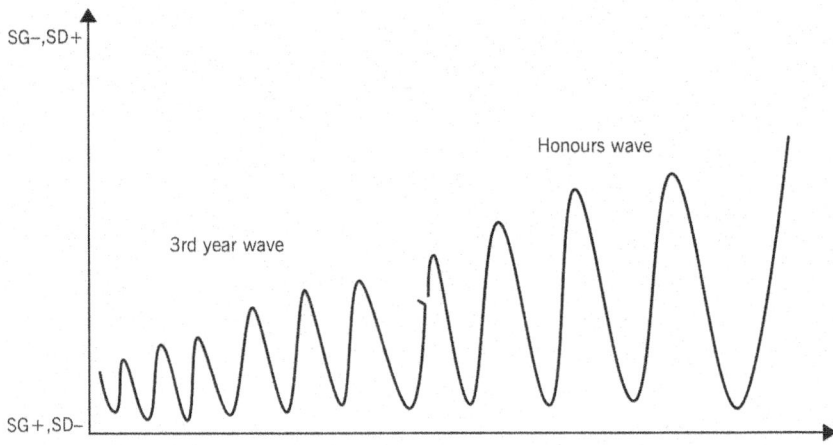

FIGURE 9.3 Possible semantic wave across both courses

build on generalized knowledge and practices in doing research will ideally give students the confidence and ability to tackle larger research projects, either professionally or academically, and continue this 'wavy' learning process down time. The lecturers concluded that to help students actually create successful research projects, and enable them to see the connections between third year and Honours, and grow their knowledge and skills, they needed to 'wave' far more consciously. They decided to create shallower waves at the start of the third year course, building towards steeper waves as the course closes, and ending on an 'up' trajectory towards generalized knowledge and understandings. These understandings and knowledge about doing research could then be picked up in Honours, recapitulated through initial class discussion, and taken further, continuing to be developed, refined and extended through the vehicle of a longer, more demanding research project.

Semantics could thus be used to map possible semantic waves that the lecturers would like to see enacted across the two courses, waving between stronger and weaker semantic gravity, to build stronger, cumulative understanding and knowledge of key concepts and research actions over time.

Semantic waves was the LCT tool used in this engagement between teaching staff and an academic developer to give lecturers a theorized, yet practical language with which to talk about their learning goals for students – a deeper, problem-oriented approach to and understanding of research methodology and methods – and the connected teaching, learning and assessment activities necessary to achieve these.

Vignette B: Improving tutor feedback-giving practices in English Studies

Giving effective written feedback can be challenging for both experienced and inexperienced tutors, especially if tutors are not given guidance on how to give feedback that connects with students' underpinning learning outcomes. This is the case in the undergraduate first-year literature English Studies course that is the focus of Vignette B. The aim of the course, ultimately, is to begin to create student learners who can think critically, independently, creatively and analytically about a range of texts. In this context, feedback plays an important role in facilitating this development through students' essay writing abilities (the essay being the vehicle through which students can demonstrate whether, and to what extent, they have mastered the requisite attributes). However, giving feedback that will effectively, and progressively, facilitate this kind of development is a daunting task. Tutors have to balance giving corrective feedback (especially in relation to textual errors) with developmental, formative feedback that is more in line with the underlying aims of the discipline as stated above. An over-focus on corrective feedback could give students misleading information about what is valued in the discipline, and lead to more cursory correction of errors in further writing, rather than deeper development of their more critical engagement with disciplinary texts.

The role of the academic staff developer in this engagement was to work with a small group of postgraduate student and professional tutors to firstly conceptualize what constitutes effective feedback in the discipline, and secondly to examine tutors' feedback-giving practices to help tutors improve the effectiveness of their feedback. This engagement arose from a concern that the feedback given to first-year students, especially, was not yielding significant improvements in students' writing and approach to reading set texts critically.

Semantics provided a useful way to open the conversation between the tutors and the academic developer about tutors' notions of 'good' writing, their concerns about their students' writing, and their sense of what was 'wrong' with both the writing and the feedback. For instance, using semantic gravity, the group could distinguish between feedback that is stronger in semantic gravity (SG+) – that which is bound to the particular essay context, such as clarification comments about the plot, or correction of specific errors – and feedback that is weaker in semantic gravity (SG–) – such as comments about the structure of an essay, or ways of framing an Introduction. For instance, a comment like 'elaborate on this point' is SG+, as it pertains to the specific text and/or essay being commented on, while a comment like 'your paragraph should have a clear topic sentence' is SG–, as it could pertain to any essay, not just the specific one being reviewed. This identification process was then taken forward into a discussion of the value of SG+ and SG– forms of feedback, and the concept of feedforward was introduced, connected to a notion of feedback needing to lean, on the whole, towards weaker semantic gravity so that students can apply the learning from the feedback on each essay to future writing.

Semantic density was then used to think about the relative complexity of the feedback given, or the ease with which students could act on the feedback to improve their writing. In this case, weaker semantic density was enacted as simple feedback (SD–), easy to act on, such as corrections of spelling errors; for instance, when the tutor crosses out an incorrectly used 'there' and writes 'their' above the comment, which indicates a straightforward replacement of one word with another. It is important to note that the success of comments also depend on whether students are given the opportunity to implement feedback (for example, between a draft and a final essay). Stronger semantic density (SD+) was enacted as feedback that would be more difficult to implement, and require more thinking through, and perhaps other knowledge, such as comments connecting parts of the plot or text to one another to reach a deeper understanding of character motivation, or an outcome in the text. For instance, when a student was asked to consider 'what is the deeper significance of this image?' in her analysis, this comment firstly needed to be unpacked (what does 'deeper significance' denote?) before being acted on (explaining and/or analyzing a point in greater detail). Implementing this comment, therefore is, comparatively speaking, not straightforward. Semantics was thus used with this group of tutors to theorize what would constitute effective written feedback in English Studies.

Once this initial theorization had been considered, the semantic plane could be used to trace the type of feedback given in practice, combining relative strengths of semantic gravity and semantic density from tutors' own feedback examples and anonymized sample student texts. This offered the tutors a visual representation of where their feedback was currently and what messages it might be sending to students, and where it should be aiming towards to help students progressively realize the underlying learning outcomes of the discipline, mentioned above. In English Studies, it can be argued that feedback should gradually progress from a prosaic code, through a rarefied code, to a rhizomatic code (van Heerden, 2018) for students to develop their ability to think critically, analytically and creatively about texts. That is, feedback should initially be relatively context-dependent (SG+) and relatively easy to implement (SD−) (prosaic code): asking students, for instance, easier to implement questions about a text which are aimed at improving or strengthening their analysis. For example, a question such as 'do you think Lady Macbeth influences Macbeth positively or negatively?' could be answered with relative ease, but it is specific to William Shakespeare's Macbeth. As students become more familiar with the expectations of the discipline and genres of reading and writing, feedback should become less context-dependent (SG−), but still be relatively easy to implement (SD−) to further facilitate students' development of the necessary attributes (a rarefied code). Tutors, for instance, could ask students relatively straightforward questions about a text in their feedback, but which have the potential to be applied to other contexts. For example, 'What type of figures of speech does the author employ, and to what effect? Think about your use of these in your writing'. As students become more confident literary scholars, feedback should become less context-dependent (SG−), as well as more challenging to implement (SD+) (a rhizomatic code), as it is through engaging with challenging feedback comments that are not bound to the particular context of the essay or text that students may be able to bring more complex meanings into their textual analyses. For instance, building on previous types of questions, the tutor could ask broader questions about a text, that could be applied to any text. For example, 'what do you

Changing curriculum and teaching practice **157**

think is the underlying theme/message of the text? It is important to consider the author's underlying aims in writing'. Ultimately, the aim of these types of questions and comments is to enable students to develop deeper and more meaningful ways of engaging with texts, without always needing overt guidance.

Plotting out the feedback of tutors and lecturers on the semantic plane enabled the group referred to in this vignette to obtain a clearer picture of current feedback practices, which in turn provided clarity on how to begin improving feedback practices. For instance, it enabled us to see if there was the desired progression or if feedback remained static. Figure 9.4 plots out the feedback a student received on six assignments, over the course of her first year of study. Each assignment was coded with a shape; each shape repeated in a lighter or darker shade of grey. The various dots on the plane represent the number of feedback comments received for each assignment. For example, there are eight light grey triangles (Assignment 6) scattered across the plane indicating that the student got eight comments for Assignment 6. As the plane shows, the feedback given throughout the year is largely grouped in the prosaic and worldly codes, with no real movement across the plane from one assignment to the next, suggesting a relatively static pattern of feedback. This, the group agreed, would not necessarily assist the student with developing the

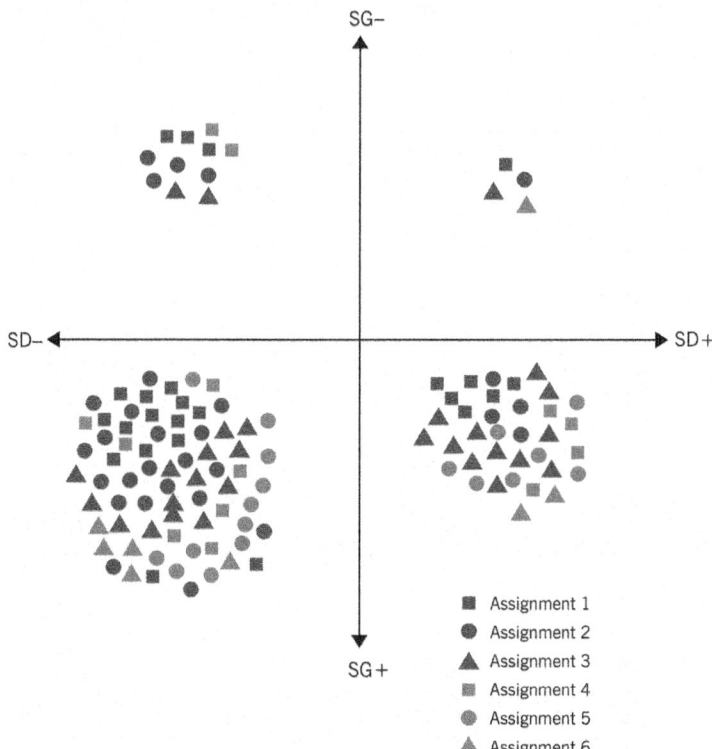

FIGURE 9.4 Plotting out feedback on the semantic plane

necessary attributes or knowledge, or make these attributes a clear goal for her to work towards. Using the semantic plane in this way indicated to the tutors the potential areas that need development by visually representing their feedback practices, and making visible gaps and missteps. In the example in Figure 9.4, this tutor would see that she needs to make feedback more complex, but still accessible for her students, as the year progresses. The academic staff developer could therefore work with the tutor, with this theorized understanding of learning and feedback, to develop effective feedforward techniques that more consciously weaken semantic gravity and strengthen semantic density over time.

Working with the semantic plane can therefore provide tutors with the opportunity to engage with their feedback-giving practices in a theorized way, which in turn could improve their feedback-giving practices. Moreover, the visual nature of the plane enables a clearer, accessible understanding of potential problems in the way feedback is currently given.

Discussion

There are three key points we would like to draw out of these vignettes, and the application of the semantic wave and semantic plane. The first is the notion of explanatory power. The practical, accessible language provided by LCT to give academic developers and lecturers alike a theorized way of unpacking seemingly complex teaching, learning and assessment problems offered us, in the work reflected on here, explanatory power. Essentially, as seen in these two vignettes, the use of the semantic wave (A) and the semantic plane (B) gave lecturers and tutors a new way of talking about student learning goals in terms of curriculum design and teaching, and assessment and feedback respectively. It enabled a focus on the learning itself, and the means to achieve that learning, rather than on what the students or lecturers/tutors were or were not doing that they already should have been doing. Other studies have shown how using the language and analytical tools offered by Semantics shifts a focus away from 'blame' on either students or lecturers or both, towards learning, teaching, and the learning environments lecturers need create to enable the most appropriate forms of learning, in the most overt and inclusive ways (see Macnaught et al., 2013; Blackie, 2014).

The second point, related to explanatory power, is the visual nature of these explanatory and analytical 'tools'. Not only could these two lecturers, and this group of tutors, obtain a language, and vocabulary, with which to analyse and critique their own teaching, or student learning, they could also 'see' (and draw) an image of their curriculum, teaching and feedback, similar to those in Figures 9.1 to 9.4. One of the most useful aspects of using LCT tools to enhance teaching and learning is their visual nature. Topographical planes and waves can be drawn to describe part of a course or a whole course; part of a lecture or series of lectures; feedback on one essay or on a whole series of essays (see Clarence, 2014; Macnaught et al., 2013; van Heerden, 2018). Thus, lecturers, tutors and also students can learn to use these tools to move into a deeper, more critical understanding of the underpinning organizing principles and learning goals within the parts and whole of their degree programme or course. This learning is exemplified in Vignettes A and B. One can zoom in, for example, to a more precise semantic wave of part of a lecture, or zoom out to a semantic plane of the course as a whole, or a larger semantic wave. This flexibility is important, because it enables academic lecturers and academic developers to make the tools work for them, rather than trying to 'shoehorn' their teaching, assessment or curriculum into a pre-existing framework that doesn't quite fit their needs.

A final point is the way in which using Semantics, or any LCT tools, offers students, lecturers and tutors something beyond 'trends' or 'tips' in teaching and learning. There have been several trends in the last couple of decades, variously named 'authentic learning', 'inquiry-focused learning', 'blended learning', 'student-centred learning' and so on. The aim here is not to critique these trends; rather, we argue that applied without a foundational sense of the organizing principles of the disciplines being learned and taught, as well as a way of seeing where one's individual course or module fits into a whole programme of learning, these trends can result in a 'hit or miss' approach to teaching and learning. If lecturers try something new, and it works in unexpected ways, or fails to work as expected, there may be a temptation to fall back onto 'common-sense' assumptions; e.g. 'this is a motivated group of students', or 'these students just don't try hard enough or read enough'. A theorized way of thinking and acting provides a 'fallback' beyond assumptions like these that take one round in circles in a vicious blame-game that focuses on being the 'right' kind of student (Boughey and McKenna, 2016), rather than on universities offering the right kinds of learning and teaching. In the two engagements we focus on in this chapter, the discussion rarely moved towards blaming students, or any other 'guilty' party; instead we were all focused on what we needed to do to enable greater student learning and success.

One can go back through the learning and teaching process using semantic gravity and semantic density, as well as allied tools such as concept mapping, to look at whether, for example, the assessment plan was clearly sequenced (see Steyn, 2012), or the waves between the classwork and the assignments were disconnected or asked students to make learning leaps they were unprepared for (Macnaught *et al.*, 2013; Maton, 2020). Theorized tools offer lecturers a way of approaching their teaching with evidence as a basis for ongoing reflection, learning and change; they enable *praxis*, by ensuring that theory does not exist in isolation, but is instead embedded within, and changes, practice (Maton, Carvalho and Dong, 2016). Eventually, lecturers can also work through this kind of thinking with colleagues, and without academic development interventions, if they are given the tools to do so, overtly and accessibly. Academic developers should not 'do staff development unto' lecturers and tutors (see Quinn, 2012): lecturers, tutors and even students should rather be equipped with theoretical and practical tools such as those discussed in this chapter as far as possible. Otherwise very little will really change in teaching and learning, and we may keep falling back onto 'common-sense' understandings that take us backwards or sideways, rather than forward.

Conclusion

This chapter argues for how academic developers can use theory, and specifically Semantics – the semantic wave and the semantic plane – to enhance teaching and learning, through enhancing curriculum design, teaching and feedback-giving practices. Through two 'vignettes' constructed using larger data sets, the chapter showed how two academic developers have used the semantic wave (A) and the semantic plane (B) to offer lecturers and tutors respectively a new way of 'seeing' their teaching and feedback and their students' possible learning. Essentially, these tools offer lecturers, tutors, students and academic developers a multilayered approach to teaching and learning, that can be made more or less complex depending on who is using the tool, and why. Semantics offers strong explanatory power, through examining how a curriculum or feedback-giving process does work, and how it should or could work, and how to traverse and close the potential gaps. It does this by enabling users of Semantics to enact a visual analysis of their curriculum or assessment – one can actually see, in a wave or plane, where the organizing principles are positioned, how the curriculum unfolds, where the assessment is pushing students towards, and where there are gaps, omissions and connections.

Finally, Semantics, and LCT as a whole, offers a theorized understanding of learning and teaching that can take us beyond applying trends and tips towards understanding which tools, trends or approaches to learning and teaching would work for which students or discipline, and why. The use of theorized, yet practical, tools to create meaningful praxis is vital as part of making higher education more open, accessible to and shared between lecturers, students, tutors, and academic development staff who seek ways of helping to enhance and develop teaching and learning within and across the disciplines.

References

Bath, D. and Smith, C. (2004). Academic developers: An academic tribe claiming their territory in higher education. *International Journal for Academic Development, 9*(1), 9–27.

Bharuthram, S. and Clarence, S. (2015). Teaching academic reading as a disciplinary knowledge practice in higher education. *South African Journal of Higher Education, 29*(2), 42–55.

Blackie, M. (2014). Creating semantic waves: Using Legitimation Code Theory as a tool to aid the teaching of chemistry. *Chemistry Education Research and Practice, 15*(4), 462–149.

Boughey, C. and McKenna, S. (2016). Academic literacy and the decontextualized learner. *Critical Studies in Teaching and Learning, 4*(2), 1–9.

Boughey, C. and McKenna, S. (2017). Analysing an audit cycle: A critical realist account. *Studies in Higher Education, 42*(6), 963–975.

Carter, S. and Laurs, D. (Eds) (2014). *Developing generic support for doctoral students: Practice and pedagogy*. London: Routledge.

Case, J.M. (2013). *Researching student learning in higher education: A social realist approach*. London: Routledge.

Clarence, S. (2014). *Enabling cumulative knowledge-building through teaching: A Legitimation Code Theory analysis of pedagogic practice in Law and Political Science* (Unpublished doctoral thesis). Rhodes University, South Africa.

Clegg, S. (2009). Forms knowing and academic practice. *Studies in Higher Education, 34*(4), 403–416.
Jacobs, C. (2007). Mainstreaming academic literacy teaching: Implications for how academic development understands its work in higher education. *South African Journal of Higher Education, 21*(7), 870–881.
Kirk, S. (2017). Waves of Reflection: Seeing knowledges in academic writing. In J. Kemp (Ed.), *EAP in a rapidly changing landscape: Issues, challenges and solutions* (pp. 109–118). Proceedings of the 2015 BALEAP Conference. Reading: Garnet Publishing.
Macnaught, L., Maton, K., Martin, J.R. and Matruglio, E. (2013). Jointly constructing semantic waves: Implications for teacher training. *Linguistics and Education, 24*(1), 50–63.
Manathunga, C. (2006). Doing educational development ambivalently: Applying postcolonial metaphors to educational development? *International Journal for Academic Development, 11*(1), 19–29.
Maton, K. (2013). Making semantic waves: A key to cumulative knowledge-building, *Linguistics and Education, 24*(1): 8–22.
Maton, K. (2014). *Knowledge and knowers: Towards a realist sociology of education*. London: Routledge.
Maton, K. (2016). Legitimation Code Theory: Building knowledge about knowledge-building. In K. Maton, S. Hood, and S. Shay (Eds), *Knowledge-building: Educational studies in Legitimation Code Theory* (pp. 1–23). London: Routledge.
Maton, K. (2020). Semantic waves: Context, complexity and academic discourse. In J.R. Martin, K. Maton and Y.J. Doran (Eds) *Accessing academic discourse: Systemic functional linguistics and Legitimation Code Theory* (pp. 59–85). London: Routledge.
Maton, K., Carvalho, L. and Dong, A. (2016). LCT in praxis: Creating an e-learning environment for informal learning of principled knowledge. In K. Maton, S. Hood and S. Shay (Eds), *Knowledge-building: Educational studies in Legitimation Code Theory* (pp. 72–92). London: Routledge.
Quinn, L. (2003). A theoretical framework for professional development in a South African university. *International Journal for Academic Development, 8*(1–2), 61–75.
Quinn, L. (Ed.). (2012). *Re-imagining academic staff development: Spaces for disruption*. Stellenbosch: SUNPress.
Shay, S. (2012). Educational development as a field: Are we there yet? *Higher Education Research and Development, 31*(3), 311–323.
Staniforth, D. and Harland, T. (2003). Reflection on practice: Collaborative action research for new academics. Educational Action Research, *11*(1), 79–92.
Steyn, D. (2012). *Conceptualising design knowledge and its recontextualisation in the studiowork component of a design foundation curriculum* (Unpublished Masters thesis). University of Cape Town, South Africa.
van Heerden, M. (2018). *What lies beneath tutors' feedback? Examining the role of feedback in developing knowers in English Studies.* (Unpublished doctoral thesis)., University of the Western Cape, South Africa.

10

A SEMANTICS ANALYSIS OF FIRST-YEAR PHYSICS TEACHING

Developing students' use of representations in problem-solving

Honjiswa Conana, Delia Marshall and Jennifer Case

Introduction

Internationally, there is growing concern about high attrition, declining enrolments and waning student interest in STEM (science, technology, engineering and mathematics) disciplines (see, for example, European Commission, 2004; OECD, 2008). In South Africa, studies on student retention and throughput in higher education show a high attrition rate at first-year level within science and technology fields, as well as low overall completion rates: only 23 per cent of students enrolled for Bachelor of Science degrees complete their studies (Council on Higher Education, 2013).

These trends internationally have led to efforts to widen access to science and technology studies, and to the adoption of curriculum reform and teaching approaches aimed at fostering the accessibility and appeal of STEM studies. Some of these efforts have focused on developing students' conceptual understanding (see, for example, Mazur, 1997); others have examined why some students leave STEM disciplines (see, for example, Seymour and Hewitt, 1997). Education research has shown that a key element of success in STEM studies is mastering the ways in which scientific knowledge is constructed and conveyed. Scientific knowledge is characterized by meaning embedded in multiple representations. Examples of such representations include diagrams, maps, flow charts, tables, graphs and mathematical equations. Scientific knowledge is also conveyed in compact nominalizations (scientific words that are dense in meaning, such as 'photosynthesis', 'acceleration', or 'differentiation') (see, for example, Lemke, 1990). Research in a range of science disciplines suggests that mastery of these representations is key, and that successful learning entails appreciating the purposes of various representations and being able to translate between them (see, for example, Cheng and Gilbert (2009) on chemistry education; Wood et al. (2007) on mathematics education; Airey and Linder (2009) on physics education).

In this chapter, we focus in particular on teaching and learning in the context of Physics, although many of the implications will hold for other science disciplines too. We illustrate the usefulness of Legitimation Code Theory (LCT), and specifically concepts from the Semantics dimension, as a framework for examining how representations are used in teaching and learning Physics. The chapter also demonstrates how the LCT method of 'semantic profiling' is useful in characterizing teaching approaches that may better enable access to science knowledge.

Developing students' use of representations in problem-solving

Physics as a discipline is centred on understanding and predicting phenomena in the natural world, through the development of idealized, abstracted models of phenomena. These models are then related back to experimental observation. Modelling phenomena in the natural world is a key aspect of doing Physics. However, research studies show that many students struggle to approach Physics problems with an understanding of modelling. One of these key studies (Van Heuvelen, 1991a) notes that expert physicists and students approach Physics problems in very different ways: the experts start with qualitative analysis (thinking about the relevant Physics principles at play) and use qualitative representations (sketches and diagrams) to understand a physical process. By contrast, students tend to move directly to mathematical equations, viewing problem-solving as 'almost entirely formula-centred – devoid of qualitative sketches and diagrams that contribute to understanding' (p. 891).

This tendency of students to focus on the mathematical aspects of problems can be linked to teaching approaches that often take for granted representations used in Physics: although problem-solving is demonstrated in lectures, often the modelling and qualitative representational aspects are glossed over, and what students see written down by the lecturer is merely the mathematical representation of the problem situation (see, for example, Leonard et al., 1996). Similarly, when lecturers use qualitative representations, such as sketches, diagrams or graphs, they often take for granted the complexity of these representations. As Fredlund et al. (2014) note, 'in many cases teachers have become so familiar with the disciplinary representations that they use that they no longer 'notice' the learning hurdles involved in interpreting the intended meaning of those representations' (p. 020129–4).

Physics educators recognize that successful Physics learning depends on understanding and using the various representational formats of the discipline (Dufresne et al., 1997; Airey and Linder, 2009). These different representations – verbal, graphical, diagrammatic or mathematical – each have different disciplinary affordances (Kress, 2010; Fredlund et al., 2012; Doran, 2016). In other words, each is able to construe meaning in a different way: for example, a sketch is good for illustrating the spatial features of a situation, whereas a graph is good for conveying the relationship between variables in a situation.

Several Physics education reform initiatives have attempted to change the traditional way in which problem-solving is often dealt with. Van Heuvelen (1991a and 1991b) argues that the explicit use of multiple representations in undergraduate Physics teaching is important to help students to begin to 'think like a physicist'. This can be achieved through creating a 'representation-rich learning environment' (Rosengrant et al., 2009, p. 010108–2), which explicitly helps students learn how to use representations, to appreciate why certain representations are useful and to see the epistemological underpinnings of these representations, thus developing students' 'meta-representational competence' (diSessa, 2004; Kohl and Finkelstein, 2008).

In this chapter, we focus on a particular area of physics, termed 'Mechanics' (which deals with concepts of motion, such as speed, velocity, acceleration, forces and so on). To tackle a mechanics problem as an expert would, students would be expected to engage with the following representations:

- a *verbal* representation – a problem statement in words (requires reading and unpacking the statement);
- a *pictorial* representation – a sketch (requires modelling the situation to capture the important features of the problem, and modelling the object of interest as a point-particle);
- a *physical* representation – a force diagram (requires visualizing the problem, identifying the system and the forces acting on it, and translating words to symbols);
- a *mathematical* representation – Physics principles and equations used to describe the situation (requires solving the problem by using appropriate mathematical representation).

To illustrate these different representations, with their different disciplinary affordances, we include an example here from a seminal paper on Physics representations (van Heuvelen, 1991a) in Figure 10.1. While the details of the problem situation are not important here, this example shows the multiple representations required for tackling such a Mechanics problem.

Having discussed the role of modelling and representations in Physics problem-solving, the next section will draw on tools from the LCT dimension of Semantics to think about the knowledge structure of Physics, and the use of representations in the teaching and learning of Physics.

LCT and Physics as a discipline

Physics can be said to epitomize a *hierarchical knowledge structure*, being a 'coherent, explicit and systematically principled structure, hierarchically organised' (Bernstein, 2000, p. 160). For example, a thorough understanding of the concept of 'electrical field' assumes knowledge of many underlying concepts and principles, such as 'force', 'field', 'electric charge' and Coulomb's Law. Not surprisingly, hierarchical knowledge structures are often mirrored in correspondingly *hierarchical curriculum structures* (Maton, 2009). So, in the case of Physics (as in so many science disciplines),

(a) WORDS

A parachutist whose parachute did not open landed in a snow bank and stopped after sinking 1.0m into the snow. Just before hitting the snow, the person was falling at a speed of 54m/s. Determine the average force of the snow on the 80kg person while sinking into the snow.

(b) PICTORIAL REPRESENTATION

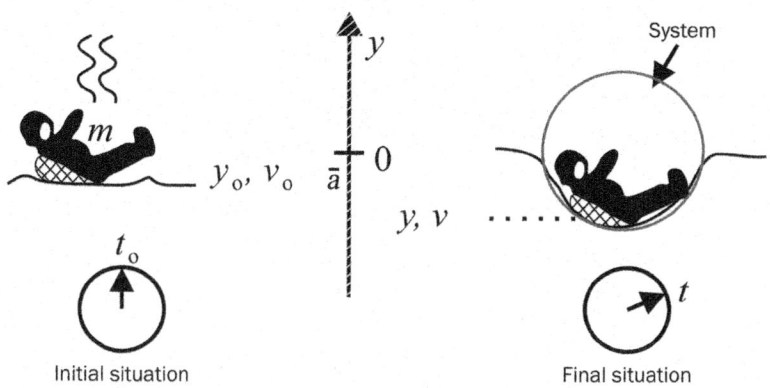

(c) PHYSICAL REPRESENTATION

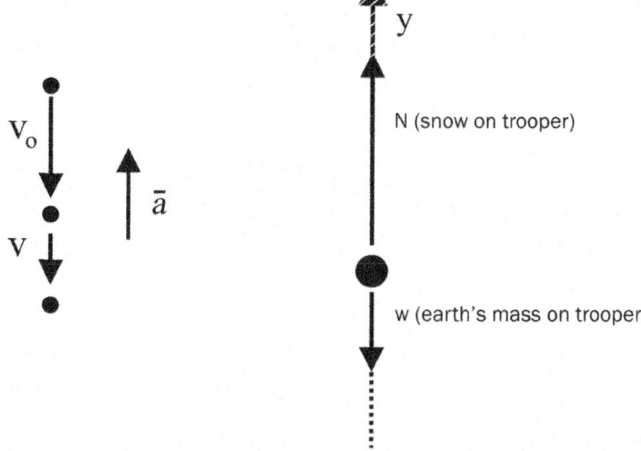

(d) MATH REPRESENTATION

$$2\bar{a}(y - y_o) = v^2 - v_o^2 \qquad \sum F_y = N - w = m\bar{a}$$

FIGURE 10.1 An illustration of the different representations needed to solve a Mechanics problem. Reproduced from Van Heuvelen, A. (1991) Learning to think like a physicist: A review of research-based instructional strategies, *American Journal of Physics*, 59, 891 (p. 892) with the permission of the American Association of Physics Teachers

the curriculum structure is hierarchical, with the junior level courses building conceptually towards the more theoretical and abstract senior level courses.

Concepts from the Semantics dimension of LCT (Maton, 2013, 2020) give us useful tools to think about Physics knowledge structure and practices. *Semantic gravity* (SG) is defined as the extent to which meaning 'is related to its context of acquisition or use' (Maton, 2009, p. 46). Semantic gravity is linked to the degree of abstraction: when semantic gravity is weaker, meaning is less dependent on its context. Physics operates with abstract, decontextualized concepts and principles, which can be said to have a weaker semantic gravity (SG−). These abstract principles can then be applied to a variety of specific physical contexts, with stronger semantic gravity (SG+). For example, the explanatory power of abstract Physics concepts (such as 'force' or 'energy') is that they can be applied to a variety of specific contexts, ranging from sub-atomic particles, to phenomena in our daily lives, to galaxies.

Semantic density (SD) examines the complexity of meaning or how many meanings are condensed within symbols (a term, concept, phrase, expression, gesture, etc.) (Maton, 2014). Physics has stronger semantic density (SD+), because meaning is condensed within the nominalizations and multiple representations (graphical, symbolic, diagrammatic, mathematical, etc.) that characterize the discipline.

In a discipline like Physics, semantic gravity and semantic density often tend to be inversely related on a semantic continuum (Lindstrøm, 2010): abstract, decontextualized concepts have weaker semantic gravity (SG−), but tend to be represented in condensed symbolic form, with stronger semantic density (SD+). For example, Newton's 2nd Law ($\vec{F}_{net} = m\vec{a}$) has weaker semantic gravity (SG−), being an abstract and generic principle, holding for all physical situations that are possible in the everyday world. Moreover, it is written in dense, symbolic form with stronger semantic density (SD+). However, it is worth noting that in some cases the relationship between semantic gravity and semantic density is more complex, and better represented as a semantic plane (see Blackie 2014, and Mtombeni 2018 for examples from Chemistry).

Maton (2013, 2020) argues that cumulative learning is enabled through variations in strengthening and weakening of semantic gravity and semantic density. These recurrent shifts in context-dependence and condensation of meaning form a *semantic wave*. In the case of Physics, this 'semantic waving' would entail explicit moving between the level of concrete (context-dependent, physical situations, SG+) and abstract (generalized principles, SG−). It would also entail explicitly unpacking (and then condensing again) the dense representations that are often taken for granted in Physics teaching (i.e. shifting between SD+ and SD−). For example, a lecture on 'energy' might start with a concrete real-life scenario of dropping a ball, and from this build towards a more abstract, generalized concept of 'mechanical energy'. This weakening of semantic gravity (from concrete scenario to abstract concept) would be accompanied by a strengthening of semantic density: the 'dropping ball scenario' would be condensed into various representations (diagrams, mathematical expressions, etc.). This upward shift on the semantic wave would then likely be followed by a downward shift: the representations, such as diagrams or mathematical expressions, would need to be explicitly unpacked for the students (weakening semantic density), and one might expect the lecturer to strengthen semantic gravity once more by moving from the abstract concept of 'mechanical energy' back to the particularities of a different real-life context. The analytical method of semantic profiling (Maton, 2020) enables us to trace these changes in the strengths of semantic gravity and semantic density over time. The semantic wave can be used to map a classroom episode, part of a lecture, a series of lectures, or an entire course.

In the next section, we draw on concepts from LCT to develop an analytical framework for examining how representations are used in teaching and learning physics.

Developing an analytical framework

For analysis in this study, the concepts of semantic gravity and semantic density were combined with the theoretical perspectives on Physics representations introduced earlier (e.g. Van Heuleven, 1991a, 1991b) to develop an analytical framework or what is referred to in LCT as a 'translation device' (see Maton and Chen, 2016; Maton and Howard, 2016). This framework offered a useful way of translating between the concepts and empirical data. This process of adapting existing frameworks for LCT Semantics studies can be seen in other LCT studies; for example, Lindstrøm (2010), Kilpert and Shay (2013) and Maton (2020).

As noted earlier, each Physics representation (verbal, graph, diagram or mathematics) has its own particular affordances: each is able to construe meaning in a different way. Representations are not inevitably related to each other in terms of semantic hierarchy. However, in the case of Mechanics, the LCT lens makes visible the recurring strengthening of semantic density (SD↑) and weakening of semantic gravity (SG↓) that occurs as one moves from the verbal representation, to the pictorial representation, then to the physical representation, and then to the mathematical representation.

Tackling a mechanics problem entails starting at the bottom of the semantic continuum (see Table 10.1) with the *verbal representation* of the concrete task situation. This would often entail concrete situations, such as the scenario illustrated in

TABLE 10.1 Semantic gravity and semantic density in relation to representations in mechanics problem solving

Semantic strengths	*Type of representation*
SG–, SD+ ↓ **SG+, SD–**	Mathematical – equations to be solved Physical – force diagram Pictorial – sketch: particle model Verbal – concrete problem statement

Figure 10.1 part (a) (or other scenarios such as a car on a slope, crates pulled by ropes or connected to pulley-weight systems). Here, semantic gravity is stronger (SG+) as the focus is on the particularities of a specific context.

The concrete situation is then modelled and simplified, and a *pictorial representation* (a rough sketch) captures the important features of the problem, including identifying the system or the significant forces acting on an object (see Figure 10.1 part (b)). In this way, the verbal representation is condensed into a sketch of the situation; semantic gravity is weakened (SG↓) and semantic density is strengthened (SD↑).

In the *physical representation* (a force-diagram), the object of interest in the problem (for example, a person, or car, or a crate) is modelled as a point-particle. The forces acting on the object are now represented as labelled vector arrows (see Figure 10.1 part (c)). Meaning has become condensed into a point-particle, arrows and dense symbolic labelling of the force vectors. Representations have become semantically denser (SD+) and more abstracted from the specifics of the problem context or the sketch (SG−).

At the level of *mathematical representation*, the situation is condensed further into dense mathematical formalism (SD+) (see Figure 10.1 part (d)). The mathematical representations are completely abstract and generic, holding for all physical situations that are possible in the everyday world (SG−). These mathematical representations are then applied to the problem-situation. Once the problem task is solved, the quantitative solution is checked by linking it back to the concrete situation. Lecturers' and students' movement between these representations can then be portrayed on semantic profiles (see Figures 10.2 and 10.3, 10.7 and 10.8). Of course, this moving along the semantic continuum is not a linear process; it is the iterative moving between representations that is key to representational fluency.

The context of the study and the methodology

This chapter draws on a larger study (Conana, 2016; Conana *et al.*, 2016), which examined two first-year undergraduate courses in a single Physics department – both courses were taught by lecturers widely regarded by their colleagues and students as excellent teachers. The one course was a more traditional mainstream course; the other, a foundation Physics course. This foundation course was designed to enable access to university for students underprepared for undergraduate science studies, many of whom are first generation in higher education (see Kloot *et al.*, 2008 for further details of foundation provision in South Africa). The foundation course allows more time and curriculum space to include some of the 'reform' initiatives detailed above, in particular a greater focus on the processes of scientific enquiry and modelling in a 'representation-rich learning environment' (Rosengrant *et al.*, 2009). Making explicit the representations used in Physics was enhanced through a collaborative partnership between the discipline lecturers and an academic literacy practitioner (see Marshall *et al.*, 2011).

Data are drawn from video-recordings of lectures and of students working on problem tasks in Mechanics, as well as from in-depth interviews with students. The video-recordings and interviews were transcribed and, as a form of data reduction, summaries of the transcriptions were prepared. These were then analysed in terms of the semantic shifts observed in the data, to construct semantic profiles of teaching approaches (see Figures 10.2 and 10.3) and of students' approaches to problem-tasks (see Figures 10.7 and 10.8). The time spent at each level on the semantic continuum is indicated on the horizontal axis of the semantic profiles. In addition, coding (in the form of line thickness) is used to indicate the different forms of interaction in the class, (with a thin line indicating where the lecturer is talking about the shifting between representations, and a thick line indicating lecturer-student interaction and engagement).

Research findings part 1: using semantic profiles to analyse teaching approaches to problem tasks

The two courses varied in the way that problem tasks were dealt with in lectures, with different degrees of explicitness about the use of representations. The problems usually had to do with situations involving objects (cars or crates) on surfaces or slopes. Starting with a verbal representation of the problem situation, the lecturer in the mainstream course tended to set up a problem orally, whereas the lecturer in the foundation course usually started with a written problem statement, which the students were required to read and interpret.

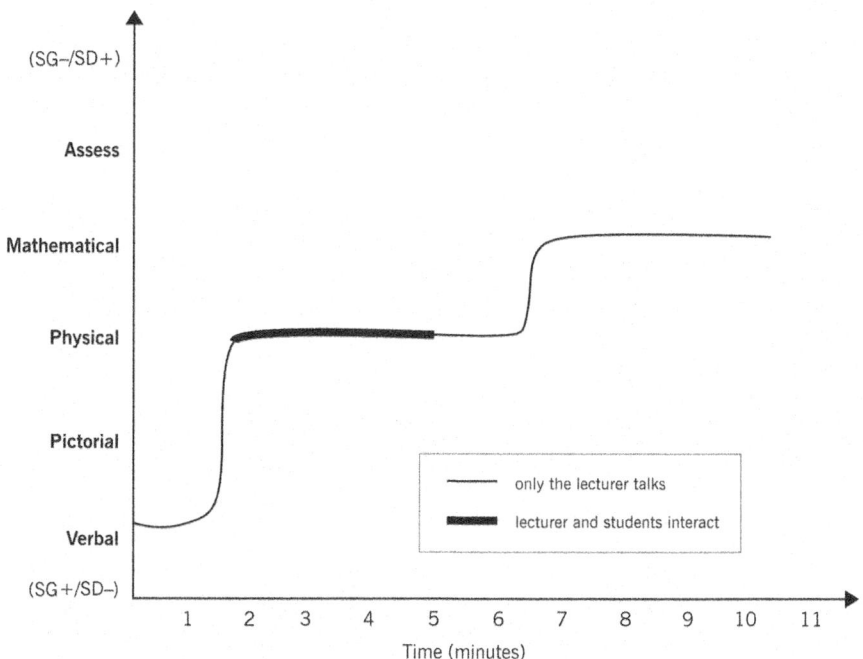

FIGURE 10.2 Semantic profile of lecture in mainstream course

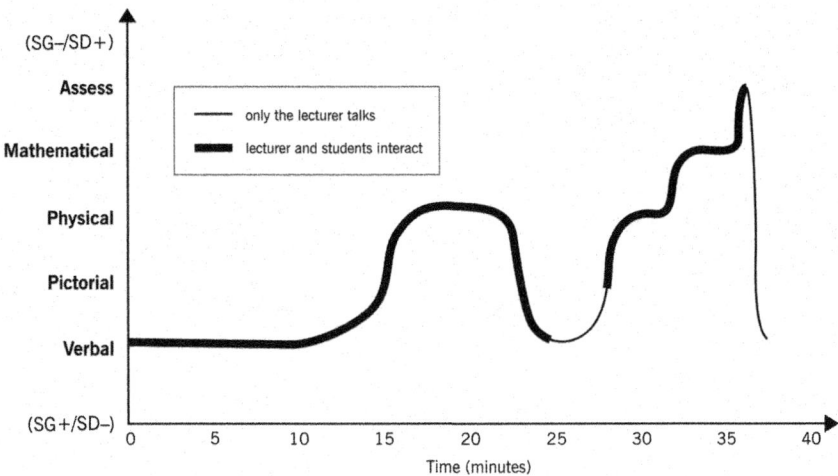

FIGURE 10.3 Semantic profile of lecture in foundation course

The semantic profiles of two lectures in the mainstream and foundation courses (see Figures 10.2 and 10.3) show the movement between representations up and down the semantic continuum. In the mainstream course (Figure 10.2), there is a rapid shift up the semantic continuum, with little time spent on qualitative representations, and the meaning of the problem context is quickly condensed into a mathematical representation.

In the foundation course (Figure 10.3), the semantic profile is flatter initially, with more time spent making sense of the verbal representation, and more time for explicit focus on modelling the problem and the detailed aspects of constructing a force diagram before moving to the mathematical representation. There is also evidence in the foundation course of 'semantic waving' – shifting up and down the semantic continuum; whereas this is less the case in the mainstream semantic profile (Figure 10.2).

The video-data from the two courses gives a finer-grained illustration of how the lecturers moved between representations in the teaching. The lecturer in the foundation course spent a lot of time guiding students explicit to move up and down the semantic continuum, unpacking and repacking representations. In this next section, we analyse in more detail this moving up and down the semantic continuum in the foundation lecture.

Moving up the semantic continuum (SG↓ SD↑)

The foundation course lecturer starts by guiding the students to draw a sketch based on the verbal problem statement (a person pushing a crate across the floor). The students identify the crate as the system of interest, and the lecturer then prompts them: 'We start with a normal sketch', he says. 'Which objects or agents will interact with my system, the crate?'. He begins to draw a sketch

A Semantics analysis of first-year physics teaching 171

(see Figure 10.4 below) and asks the students to identify the significant forces. A student calls out 'gravity' and the lecturer writes 'gravity $\vec{F}_{g\,EconC}$' and points out the vector sign on top. He then asks, 'It's the force of what what on what?', and then moves from the verbal statement ('It's the gravitational force of the Earth on the crate') to the more condensed symbolic representation $\vec{F}_{g\,EconC}$. Then, he explicitly shows the students how meaning is condensed in this symbolic format $\vec{F}_{g\,EconC}$:

> I'm not just labelling this as the gravitational force, I'm identifying the agent which is the result or causes this force. So, in other words, the Earth (points to the symbol E) is responsible for this gravitational force (points to $\vec{F}_g$) on the system, that is, the crate (points to symbol C).

Here (at about minute 14 on Figure 10.3), we see the lecturer explicitly condensing as he moves from the verbal representation to the pictorial representation (Figure 10.4) and strengthens semantic density (SD↑). By way of contrast, in the mainstream lecture on a similar problem task, the dense symbolic representation F_g is taken-for-granted and glossed over (as *'the most obvious force is $\vec{F}_g$,' $\vec{F}_g$*). There is no explicit discussion about the meaning condensed in the symbol .

In the foundation lecture, the lecturer continues to move up the semantic gravity continuum by translating the sketch into a force diagram (see Figure 10.5 below). The real-life, extended object (in this case, the crate) is modelled as a point-particle and represented as a dot on the force diagram. Here, as the lecturer further abstracts from the crate to the point-particle (SG↓) and condenses meaning into an assemblage of arrows and symbols (SD↑), he points to the underlying epistemological feature of Physics, i.e. the idea that Physics provides us with simplified models for making sense of the complex physical world.

As students are working in groups drawing their force diagrams, the lecturer reminds them: 'Remember... what is the main purpose of the [force diagram]? We were trying

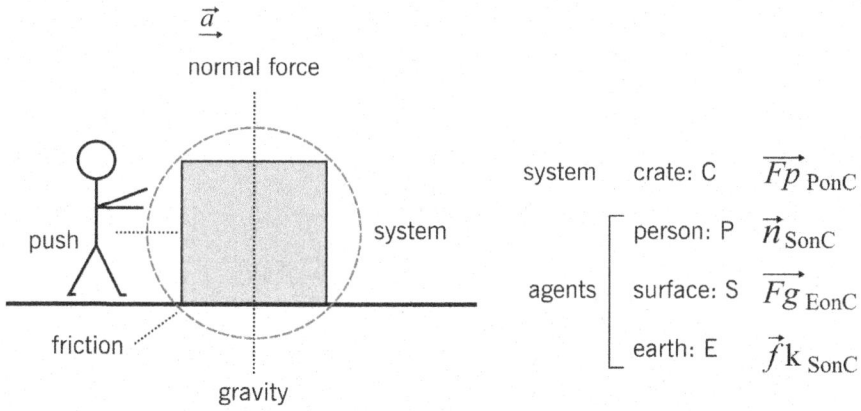

FIGURE 10.4 Pictorial representation – sketch of the problem scenario

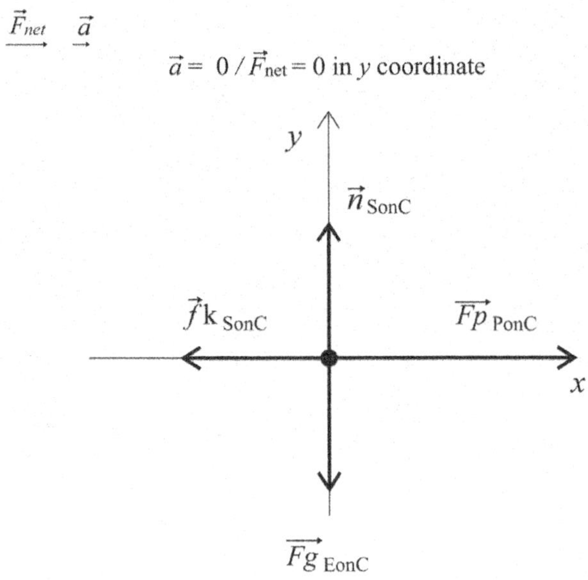

$\vec{F}_{net}$ $\vec{a}$

$\vec{a} = 0 / \vec{F}_{net} = 0$ in y coordinate

$\vec{n}$ SonC

$\vec{f}k$ SonC $\vec{F}p$ PonC

$\vec{F}g$ EonC

FIGURE 10.5 Physical representation – force diagram of the problem scenario

to identify the significant forces acting on the system, and the relative sizes of them.' Here, there is evidence of the lecturer attending to what Kohl and Finkelstein (2008, p. 11) call 'meta-representational competence', that is, discussing the purpose of representations and 'knowing what different representations are useful for'.

Moving down the semantic continuum (SG↑ SD↓)

At this point (at about minute 22 on Figure 10.3), the foundation lecturer prompts the students to check their force diagrams to see whether they correspond correctly to the physical situation of the problem task. He reminds the students that the force diagram is not merely a procedure to follow mindlessly: 'You need to remember that the [force] diagram is not just some lifeless thing; it must reflect the physical situation'. Here, he guides the students to unpack the dense meaning encapsulated in the abstract force diagram (SG–, SD+) to check it out against the verbal representation of the concrete situation (SG+, SD–).

Moving up the semantic continuum again (SG↓ SD↑)

Here (at about minute 26 on Figure 10.3), the lecturer moves back up the semantic continuum to represent the meaning in the force diagram in mathematical form (see Figure 10.6 below). At this stage, meaning is at its most abstract and generic (SG–): the mathematical representation of Newton's 2nd Law, ($\vec{F}_{net} = m\vec{a}$) (represented below as N11), applied here to the particular problem situation.

N11: $\Sigma \vec{F}_y = \vec{n}_{SonC} + \vec{Fg}_{EonC} = 0$

(a = 0 / $\vec{F}_{net}$ = 0 in y coordinate)

N11: $\Sigma \vec{F}_x = \vec{f}k_{SonC} + \vec{Fp}_{PonC} = m\vec{a}_x$

FIGURE 10.6 Mathematical representation of problem scenario

In summary, a Semantics analysis of teaching approaches (as captured in the semantic profiles in Figures 10.2 and 10.3), indicated that the foundation course showed more evidence of *semantic waving*, that is, recurrent shifts in context-dependence and complexity of meaning on the semantic continuum. There was more movement between representations, and the video data gave fine-grained evidence of the lecturer supporting students' learning through the careful unpacking and repacking of dense representations.

Research findings part 2: using semantic profiles to analyse students' approaches to problem tasks

In the second part of the study, several student groups were observed tackling Physics problem tasks on the same Mechanics topic as in the lectures above. In this part of the chapter, we examine the semantic profiles for two of these student groups, one in the mainstream course and one in the foundation course. Figure 10.7 and Figure 10.8 below present the semantic profiles for the mainstream and foundation student groups respectively.

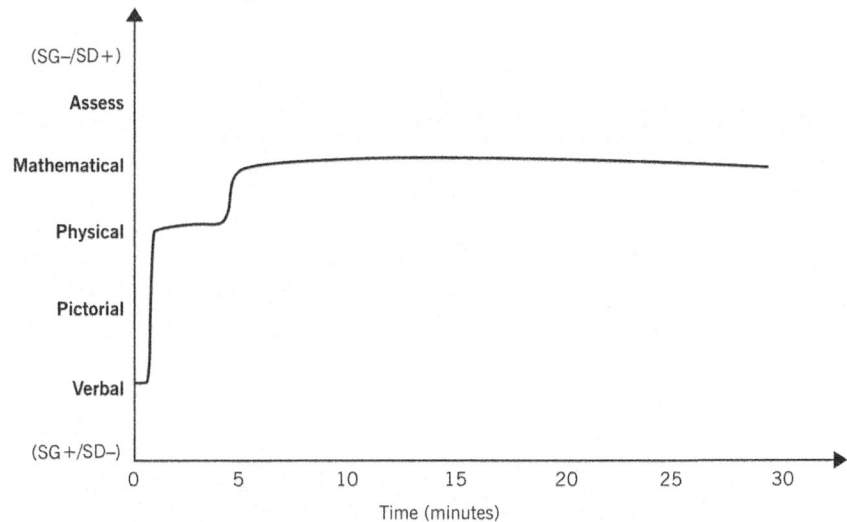

FIGURE 10.7 Semantic profile of students tackling a task in the mainstream course

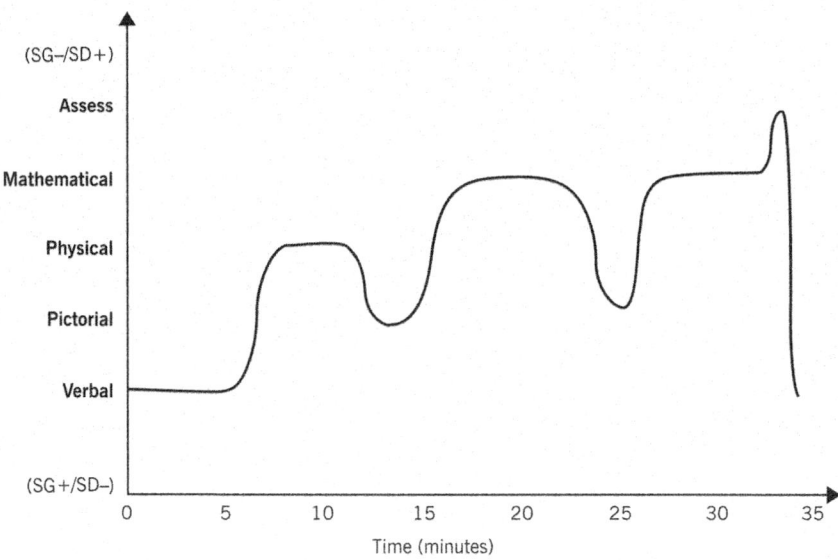

FIGURE 10.8 Semantic profile of students tackling a task in the foundation course

The semantic profile for the foundation group (see Figure 10.8) is flatter initially than in the mainstream case, indicating that the students spend more time discussing and unpacking the verbal representation of the problem. Only once they are clear about the problem statement, do they go on to model the problem situation in a sketch, before drawing a force diagram. The semantic profile for the foundation group shows shifts up and down the semantic continuum as the students tackle the task. They draw the force diagram, then shift to and fro on the semantic continuum as they modify the diagram based on their modelling of the situation, and then move to a mathematical representation.

In contrast, the mainstream group (see Figure 10.7) move swiftly up the semantic continuum to draw a force diagram and then move to the mathematical representation of the problem. At this point, they encounter confusion about the problem situation (whether the object is accelerating or not). This confusion at the abstract, mathematical representation stage of the problem arises because they have not spent enough time reading and making sense of the concrete problem situation. The mainstream students do not move up and down the semantic continuum in the same way as the foundation students do, but spend most of the time at the abstract mathematical representation level.

Video-data provides further insight into students' use of disciplinary representations. For example, the two groups use force diagrams in different ways. In the mainstream group, the force diagrams were drawn mechanically, and were not really put to use in setting up the mathematical representations, despite the function of force diagrams being to help in the move from the concrete situation to a mathematical representation (Rosengrant et al., 2009). When asked about the use of the force diagram representation, one student in the mainstream group noted that 'I would generally draw or just sketch something'. This comment reveals a blurring of the distinction between a sketch and a force diagram, suggesting that the different purposes of these representations are not apparent to the student. Furthermore, the mainstream students seem unclear of the modelling implications of representing an object as a point particle; they note that: 'This [the point particle representation] will just confuse us' ... 'the dot will be difficult to see'. By contrast, the student group in the foundation course began by modelling the crate as a point particle. They took great care drawing their force diagrams, so that the relative sizes of the force vectors represented details of the concrete, physical situation: 'The [force] diagram gives you an indication of the relative sizes of the forces so you know that the system is at rest or moving [accelerating] ...'. These foundation course students also showed a greater degree of 'meta-representational competence' (Kohl and Finkelstein, 2008) in being able to articulate the purpose of the force diagram: 'You have to draw a [force diagram] because it makes it easier to calculate ... it helps you to see which forces are in the x and y direction'.

This nascent development of meta-representational competence in students can be seen as helping student to 'thinking like a physicist' (Van Heuvelen, 1991a) and to develop fluency in moving between representations (Airey and Linder, 2009). The Semantics analysis helps us to see how students approach the problem tasks, as captured in the semantic profiles in Figures 10.7 and 10.8. These show that there was more semantic waving in the foundation group (that is, moving between representations) in contrast with the mainstream group, who spent most of the time at the abstract mathematical representation level.

Discussion and conclusion

In this final section, we summarize the findings from the study and draw out some more general implications for undergraduate science teaching. The analysis of the semantic profiles (Figures 10.2 and 10.3; Figures 10.7 and 10.8) showed that teaching approaches influenced how students tackled problem tasks: in the foundation case, the more explicit focus on the representations used in Physics, and more semantic waving (i.e. moving up and down the semantic continuum) in the teaching, was reflected in the way the students tackled Physics tasks. On the foundation students' semantic profile, there were more shifts between representations, and these students showed evidence of beginning to develop what Kohl and Finkelstein (2008) call 'meta-representational competence', that is understanding the purpose of representations and 'knowing what different representations are useful for' (p. 11). If 'thinking like a physicist', as noted earlier, entails the use of qualitative analysis, modelling and qualitative representations to understand a physical process, rather than moving straight to mathematical representations, then students' problem-solving practices in the foundation group were more congruent with expert physicist practices.

Our findings support other studies that show that a 'representation-rich learning environment' (Rosengrant et al., 2009, p. 010108–2) can support students learning how to use representations. As Blackie (2014) notes, this approach does not necessarily require a slower pace. Rather, it requires careful pedagogical attention to the use of representations in a discipline, to explicitly using different kinds of representations with students, and attention to the features of representations that students struggle with. At a more 'meta'-level, it also requires a focus on why certain representations are used when, and on the epistemological underpinnings of representations (for example, modelling as a point particle). In this way, students' 'meta-representational competence' (diSessa, 2004; Kohl and Finkelstein, 2008) is developed.

The method of semantic profiling was extended in this study, using coding to indicate the different forms of interaction in the class (with a thin line indicating lecturer talk, and a thick line indicating lecturer-student interaction and engagement). The semantic profiles (Figures 10.2 and 10.3) indicate that in the foundation course, the students themselves were largely engaged in moving up and down the semantic continuum, and enacting the shifts between representations in class, rather than observing these being demonstrated by the lecturer (as was mostly the case in the mainstream course). This sort of interactive engagement has been shown by Physics education research to be important for Physics learning (Hake, 1998; Wieman and Perkins, 2005; Mazur, 2009; Fredlund et al., 2012). Therefore, being able to map student engagement on the semantic profiles proved to be a very useful tool.

Although the focus of our analysis in this chapter was undergraduate Physics, there are some useful implications for undergraduate science teaching more generally. The LCT concepts and tools offer useful insights into developing students' use of representations and improving science teaching:

First, the concept of semantic gravity focuses attention on the need for teaching to use a wide semantic range between the concrete and the abstract, and not to remain at the level of the abstract, as science teaching often tends to do. For example, for Physics, this would mean ensuring successive shifts between concrete scenarios and abstract principles; for Chemistry, this might similarly mean using the full range of micro-level, macro-level and symbolic representations (see, Johnsone, 1982; Mtombeni, 2018).

Second, the concept of semantic density highlights the dense terminology and representations used in science and the need for teaching to more explicitly unpack features of these representations, which are often taken for granted in teaching. For example, a Physics lecturer might draw a force diagram, and assume that students understand what the arrows and dot represent; a Chemistry lecturer might use a 'ball-and-stick' model of a molecule, and assume that students understand what the ball and sticks represent; a Mathematics lecturer might assume that students understand what the slope of a graph represents. Explicit focus on representations is important since research shows that students' struggle to master representations and their fluency with representations often develops over an extended period of time (Eriksson et al., 2014).

Third, the LCT method of semantic profiling provides a useful visual portrayal for educators of how the strength in semantic gravity and semantic density vary over time in science lesson or science task. They are also able to offer a useful portrayal of the extent of student engagement in a lesson; this is significant since research shows that developing representational fluency takes time and student engagement.

Working with science faculty colleagues, we also have found semantic profiling to be a productive professional development tool for stimulating lecturers' reflections on their teaching and classroom approaches (see also Clarence, 2016). In conclusion, the tools of Semantics proved very powerful in representing undergraduate classroom teaching practices, and in fostering engagement and discussion among colleagues about teaching approaches that better enable access to the science disciplines.

References

Airey, J. and Linder, C. (2009). A disciplinary discourse perspective on university science learning: Achieving fluency in a critical constellation of modes. *Journal of Research in Science Teaching*, 46, 27–49.

Bernstein, B. (2000). *Pedagogy, symbolic control and identity: Theory, research, critique* (Revised edn). Oxford: Rowman and Littlefield.

Blackie, M. (2014). Creating semantic waves: using Legitimation Code Theory as a tool to aid the teaching of chemistry. *Chemistry Education Research and Practice*, 15(4), 462–149.

Cheng, M. and Gilbert, J.K. (2009). Towards a better utilization of diagram in research into the use of representative levels in chemical education. In J.K. Gilbert and D.F. Treagust (Eds), *Multiple representations in chemical education* (pp. 55–73). Dordrecht: Springer.

Clarence, S. (2016). Exploring the nature of disciplinary teaching and learning using Legitimation Code Theory Semantics. *Teaching in Higher Education*, 2(2), 123–137.

Conana, C.H. (2016). *Using semantic profiling to characterize pedagogical practices and student learning: A case study of two introductory physics courses*. (Unpublished doctoral thesis). University of the Western Cape, South Africa.

Conana, H., Marshall, D. and Case, J. (2016). Exploring pedagogical possibilities for transformative approaches to academic literacies in undergraduate Physics. *Critical Studies in Teaching and Learning*, 4(2), 28–44.

Council on Higher Education (CHE). (2013). *A proposal for undergraduate curriculum reform in South Africa: The case for a flexible curriculum structure. Report of the Task Team on Undergraduate Curriculum Structure*. Pretoria: Council on Higher Education. Retrieved from www.che.ac.za/media_and_publications/research/proposalundergraduate-curriculum-reform-south-africa-case-flexible.

diSessa, A.A. (2004). Metarepresentation: native competence and targets for instruction. *Cognition and Instruction*, 22, 293–331.

Doran, Y. (2016). *Knowledge in physics through mathematics, image and language*. (Unpublished doctoral thesis). University of Sydney, Australia.

Dufresne, R.J., Gerace, W.J. and Leonard, W.J. (1997). Solving physics problems with multiple representations. *The Physics Teacher*, 35(270), 270–275.

Eriksson, U., Linder, C., Airey, J. and Redfors, A. (2014). Introducing the anatomy of disciplinary discernment: An example from astronomy. *European Journal of Science and Mathematics Education*, 2(3), 167–182.

European Commission. (2004). *Europe needs more scientists!* Brussels: Directorate-General for Research, High Level Group on Human Resources for Science and Technology in Europe.

Fredlund, T., Airey, J. and Linder, C. (2012). Exploring the role of physics representations: An illustrative example from students sharing knowledge about refraction. *European Journal of Physics, 33*, 657–666.

Fredlund, T., Linder, C., Airey, J. and Linder, A. (2014). Unpacking physics representations: Towards an appreciation of disciplinary affordance. *Physical Review Special Topics – Physics Education*, 10, 020129, 1–13.

Hake, R. (1998). Interactive-engagement versus traditional methods: A six-thousand student survey of mechanics test data for introductory physics courses. *American Journal of Physics*, 66(1), 64–74.

Johnstone, A.H. (1982). Macro- and micro-chemistry. *School Science Review*, 64, 377–379.

Kilpert, L. and Shay, S. (2013). Kindling fires: Examining the potential for cumulative learning in a journalism curriculum. *Teaching in Higher Education*, 18(1), 40–52.

Kloot, B., Case, J.M. and Marshall, D. (2008). A critical review of the educational philosophies underpinning Science and Engineering foundation programmes. *South African Journal of Higher Education*, 22(4), 799–816.

Kohl, P.B. and Finkelstein, N.D. (2008). Patterns of multiple representation use by experts and novices during physics problem solving. *Physical Review Special Topics: Physics Education Research*, 4: 010111, 1–13.

Kress, G. (2010). *Multimodality. A social semiotic approach to contemporary communication.* London: Routledge Falmer.

Lemke, J.L. (1990). *Talking science: Language, learning and values.* London: Albex Publishing.

Leonard, W.J., Dufresne, R.J. and Mestre, J.P. (1996). Using qualitative problem solving strategies to highlight the role of conceptual knowledge in solving problems. *American Journal of Physics*, 64(12), 1495–1503.

Lindstrøm, C. (2010). *Link maps and map meeting: A theoretical and experimental case for stronger scaffolding in first year university physics education.* (Unpublished doctoral thesis). University of Sydney, Australia.

Marshall, D., Conana, H., Maclons, R., Herbert, M. and Volkwyn, T. (2011). Learning as accessing a disciplinary discourse: Integrating academic literacy into introductory physics through collaboration partnership. *Across the Disciplines*, 8(3). Retrieved from https://wac.colostate.edu/docs/atd/clil/marshalletal.pdf.

Maton, K. (2009). Cumulative and segmented learning: Exploring the role of curriculum structures in knowledge-building. *British Journal of Sociology of Education*, 30(1), 43–57.

Maton, K. (2013). Making semantic waves: A key to cumulative knowledge-building. *Linguistics and Education*, 24(1), 8–22.

Maton, K. (2014). *Knowledge and knowers: Towards a realist sociology of education.* London: Routledge.

Maton, K. (2020). Semantic waves: Context, complexity and academic discourse. In J.R. Martin, K. Maton and Y.J. Doran (Eds) *Accessing academic discourse: Systemic functional linguistics and Legitimation Code Theory* (pp. 59–85). London: Routledge.

Maton, K. and Chen, R.T-H. (2016). LCT in qualitative research: Creating a translation device for studying constructivist pedagogy. In K. Maton, S. Hood and S. Shay (Eds), *Knowledge-building: Educational studies in Legitimation Code Theory* (pp. 27–48). London: Routledge.

Maton, K. and Howard, S.K. (2016). LCT in mixed-methods research: Evolving an instrument for quantitative data. In K. Maton, S. Hood and S. Shay (Eds), *Knowledge-building: Educational studies in Legitimation Code Theory* (pp. 49–71). London: Routledge.

Mazur, E. (1997). *Peer instruction: A user's manual.* Upper Saddle River, NJ: Prentice Hall.

Mazur, E. (2009). Farewell, lecture? *Science*, 323(5910), 50–51.

Mtombeni, T. (2018). *Knowledge practices and student access and success in General Chemistry at a Large South African University* (Unpublished doctoral thesis). Rhodes University, South Africa.

OECD. (2008). *Encouraging student interest in science and technology studies*. Global Science Forum. Paris: OECD.

Rosengrant, D., Van Heuvelen, A. and Etkina, E. (2009). Do students use and understand free-body diagrams? *Physical Review Special Topics: Physics Education Research*, 5, 010108, 1–13.

Seymour, E. and Hewitt, N.M. (1997). *Talking about leaving: Why undergraduates leave the sciences*. Boulder, CO: Westview.

Van Heuvelen, A. (1991a). Learning to think like a physicist: A review of research based instructional strategies. *American Journal of Physics*, 59(10), 891–897.

Van Heuvelen, A. (1991b). Overview: Case study physics. *American Journal of Physics*, 59(10), 890–907.

Wieman, C.E. and Perkins, K.K. (2005). Transforming education. *Physics Today*, 58(11), 36–42.

Wood, L.N., Joyce, S., Petocz, P. and Rodd, M. (2007). Learning in lectures: Multiple representations. *International Journal of Mathematical Education in Science and Technology*, 38(7), 907–915.

11
FROM PRINCIPLE TO PRACTICE

Enabling theory–practice bridging in engineering education

Karin Wolff

Introduction

Science, Technology, Engineering and Mathematics (STEM) professionals are crucial to addressing global sustainable development issues (UNESCO, 2010), but represent the most pressing higher education (HE) challenges, with evidence of poor retention and graduation rates, as well as employer feedback on graduates' lack of 'soft and technical skills' (manpowergroup.com, 2015). Widespread initiatives to address challenges in STEM education include systematic curriculum redesign, foundational learning support for first-year students, a more concerted effort to address the theory–practice divide through work-integrated learning (WIL) approaches (Winberg et al., 2013) and, more recently, a focus on the professional development of STEM educators (Winberg et al., 2019). However, each initiative is beset with its own challenges: curriculum redesign sees a consistent uncomfortable straddling of the how-much-theory and how-much-practice divide; foundational support restricted to the first year does not acknowledge the challenge of 'epistemic transitions' (Shay, Wolff and Clarence-Fincham, 2016); WIL approaches require significant resources and collaboration (Mutereko and Wedekind, 2016); and STEM professional development for educators has tended to be generic and untheorized (Winberg et al., 2019).

Engineering encompasses all of the STEM disciplines and is the ideal field to illustrate the challenges in STEM education. An engineering curriculum represents the 'epistemic transition' from the natural [and mathematical] sciences to the engineering sciences, to the sciences of design, and the practice of application (Shay et al., 2016) using dynamically evolving technologies. Each stage entails significantly different kinds of knowledge and practices, which are more complex than captured by the terms 'theory' and 'practice'. Engineering educators often work in sub-fields which have tended to valorize their specialist science-based knowledge in such a way as to lead to 'silo' curricula, with a focus on specializations such as physics (in engineering), mechanical engineering or computer science, for example. And yet, even an ostensibly common concept such as thermodynamics, when seen through the eyes of different engineering academics, results in student learning challenges shaped by different educator paradigms (Christiansen and Rump, 2008).

The challenges in engineering education, I suggest, are exacerbated by 'knowledge-blindness' (Maton, 2014) – blindness to the organizing principles of different forms of knowledge and the concomitant implications for teaching, learning and practice in context. Bernstein referred to the 'regionalization' of knowledge (2000) – the combinations of different pure disciplines such as Physics and Mathematics into complex 'regions', such as Engineering (or the health sciences for that matter) – and proposed that 'regions' require a curriculum based on *integration* with lateral staff relations rather than a *collection* (Bernstein, 1977) of 'siloed' specializations. The focus for this chapter is the professional development of engineering academics through: (1) the creation of 'integrated spaces'; and (2) the introduction to empirical, theoretically informed ways of understanding different knowledge practices.

Legitimation Code Theory (LCT) is used as an accessible analytical framework to demonstrate *how engineering academics can be assisted in addressing the theory–practice divide in engineering curricula*. The chapter draws on one of ten international collaborative projects to enhance existing engineering educator capacity (known as EEESCEP), funded by the South African Department of Higher Education and Training (DHET). The first section provides the contextual background to the significance for educators of understanding engineering knowledge practices. This is followed by an elaboration on the framework and LCT Specialization instrument: *the epistemic plane*. The third section showcases an example of engineering practice analysis, which is then applied in four engineering educator curriculum and pedagogy case studies in two distinct institutional contexts.

Problem context and literature: complexities for twenty-first century engineering educators

'Engineering is … a profession devoted to harnessing and modifying the three fundamental resources that humankind has available for the creation of all technology: energy, materials, and information' (Feisel and Rosa, 2005, p. 121). Working effectively with these three fundamental resources entails a grasp of the physics and mathematics which are applicable in different ways to energy and materials, as well as the literacies and logic-based disciplines underpinning the collection and processing of information using technologies. These are significantly different forms of knowledge which are brought into a synergistic relationship in order to engage in the central 'engineering endeavour' of problem-solving (Sobek and Jain, 2004). Engineering educators are primarily responsible for producing 'problem-solving' graduates using curricula aligned to the International Engineering Alliance graduate profiles (IEA, 2013). Although these profiles are intended to provide a 'holistic' framework for professional achievement, the generic problem-solving descriptors are open to contextual interpretation. While educators cannot prepare a graduate for all contexts in a rapidly changing technology-driven profession, labour market demands mean that academics must address consistent industry feedback on graduate inability to 'apply theory' (Griesel and Parker, 2009) and take seriously the 32 per cent of 40,000 employers world over who have cited lack of technical skills (manpowergroup.com, 2015) as the main reason not to employ graduates. These complaints highlight the science–engineering disjuncture (Bernold et al., 2007) and difficulties in a curriculum that is required to 'face both ways' (Barnett, 2006) – towards the disciplinary basis as well as the world of work.

The theory–practice divide in engineering education

In South Africa (the site of the research) the balance between theoretical and practical engineering qualifications has shifted considerably over the past five decades with the Universities of Technology (UoTs) – originally technical colleges – demonstrating increasing 'academic drift' and the employment of fewer academics with actual industrial experience (Winberg, 2005). In contrast, one finds many of the traditional research-intensive universities demonstrating 'vocational drift' with forms of progressive, practice-orientated teaching and learning similar to those seen in the USA where engineering retention and graduation rates have steadily been declining (Porter and Roessner, 2006). Although these latter shifts indicate an attempt to enable a graduate to practice in the profession, it is one that is changing dramatically with both the exponential development of computer-based 'smart' technologies and simultaneous patterns of rapid technological obsolescence (UNESCO, 2010; Felder, 2012). Few engineering educators today have the necessary exposure to these practices in real world contexts, challenging their ability to provide meaningful opportunities for their students to acquire relevant, technical expertise.

A critique of overly practical curricula, however, is that they risk constraining learning to particular contexts, and deny students access to forms of theoretical knowledge (Wheelahan, 2009) necessary to deal with complexity. 'Recreating the everyday world in the curriculum … [threatens the] sense that there are bodies of knowledge that are worth acquiring and that give us real insight into the natural and social world' (Allais, 2014, p. xv). In this chapter, I suggest that engineering educators wishing to understand the relationship between theory and practice in their curricula and pedagogy need to overcome pervasive 'knowledge-blindness' (Maton, 2014) through collective access to explanatory research and instruments.

Engineering educator support

Academic development (AD) initiatives in South Africa shifted from primarily student support to professional learning for 'under-prepared' academic staff in 1994 (Leibowitz et al., 2017). A recent review of the global literature on AD for STEM educators (Winberg et al., 2019) reveals that most initiatives (whether formal or informal) are at best generic and usually conducted by social scientists. Workshops, seminars and short courses are generally designed around classroom management strategies, constructivist approaches to aligning teaching to outcomes, the introduction of general pedagogic frameworks and a strong move towards 'reflective practice' to enable faculty to understand and transform their practices (Froyd et al., 2007). A few notable AD initiatives specifically for engineering educators are the use of engineering pedagogy methodologies for curriculum design, such as the popular Conceive-Design-Implement-Operate (CDIO) used in engineering design projects (Chuchalin et al., 2015). There are also engineering research approaches such as the research-knowledge utilization (RKU) project which seeks to map discipline-based research innovations to those applicable to STEM education (Porter and Roessner, 2006). Another approach is the use of engineering systems metaphors to analyse curriculum and pedagogy (Auret and Wolff, 2018). Such approaches are more likely to interest engineering academics (Felder et al., 2011) given that they draw on familiar discourses through which to address educational challenges. However, although these initiatives mark a welcome attempt to overturn the predominant 'knowledge-blindness' evident in the professional learning support of engineering educators, there are more effective ways to explicitly 'see' how theory and practice are related.

Research context

The South African education ministry launched a programme to specifically enhance engineering education provision, known as the Existing Engineering Educator Staff Capacity Enhancement Project (EEESCEP). In the first round there were ten international collaborative projects dedicated to a range of AD initiatives. These included master classes on teaching engineering-specific concepts, postgraduate engineering education programmes, and in this case teaching towards 'Engineering in Context' (EiC). The EiC project was a collaboration between two previously disadvantaged UoTs (one urban and one rural), a research-intensive 'historically white institution' and an international Applied Sciences university. The EiC purpose was to introduce South African engineering academics to each other and to educational approaches that were both theorized and practical. Participating staff across the three South African institutions were supported and mentored by AD facilitators and researchers, who introduced theorized, reflective practices as well as case studies demonstrating the theory–practice relationship 'in context'.

Theory–practice engineering research

The EiC project used case studies to demonstrate the synergistic and supportive relationship between the collaborating international academics and their industry partners, where students engaged with real world problems on industrial projects. Prior research on engineering problem-solving, entailing a total of 41 case studies across all engineering sectors in South Africa, explicitly examined the relationship between different forms of knowledge in the context of industrial practice (Wolff, 2018). This research produced sets of illustrative 'problem-solving maps' representing how engineering practitioners draw on different forms of disciplinary knowledge when they solve real world problems. The 'maps' – based on transcriptions of interviews with technicians, technologists and engineers in industrial sites – sought to reveal the *what* and *how* of the problem-solving process as participants approached, analysed and solved technical problems. The mapping was illustrated using an analytical tool from the Legitimation Code Theory dimension of Specialization: the *epistemic plane*. These maps and the LCT tool were the primary resources used in supporting EiC participants at the collaborating institutions.

Theoretical framework

Legitimation Code Theory (LCT) describes, interprets and counters invisible social structures that shape, *inter alia*, educational achievement and social mobility. LCT sees forms of knowledge as having structural properties that have structuring effects on practices (Maton, 2014, 2016). Key to working effectively with all knowledge forms is the ability to recognize and realize their 'codes'. LCT has developed a multi-dimensional toolkit for the analysis of 'codes' underlying practices (e.g. Maton, 2014, 2016, 2020; Maton and Howard 2018). Here I shall draw on the Specialization dimension and specifically the concept of *epistemic relations*, an ideal tool to overcome the binary theory–practice distinction because it can visually capture the nature of the relationship between the 'what' and 'how' of a practice.

To explain, Specialization begins from the simple premise that all practices are about or oriented towards something and by someone (Maton, 2014, 2016). One can, therefore, analytically distinguish: *epistemic relations* between practices and their object (that part of the world towards which they are oriented); and *social relations* between practices and their subject (who or what is enacting the practices). Second, epistemic relations can be further distinguished into *ontic relations* between knowledge claims and their object of study, and *discursive relations* between knowledge claims and other knowledges (Maton, 2014, p. 175). Each can be independently stronger (+) or weaker (−). Figure 11.1 is an annotated interpretation device used to analyse industrial problem-solving processes. Here *ontic relations* or OR (vertical axis) describes the relative strength of the identity of a phenomenon – the *what* of the knowledge practice being considered – and *discursive relations* or DR (horizontal axis) describes how strongly the approach to the phenomenon is bounded, or how 'fixed' or 'open' the *how* is. The two axes of stronger/weaker continua give us four *insights* or ways of seeing knowledge practices.

A useful way of demonstrating a practice based on *purist insight* is to simply throw an object into the air and ask the observers what phenomenon they observe. The answer across multiple contexts (irrespective of language or culture) is always 'gravity'. This is a phenomenon with a stronger internal identity (OR+) and which the field agrees is represented by a fixed set of rules (DR+). Much of the natural science-based content of our curricula is dependent on *purist insight*. However, to

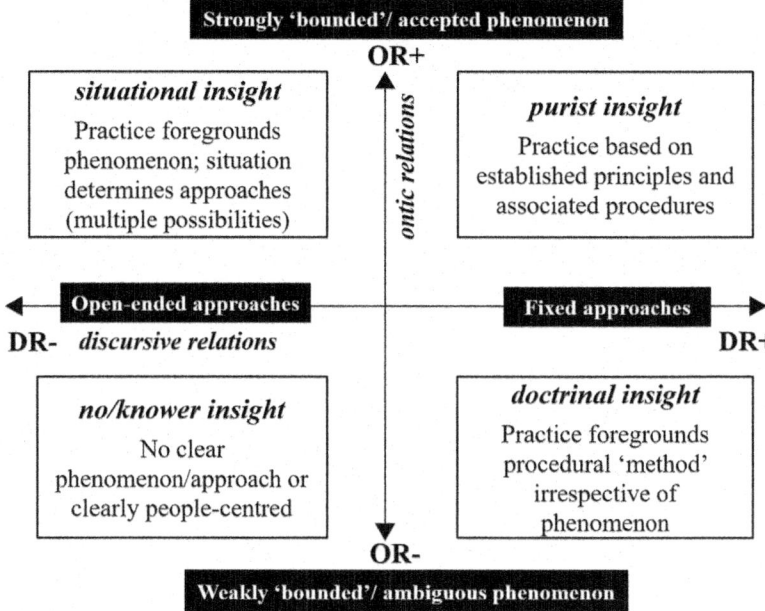

FIGURE 11.1 Annotated epistemic plane

Source: adapted from Maton, 2014, p. 177

work with a concept like gravity, we rely on mathematics. Here, it is important to know that the different mathematical 'languages' each have their own rules, and these are more important to 'fix' in place before we use the mathematics on something else.

Where the rules or methods are more important than the phenomenon, we speak of drawing on *doctrinal insight* (OR−, DR+). This is the case for any well-defined and accepted method, such as the Scientific Method or the process of integration in Calculus. A great deal of learning in the 'apply theory' phase of our engineering programmes takes place in this quadrant. Now let us say we want to maximize the use of the phenomenon of gravity on a children's playground. Where is the playground? Who are the children? Many factors are going to determine materials, cost and safety, thus requiring *situational insight* (OR+, DR−). The phenomenon is clear, but the methods are more open-ended. This example already moves us into the fourth quadrant – *no/knower insight* (OR−, DR−). When we lose sight of the phenomenon in question and cannot identify possible approaches, the knowledge practice is said to draw on *no insight*. Alternatively, if the practice is not about knowledge (*epistemic relations*), but *knowers* in the system, then we need a different tool to understand the implications for practice where *social relations* are foregrounded.

In the EiC research context, the LCT Specialization *epistemic relations* instrument became an invaluable tool for engineering educators for several reasons. Firstly, the graphic depiction of a state or process is an accessible discursive tool for STEM practitioners in general, given their familiarity with the epistemic plane. Secondly, differentiating between different phenomena according to levels of consensus (in other words, relative *ontic relations* strengths) is key to understanding the epistemic transitions across a professional qualification. Natural science phenomena demonstrate stronger *ontic relations* in that the field has reached greater consensus about the identity of such concepts as gravity, forces and heat exchange, and one would find relatively standardized references to these in typical university texts. In contrast, the engineering sciences demonstrate slightly weaker *ontic relations* where the field is emerging or competitive – such as in the use of different polymer materials in manufacturing engineering. When it comes to the use of technologies, the epistemic transition is along the *discursive relations* axis in that there are far more possible approaches given the sheer volume of programming platforms and languages underpinning competing technologies. The third advantage of the *epistemic plane* as a tool for engineering educators is its ability to illustrate 'code shifting' (Maton, 2014). Code shifting is about change – the key ingredient for the development of 'problem-solving' abilities: a change in conditions or perspectives or approaches or effects. The *epistemic plane* is the primary analytical tool used to introduce the EiC participants to empirical research on engineering problem-solving so as to address the theory–practice challenge in education.

Research methodology

The two institutional contexts selected for this chapter are labelled A and B. Group A consists of ten engineering academics at a medium-sized, research-intensive university who are engaged in efforts to improve the teaching of subjects in four-year engineering Bachelor's degrees. Although the teaching is rooted in disciplinary fundamentals covered during lectures, and there are opportunities for 'application' during tutorials and basic practical laboratory work, the faculty is actively involved in experimenting with technologies to reduce staff workload, improve student learning, and enable better technical skills development. Group B is from a UoT: an entire department teaching industrial engineering who are busy redesigning their diploma qualification, as well as a participant from mechanical engineering. Engineering retention and graduation rates are low at institution B (CHE, 2015), and given that it caters to school leavers with lower levels of academic achievement, there has been an increase in attention to theoretical fundamentals.

The *epistemic plane* has been used to illustrate the research design for this chapter (Figure 11.2). Each AD case study entails either a curriculum, teaching, learning or assessment challenge for educators in one of the two institutional contexts. Secondly, each selected AD case study illustrates a key finding from the local engineering problem-solving research. A single comprehensive industrial case study has been selected to illustrate the range of problem-solving findings. Each finding relevant to a particular AD case is presented by way of a brief summary. The key focus is the educators' interpretation of the significance of the tool and finding in relation to

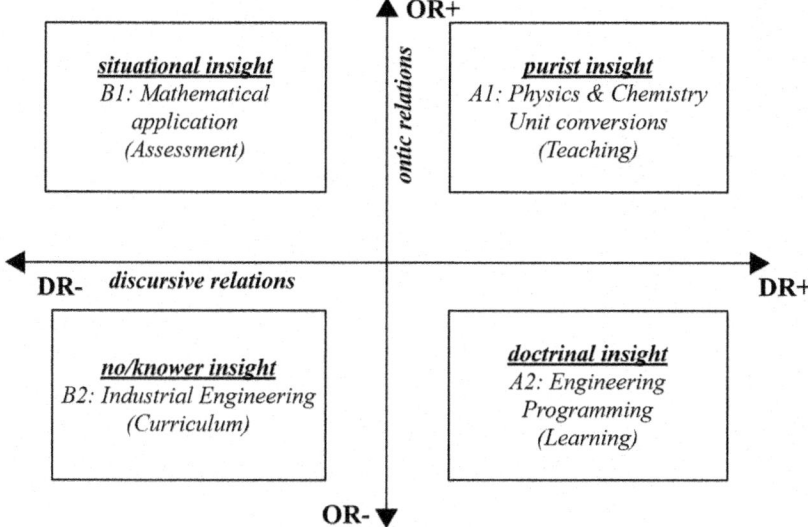

FIGURE 11.2 Epistemic plane mapping of the AD case studies

solving the educational challenge in question. Data for the AD case studies are drawn from participant and researcher observation notes, interviews, workshop surveys and curriculum texts.

Using theory and research in engineering academic development

Engineering problem-solving exemplar

A case study from the Oil and Gas sector was selected to demonstrate the application of the epistemic plane to analyse a complex problem-solving process. A mechatronics maintenance technician with two years' experience on an off-shore drilling rig faced the following problem (abridged):

> During REW (Reservoir Evaluation and Wireline) several tools go to the bottom of the well miles away from the surface. In order to send electrical signals for evaluation of the [rock] formation, we use a tool string head that is connected to an electrical cable from a control room. [Without the assistance of technicians with more experience], I had to find **why the electrical signal is not flowing** through the head to the tool string ... [using electrical diagrams and computer data].

The full problem-solving analysis (Figure 11.3) starts with his (1) approach as he contextualizes the problem *situation*. He then moves into (2a) the *knower* quadrant by establishing the staffing arrangements [not detailed in the extract]. He refers to

188 Karin Wolff

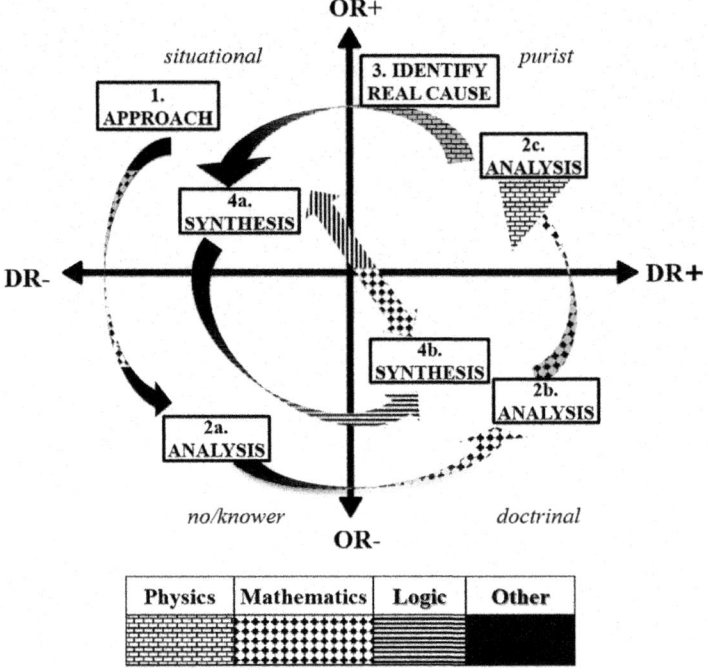

FIGURE 11.3 Engineering problem-solving in the Oil & Gas sector

several (2b) *doctrinal* procedures gathering data from electrical diagrams to data sheets, and then shifts into (2c) the *purist* quadrant to establish why the 'electrical signal is not flowing'. In the second extract, he describes the physics basis of the problem in analytical detail, while weaving the mathematical (*doctrinal*) analysis into his explanation:

> The sonic log measures interval transit time (Δt) of a compressional sound wave traveling through one foot of formation. [It] consists of one or more sound transmitters, and two or more receivers. Interval transit time (Δt) [depends on lithology and porosity and] is the reciprocal of the velocity of a compressional sound wave.

Each of these physics concepts requires the grasp of a different set of relations between units, values and representations, such as the **v** for velocity (which is metres per second) and V for volume (associated with porosity), which is metres cubed. These underpin his understanding of *what* information the signal should be transmitting. However, the actual transmission of the signal is based on entirely different physics: that of electricity (in which we find another 'V' for voltage!). It is here that his problem is located: the tool is not sending a signal. Extract three establishes the third discipline on which he draws: computer-based logic.

> The company has a new method of testing the electronics [so] I connected the tools ... to the computer (acquisition system) to check the functionality [of the tool string head]. This new technology came to reduce costs ... to avoid replacing electronic boards that are working perfectly but [which] we cannot see.... It makes every task more difficult to find errors and ... we are not allowed to use internet.

The technician is required to interpret the problem via a computer interface. This consists of geological imaging software (of which there are dozens) using three-axis single-sensor seismic hardware and software. The user cannot see *why* the signal is not flowing, only that there is a missing reading. These readings are in the form of thousands of lines representing rock formation information captured using sound and light which produce analogue waves. Each wave is digitized into a voltage signal which produces 'lines' on the computer screen. These can be misinterpreted if the resolution is incorrect and if the user does not know what the line represents.

To solve the problem, the technician shifted back and forth between (4a) all the elements on the tool string head and data acquisition system, and (4b) the doctrinal rules of each single feature, from hardware connections (*what* is connected to *what*) to software data in multiple alpha–numeric and graphic languages. He finally determined that one of the three sensors on the tool head string was faulty, and this was then replaced. This problem-solving case study demonstrates a range of significant research findings for what exactly the theory–practice relationship looks like in real industrial sites, and how disciplinary thinking comes into play. Four key findings from all the engineering problem-solving case studies are represented in this single exemplar. In the following sections, each finding is used to demonstrate its usefulness and application to a particular EiC issue.

AD Case study A1: Teaching of fundamental principles

> Finding 1: Successful problem-solvers engage in explicit code-shifting behaviour, moving across the epistemic plane and using all four insights, but never lose sight of the fundamental principles.

A key feature in the problem-solving exemplar is the technician's ability to identify the principles behind any particular moment in his process, from the function of the sonic log to the physics of signal transmission and the digital readings on the computer.

A1 Teaching the fundamentals of unit conversions

Group A1 consisted of four lecturers who taught a first-year Bachelor of Science in Chemical Engineering course. Their challenge was consistently poor student performance on unit conversions and estimations tests, which are regarded as a 'core competency' for engineering students. The team had compiled an online bank of randomized practice questions assuming that unit conversions mainly required doctrinal insight, such as simply converting from feet to metres. A series of AD sessions using the epistemic plane (Figure 11.4) enabled the team to interrogate the questions they had set. It soon emerged that the questions had hidden assumptions about student prior experience (knower insight) or the understanding necessary for 'derived units' (combinations of the base units such as kilograms, metres and seconds), which relies on purist insight.

Using the epistemic plane, the team reframed and categorized the questions so as to be able to identify more accurately what exactly the 'knowledge gap' was and how best to address this. Student responses indicated that the primary challenge was the understanding of the physics principle behind a specific scientific unit (purist insight). Just the frequency of the letter 'v' in the sonic log case study and its reference to multiple physics concepts was a useful reminder for these academics of the importance of creating opportunities for their students to develop a stronger grasp of the concepts. The AD initiative enabled 'a more nuanced view of the kinds of difficulties students confront when engaged in synthesizing different forms of science-based knowledge' (Tadie *et al.*, 2018, p. 1048).

AD Case study A2: Learning in programming classes

Finding 2: Working with logic-based technologies entails iterative, diametrical code shifting between the situation (with all its possibilities) and the doctrinal rules of a selected approach.

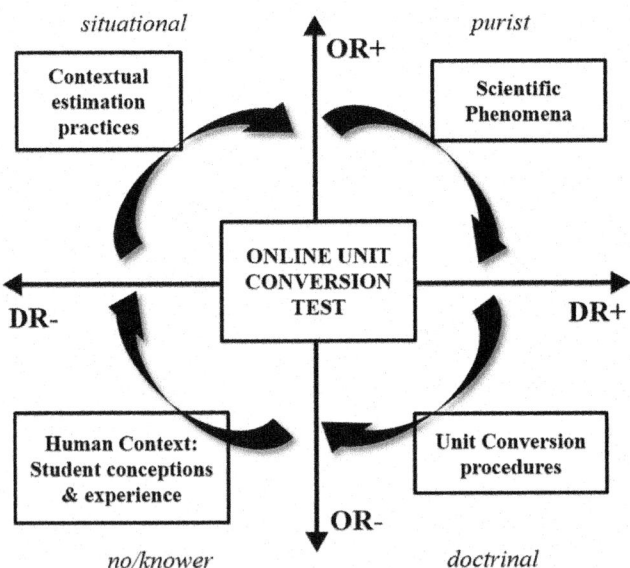

FIGURE 11.4 Group A1 Unit conversion code shifting.

The iterative diagonal code-shifting pattern between the *situational* and *doctrinal* insights is the most common pattern across all the successful engineering problem-solving case studies involving computer-based technologies. And yet, it is the primary complaint among employers and educators: the inability to move from fixed to open-ended approaches.

A2 Programming learning challenges

Lecturer A2 teaches programming to all engineering first-year students (±1000). The problem for students was that the handwritten programming assessments resulted in delayed feedback and an enormous workload for teaching assistants. For the lecturer, this form of initial logic-based learning was ineffective, as it emerged in later stages of the qualification as a consistent inability to adapt to new programming challenges and platforms. Lecturer A2 had already introduced a Moodle® extension called *CodeRunner*® to ease the marking workload and to provide students with immediate feedback. He was interested in understanding why this was proving effective, and the industrial case study helped to confirm the importance of iterative code-shifting practice.

Using the epistemic plane (Figure 11.5), he could analyse the benefits of the automated programming teaching tool. The *CodeRunner*® system itself is located in the situational quadrant in that it is able to handle a number of programming languages and enables teachers to set a range of question types, from 'write a function' to 'write a program' (Lobb and Harlow, 2016). Writing a specific function enables

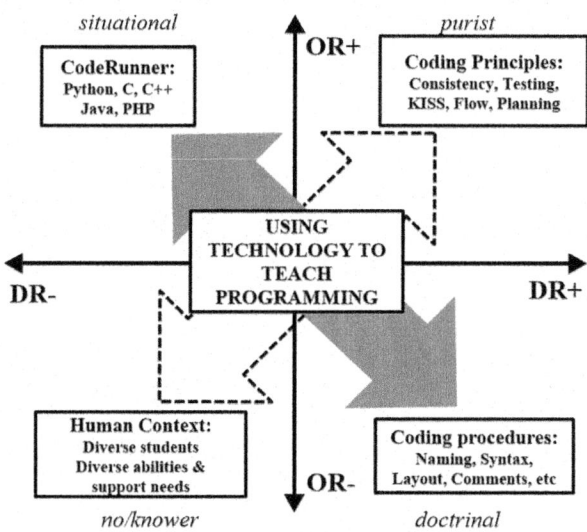

FIGURE 11.5 Lecturer A2 supporting Programming learning using the epistemic plane

Source: Wolff, 2017

students to practice accuracy in the doctrinal quadrant, but writing a whole programme shifts their thinking into the situational quadrant. This iterative move, furthermore, develops their understanding of key programming principles (purist) such as consistency and simplicity.

A further benefit was that a 'learner-centred' approach (students working independently and at their own pace) is particularly important in contexts where students have significantly different degrees of familiarity with computers prior to entry into the HE system.

AD Case study B1: Assessing mathematical code shifting

> Finding 3: Mathematics references occur in all insight quadrants and represent different mathematical languages.

The sonic log technician draws on mathematics in several different ways: the simple arithmetic required to measure time and activities; the algebra of different kinds of functions to relate voltage signals to time; the Calculus to determine rates of change in the voltage or sonar signals; the geometric representation of the signals as having magnitude and direction; the 'logic-based' topology of the system as a whole. Each of these forms of mathematics underpins the different code-shifting stages across the *epistemic plane*.

Mathematics teaching, learning and assessment challenges

Lecturer B1 at the university of technology teaches the 3rd and final mathematics course in a mechanical engineering diploma programme. Mathematics is the single largest cause of attrition in engineering programmes (Bernold *et al.*, 2007). Having spent a number of one-to-one AD sessions interrogating her context and familiarizing herself with the industrial case studies, she initiated a competitive group assessment task designed to 'stretch' her students' thinking:

> The following differential equation describes a unique structure found on the premises of our department. [Equation]. Using your knowledge of Strength of Materials and Mathematics, identify the structure and its precise location.

Her knowledge of the Unit Conversions challenge (A1 case study) led her to enrich the task by explicitly building in unit conversion opportunities for students:

> given that the structure carries a point load (at $x = L$) of 44 imperial gallons of fluid that has a density of $895 \, kg/m^3$.

Lecturer B1 expected the students to start with what they knew. In this task, the known lay in the clue: a 'fluid' that has a certain density and a load of 44 imperial gallons (purist). The first step would be to consult density tables (on the Internet) and find that hydraulic fluid matches the given density most accurately (doctrinal).

The second step would be to convert the gallons to litres (roughly 200 litres) and then 'imagine' how large that might be. Knowing the rough size and type of fluid should lead them to considering the environment (situational). Where might they find hydraulic fluid at their department? On locating the actual 'drum', they could identify the supporting structure which the differential equation described.

Her epistemic plane mapping of the task intention (Figure 11.6) and observation of student behaviour enabled her to determine which students had challenges in which particular 'codes' or insights. Some did not convert from imperial to metric (the system we use in South Africa) and so assumed they were looking for a smaller structure. Others started to work directly with the equation (doctrinal). Several students, however, had a clearly 'situational' orientation and left the classroom to see if they could find the mystery structure, following the 'fluid' clue.

Student feedback on the exercise revealed the following:

> I found it fascinating how one simple equation can represent a real structure!
>
> I learnt more about maths and other engineering subjects because it made me do research and be open-minded.

This example is an excellent beginning to enable lecturers to explicitly encourage mathematical code shifting.

Case study B2: Redesigning a holistic curriculum

> Finding 4: All insights play a part in effective problem-solving and need to be explicitly captured in the curriculum.

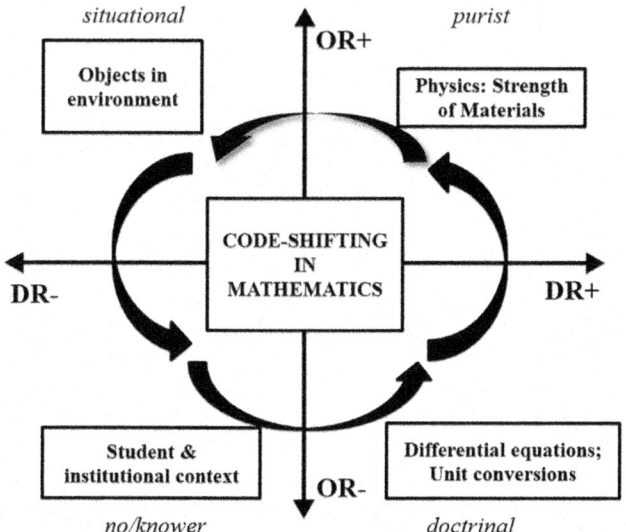

FIGURE 11.6 Lecturer B1 Mathematical code shifting

The sonic log technician case study is but one of 41 in which it has become clear that the different disciplines require different insights and that effective solving problems means code shifting around the epistemic plane.

Industrial engineering curriculum challenges

The university department for this AD case study was under pressure to redesign their technician qualification aligned to 11 standardized exit level outcomes (or graduate attributes). The first AD workshop revealed that they had vastly differing interpretations of the key qualification outcomes. In four sub-groups, staff discussed what kind of insight was most important for each outcome and mapped these onto the epistemic plane. It emerged that the only two outcomes on which all agreed were: 1) that the 'application of engineering principles' entailed all four insights, and 2) that 'knowledge of natural, mathematical and engineering sciences' were seen as purist/doctrinal. The use of appropriate techniques/tools (Outcome 5) was variously regarded as situational, or merely doctrinal, or dependent on the person (knower). Similarly, the ability to 'conduct investigations' (Outcome 4) was situated in all four different insight quadrants. The exercise not only established that each academic is a *knower* in his/her own right with different perspectives on concepts, but also enabled reflection on their students' possible experience: different conceptions of what they are learning with academics assuming that the terms and concepts are standard. The divergence in their interpretations led to critical engagement with what the 'insights' really mean for their context and profession. The department found the tool and the industrial case studies so useful that they used the *epistemic plane* as a blank slate to establish the key principles, procedures, possibilities and 'people' relevant to the redesign of their qualification. Figure 11.7 captures a few of the central ideas that have begun to emerge in their work.

A defining moment for me as an AD practitioner was when the department moved well beyond the 'content' to redefine the 'principles' underpinning their new qualification. They agreed, collectively, that *Ubuntu* is a key engineering principle. The word means 'human mutuality' and implies a shared humanity (Mbembe, 2011). This term transcends those captured in the formal qualification specifications, and speaks to the emergence of a shared philosophy, not only in the department, but in our collective endeavour to bring about true transformation in the HE system.

Concluding remarks

An industrial case study exemplar has been used to demonstrate how theoretically informed empirical research can assist engineering educators in understanding the importance of different disciplinary ways of thinking in different contextual knowledge practice sites. Using LCT's *epistemic plane* as a mediating device, staff in different AD contexts were able to interrogate their existing curriculum, teaching, learning and assessment practices. The key finding in the industrial case studies – the significance of code shifting to successfully solve complex socio-technical

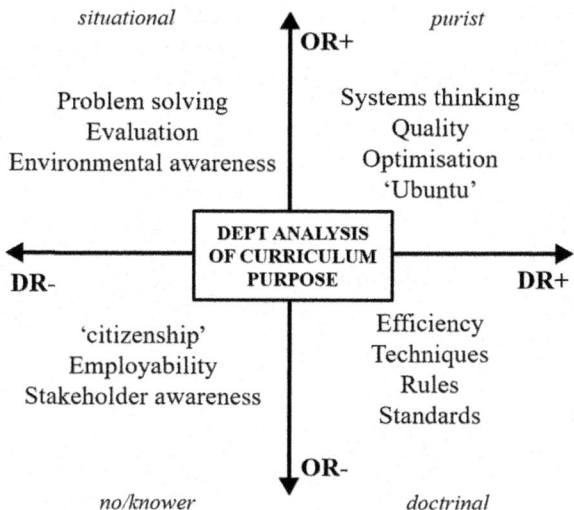

FIGURE 11.7 Group B2 discussion on curriculum purpose

problems – was translated into a range of pedagogic initiatives. These include the redesign of unit conversion teaching to more effectively identify student knowledge gaps (A1); the effective use of a software platform to enable diagonal code shifting between different possibilities and fixed procedures (A2); the stretching of a mathematics assessment task to include open-ended problem-solving (B1); and the redesign of a curriculum (B2) that recognizes how important it is to shift from the right-hand side of the *epistemic plane* into the more open-ended side, which is what employers most value.

Acknowledgement

This research was funded by the South African Department of Higher Education and Training's 'Engineering Education Existing Staff Capacity Enhancement program', with support from the Newton Fund and the Royal Academy of Engineering.

References

Allais, S. (2014). *Selling out education: National qualifications frameworks and the neglect of knowledge*. Rotterdam: Sense.

Auret, L. and Wolff, K. (2018, April). A control system framework for reflective practice: Design-based research applied to process control teaching. In *2018 IEEE Global Engineering Education Conference (EDUCON)* (pp. 100–108). IEEE.

Barnett, M. (2006). Vocational knowledge and vocational pedagogy. In M. Young and J. Gamble (Eds), *Knowledge, curriculum and qualifications for South African further education* (pp. 143–157). Cape Town: HSRC Press.

Bernold, L., Spurlin, J. and Anson, C. (2007). Understanding our students: A longitudinal study of success and failure in engineering with implications for increased retention. *Journal of Engineering Education, 96*(3), 263–274.

Bernstein, B. (1977). *Class, codes and control, Volume III: Towards a theory of educational transmissions*. London: Routledge and Kegan Paul.

Bernstein, B. (2000). *Pedagogy, symbolic control and identity: Theory, research, critique*. (Revised ed.). London: Rowman and Littlefield.

Christiansen, F.V. and Rump, C. (2008). Three conceptions of thermodynamics: Technical matrices in science and engineering. *Research in Science Education, 38*(5), 545–564.

Chuchalin, A., Tayurskaya, M. and Malmqvist, J. (2015). Faculty development programme based on CDIO framework. Interactive Collaborative Learning (ICL), 2015 International Conference. IEEE, 441–447.

Council on Higher Education (CHE). (2015). *Vital Stats Public Higher Education 2013*. Pretoria: Council on Higher Education.

Feisel, L. and Rosa, A. (2005). The role of the laboratory in undergraduate engineering education. *Journal of Engineering Education, 94*(1), 121–130.

Felder, R. (2012). Engineering education: A tale of two paradigms. In, B. McCabe, M. Pantazidou and D. Phillips (Eds), *Shaking the foundations of Geo-Engineering education* (pp. 9–14). Leiden: CRC Press. Retrieved from www.engr.ncsu.edu/wp-content/uploads/drive/196QvnYsMz9QawFvoJwRfed8nXFGeVt7G/2012-TwoParadigms.pdf.

Felder, R.M, Brent, R. and Prince, M.J. (2011). Engineering instructional development: Programs, best practices, and recommendations. *Journal of Engineering Education, 100*(1), 89–122.

Froyd, J., Layne, J., Fowler, D. and Simpson, N. (2007). Design patterns for faculty development. Milwaukee: 37th ASEE/IEEE Frontiers in Education Conference.

Griesel, H. and Parker, B. (2009). *Graduate attributes: A baseline study on South African graduates from the perspective of employers*. Pretoria: Higher Education South Africa.

IEA. (2013). Graduate Attributes and Professional Competency Profiles. International Engineering Alliance. Retrieved from www.ieagreements.org.

Leibowitz, B., Bozalek, V., Garraway, J., Herman, N., Jawitz, J., Muhuro, P., Ndebele, C., Quinn, L., van Schalkwyk, S., Vorster, J-A. and Winberg, C. 2017. *Learning to teach in Higher Education in South Africa: An investigation into the influences of institutional context on the professional learning of academics in their roles as teachers*. HE Monitor No. 14, April 2017. Pretoria: South Africa: South African Council on Higher Education.

Lobb, R. and Harlow, J. (2016). Coderunner: A tool for assessing computer programming skills. *ACM Inroads, 71*(1), 47–51.

manpowergroup.com. (2015). *Talent Shortage Survey*. USA: The Manpower Group.

Maton, K. (2014). *Knowledge and knowers: Towards a realist sociology of education*. London: Routledge.

Maton, K. (2016). Legitimation Code Theory: Building knowledge about knowledge-building. In K. Maton, S. Hood and S. Shay (Eds), *Knowledge-building: Educational studies in Legitimation Code Theory* (pp. 1–24). London: Routledge.

Maton, K. (2020). Semantic waves: Context, complexity and academic discourse. In J.R. Martin, K. Maton and Y.J. Doran (Eds), *Accessing academic discourse: Systemic functional linguistics and Legitimation Code Theory* (pp. 59–85). London: Routledge.

Maton, K. and Howard, S.K. (2018). Taking autonomy tours: A key to integrative knowledge-building, *LCT Centre Occasional Paper 1*: 1–35.

Mbembe, A. (2011). Democracy as a community of life. In J. De Gruchy (Ed.), *The humanist imperative in South Africa* (pp. 187–194). Stellenbosch: SUN Press.

Mutereko, S. and Wedekind, V. (2016). Work integrated learning for engineering qualifications: A spanner in the works? *Journal of Education and Work, 29*(8), 902–921.

Porter, A. and Roessner, D. (2006). A systems model of innovation processes in university STEM education. *Journal of Management and Social Sciences, 2*(2), 154–170.

Shay, S., Wolff, K. and Clarence-Fincham, J. (2016). Curriculum reform in South Africa: More time for what? *Critical Studies in Teaching and Learning 4*(1), 74–88.

Sobek, D.K. and Jain, V.K. (2004). The engineering problem-solving process: good for students? In *Proceedings of the 2004 American Society for Engineering Education Annual Conference & Exposition*. 20–23 June 2004, Salt Lake City, Utah, 9.1256, pp 1–15.

Tadie, M., Pott, R., Goosen, N., Van Wyk, P. and Wolff, K.E. (2018, April). Expanding 1st year problem-solving skills through unit conversions and estimations. In *2018 IEEE Global Engineering Education Conference (EDUCON)* (pp. 1035–1043). Santa Cruz de Tenerife: IEEE.

UNESCO. (2010). *Engineering: Issues, challenges and opportunities for development.* Paris: UNESCO.

Wheelahan, L. (2009). The problem with CBT (and why constructivism makes things worse). *Journal of Education and Work, 22*(3), 227–242.

Winberg, C. (2005). Continuities and discontinuities in the journey from technikon to university of technology. *South African Journal of Higher Education, 19*(2), 189–200.

Winberg, C., Engel-Hills, P., Garraway, J. and Jacobs, C. (2013). Professionally-oriented knowledge and the purpose of professionally-oriented Higher Education. In Council on Higher Education, *The aims of Higher Education – Kagiso 9* (pp. 98–119). Pretoria: South African Council on Higher Education.

Winberg, C., Adendorff, H., Bozalek, V., Conana, H., Pallitt, N., Wolff, K., Olsson, T. and Roxå, T. (2019). Learning to teach the STEM disciplines in higher education: A critical review of the literature. *Teaching in Higher Education, 24*(8), 930–947.

Wolff, K. (2018). Theory and practice in the 21st century engineering workplace. In S. Allais and Y. Shalem (Eds), *Knowledge, curriculum and preparation for work* (pp. 182–205). London: Sense.

12
BUILDING THE KNOWLEDGE BASE OF BLENDED LEARNING

Implications for educational technology and academic development

J.P. Bosman and Sonja Strydom

Introduction

Our approach and interest in the topic is guided by an attempt to contribute to the knowledge-building of blended learning in the diverse higher education (HE) contexts in South Africa. To gain insight into the relevance of technology-enhanced teaching and learning practices in HE provided the rationale for the study. We are furthermore interested in the impact such practices and insights have on academic development (AD) practices since it is increasingly expected of academic developers to gain additional insights and knowledge in the field of educational technology, which includes knowledge of blended learning as a pedagogical approach.

The field of educational technology in higher education: setting the scene

Our AD work is situated in the field of educational technology which is viewed as a young and emerging field. In general, optimism and beliefs in the transformative potential of educational technologies are evident in the literature. However, the field is also challenged by: (a) limited theory development, especially in terms of the connection between Information Communication Technologies (ICTs) and disciplinary knowledge practices (Czerniewicz and Brown, 2007; Maton and Howard, 2016; Oliver, 2013); (b) a need to further a variety of methodological approaches and philosophical perspectives at a scholarly level (Bulfin et al., 2014; Surry and Baker, 2016); (c) knowledge-blindness where limited attempts are made to explore the knowledge practices within the field (Howard and Maton, 2011; Maton, 2014); and (d) mapping the field and terrain of educational technology (Czerniewicz, 2008, 2010; Rushby and Surry, 2016).

One of the main elements that complicates the field of educational technology is the tendency to place emphasis on applied elements, which results in limited development of theory (Hannon and Al-Mahmood, 2014). Very often, the field is mirroring so-called 'common-sense assumptions' which are mainly focused on design, implementation and evaluation (Jones and Czerniewicz, 2017), inevitably resulting in approaches that emphasize a false dichotomy (Jackson, 2014) whereby either knowing *or* knowers are investigated (Howard and Maton, 2011), rather than both.

From an agentic perspective, academics, instructional designers and academic developers experience the emergence of the field at different levels. For instance, it is expected of academics to adhere to the needs of the twenty-first century workforce and participate in the development of student graduate attributes in their respective curricula. Technology, in its many forms and functions, is expected to remain one of the key elements in the development of student skills in the twenty-first century. Mapped against such a background, including contextual institutional and societal needs and the individual needs of academics, the involvement and work of the instructional designer and academic developer becomes more complex and multi-faceted. For instance, AD requires knowledge and understanding of theory, praxis, structure and agency to fully engage in the evolving field of educational technology. From an AD perspective, those involved in curriculum development and design, teaching and learning and other HE-related issues no longer have the luxury of avoiding technology and knowledge thereof. This work therefore asks of teaching and learning specialists to become knowledgeable about a variety of technology-related aspects such as a general understanding of theory underpinning technology-integration in the curriculum, a working knowledge of different approaches and tools to be considered for teaching and learning, and a critical awareness of the potential and pitfalls associated with such interventions. Despite these epistemological challenges within the educational technology field, the integration of technology into the HE curriculum remains active and is gaining global momentum.

Educational technology in South Africa: a voice from the South

In recent years, the majority of HE institutions in the West have invested heavily in educational technology in terms of infrastructure and support (Price and Kirkwood, 2014). This process is also gaining momentum in the South (e.g. South Africa) where the potential of such technologies is perceived in terms of addressing particular educational demands such as large student cohorts, unsatisfactory curriculum design, multilingual issues for non-native speakers and ill-preparedness of students for the academic expectancies of higher education (Jaffer, Ng'ambi and Czerniewicz, 2007). Furthermore, it has been argued that the integration of technology into the curriculum could further assist in the alignment of workplace needs and preparing students to develop twenty-first century skills (i.e. the ability to respond to continuous changes in the workplace) (Bozalek *et al.*, 2013). In addition, the #feesmustfall movement in South Africa that led to student protests and teaching disturbances in 2015 and 2016 contributed to many HE institutions considering blended and/or online approaches to assist students in their preparation for assessments and examinations. These approaches enabled many students and lecturers to remain in contact despite not having face-to-face contact. Many of above-mentioned reasons are of course not unique to HE institutions in the South, but form part of a global need to prepare students for rapid changes in modern society.

Thus, it is expected that technology-enhanced learning, and blended learning specifically, has the potential to address a number of real issues and challenges within HE institutions. But this requires a carefully constructed process of re-evaluating and redesigning the curriculum to address such context-specific and challenges (Bozalek *et al.*, 2013).

An institutional blended learning short course: an overview

In terms of this particular case study at our university, the sustainable integration of educational technologies to potentially assist in richness and reach (i.e. enriching the learning experience of students and attempting to reach more students) was enhanced by one of the institution's strategic outcomes that emphasized continuous programme renewal. At a broader strategic level, these expectations and priorities relate to the potential of information communication technologies (ICTs) in HE to contribute and promote change (Czerniewicz *et al.*, 2006).

We find that academics often struggle to see the transformative potential of technology-enhanced pedagogies and choose to maintain traditional approaches and pedagogies (Salmon, 2005) through integrating by means of substitution or mirroring existing face-to-face practices in an online mode (Kirkwood and Price, 2013). Due to this reality, and the complex nature of learning technologies and their affordances, we are very aware that academics and instructional designers (including academic developers) inevitably tend to focus more on the tools and technology instead of pedagogy (Salmon, 2005). A further complexity remains in the notion of e-pedagogy, the difficulties in meaning making and understanding this relatively young and emerging field (Sharpe *et al.*, 2006). Based on this, we decided to develop a professional development short course for academic lecturers in an attempt to address some of these challenges and to introduce them to the theory and praxis of blended learning. In addition, we wanted to model a transformative pedagogical approach while introducing lecturers to the theory and practices of blended learning.

A number of factors and pointers were at play during our conceptualization of the short course. Firstly, we were aware of the notion and role of blended learning within the broader educational technology field. We realized that many fields within HE are at play when considering a blended approach. These include the role and function of IT systems, the emerging field of educational technology, teaching and learning, AD, design approaches, information science and so forth. To accommodate or at least acknowledge and translate the influence of all these interrelated aspects in a meaningful way within one short course, was an exciting yet challenging opportunity.

We wanted lecturers to experience and understand the notion of blended learning at a theoretical and practical level. Over an eight-week period participants firstly participated in a face-to-face session where the theoretical underpinnings of blended learning were introduced and explored. This first workshop drew on a number of theoretical approaches to assist in knowledge development of the notion of blended learning. The work of Gilly Salmon (2013) related to curriculum design, e-tivities and curriculum-mapping provided academics with a broad framework within which they could start to explore approaches of technology integration into the curriculum. The Conversational Framework of Diana Laurillard (2012) also contributed to a theoretical but practical process of starting to integrate technologies into learning activities. This session also served the purpose of participants getting to know each other and familiarizing themselves with the online approaches and platform. This was followed by a four-week fully online experience where academics were introduced to topics such as online videos, iSpring, the Google suite and e-assessment. A final face-to-face workshop concluded the course where participants had the opportunity to reflect on their learning experiences and to receive support with their written capstone assignment.

While we conceptualized and designed the course, we attempted to model a blended approach by means of the structure of the course, but equally also in terms of what was expected of facilitators and participants (students) during such a mode of delivery. Another important aspect for us was to attempt to weave between the abstract and the practical during the duration of the course.

Based on learning design principles, we used a standard format for all online sessions and encouraged the use of different online tools, approaches and the development of an online community of practice. Each week participants had to engage with theoretical principles and frameworks associated with the weekly topic, but they also had to produce an online artefact to encourage practical engagement with such tools and approaches. The capstone assignment required participants to integrate any aspect of new knowledge they had acquired during the course into a proposal to their head of department for introducing blended learning into a specific faculty-related module or programme.

Uncovering knowledge and knower practices in the course

It was during our engagement with this course that we became increasingly aware of the need to interrogate knowledge and knower practices across our field of educational technology (Maton, 2014). Related to our short course, we as facilitators (i.e. academic developers) were interested in the manner in which we approach the introduction of blended learning theory and practice, the languages of legitimation we employ, as well as strategies we value in our attempts to legitimize the organizing principles of our field.

By drawing on the dimension of Specialization (Maton, 2014), we could acknowledge that our practices were oriented towards specifically something and were enacted by someone. In short, the way we presented and facilitated the short course was oriented towards *epistemic relations* (between knowledge and its objects of study) and *social relations* (between knowledge and its subjects). By interrogating this, we were able to identify and explore what we as facilitators legitimize as knowledge (*epistemic relations*) and who can be viewed as legitimate knowers (*social relations*). With the aid of the specialization plane, the differences between legitimized knowledge and knowers can be examined through four principal specialization codes.

As detailed in Maton (2014, 2016) the *specialization plane* (Figure 12.1) includes four main codes:

- *knowledge codes* (ER+, SR−), where possession of specialized knowledge, principles or procedures concerning the practice of blended learning is emphasized as the basis of achievement, and the attributes of blended learning practitioners are downplayed;
- *knower codes* (ER−, SR+), where specialized knowledge of blended learning practices and theory are downplayed and the attributes of blended learning practitioners are emphasized as measures of achievement;
- *élite codes* (ER+, SR+), where legitimacy is based on both possessing specialist knowledge of blended learning practice and being the right kind of blended learning knower; and
- *relativist codes* (ER−, SR−), where legitimacy is determined by neither specialist knowledge of blended learning practice nor knower attributes – 'anything goes'.

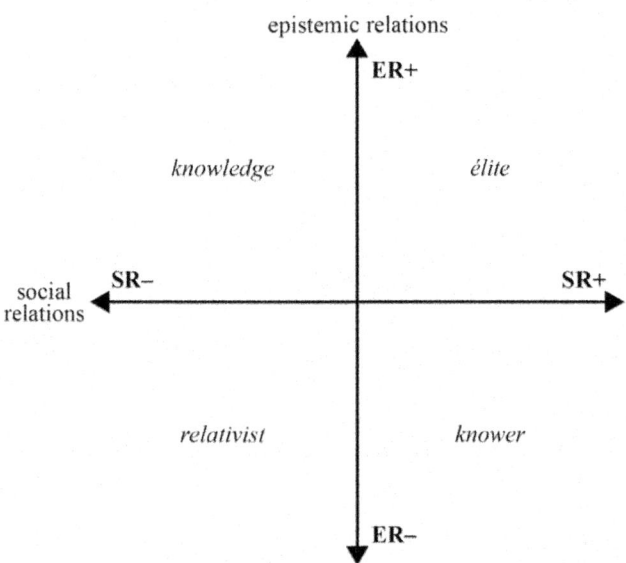

FIGURE 12.1 The specialization plane

Source: Maton, 2014, p. 30

Being guided by the four codes of the Specialization dimension, we were able to identify the aspects we as facilitators legitimized throughout the short course while introducing academics to new knowledge related to blended learning.

The knowledge base of blended learning

To understand the relevance and use of blended learning as a specific pedagogical approach within the educational technology field we decided to ask two core questions, namely 'What is the knowledge base of blended learning?' and 'How does it speak to the field of educational technology?' In this section, we look at the first question regarding the knowledge base of blended learning. We report how we made the invisible knowledge principles of blended learning visible by showing how we: (a) analysed the data in terms of emerging themes that indicate stronger and weaker epistemic relations and social relations; (b) developed what is known in LCT as a 'translation device' that serves as a 'bridge' between theory and data; and (c) then mapped the blended learning specialization codes on the specialization plane to highlight the knowledge base valorized by the facilitators in the course.

Thematic analysis of the data according to stronger or weaker ER and SR

The data represented the anonymized transcriptions of audio recordings of two full days of teaching during face-to-face workshops as part of the Blended Learning Short Course. It also included facilitator posts on the discussion forums in the course on the learning management system. Only the facilitators' 'voices' or posts are analysed here.

Inductive thematic analysis was used to identify the broad concepts of *epistemic relations* (ER) and *social relations* (SR) as a lens. The following broad concepts were identified through an iterative movement between the data and the lens and then clustered according to ER affinities (possession of specialized knowledge, skills, procedures) or SR affinities (disposition of the knower, including natural talent), as seen in Table 12.1.

Blended learning: external language of description and translation device

To be able to develop a translation device for blended learning we first needed to build an 'external language of description'. 'Internal languages of description' relate to theoretical concepts and how they are linked or interrelated (Maton, 2014, p. 27). 'External languages of description' show how such theoretical concepts relate to referents beyond the theory employed. A translation device helps to engage with data and to 'translate' the interplay between theory and data, highlighting the relation between theory and data (see Maton and Chen, 2016; Maton and Howard, 2016). The purpose of a translation device is to assist in the analysis of the research

TABLE 12.1 Broad themes/concepts from the data with ER or SR affinities

Epistemic relations affinity concepts	Social relations affinity concepts
Theoretical concepts: The focus is on theoretical concepts and frameworks from the fields of blended learning, teaching and learning (pedagogy) or design.	**Expert others:** Reference is made to the importance of blended learning knowers like course facilitators, seminal researchers and blended learning academic developers.
Educational technology: The focus is on different kinds of educational technology and how they are applied to blended learning.	**Peers:** The role of other academics engaged with technology and blended learning practitioners and how they can further participants' knowledge about blended learning is foregrounded.
Knowledge building: Any reference to the importance of knowledge in different fields and discipline and how that relates to blended learning.	**Individual disposition:** The individual blended learning practitioner's dispositions and "feel" for blended learning and their willingness to innovate, change and to try new approaches are emphasized.
Pedagogical practices: References to specific blended learning practices which include processes around and application of blended learning.	**Students:** The role that students' needs and perspectives play in practicing blended learning is mentioned. The students are implied as legitimate knowers in the sense that their potential insights into blended learning (e.g. around the use of specific technologies) are acknowledged.
Scholarly approach: Emphasis is placed on the importance of a scholarly approach to blended learning which can include reflecting on your own innovation up to research in the field of blended learning.	N/A
Context and culture: The influence of the practitioner's academic environment (in terms of a supporting or innovative culture of "doing things") as well as the broader institutional context on how blended learning is practiced is emphasized.	N/A

problem – in this case, uncovering the underlying knowledge base of blended learning. This enabled us to relate the LCT dimension of Specialization to an analysis of our practice of teaching blended learning. For Specialization, it is important to describe what we mean by epistemic relations (ER) and social relations (SR) in terms of blended learning. Table 12.2 and Table 12.3 show how the broad concepts identified from the thematic analysis can be used to create an external language of description with indicators of stronger or weaker epistemic relations (Table 12.2) and social relations (Table 12.3) in the data.

In this way, we are able to use how we introduce and conceptualize blended learning (concepts) to 'explore the organizing principles' of the knowledge base underlying our practice of Blended Learning (Maton, 2016, p. 7). To simplify it for other practitioners one could say that for discovering *epistemic relations* one needs to see how much one focuses on the specialized knowledge which includes specialized concepts from the fields of educational technology, teaching and learning, as well as design. A focus on and sensitivity to knowledge (and other knowledge domains), specialized knowledge practices around the use of educational technologies and how to apply them in practice in a specific context and with a scholarly approach are other indicators for stronger epistemic relations. As to *social relations* one could look at how strongly the importance of peers, other knowers (like experts, teachers and support staff), own disposition towards educational technology as well as the influence of students come to the fore when analyzing one's own practice.

Uncovering the legitimizing epistemic relations and social relations, conceptualized as specialization codes enabled us to create a translation device for blended learning knowledge as part of the educational technology field. In Table 12.4 the translation device for blended learning is put forward with exemplary quotes from the data.

The next questions are in which plane the knowledge base (of the facilitators) mostly resides, how the knowledge base moves between the quadrants of the plane, and if there is a difference in the different teachers' ('voices') *basis* for their practice (i.e. the way blended learning knowledge is legitimized or valorized). Here code matches and clashes are important indicators for the way a team of teachers might represent a more coherent and flowing (i.e. more code matches) or a more fragmented (i.e. more code clashes) process of knowledge building. It of course also points to what each of these teachers valorize individually.

Blended learning: specialization plane

Blended learning's knowledge base inhabits and traverses all the codes, i.e. *knowledge codes* (ER+, SR−), *knower codes* (ER−, SR+), *élite codes* (ER+, SR+) and *relativist codes* (ER−, SR−). To do the Specialization analysis we looked at the data in terms of stronger or weaker ER and SR and coded according to what a specific quotation represented in terms of a specialization code. The following table (Table 12.5) provides examples from the data and how it was interpreted in terms of the

TABLE 12.2 External language of description for epistemic relations

Epistemic relations (ER)			
Concept manifested as		Indicators	Example quote
Theoretical concepts	ER+	Knowledge of/learning about blended learning, T&L and design theoretical frameworks and concepts	This is where it all comes together because we have our theory of learning. We know now that we have to design something. We've looked at pedagogy, we have the TPAC … you know content knowledge, technology knowledge, pedagogical [unclear] knowledge have somehow come together (1:169)
	ER−	Downplaying the importance of theoretical concepts and frameworks regarding blended learning, T&L and design	I'm not asking for the deep, philosophical discussions but because the assignment does have an aspect of thinking theoretically about blended teaching and learning, there might be one or two questions that you are really pondering over and wondering about the theory (1:245)
Educational technology	ER+	Focus on specialized knowledge of different educational technologies, their affordances and applications	The idea was to there, write the second 55-word story on your blog. But be it as it may, you all engaged there and articulated something, integrated the tool with your own thoughts (1:291)
	ER−	Valorizing the use of educational technology without a clear sense of the affordances and how it relates to the practice of blended learning (using EdTech because of "hype")	This is one of the great features of Google docs. You don't need an account to access it. You only need an account when you want to create a new document. Thus, if you want someone to edit, comment on or simply view a document that is in your Google drive you simply share the direct link from the doc with them (2:15)
Knowledge building	ER+	Expertise in knowledge building and knowledge domains like other disciplines and how it is integrated in understanding blended learning is legitimized	You are touching on the 'blend' necessary to consider learning technologies: enhancing your own knowledge domains with careful consideration of the affordances of each tool available (2:5)
	ER−	The influence of different knowledge domains and disciplines on the way blended learning is practiced is downplayed or is absent	we have a more of a holistic experience in terms of programmme renewal. But for the purpose of our course, we are focusing predominantly on what we call e-tivities, e-learning activities, if you like, in the sense (1:57)

Practices	ER+	Knowledge of very specific skills in integrating blended learning concepts in educational practice (includes specialized skills of using educational technology) are emphasized	as a Psychology Lecturer, I want to teach Behaviorism and I want to use the Discussion Forum. So I know how to create the discussion Forum and I know about the content about behaviorism and how do I integrate the two that it makes sense? (1:120)
	ER−	blended learning Practices are relativized or brushed over or seen as taken for granted – seen as saving time or being more effective	this notion of working smarter, saving resources, more free time, lecturers can free up time, express myself more clearly, I think is an interesting one that has come out from particular group and one that we will definitely be revisiting throughout the course (1:44)
Scholarly approach	ER+	Knowledge about or valorizing the importance of research in blended learning	that is where your research aspect can come in as well and also, what they argue there and what they highlight is that one then obviously, you need to reflect on that as well (1:209)
	ER−	Downplaying scholarly approaches or focusing on "just doing" blended learning	This assignment, we have tried to make as useful to your practice as possible. It mustn't be something that you do on a theoretical level and then file it somewhere and say, "okay, I got a certificate and that's it." It must be something that you can use in your practice (1:330)
Context and culture	ER+	A focus on how theories and frameworks of institutional and contextual culture can affect blended learning practice	in your particular context, what are the things or aspects that need to be in place in order for successful blended learning integration to take place, whether it is at the modular level, the programme level or whatever the case might be (1:96)
	ER−	The institutional and academic environment of the blended learning practitioner is deemed as having an impact on blended learning practice (like workload)	I think the workload thing is a touchy subject, is the fact that it takes time to create these things. (1:282)

TABLE 12.3 External language of description for social relations

Social relations (SR)

Concept	manifested as	Indicators	Example quote
Expert others	SR+	Expert scholars', Facilitators' and BLCs' BL knowledge, skills, practices and support deemed important for learning about and doing BL	the coordinators are really your best friend when it comes to blended learning in your faculty. So, it makes sense that they are here today because that is how we get things done is we work together in teams (1:238)
	SR−	The role of expert others as legitimate knowers of BL is downplayed or absent	So we've got the – we've got Morton's Alignment. It might that you argue that you know, in terms of a lesson plan it makes much more sense for me to triple align it. But it might be that I say, you know what, I'm going to start small and I'm going to use Twitter for the first time (1:212)
Peers	SR+	Engagement with and searching out knowledge of/support from peers (course cohort/alumni/other perceived BL knowers) with regards to BL	we have a nice range from all the faculties and from the Postgraduate Development Unit this time round that we can, we can learn a lot from each other (1:23)
	SR−	Downplaying the role of peers as legitimate BL knowers or focusing on experts or individuality	There isn't anyone who is working with the exact same students all the time as the next person. You know, unless the two of you are standing in front of the same class, giving the same lecture you know, speaking in tandem, you all have different contexts and your students have different needs. (1:268)
Individual disposition	SR+	Individual disposition (feelings, "feel for", critical reflection, choices, context) foregrounded as important for developing BL practices	our pedagogical approach and that comes back to our own teaching and learning philosophies, the way in which we engage with our students; the way in which we transfer knowledge; the way in which we share knowledge. So, it's perhaps a very personal thing, our lecturers on pedagogical approaches in a sense (1:197)
	SR−	Individual disposition as important to becoming a BL knower is downplayed – "anyone can do it"	at the end of this there will be at least one thing that you have discovered about your context and about the way that you do things that will be different and you know if you've learnt one new thing within the course, then we are happy (1:20)
Students	SR+	Students' needs and perspectives are taken into account with regards to BL – students are accepted as legitimate BL knowers	we speak about what is the purpose, what is the point of this? What is the need that I'm meeting [unclear] for my students, the learning needs? (1:262)
	SR−	Students' needs and perspectives are relativized or negated in terms of blended learning	start the students on peer assessment from early on so that they can get used to marking before they get to the 4th year (2:21)

TABLE 12.4 Blended learning: Translation device for specialization codes (ER+/−, SR+/−)

Specialization code	Indicators	Example quote from data
knowledge code (ER+, SR−)	Specialized knowledge of blended learning related concepts, skills and procedures are emphasized and the disposition and attributes of blended learning practitioners are downplayed.	we need to understand one more thing and this is a thing that's quite unique or has become unique to the field of educational technology or learning technology and this is the concept of affordance (1:170)
knower code (ER−, SR+)	Blended learning knower disposition in relationship to other actors are foregrounded and blended learning knowledge, skills and practices are downplayed.	By networking and looking at each other, we're also going to learn a lot and there's lots of experience already in the room (1:27)
élite code (ER+, SR+)	Blended learning practice comprises a blend of blended learning knowledge and a blended learning knower disposition.	But I think we are connecting it now back to the language that we've now learnt, which I think is powerful. There's all the colleagues in the faculties, the blended learning support, colleagues, they are using this concept, these ideas. You are living in that place so we can talk together and we can get somewhere (1:180)
relativist code (ER−, SR−)	A downplaying of both blended learning knowledge, skills and practices and knower dispositions – usually when educational technology (on its own) is foregrounded or valorized.	with SUNlearn [the Moodle based learning management system], this is called a book in SUNlearn. It's like an e-book or in text form if you like. And we actually quite want to use this rather than word documents or PowerPoints. So, you can actually create a nice online textbook if you like (1:50)

TABLE 12.5 Quotes from the data that show examples of each of the four specialization codes

Quotation	ER	SR	Specialization code
we have the teaching and learning knowledge, theory of learning, the theory of teaching and learning that we have a basic understanding of that (1:117)	1	−1	knowledge code
So that's where you can discuss then with people from previous courses as well and get ideas from them too (1:22)	−1	1	knower code
we'll be working on the Learning Designer, which JP introduced at the first workshop and this is where you will be working closely with the coordinators that are here. They have worked with the Learning Designer with other lecturers and on their own and they can assist then in helping you plan how you're going to use it, what you're going to do on the Learning Designer and you're going to start actually designing a module or a theme within your course (1:241)	1	1	élite code
The tool we are using is called Socrative.... It's free so I've signed up then I created quizzes. You can go to quizzes that you can send your students to. But for this pedagogy that I've designed or cwhose, we are going to participate in a race (1:162)	−1	−1	relativist code

BL external language of description to get to the specialization code. For stronger epistemic relations (ER+) or social relations (SR+) we assigned a 1 and for a weaker epistemic relations (ER−) and social relations (SR−) we assigned a − 1.

After coding all the data we calculated the average percentages of each of the specialization codes to be able to map them on the quadrants (knowledge, knower, elite, relativist). Analysis of the data using the blended learning translation device demonstrated that when the three most prominent voices in the course were analysed as a whole, knowledge codes were the strongest basis for teaching blended learning, followed by relativist codes, knower codes and slight references to élite codes. Table 12.6 shows the percentages for all the data.

Having these percentages made it possible to map the knowledge base of blended learning in terms of our practice demonstrated in the facilitation of the short course on the specialization plane. Figure 12.2 shows the mapping and indicates that in terms of all the facilitators' teaching on the course, the knowledge base of blended learning lies spread across the knowledge and relativist code quadrants.

TABLE 12.6 Percentages of the different specialization codes in terms of facilitator voices

Élite code	knower code	relativist code	knowledge code
8,5	16,0	30,5	45,0

Building blended learning **211**

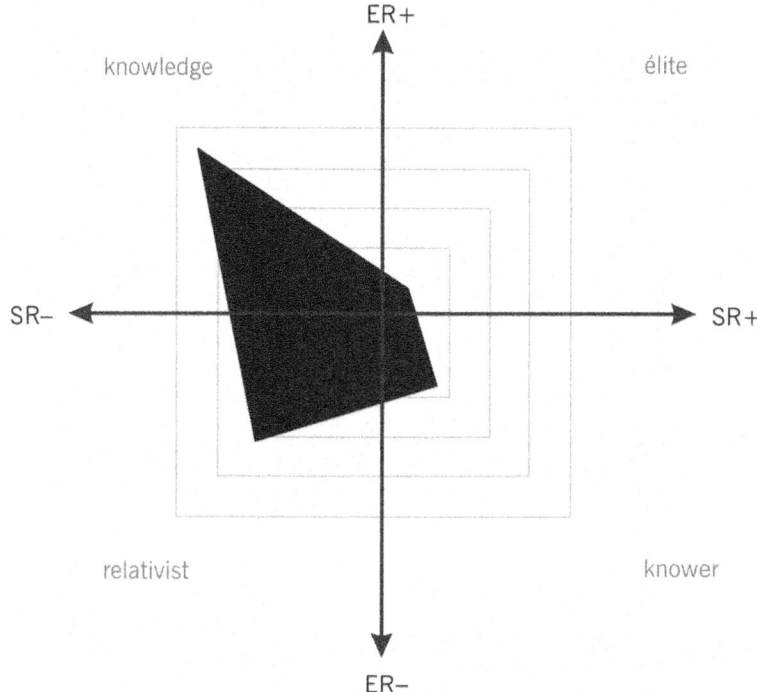

FIGURE 12.2 All voices: The specialization plane for the knowledge base of blended learning from the perspective of all teachers' voices analysed as a unit

When analysed separately, the three main teaching voices (A, B and C; see Figure 12.3) highlighted similarities but also some differences. The similarities are that all three voices inhabit all areas of the specialization plane in their references about the knowledge base of blended learning. Voice A and C are almost similar in profile, placed in the knowledge domain, while Voice B is different in that the relativist and knower domain are inhabited more.

Examples from the data of the different voices are represented in Table 12.7.

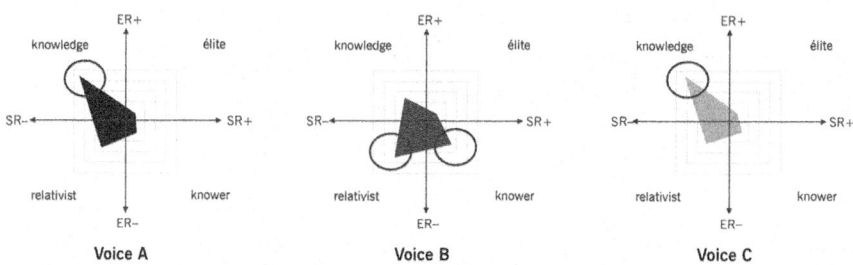

FIGURE 12.3 Voice A, B and C: Specialization planes for the knowledge base of blended learning when analyzed separately for three main teaching voices

TABLE 12.7 Examples from the data indicating the code matches and clashes between Voices A, B and C

Voice	Example from the data	Specialization code
Voice A	we want to delve into the concept of blended learning on a conceptual basis (1:48)	knowledge code
	Okay, so I don't know who's registered on the Facebook page for example. That is a very informal, just an interesting space to be and there are some active and less active participants there. But that's an interesting space to join (1:316)	relativist code
Voice B	believe me, it is something that is doable and we've seen it now with over 140 people, 140 lecturers, support staff at the university over the past couple of years. And we've built a nice community (1:7)	knower code
	because the students stay connected with the use of technology but lecturers as well. Is it similar? Us to have more free time. That would be quicker assessment, working smarter, freeing up time. More pleasant learning (1:41)	relativist code
Voice C	Mixing different technologies…. That's very important, so it's focusing on the outcome, outcome is central, learning outcomes are central and then where they are appropriate (1:76)	knowledge code
	when you start to design and especially if it's the first time that you start to integrate these technological tools, I'll suggest that we start to use this … just for once or twice or three times, just to get the feel of that and it will become a habit, something naturally later on as well (1:130)	relativist code

Uncovering this knowledge base of blended learning as it is realized at our institution is fascinating and important as it indicates it is mainly structured as a knowledge field, that is supported by relativist-code, knower-code and even élite-code notions. The fact that all three voices share preferences in terms of specific knowledge structures shows how participants probably have a code-matching experience when learning from these facilitators. Essentially, the focus on knowledge and also how one should teach through 'semantic waves' (Maton, 2013) or weaving (as we see below) is to be expected to a certain extent as the team have been investigating, and specifically trying to use, a focus on knowledge as well as creating 'semantic waves' in the design of the course. Acknowledging this, knowledge could be viewed as the more semantically dense and abstract concepts that are unpacked and made more concrete through less semantically dense, relativist examples, tools, tips and tricks to meaningfully connect it all as a practical knowledge. The presence of a knower focus points to the emphasis in the course on the importance of support from expert blended learning coordinators and the facilitators who are assigned to course participants for support in integrating the knowledge into practice.

The slight code clashes between Voice A and C on the one hand and Voice B on the other could indicate a substantive theoretical difference in the understanding of blended, learning, or it could be that Voice B's teaching topics (as well as where these was taught in the course) were more geared towards the application of the theory (knowledge domain focus) to the practice (relativist) and also how to get help and support in doing this practical knowledge application of blended learning (knower focus).

This analysis shows that blended learning (as encountered and taught at our institution) is a practical or situated knowledge in that it meaningfully combines different specialization codes towards enabling professional practice (Winberg et al., 2013, p. 106). The participants are practicing academics and so our approach is not dissimilar to work in integrated or professional learning approaches. The combination of knowledge codes, relativist codes and knower codes in the curriculum and pedagogy describes this practical knowledge approach.

In the next section, we will interrogate: (a) what this knowledge means for pedagogical practice; (b) how this knowledge illuminates the field of educational technology; and (c) how it interacts with the nexus of AD and is relevance for diverse HE contexts.

The practice of teaching blended learning

As we answered what the knowledge base of blended learning is, we also started to look at the practice of teaching a blended learning course. Over the years the Blended Learning Short Course has become a modelling environment where the participants can experience what it means to learn and teach in a blended mode. As such the 'way' we teach the course points to the way that participants could imagine their own blended learning teaching practice. Our pedagogical approach informs the pedagogy of the participants.

As such a next step was to look at how and when the different blended learning knowledge practices happened throughout the course. Plotting the differing use of specialization codes over time uncovered an interesting and potentially powerful pedagogical strategy. The use of specialization codes throughout time, highlighted a picture of dynamic movement. The teaching would start in a relativist code and then quickly shift to a knower code and from there to an élite code. It would return to knower, back to élite, then to relativist, then to élite just to stay for a while in knower code blended learning teaching (with a quick foray into elite). We would then dwell in knowledge and subsequently enter a block of relativist code just for the whole sequence to repeat throughout the two days of teaching. The code shifts through time suggests a kind of teaching 'tapestry', and one could suggest that a pedagogical strategy of specialization code 'weaving' is prevalent.

That we teach this way is not surprising as the course deliberately integrates aspects of theory and practice and also different educational technologies. The course starts with reference to educational technologies as an ice-breaker and to pique participants' interest in blended learning (relativist code). We then refer to who we are as facilitators, who the participants are as practitioners and how the support from the blended learning coordinators in the different faculties works (knower code). The theoretical basis of blended learning as consisting of concepts and practices (knowledge code) combined with a certain disposition and knowing who the leaders in the field are (knower perspectives) are then highlighted (élite code).

To us, this practice of weaving through all the codes is an important part of the way that the knowledge base of blended learning is created. As we have seen the three main 'voices' emerging from the analysis do slightly differ in their use of particular specialization codes. These code clashes are mitigated by this incorporation of a specialization code-weaving pedagogical practice that provides participants with a unified and coherent (although polyvalent) knowledge building experience. We can therefore say that blended learning (as taught at our institution) as a practice of the educational technology field is: (a) predominantly a knowledge-code region, (b) with relativistic-code tendencies, (c) that makes room for knower-code approaches, and (d) weaves the codes together towards practice-based knowledge-building.

What does this mean for the broader educational technology field?

Now that we have mapped our own local knowledge practice of blended learning it is possible to return our perspective to the broader field of educational technology. Being a relatively young field complicates the manner in which we describe and conceptualize what we do. This tends to be confusing for even practitioners in the field. Therefore, it is not uncommon to find terminology such as Educational Technology, Blended Learning, Instructional Design, Learning Science, Technology Enhanced Learning, Learning Technologies, Online Learning Design, e-Learning, Audio-Visual Learning, and ICT Integration in Teaching and Learning in the literature and practice. These terms represent different groupings in the field who are all vying for attention and influence through publications and professional associations to be custodians of the future of the field. This echoes the struggle for control of the educational technology field towards determining the 'ruler of legitimacy' and the controller (through the 'comparative values of specialization codes') of the structuring of the field (Maton, 2014, pp. 52–53).

How one speaks and the concepts one uses are often 'inherited' as part of the specific approach one started out with. In the USA the chance that you will describe yourself as an Instructional Designer or Audio-Visual expert in teaching and learning is bigger than in the UK where you will refer to learning technologies or Australia where educational technologies reign supreme. In South Africa, there is currently a building of consensus that blended learning (or even hybrid learning) is what we should call our approach in teaching and learning. The problem is that it is challenging to grasp the similarities as well as the differences without insight into the knowledge practices of the different groupings. Czerniewicz (2008) started a similar process of mapping the terrain of educational technology using Bernstein as 'cartographer'.

Clarifying some of the bigger picture issues raised in this chapter will help build a shared language. Agreement on the key elements of the new domain, and agreement about ways of seeing will help build the internal consistency in the field. With researchers and professionals from such a wide range of backgrounds, coherent articulation and integration are necessary. While field formation cannot be prescribed, the process can be made explicit. Sufficient consensus is needed to enable communication among educational technology researchers and professionals, and in order to build a credible, legitimate and distinguished knowledge field (Czerniewicz, 2008, p. 177).

By using LCT's Specialization dimension, we have extended the possibilities of mapping the field and in this way are able to clarify differences and similarities in the field. Through mapping our own understanding of the knowledge base of blended learning, we have provided a starting point for other approaches to do the same. We argue that the educational technology field could potentially evolve through debate and engagement regarding the 'plotting' of different approaches based on their valorized knowledge structures. For instance, Instructional Design and Learning Science could potentially be situated as knowledge codes. Similarly, we observe the relativist code approaches of Audio-Visual and ICT groupings, the strong knower code postmodern approaches, and the élite code of Technology Enhanced Learning and Online Learning Design practitioners. We could possibly also map Learning Technology proponents as similar to blended learning in that there is an intersection of all the codes.

Making the invisible knowledge practices of the different approaches visible strengthens the field, and potentially gives us a language with which we can uncover our own (often hidden) understanding of what we do and why we do it. It also has explanatory power regarding the very tangible code clashes between groups who often use the same terminology (e.g. instructional designer, or blended learning coordinator, or even educational technologist) but mean different things. Whether it is designing educational technology curricula, participating in global research projects, or building associations and networks, understanding and acknowledging which knowledge practices we are valorizing and legitimizing is important and can provide insight and open up possibilities for deliberation and collaboration.

What does this mean for blended learning academic developers in the field of educational technology?

By first mapping one's own approach in terms of LCT Specialization enables the academic developer engaged with blended learning to situate their underpinning knowledge practice in relation to or in distinction of other approaches. This enables a scholarly approach to the teaching of blended learning and also informs the pedagogical choices made in the field of reproduction (the space where teaching and learning takes place – where choices are made about how to integrate technology into the curriculum) (Maton, 2014).

Blended learning academic developers who are interested or convinced by our approach could immerse themselves in the tools we put forward in this chapter, namely (a) familiarization with the external language of description; (b) contemplation of the Specialization translation device for blended learning; and (c) interrogation of the constant movement ('weaving') between the knowledge code, relativist code and knower code as teaching practice. Doing this will enable a curriculum design and knowledge practice that takes knowledge seriously and uses Specialization as a powerful tool towards knowledge-building and building the field.

What does it mean for the broader HE academic development field in South Africa?

As mentioned earlier, the role of academic developers now inadvertently includes having to come to grips with the meaningful integration of educational technology in teaching and learning. As such the binary relationship between, for example, 'general' HE advisors and 'blended learning advisors' that has been a lived experienced for many, is showing signs of weakening, and a more useful openness to integrated and multi-faceted approaches (that includes an educational technology focus), is gaining ground. Being able to start to surface the emerging knowledge base of blended learning, by better mapping the educational technology field, could benefit the broader field of academic development related to teaching and learning practices in particular.

The movement towards analyzing and theorizing the knowledge base of blended learning and educational technology as part of the broader higher education academic development field, starts addressing the knowledge-blindness within the educational technology field. By 'knowledge-blindness' we mean the process of examining the different forms of knowledge and how it influence different contexts and situations (Maton, 2014, pp. 3–8). Such engagements pave the way for academic developers specializing in educational technology to move closer to general HE practitioners and researchers in the field. It provides a (better) language, and encourages the sharing of practice through a scholarly approach. It also becomes a case of the critical importance of commensurability, mutual understanding and problem-solving within the broader field. Czerniewicz (2010, pp. 13–14) makes the point very strongly:

> In order to build knowledge, there needs to be a conscious acknowledgement of commensurability. There is a crucial distinction to educational technology – mapping the terrain to be made between considering the field to have different perspectives rather than different paradigms. While paradigms tend to be mutually exclusive, perspectives suggest a shared interest in solving common problems, albeit in different ways, and a commitment to mutual understanding using different approaches. Different perspectives have the potential to shed light on overlapping or mutual problems.

We suggest that Czerniewicz's (2010) narrower focus on educational technology could be broadened to speak to the bigger field of academic development in HE. Especially in the global South, there are so many pressing problems in HE, that a commitment to bringing in more perspectives (not exclusive paradigms, also from an educational technology side) to find meaningful and lasting educational solutions is long overdue. A first important step is to make our practices, knowledge bases, theorizing and processes explicit. Then one can start addressing general challenges such as transformation, or more specific challenges such as the quality of mobile apps for collaborative knowledge building.

Conclusions

Analyzing and mapping the knowledge base of blended learning and the field of educational technology through specialization codes creates new possibilities of commensurability in the field of academic development. Blended learning as developed and taught at Stellenbosch University, is shown here to be a knowledge informed, knower supported and in the end a very practical knowledge. This practical knowledge can join hands with other AD knowledge practices to address the many challenges in a diverse and dynamic higher education landscape. This is especially relevant due to the shifting roles of academic developers in the ever-growing digitization of higher education.

To this end this analysis of our blended learning teaching/AD practice through LCT lenses joins the growing sharing of practice in the teaching and learning sphere. We add our voice to Vorster and Quinn's (2015) analysis of their academic development course, to Maton, Carvalho and Dong's (2016) insights into a good informal e-learning approach, and to Shay and Steyn's (2016) deeper understanding of vocational learning.

Lastly, the mere focus on knowledge in the field of educational technology has opened up other possible avenues of research and practice. In the educational technology field the concept of the different affordances of technologies for learning is gaining ground. A practitioner or researcher would interrogate how a particular technology could afford a certain outcome or effect and design a learning experience around this insight. What is possibly missing though is a renewed focus on the affordances of knowledge. How do (different) educational technologies build knowledge? What kind of knowledge-building is supported by what kinds of educational technologies? This emerging way of thinking and doing is not only for researching teaching and learning practices, but could also potentially be used for designing teaching and learning and/or knowledge-building experiences.

By starting on the path to being cured of knowledge blindness in the practice of blended learning and in the field of educational technology, one can assist others through knowledge-sensitive academic development practices to teach in powerful knowledge-affirming ways.

References

Bozalek, V., Ng'ambi, D. and Gachago, D. (2013). Transforming teaching with emerging technologies: Implications for higher education institutions. *South African Journal of Higher Education*, *27*(2), 419–436.

Bulfin, S., Henderson, M., Johnson, N.F. and Selwyn, N. (2014). Methodological capacity within the field of 'educational technology' research: An initial investigation. *British Journal of Educational Technology*, *45*(3), 403–414.

Czerniewicz, L. (2008). Distinguishing the field of educational technology. *The Electronic Journal of E-Learning*, *6*(3), 171–178.

Czerniewicz, L. (2010). Educational technology – mapping the terrain with Bernstein as cartographer. *Journal of Computer Assisted Learning*, *26*(6), 523–534.

Czerniewicz, L. and Brown, C. (2007). Disciplinary differences in the use of educational technology, paper presented at ICEL 2007: 2nd International Conference on E-Learning.

Czerniewicz, L., Ravjee, N. and Mlitwa, N. (2006). ICTs and the South African higher education landscape. Retrieved from https://telearn.archives-ouvertes.fr/hal-00190317/document.

Hannon, J. and Al-Mahmood, R. (2014). The place of theory in educational research. *Rhetoric and reality: Critical perspectives on educational technology* (pp. 1–6). Dunedin, NZ: Ascilite.

Howard, S. and Maton, K. (2011). Theorising knowledge practices: A missing piece of the educational technology puzzle. *Research in Learning Technology*, *19*(3), 191–206.

Jaffer, S., Ng'ambi, D. and Czerniewicz, L. (2007). The role of ICTs in higher education in South Africa: One strategy for addressing teaching and learning challenges. *International Journal of Education and Development using ICT*, *3*(4), 131–142.

Jackson, F. (2014). Knowledge and knowers by Karl Maton: A review essay. *Journal of Education*, *59*, 127–146.

Jones, C. and Czerniewicz, L. (2017). Theory in learning technology. *Research in Learning Technology*, *19*(3), 173–177.

Kirkwood, A. and Price, L. (2013). Technology-enhanced learning and teaching in higher education: What is 'enhanced' and how do we know? A critical literature review. *Learning, Media and Technology*, *39*(1), 6–36.

Laurillard, D. (2012). *Teaching as a design science: Building pedagogical patterns for learning and technology*. London: Routledge.

Maton, K. (2013). Making semantic waves: A key to cumulative knowledge-building, *Linguistics and Education*, 24(1): 8–22.
Maton, K. (2014). *Knowledge and knowers: Towards a realist sociology of education*. London: Routledge.
Maton, K. (2016). Legitimation Code Theory: Building knowledge about knowledge-building. In K. Maton, S. Hood and S. Shay (Eds), *Knowledge-building: Educational studies in Legitimation Code Theory* (pp. 1–24). London: Routledge.
Maton, K. and Chen, R.T.-H. (2016). LCT in qualitative research: Creating a translation device for studying constructivist pedagogy. In K. Maton, S. Hood and S. Shay (Eds), *Knowledge-building: Educational studies in Legitimation Code Theory* (pp. 27–48). London: Routledge.
Maton, K., Carvalho, L. and Dong, A. (2016). LCT in praxis: Creating an e-learning environment for informal learning of principled knowledge. In K. Maton, S. Hood and S. Shay (Eds), *Knowledge-building: Educational studies in Legitimation Code Theory* (pp. 72–92). London: Routledge.
Maton, K. and Howard, S. (2016). LCT in mixed-methods research: Evolving an instrument for quantitative data. In K. Maton, S. Hood and S. Shay (Eds), *Knowledge-building: Educational studies in Legitimation Code Theory* (pp. 49–71). London: Routledge.
Oliver, M. (2013). Learning technology: Theorising the tools we study. *British Journal of Educational Technology*, 44(1), 31–43.
Price, L. and Kirkwood, A. (2014). Using technology for teaching and learning in higher education: A critical review of the role of evidence in informing practice. *Higher Education Research and Development*, 33(3), 549–564.
Rushby, N. and Surry, D.W. (2016). Mapping the field and terminology. In N. Rushby and D.W. Surry (Eds), *The Wiley handbook of learning technology* (pp. 1–10). Chichester: Wiley Blackwell.
Salmon, G. (2005). Flying not flapping: A strategic framework for e-learning and pedagogical innovation in higher education institutions. *Research in Learning Technology*, 13(3), 201–218.
Salmon, G. (2013). *E-tivities: The key to active online learning*. New York: Routledge.
Sharpe, R., Benfield, G. and Francis, R. (2006). Implementing a university e-learning strategy: Levers for change within academic schools. *Research in Learning Technology*, 14(2), 135–151.
Shay, S. and Steyn, D. (2016). Enabling knowledge progression in vocational curricula: Design as a case study. In K. Maton, S. Hood and S. Shay (Eds), *Knowledge-building: Educational studies in Legitimation Code Theory* (pp. 138–157). London: Routledge.
Surry, D.W. and Baker, F.W. (2016). The co-dependent relationship of technology and communities. *British Journal of Educational Technology*, 47(1), 13–28.
Vorster, J. and Quinn, L. (2015). Towards shaping the field: Theorising the knowledge in a formal course for academic developers in Higher Education. *Higher Education Research and Development*, 34(5), 1031–1044.
Winberg, C., Engel-Hills, P., Garraway, J. and Jacobs, C. (2013). Professionally-oriented knowledge and the purpose of professionally-oriented Higher Education. In Council on Higher Education, *The aims of Higher Education – Kagiso 9* (pp. 98–119). Pretoria: South African Council on Higher Education.

13

LEGITIMATE PARTICIPATION IN PROGRAMME RENEWAL

The role of academic development units

Gert Young and Cecilia Jacobs

Introduction

Academic development (AD) units are generally understood to concern themselves with 'the improvement, support and development of teaching, learning, assessment and curriculum, the enquiry into, investigation of and research into higher education, and informed debate and promotion of the scholarship of teaching and learning into higher education goals and practices' (Bath and Smith, 2004, p. 14). This can be achieved in various ways including support for the professionalization of university teaching through staff development. While this may seem a relatively uncomplicated pursuit, AD units face numerous conceptual, structural and practical challenges (Gosling, 1996, 2001; Challis et al., 2009; Holt et al., 2011; Green and Little, 2013). This is certainly also true in the South African context (Boughey, 2009), where some of the conceptual challenges relate to different understandings within institutions of what constitutes quality teaching, learning, professionalization and development (Quinn, 2012a, 2012b), some of the structural challenges refer to organizational positioning, structuring and reporting lines of AD units (Gosling, 2009), and some of the practical challenges stem from a common experience of constantly being under-staffed and under-resourced (Challis et al., 2009; Gosling, 2009).

As a result of many of these challenges AD units and faculties experience their interactions in various modalities ranging from opposition to cooperation (Naidoo, 2012), probably best expressed by Gosling's characterization of AD work as reflecting 'unremitting contradiction' (2009, p. 5). Challis, Holt and Palmer (2009) suggest that academic developers and lecturers often conceive different roles for AD units in terms of the general functions of these units and Gosling's (2009) survey of directors of AD units in South Africa confirms this. In the South African higher education context 'faculty' refers to a structure within the university that houses a particular discipline (e.g. the faculty of Arts and Social Sciences) For example, academic developers tend to view professional learning and development as the responsibility of lecturers but supported by academic developers, while many lecturers view learning and development as 'programming that educational developers are responsible for' (Wilcox, 1998, p. 99). Such perceptions of AD by lecturers are associated with a view of teaching (and related activities such as curriculum development) as being based on common-sense knowledge rather than based on a rigorously developed body of knowledge produced in a systematic way (Rowland, 2002). These different conceptions also suggest different perceptions about the identity and status of AD units and academic developers (Leibowitz et al., 2017).

It is to be expected that with such different views, interaction between AD units and faculties is at times characterized by contestation. What is not always clear is the nature of and explanation for this contestation. To investigate the nature of this contestation, we use this chapter to explore its manifestation in programme renewal interaction. In the context of our research, programme renewal refers to a continuous and wide range of activities designed to improve the quality of the programmes offered by a higher education institution, the purpose of which would be to respond to educational, knowledge and societal needs (Bitzer and Costandius, 2018). This includes (but is not limited to) rethinking the outcomes of programmes, the content of specific courses as well as the sequencing of these courses, the modes employed to conduct teaching and learning (e.g. face-to-face, online, blended, etc.), assessment practices and the relation between the programmes offered and societal and market needs. These activities all suggest a variety of stakeholders in programme renewal. Bitzer and Costandius (2018) for example, suggest (implicitly and explicitly) that activities could involve teaching staff, curriculum researchers, renewal experts, institutional strategists, market stakeholders and even staff who design preparation programmes for university academics. Programme renewal can thus justifiably be described as a form of social interaction that, like most other forms of social interaction, can be characterized by competition or cooperation (or a great number of positions in between).

One of the general roles of AD units in South Africa is acting in an advisory capacity in programme renewal in faculties. In general the support provided by AD units can be described as scholarly, meaning that the support is based on systematic explorations of teaching, learning and curriculum practices that are theoretically informed, rather than intuitive or purely experiential (Leibowitz, Bozalek and Khan, 2017, p. 2). As both the AD units and faculties approach programme renewal from a basis of knowledge, albeit different kinds of knowledge (Bath and Smith, 2004), the interaction has significant potential for tension. It is our contention that lecturers approach programme renewal from a disciplinary knowledge base, while academic developers approach programme renewal from a knowledge base that draws on curriculum theory. Any exclusive claims to knowledge contributions in programme renewal sets up the interaction between academic developers and lecturers as one in which both parties attempt to make legitimate contributions from their respective knowledge bases. Since the purpose of this study was to interrogate the different conceptions, of these two groups, regarding what constitutes 'legitimate participation' in programme renewal, the Legitimation Code Theory (LCT) dimension of Specialization offers a particularly useful framework for analyses.

We start this chapter with some brief comments on the institutional (Stellenbosch University) and national (South Africa) contexts in which this study is situated. While our study is located in a very specific context and probably reflects some aspects that are functions of this unique context, the nature of the relationship between academic developers and lecturers and how this relationship influences and is influenced by common higher education activities (like programme renewal) are phenomena that are widely experienced and acknowledged. Our brief contextualization is followed by a description of the methodology employed. After providing the necessary methodological parameters we explain in more detail how and why we used Specialization for our analysis. Finally, we conclude with some recommendations for both practice and research.

Methodology

The context for this study is a research-intensive university in South Africa, where programme renewal has been identified as a strategic priority of the university and an institutional curriculum renewal project is being driven at the Deputy Vice Chancellor level at the university. This institutional curriculum renewal project, now in its fourth year, involves all of the ten faculties at the university and is the focus of the study reported in this chapter. The AD unit at the university plays an advisory role in the institutional curriculum renewal project. The practice of programme renewal, as experienced through the institutional curriculum renewal project, continues to represent an area of interaction between the academic developers and lecturers and is thus one space in which the relationship between these role-players finds expression, ranging from cooperation to competition. From our experience, as academic developers in the institutional curriculum renewal project, we conjectured that the academic developers from the AD unit and the lecturers from the faculties were understanding the practice of programme renewal differently, valuing different aspects of the practice of programme renewal and perceiving different roles and legitimacies for the AD unit in programme renewal. We thus set out to explore the conception of these differences empirically using LCT.

LCT is a sociological approach which reveals the organizing principles underlying practices (Maton, 2014, 2016). As higher education comprises a range of academic fields/disciplines where academics *cooperate* and/or *struggle* for status and resources in their fields/disciplines, we chose LCT as an analytical framework because it enabled us to engage with our empirical work and demonstrate the underlying principles of this cooperation and/or struggle for what was considered legitimate in the practice of programme renewal.

Howard and Maton (2011) have argued that in the absence of sound theoretical frameworks, research is likely to be repetitive and fragmented. This in turn prevents researchers from making advances in building knowledge. While there have been significant amounts of empirical research on the role and status of academic developers, AD units and academic development as a practice or profession in higher education, much of this research has been highly contextualized and descriptive. Gaining a better understanding of the problem of the positioning of academic development in higher education requires more explicit theorization (Shay, 2012) and a better grasp of the principles underlying practices such as programme renewal, rather than descriptions of the actual enactments. We therefore drew on LCT to provide us with instruments to understand the underlying principles that dictate the positioning of academic development with regard to the practice of programme renewal. In applying these concepts, Maton (2014, 2016) suggests that the reasons for cooperation and/or struggle about what is considered legitimate knowledge practices are uncovered. In this study we have identified programme renewal as a knowledge practice and we apply the LCT dimension of Specialization to investigate *how* and *why* lecturers and academic developers engage in programme renewal, and what is considered legitimate programme renewal practice within their respective contexts. The balance of power across programme renewal practices shape what *is* or *is not* possible in particular contexts, such as AD units and faculties/academic departments. In this study we describe the object of the study as an attempt to interrogate the different conceptions of academic developers and lecturers regarding what constitutes 'legitimate participation' in programme renewal. The research-related questions were framed as:

- What is regarded as 'legitimate participation' in programme renewal from the perspectives of academic developers and lecturers?
- What are the differences and similarities in how academic developers and lecturers understand 'legitimate participation' in programme renewal?
- What are the implications of these differences and similarities for the role of AD units in programme renewal?

We chose the dimension of Specialization, as this dimension is premised on the claim that every knowledge practice (such as programme renewal) is about or oriented towards something and by someone (see Maton 2014, 2016; Maton and Chen 2020). One can, therefore, analytically distinguish: *epistemic relations* between practices and their objects (that part of the world towards which they are oriented); and *social relations* between practices and their subjects (who or what is enacting the practices). Since we were interested in finding out what was valued in the practices and processes of programme renewal for academic developers and lecturers, and we conjectured that these two groups might be valuing different things, the analytical tools of Specialization helped us to uncover this. Specialization helped us to see what was valued in the practice of programme renewal, and what legitimated this process for the people involved in it. In our data we identified *epistemic relations* and *social relations* in the following way:

- *epistemic relations:* participants understood the practice of programme renewal in relation to the knowledge that underpins the process;
- *social relations:* participants understood the practice of programme renewal in relation to the knowers involved in the process and their dispositions (i.e. those with expertise in and experience of the process of programme renewal).

When considering the structure of a social field (including the one we explore here), LCT conceptualizes different strengths of social relations as 'gazes' (Maton, 2014, pp. 86–105, 171–195). These represent different kinds of knowers, or, put differently, different ways of recognizing what is valued (Ellery, 2018, p. 26). The gazes Maton (2014) explores are 'born', 'social', 'cultivated' and 'trained'. Briefly the *trained gaze* represents the weakest social relations, *born gazes* the strongest, *social gazes* are weaker than born gazes, and *cultivated gazes* are weaker than social gazes (Maton, 2014, p. 95). A born gaze is said to be that of a legitimate knower that is 'naturally' talented. A social gaze is less exclusive but still strongly bounded as it is based on socially constructed categories. The cultivated gaze is one of a knower that has, through experience, guidance and exposure become a legitimate knower. Finally, the trained gaze is that of a legitimate knower that has become such through systematic development and training. The value of these distinctions is that they allow us to understand how and why different knowers value certain knowledge practices.

In order to analyse what legitimated the practices and processes of programme renewal for academic developers and lecturers at the university, we drew on three different data sets. We conducted ten focus group sessions across the ten faculties at the university, focusing on the process of programme renewal. This was followed by individual interviews with three faculty-based programme leaders, who were purposively selected based on the data arising from the focus group interviews. Interviews were also conducted with seven academic developers. All interviews and focus group sessions were recorded and transcribed. We completed an initial *soft-eyes* coding to establish what academic developers and lecturers regarded as 'legitimate participation' in programme renewal. The views of the participants from these two groups were coded into themes representing what was valued in the practice of programme renewal. The following broad themes emerged from the first iteration of data analysis: knowledge of disciplinary content; knowledge of market/industry needs; knowledge of the public good; knowledge of administrative procedures for programme renewal; knowledge of curriculum design, pedagogy and assessment; knowledgeable people with enabling dispositions.

A second iteration of analysis was then completed, where these broad themes were coded using *epistemic relations* (ER) and *social relations* (SR) as coding categories. The knowledges underpinning the practice of programme renewal (knowledge of: disciplinary content; market/industry needs; the public good; administrative procedures for programme renewal; curriculum design, pedagogy and assessment) were coded as ER. The knowers underpinning the practice of programme renewal (those with expertise and experience in programme renewal; those with enabling dispositions/attitudes towards programme renewal) were coded as SR.

Table 13.1 illustrates how the broad themes from the first iteration of data analysis were translated into the Specialization categories of *epistemic relations* and *social relations*. Column 1 of the table describes what *epistemic relations* (ER) and *social relations* (SR) looked like in our data – in other words what was valued in the practice of programme renewal. Column 2 of Table 13.1 are examples of data from the focus group discussions and interviews which foregrounded ER and SR.

The quotations foregrounding ER illustrate a *knowledge code*, where possession of specialized knowledge, principles or procedures are emphasized as the basis of successful programme renewal, and the attributes and expertise of knowers are downplayed. From the data it appears that five different kinds of knowledge legitimate the process of programme renewal. The quotations foregrounding SR illustrate a *knower code*, where specialist knowledge is less significant and instead the attributes and expertise of knowers are emphasized as the basis of successful programme renewal. From the data it appears that certain kinds of knowers are needed for programme renewal, those with expertise in curriculum renewal, and that it is the attitudes and dispositions of the participants in the process of programme renewal that are important. The above analysis provides some answers to our first research question: *What is regarded as 'legitimate participation' in programme renewal from the perspectives of academic developers and lecturers?*

Analysis

Our first two iterations of data analysis revealed what was valued in the practices and processes of programme renewal across both groups, the academic developers and the lecturers. Since our conjecture was that these two groups might be valuing different things, a third iteration of data analysis was undertaken, where we explored the differences and similarities in how these two groups understood *'legitimate participation'* in programme renewal. Epistemic relations (ER) and social relations (SR) may be more strongly or weakly emphasized as the basis of successful programme renewal, and these continua of strengths can be visualized as axes of the *specialization plane* in which one can identify four principal specialization codes, as illustrated in Figure 13.1.

In Figure 13.1 we have located programme renewal as a knowledge practice on the specialization plane. The top left quadrant foregrounds stronger epistemic relations and weaker social relations as the basis of successful programme renewal: a *knowledge code*, where (in this study) possession of specialized knowledge, principles or procedures are emphasized as the basis of successful programme renewal, and the expertise and attributes of knowers are downplayed. In the bottom left quadrant neither epistemic relations nor social relations are emphasized as the basis of successful programme renewal: a *relativist code*, where neither the possession of specialized knowledge nor the expertise and attributes of knowers are regarded as important for successful programme renewal. The bottom right quadrant foregrounds weaker epistemic relations and stronger social relations as the basis of successful programme renewal: a *knower code*, where the attributes, personal experiences and expertise of

TABLE 13.1 Translation device

Indicators (ER and SR)	Examples of supporting data
ER.: Successful programme renewal is dependent on: • knowledge of disciplinary content (ER1) • knowledge of market/industry needs (ER2) • knowledge of the public good (ER3) • knowledge of administrative procedures for programme renewal (ER4) • knowledge of curriculum design, pedagogy and assessment (ER5)	• The perception of the current, the average lecturer in a faculty, to him programme renewal is content orientated if not driven ... I think it's simply because we're focusing too much – the starting point it too often the content. (lecturer) [ER1] • The industry is so powerful, they put probably 45, 50 million rand a year through this faculty ... and now that's our point of departure so when you develop a curriculum we say, O.K. you must meet their requirements because they fund us and they employ the students. (lecturer) [ER2] • For programme renewal we need to know what the needs are out there, what the needs are in higher education as well as what the needs of are the students. It is not just about content but also about ... delivering students that make a difference in society. (academic developer) [ER3] • ... it involves paper work .... and I think people are scared of paper work. They don't like administration and they've been researchers out there and they want to crack on with their science. They're not actually interested in getting involved in any of this stuff, and NQF levels, and education and things, and paperwork and form A's and institutional processes and meetings and committees. (lecturer) [ER4] • The same goes for us as academic advisors, we that are supposed to have the knowledge about what counts as excellent teaching and learning. (academic developer) [ER5]
SR: Successful programme renewal is dependent on: • knowers/experts in curriculum renewal (SR1) • people with enabling dispositions (SR2)	• For programme renewal one also needs knowledgeable people – experts in the art of curriculum development, assessment strategies and appropriate modes of delivery (lecturer) [SR1] • I feel that [the academic developer] helped... by showing, 'listen this is not so bad, you can do it, you know, and this is actually quite easy, this is how you start'. So not only providing the knowledge, but making it accessible by saying, 'Guys, you can actually do it, see you're halfway there, you've already done this'.... So I felt that that was really important. (lecturer) [SR2]

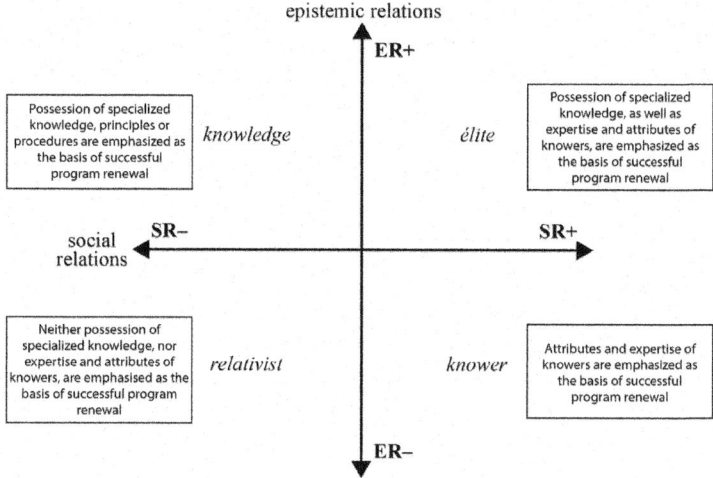

FIGURE 13.1 The specialization plane

Source: adapted from Maton, 2014, p. 30

the knowers are emphasized as the basis of successful programme renewal and specialized knowledge is less significant. The top right quadrant foregrounds stronger epistemic relations and stronger social relations as the basis of successful programme renewal: an *élite code*, where both specialized knowledge and being a knower with the necessary expertise and attributes for successful programme renewal, are emphasized.

In the third iteration of data analysis the differences and similarities in how the academic developers and the lecturers understood *'legitimate participation'* in programme renewal was revealed.

The academic developers

Academic developers seemed to express preference for specialized knowledge and practices (*epistemic relations*) in their thinking about programme renewal. They acknowledged a collection of sets of knowledges that structure programme renewal knowledge. The first of these knowledges we refer to as *disciplinary content knowledge [ER1]*, which refers to academic developers' acknowledgement of disciplinary knowledge as essential to programme renewal, as evidenced in this quotation:

> We bring something but other colleagues bring something else. They bring the Math, the Science, the Law. The disciplines are not something we necessarily have access to. But it is knowledge without which programme renewal cannot happen.
>
> (AD2)

The designation of interviewees was done in the order that the interviews were conducted. Thus 'AD' signifies the second academic developer who was interviewed. What is referenced here is the content, that part of the discipline that is often objectified. While academic developers are of course not the agents of disciplinary knowledge, they consider it to be essential. Which does not mean that disciplinarity is viewed as unproblematic. Reimann (2009) argues that academic developers, even though they may not be disciplinary experts, can support academics in programme renewal efforts by engaging them in discussions about the 'ways of thinking and practicing' in their disciplines.

A next set of collected knowledges we broadly refer to as *knowledge of curriculum design, pedagogy and assessment [ER5]*. This encapsulates knowledge of teaching, learning, assessment, and general knowledge of the discipline of Higher Education Studies (Bath and Smith, 2004), as evidenced in these quotations:

> We got a little working group together and each had their own responsibility. I was asked to look at pedagogy and the role it would play in realising this new program.
>
> *(AD4)*

> For me it is more than content and just changing content. So I think as advisors, we are supposed to have the knowledge of what good teaching and learning is and specifically what good teaching and learning is in that Department and Faculty. We should play a role in helping Departments establish good teaching and learning so they can deliver the best possible programme for students.
>
> *(AD5)*

These examples from the data illustrate that this particular kind of knowledge is viewed as essential to academic developers in any claim of legitimacy of programme renewal practices. Academic developers claim legitimacy based on specialized knowledge. This includes knowledge of teaching and learning, which is distinguished from discipline-specific knowledge and knowledge about institutional processes and requirements for programme renewal. The challenge academic developers experience is related to the extent that lecturers accept this specialized knowledge as a legitimate basis for programme renewal practices.

A next set of collected knowledges we broadly refer to as *knowledge of administrative procedures [ER4]*. From the data it was apparent that academic developers value the required processes and associated knowledge of these administrative processes, but not as an end in itself but as a means to an end. In as far as the processes create the potential for reflective engagement in programme renewal, the associated knowledge is valued, as evidenced in these quotations:

> And then there are of course the technical things – forms, processes etc. I sometimes think that when they get us in, the Departments are thinking

about the easiest, the quickest way to get these technical things done. But of course we look deeper at these things to what are the implications for teaching and learning and to how teaching and learning can be advanced.

(AD3)

What I eventually did was to use the forms and institutional requirements as a tool to get them to do it. At least it got them thinking. When they first did the recurriculation they thought that once the thinking was done, they were finished. But then they had to fill in the forms as required by the University, that is where the struggle came. I helped and in the end they understood that it was necessary. Not just as some formal process but as something important to ensure that they actually apply good teaching and learning principles.

(AD1)

We also found other sets of knowledges, such as *knowledge of the public good [ER3]*, valued by academic developers, but these often overlapped with one of the aforementioned knowledges. This set of knowledges is acknowledged by Bitzer and Costandius (2018) and is evidenced by statements such as: '*We need to consider how to align programme renewal with the transformation needs of our country*', and '*programme renewal needs inputs that will ensure that through the programme students will be equipped to make a difference to society*'. This signals an area for further exploration.

Apart from thinking about *what* constitutes legitimate programme renewal practice, academic developers also suggested that *who* engages in these practices, is also important to its legitimacy. However, the *social relations* seemed less conceptualized and apparent than the *epistemic relations* in the underlying structure of legitimate programme renewal as conceived by academic developers. Where *social relations* featured in the data, *experience* and *identity* were highlighted as two important and explicit acknowledgements of the knower, as evidenced by the below:

> There is value in saying we've tried this and that before and it works, or does not.
>
> We must remember that we are educational advisors. While we are related to an academic discipline we are different to academics. Not just our discipline but also our reason for existence is different.
>
> *(AD5)*

All fields include particular gazes (Maton, 2014, p. 96). This means that in academic developers' conceptualization of the field, gazes offer a further analytical tool to improve understanding of how authenticity is judged. For some academic developers association with a particular faculty as well as is an essential part of legitimate participation in programme renewal. One, for example, stated that 'I think it is the fact that I have a background in the faculty. That, not only what I know, already opens doors. It plays a role in me being accepted in the faculty' (AD1). Others again valued particular social positions, particularly those based on standpoint theories. Expressions like those which follow are common:

> The 'buzz word' in higher education at the moment is transformation. And I think our role in programme renewal is to ensure that programs pursue transformation. We have to have a view on social justice and transformation, not just knowledge, if we are going to contribute to programme renewal.
>
> *(AD6)*

> For me it is about the student and how we can change society.
>
> *(AD5)*

So, valuing particular kinds of knowers is apparent in academic developers' understanding of legitimacy. What appears interesting (but requires further investigation) is that those relatively new to academic development work subscribe to trained gazes (weaker social relations and stronger epistemic relations) while those that have clear academic development career trajectories value those gazes with stronger social relations (cultivated and social gazes).

So, it appears that for academic developers, legitimate programme renewal practices require stronger *epistemic relations* that are based on particular sets of distinguishable knowledges, as well as stronger *social relations*, expressed as the enactment of specific identities. However, the data shows more of an emphasis on the *epistemic relations* than the *social relations* for this group.

The lecturers

We turn now to the structuring of programme renewal knowledge as expressed by the lecturers. Our analysis of the data suggests that lecturers also valued the three types of knowledges we identified in the academic developer data, but they understood these differently to the academic developers. For example, for the type of knowledge we earlier referred to as *disciplinary content knowledge [ER1]*, there was a slightly different understanding of this, particularly from those lecturers teaching on professional programmes, such as Law and AgriSciences. The notion of *disciplinary knowledge* was expanded to include another kind of knowledge, knowledge of market/industry needs *[ER2]*, as evidenced in the quotation below:

> In terms of colleagues they obviously had the subject knowledge ... I think the technical knowledge is very important because that is what industry buys from us and it is clear when you put together a programme delivering certain knowledge and skills that we need to – you can't let a student leave a programme without that base, so the knowledge comes first.

One participant described how they had a professional degree (one oriented towards a specific profession) and how this degree was in competition with another non-professional degree they had recently started offering. The programme renewal process, he explained, had to 'know' the context for which the degrees were instituted and who the likely audience for these two degrees would be. Without this knowledge one or both of the degrees run the risk of becoming irrelevant.

The set of collected knowledges that we broadly referred to earlier as *knowledge of curriculum design, pedagogy and assessment [ER5]* was also evident in the data emerging from the lecturers, who also considered it an essential part of legitimate programme renewal practice, as evidenced in the two quotations below:

> I think we didn't have the in-house knowledge and know-how and probably practice in how to go about this task in a sound educational way, one could almost say. So I found that I could rely on her (academic developer) to provide me with that subject knowledge.

> So, there's for me a lot of empowerment if you can create an island situation and concentrate just on this one thing that we call the renewal or the renewing of the Master of (discipline) by getting experts (academic developers) to come and explain the theory behind what we are busy doing, explaining the process that we will be following.

Finally, the valuing of *knowledge of administrative procedures [ER4]* was different for lecturers than it was for the *academic developers*. Whereas the *academic developers* understood the procedures as a means to an end, lecturers often viewed these as an end in itself. So, the procedures were regarded as important because they were required by the institution and not because they were a tool or mechanism that supported critical engagement with curriculum, as illustrated in the quotation below:

> Remember you are working here with a group of scientists. We are very pragmatic. So we like it when there is a bit of structure and a recipe, a method for how to do it, particularly when it is something of an educational nature, it is a very woolly matter for us lecturers.

In the data set generated by the lecturers we also found indications of the importance of *social relations* in programme renewal practices, but here again it seemed a lot less apparent than the *epistemic relations* in the underlying structure of legitimate programme renewal. Again *identity*, as well as personal experience, featured as significant, as evidenced in these two quotations:

> And it would be my role (programme coordinator) to coordinate that process, to talk to colleagues. It's not possible for faculty (management) or the (AD Unit) to talk to my programme, to people teaching in the modules. Only us that teach will know best what can work or not work.

> Well in the first place it's people. So there's people e.g. when I sit around a table and I listen to a person like X and she refers to (a book). There's immediately a person reflecting on a book that meant a lot to her and the fact that it meant a lot to her gained my interest and then, you know, I want to go and read it.

Turning briefly to the issue of gazes, we can say from our data that when it comes to knower codes, lecturers strongly value those that have stronger epistemic relations and weaker social relations; in other words, cultivated gazes. Given the narrative of 'content equals curriculum' that often characterizes lecturer conceptualizations (see next section), this makes sense.

So, it appears that for lecturers, legitimate programme renewal practices also require stronger *epistemic relations* that are based on particular sets of distinguishable knowledges. Legitimate programme renewal practices also require stronger *social relations* that are expressed as the enactment of specific identities. However, as with the academic developers, the data shows more of an emphasis on the *epistemic relations* than the *social relations* for the lecturers.

The above analysis provides some answers to our second research question: *What are the differences and similarities in how academic developers and lecturers understand 'legitimate participation' in programme renewal?* We now turn to our third research question: *What are the implications of these differences and similarities for the role of AD units in programme renewal?* and offer a possible explanation for the contestation referred to in the introduction to our chapter.

Discussion

From the data analysis it appears that programme renewal knowledge is generally regarded by both academic developers and lecturers as representing a practice that is more strongly legitimated through *knowledge codes* than *knower codes*. In the previous section we argued that both sets of actors value stronger *epistemic and social relations* in programme renewal, even though the *social relations* are considered less important for the practice of programme renewal. In the context of our data, this would suggest an *élite code*, across both data sets. Thus we do not find an explanation for contestation in a code clash, as we had at first conjectured. The medium, as Maton (2000) states, is also a message. In the case of our research this means that the structure of programme renewal knowledge and practices is not just a by-product, some sort of epiphenomenon, of a particular outcome. In the way in which it is done, we also see something of what it means. From the analysis we found some overlaps and differences between how academic developers and lecturers conceive of and practice programme renewal. We found that both groups claim a specialized knowledge base as essential to programme renewal. This does, however, not mean simple correspondence between the conceptualizations of the academic developers and the lecturers, since they did not hold similar views, similar approaches and similar judgements of value. How then do we account for the struggle for control of the mechanism that defines 'successful' programme renewal practice?

Both the lecturers and the academic developers claimed that specialized knowledge was essential to programme renewal, so it appears that the contestation around programme renewal, that often characterizes the work of AD units, does not result from a code clash. The data suggests that the legitimation of programme renewal practices by lecturers and academic developers is characterized by *code matching* but that the *epistemic relations* differ for different groups of actors. Both groups appear to value what LCT refers to as *knowledge codes* but the *objects* to which this knowledge is oriented, differ between these two groups of actors. In terms of *disciplinary knowledge* both academic developers and lecturers consider disciplines as bounded and governed by particular characteristics. However, the contestation is more than just a matter of epistemology. What sets disciplines apart are not just *how* knowledge is constructed in them but also *what* the knowledge actually is. Returning to the idea that the structure of programme renewal knowledge tells us something about programme renewal knowledge itself, we conclude that where programme renewal knowledge is reduced to disciplinary knowledge, and other specialized forms of knowledge (such as knowledge of curriculum design) are either not acknowledged or seen as only procedural practices, the view that *curriculum equals content* tends to hold sway. The perception among academics that most forms of knowledge other than the disciplinary are of less importance in curriculum development (because, so the argument goes, they lack the intellectual rigour of disciplinary knowledge), is well documented (Gosling, 2003). The understandings of the lecturers tended towards this view.

Academic developers, on the other hand, valued disciplinary knowledge (although they acknowledged that they were not the agents of this knowledge); knowledge of curriculum design; and to a lesser extent, knowledge of administrative procedures. In the case of the lecturers we found that what was most valued was the disciplinary knowledge and the belief that the disciplinary expert was the agent of this knowledge. There was a more limited valuing of the knowledge of curriculum design, but often in the sense described by Malcolm and Zukas (2001), as merely the application of theoretical knowledge and not the continued theorized development and critique of teaching and learning thinking. Many lecturers also considered academic developer participation in the administrative procedures as legitimate, particularly their facilitation of the institutional processes. In particular they attached value to the increased administrative capacity that the involvement of academic developers often provided. In this regard academic developers were often seen as the ones to complete the required forms and to manage the administration through the institutional processes.

It appears then that what can legitimately be described as programme renewal knowledge and practice, depends on how actors view curriculum. If curriculum is the equivalent of content, then knowledge about it is to be found in the content of the discipline. If it is viewed as a dynamic interaction between disciplinary content knowledge; knowledge of curriculum design; knowledge of administrative procedures; as well as the attitudes and dispositions of the actors, then it is conceivable that different knowledge bases are acknowledged as part of programme renewal knowledge. This has implications for who can claim to be producing programme renewal knowledge. If curriculum is narrowly understood as disciplinary content, then only disciplinary specialists can produce programme renewal knowledge. However, if curriculum is understood more broadly as the interaction of various knowledges (disciplinary content knowledge; knowledge of curriculum design; knowledge of administrative procedures; as well as the attitudes and dispositions of the actors) in the contexts of higher education and the specific institution, then a more collaborative approach is required to produce programme renewal knowledge.

Recommendations

For practice

These findings have implications for how the role of AD units are understood. If academic developers and lecturers make different claims to legitimacy concerning the engagement of the AD units in the practice of programme renewal, what are the implications for how the role of AD units is legitimated or challenged? The analysis of the findings point to tentative recommendations towards more successful programme renewal practices. It is clear that the practice of programme renewal is contested terrain and all parties have to accept that some contestation is inevitable. This could open up productive spaces for interrogating questionable programme renewal practices and challenging narrow understandings of the knowledge bases and practices underpinning the processes of programme renewal. If one is to promote a broader understanding of curriculum, which includes the interplay of disciplinary content knowledge, as well as knowledge of curriculum design and administrative procedures, then a collaborative approach to programme renewal is recommended. This suggestion is in line with the argument that academic development work should be done by experts but within disciplines (Ashwin, 2006; Löytönen, 2017), rather than as generic stand-alones. Such collaboration would bring together actors, such as disciplinary experts and academic developers, who embody these types of knowledges. However, such collaboration would need to be premised on an understanding that different knowledge bases inform programme renewal practices and knowledge. Establishing such a premise for the practice of programme renewal might require the subverting of established curriculum procedures and consciously creating spaces to insert theoretical knowledge and reflection into the practice of programme renewal. Furthermore, there appears to be the need to engage institutions on the role of AD units, particularly in the practice of programme renewal.

For further research

In writing this chapter we have also reflected on how LCT could be harnessed to facilitate academic development. We have attempted to illustrate how LCT, specifically concepts from the dimension of Specialization, was used to better understand the process of curriculum development, and the associated practice of programme renewal. This analysis and the initial findings are pointing to differences in what two groups of actors, the lecturers and the academic developers, value in the practice of programme renewal, as well as differences in what they consider to be legitimate programme renewal. One of the difficulties we experienced in using the tools within the dimension of Specialization was struggling to separate analytically the epistemic relations and social relations, as they were so enmeshed in the data. We particularly struggled with the coding of social relations in the empirical data, as they were so enmeshed with epistemic relations, especially when we were analyzing the knowledge of administrative procedures. We suspect that some of this confusion can be cleared by the use of gazes (Maton, 2014) for further analysis.

Another part of the LCT toolkit that we believe will contribute to our understanding is the '4-K model' (Maton, 2014, pp. 171–195). One response might be to introduce the model to explore social relations in a more nuanced way. Another response might be to layer another dimension onto the analysis of the data, to analyse more deeply what was happening within a knowledge code. We also considered expanding the data set to include curriculum documents, such as the Form As and Bs referred to in the data. We also found it necessary to nuance our analysis beyond what Specialization makes obvious. For example, our analysis showed the necessity of unpacking 'knowledge' to distinguish between different kinds of legitimate knowledges.

In conclusion, we started this chapter with the suggestion that the work that AD units do in universities is often characterized by contestation and we conjectured that this can, at least in part, be accounted for by the different views academic developers and lecturers hold of the status, identity and knowledge base of AD units. Specialization offered us a tool to both frame this conjecture and investigate it.

References

Ashwin, P. (2006). The development of learning and teaching in higher education: the changing context. In P. Ashwin (Ed.), *Changing higher education: The development of learning and teaching* (pp. 3–15). London: Routledge.

Bath, D. and Smith, C. (2004). Academic developers: An academic tribe claiming their territory in higher education. *International Journal for Academic Development, 9*(1), 9–27.

Bitzer, E. and Costandius, E. (2018). Continuous programme renewal and critical citizenship: Key items for the South African higher education curriculum agenda. *Transformation in Higher Education, 3*(0), a37.

Boughey, C. (2009). *A meta-analysis of teaching and learning at the five research intensive South African universities not affected by mergers*. Pretoria: Council on Higher Education.

Challis, D., Holt, D. and Palmer, S. (2009). Teaching and learning centres: Towards maturation. *Higher Education Research and Development, 28*(4), 371–383.

Ellery, K. (2018). Legitimation of knowers for access in science. *Journal of Education, 71*, 24–38.

Gosling, D. (1996). What do UK Educational Development units do? *International Journal for Academic Development, 1*(1), 75–83.

Gosling, D. (2001). Educational development units in the UK – what are they doing five years on? *International Journal for Academic Development, 6*(1), 74–90.

Gosling, D. (2003). Philosophical approaches to academic development. In H. Eggins and R. Macdonald (Eds). *The scholarship of academic development* (pp. 70–79). Milton Keynes: Society for Research into Higher Education and The Open University Press.

Gosling, D. (2009). Educational development in the UK: A complex and contradictory reality. *International Journal for Academic Development, 14*(1), 5–18.

Green, D.A. and Little, D. (2013). Academic development on the margins. *Studies in Higher Education, 38*(4), 523–537.

Holt, D, Palmer, S and Challis, D. (2011). Changing perspectives: Teaching and learning centre's strategic contributions to academic development in Australian higher education. *International Journal for Academic Development, 16*(1), 4–17.

Howard, S.K. and Maton, K. (2011) Theorising knowledge practices: A missing piece of the educational technology puzzle. *Research in Learning Technology, 19*(3): 191–206.

Leibowitz, B., Bozalek, V. and Kahn, P. (2017). *Theorising Learning to Teach in Higher Education*. Abingdon: Routledge.

Löytönen, T. (2017). Educational development within higher arts education: An experimental move beyond fixed pedagogies. *International Journal for Academic Development, 22*(3), 231–244.

Malcolm, J. and Zukas, M. (2001). Bridging pedagogic gaps: Conceptual discontinuities in higher education. *Teaching in Higher Education, 6*(1), 33–42.

Maton, K. (2000). Languages of legitimation: The structuring significance for intellectual fields of strategic knowledge claims. *British Journal of Sociology of Education, 21*(2), 147–167.

Maton, K. (2014). *Knowledge and knowers: Towards a realist sociology of education*. London: Routledge.

Maton, K. (2016). Legitimation Code Theory: Building knowledge about knowledge-building. In K. Maton, S. Hood and S. Shay (Eds), *Knowledge-building: Educational studies in Legitimation Code Theory* (pp. 1–24). London: Routledge.

Maton, K. and Chen, R.T-H. (2020). Specialization codes: Knowledge, knowers and student success. In J.R. Martin, K. Maton and Y.J. Doran (Eds), *Accessing academic discourse: Systemic functional linguistics and Legitimation Code Theory* (pp. 35–58). London: Routledge.

Naidoo, A. (2012). Leading curriculum renewal in a faculty of education: A story from within. *Perspectives in Education, 30*(2), 71–80.

Reimann, N. (2009). Exploring disciplinarity in academic development: Do 'ways of thinking and practicing' help higher education practitioners to think about learning and teaching? In C. Kreber (Ed.), *The university and its disciplines: Teaching and learning within and beyond disciplinary boundaries* (pp. 84–95). Abingdon: Routledge.

Rowland, S. (2002). Overcoming fragmentation in professional life: The challenge for academic development. *Higher Education Quarterly, 56*(1), 52–64.

Shay, S. (2012). Educational development as a field: Are we there yet? *Higher Education Research and Development, 31*(3), 311–323.

Quinn, L. (2012a). Enabling and constraining conditions for academic staff development. In L. Quinn (Ed.), *Re-imagining academic staff development: Spaces for disruption* (pp. 27–50). Stellenbosch: SUNPress.

Quinn, L. (2012b). Understanding resistance: An analysis of discourses in academic staff development. *Studies in Higher Education, 37*(1), 69–83.

Wilcox, S. (1998). The role of the educational developer in the improvement of university teaching. *The Canadian Journal of Higher Education, 28*(1), 77–104.

14
DECOLONIZING THE SCIENCE CURRICULUM
When good intentions are not enough

Hanelie Adendorff and Margaret A.L. Blackie

Introduction

In many parts of the world, particularly those territories under colonial rule in the mid-1800s and later, formal education had been a major part of the transplanting of knowledge from the dominant territory to the colonized territory. It was intentional move to 'civilize' the native peoples and seen as an unqualified good. The post-World War II era saw the decolonization of territories around the globe in a formal political sense. But it took several decades before questions began to arise around the nature of formal education itself and its powerful cultural influence (Bray, 1994). It is only really in the last 20 years that academic inquiry has begun to probe the potentially destructive nature of a 'colonized' curriculum. In the English speaking academic world these questions are gaining traction across the Commonwealth. South Africa has been a latecomer to the conversation, perhaps because the move to majority rule occurred relatively recently. It is only as the 'born frees' have entered the higher education space that the cracks in the foundation of the 'Rainbow Nation' have become undeniable.

The conversation around decolonization of higher education curricula hit South Africa by storm with the #RhodesMustFall and subsequent #FeesMustFall campaigns.[1] Prior to this, decolonization conversations, if they were happening at all, in higher education institutions, were limited to small pockets of interest. The advent of the countrywide student protests beginning in 2015 has meant a far wider engagement with decolonization. The level of response and engagement across the academic spectrum is widely variant, and rather shallow reactionary responses both strongly in favour and strongly resistant have tended to dominate thus far. Between disciplines there are also varied positions. While the humanities and arts faculties easily recognize the presence and influence of Western ideology in their curricula, for the most part the decolonization of science curricula is a far less obvious project.

The lack of understanding by both staff and students for where the problem lies and how science can have a colonizing influence has prompted us to use Legitimation Code Theory to help us reflect on what is at stake in these conversations. Our intention is to provide a framework which can be used by both staff and students to facilitate explorations which could in fact lead to a richer science curriculum.

Ordinarily this kind of chapter in an education research book would begin by situating the argument in the current literature and thereby signally the intellectual antecedents of the argument. It is our hope and intention to provide a document which can used by STEM educators in the higher education to foster meaningful and critical engagement with the conversation around decolonization of curricula. To this end we have chosen begin rather by explaining our entry into the problem, the insight given by the employment of concepts from the Specialization and Autonomy dimensions of Legitimation Code Theory (LCT) to reveal the points of conflict, confusion and where care must be taken in proceeding. Beyond LCT itself, the engagement with the education per se has been kept to a minimum precisely to lower the threshold of entry to the conversation for STEM educators.

Nonetheless, we must take as our point of departure that science is not perceived as philosophically neutral. From some quarters, science has come under fire for the colonial and colonizing nature of its curricula, which arguably leads to epistemic violence (Heleta, 2016b). It is worth noting that many academic scientists find the lack of neutrality of scientific education to be almost unthinkable given the presumed objectivity of the scientific method. We hope that this chapter will reveal something of the complexity at the heart of the decolonization conversation.

This chapter will use the LCT dimensions of Specialization and Autonomy to analyse the content of some of these decolonization calls, and current responses as well as approaches to decolonizing the science curricula at Stellenbosch University (SU). The lens of LCT offers valuable insight into decolonization of science curricula, and shows why current decolonization attempts might be perceived as perpetuating past injustices despite every intention to respond positively and effectively.

Our entry into the conversation

While the far reaching implications of decolonizing curricula has become the major focus of our interest. Our use of LCT to more productively engage with the potential decolonization of science began with a conversation around a short video clip which caused a major ruckus on social media under #ScienceMustFall (#SMF). The clip featured a black female student from the University of Cape Town in a discussion panel on the need for decolonization of curricula. She began by stating that 'science as a whole is a product of Western modernity and the whole thing should be scratched off'. She then went on to illustrate what she meant by using the example of the belief that it was possible for magic to cause a lightning strike on another person. At this point a white male interjected saying 'It's not true'. Immediately the chair of the panel intervened to force an apology from the white male. The black female student responded with comments on the problem of the imposition of gravity by Newton. The sequence which lasted just over four minutes caused a furore on social media.

It was clear in the social media storm in the days and weeks that followed that neither of the two significant camps in the highly polarized discourse appeared to grasp was at stake for the other camp. The reason for this major mismatch seemed to be explicable using the Specialization dimension of LCT (see Figure 14.1). Specialization is concerned with what counts as a legitimate knowledge claim. It starts from the position that every practice is about or oriented towards something and by someone (Maton, 2014, 2016; Maton and Chen, 2020). It thus sets up: relations concerned with knowledge, called *epistemic relations* (ER) and relations concerned with knowers or *social relations* (SR).

Different practices emphasize these relations in different ways. Practices may more strongly or weakly emphasize epistemic relations and/or social relations as the basis of legitimacy. The relative strength of the two relations together give the *specialization code*, and we can analyse practices in terms whether they emphasize one, both or neither as the basis for status and achievement.

Where practices emphasize the possession of specialized skills, knowledge and procedures as the basis for success (stronger epistemic relations) and downplay the attributes of who is speaking or who is making the claim (weaker social relations), we have a *knowledge code*. Conversely, if what you are studying and how is less important (weaker epistemic relations) and it is more important who you are – such as having the right cultivated dispositions, or the right sensibility or right social category (stronger social relations) – we have a *knower code*. We can also have both weaker epistemic relations and weaker social relations (anything goes) or a *relativist code*, and both stronger epistemic relations and stronger social relations (have to have right knowledge and dispositions) or an *élite code*.

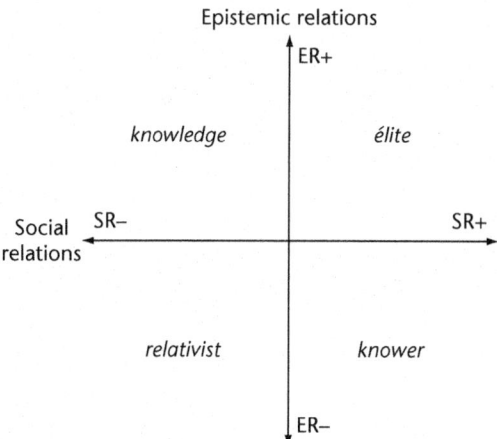

FIGURE 14.1 The specialization plane

Source: Maton, 2014, p. 30

Social fields can thus be understood as *knowledge–knower structures* (Maton, 2014, pp. 65–85). For example, science can be characterized as a knowledge-code field. Such fields exhibit *hierarchical knowledge structures* and *horizontal knower structures*, where it is the explanatory power of the axioms and theorems that is valued. The social profile of the scientist is held to be irrelevant to their scientific contribution – anyone can claim legitimate knowledge so long as they use the appropriate scientific principles and procedures. In contrast, the humanities can be characterized as having a *horizontal knowledge structure* and *hierarchical knower structure* – a systematically organized hierarchical system of knowers based on the ideal knower. In such fields, the knowledge is subservient to the knower, serving only to build more legitimate knowers (Maton, 2014). Knowledge-code fields, such as science, expand by integrating new theories into the hierarchical framework, ultimately aiming for the fewest possible axioms incorporating the largest possible range of empirical phenomena. In contrast, knower-code fields such as the humanities, expand by integrating more knowers at lower levels, and across an expanding range of different dispositions.

To fully understand these fields, and especially knower-code fields, we need to consider the possible stance or 'gazes' that actors can assume in them. To this end, Maton (2014) identifies four gazes along a continuum of increasing strength of social relations.

1. *trained gazes* with weaker social relations (SR−) and stronger epistemic relations (ER+). This gaze is typically at one end of the continuum and is associated with knowledge-code practices;
2. *cultivated gazes*, which are typically associated with knower-code practices and acquired by long immersion that cultivates the legitimate dispositions of the knower;
3. *social gazes*, also typically associated with knower codes, are acquired by virtue of one's location in society such as one's class position, or one's social category, e.g. being black or female;
4. *born gazes* which are found at the end of the knower continuum with the strongest social relations (SR+) and weakest epistemic relations (ER−).

For the purpose of this study, what is termed in LCT a *translation device* was designed to bring the theory to bear on the data. A translation device makes explicit how concepts are realized within an object of study (see Maton and Chen, 2016; Maton and Howard, 2016). Here epistemic relations were defined as any reference to the explanatory power of scientific theory and the use of the scientific process. Cases emphasizing this were coded as stronger epistemic relations (ER+), for example 'the eminent cyber journal, *The Conversation*, has published an article promoting the "decolonization" of Mathematics, arguably the "purest" of the sciences' (Cameron, 2016). Cases downplaying the scientific process or explanatory power of theories were coded as weaker epistemic relations (ER−), for example 'decolonizing science would mean doing away with it entirely and starting all over again to deal with how we respond to environments and how we understand it' (UCT Scientist, 2016).

Manifestations of social relations were defined as any reference to personal experience, personal knowledge and valuing of the personal. Cases emphasizing this were coded as stronger social relations (SR+), for example 'accommodate knowledge from our perspective' (UCT Scientist, 2016), and cases downplaying the personal were coded as weaker social relations (SR−), for example 'this video indicates a Fallist, decolonized view within which beliefs are the rule and the new Afrocentric science acts merely as a confirmatory tool to help the "re-educated and decolonized-minded" to reinforce beliefs within safe, sacred spaces' (Cameron, 2016).

Analyzing the #SMF debate with Specialization and gazes

The opinions expressed in the four-minute video clip can be characterized as a knower code. We see stronger social relations (SR+) with statements such as 'the whole thing is a product of Western modernity'. Here, who it is that makes the claim is held as more important than the content of the claim and thus this clip exhibits weaker epistemic relations (ER−), in quotes such as 'we can do more as new knowledge producers, as people who have been given the benefit to reason or whatever people say we do when we think or rationalize'. The same emphasis on social relations (SR+) is seen the speaker's statement that:

> Western modernity is the direct antagonistic factor to decolonization because Western knowledge is totalizing. It is saying that it was Newton and only Newton who knew or saw an apple falling and then out of nowhere decided that gravity existed and created uh an equation, and that is it, for the rest … whether people knew Newton or not or whether that ever happens in Western Africa Northern Africa, that thing is the only way to explain gravity is through Newton who sat under a tree and saw an apple fall.

When we look at the response of Professor Tim Crowe (Crowe, 2016), selected as an example of the typical science response in the online conversation, we see a knowledge code. His statement that 'this video indicates a Fallist's decolonized view within which beliefs are the rule and the new Afrocentric science acts merely as a confirmatory tool to help the re-educated and decolonized-minded to reinforce beliefs' shows weaker social relations (SR−). In the following statement we see stronger epistemic relations (ER+):

> I believe that universities ought to be marketplaces of ideas, among many other things. Without the give and take of intellectual discourse and debate, universities devolve into nothing more than glorified training colleges. Meaningful post-graduate education and research become unfulfilled dreams.

This example is chosen because it is written by an established scientist writing from the perspective of a scientist. There is a clear dismissal of the Fallist position out of a recognizable scientific (ER+, SR−) position, but there is no attempt to critique the 'obvious' neutrality of science.

These two positions, which are seen playing out in most of the responses to the two-hour meeting between the UCT Science Faculty and 'Fallists' (UCT Scientist, 2016), constitute a *code clash*. In such a 'code clash' between different bases of legitimacy it is almost impossible to find common ground because the nature of the ground itself is contested although not explicitly. More recently, the conversations around the decolonization of science have evolved into a more scholarly space. Nonetheless, the powerful caricature of the 'Science Must Fall' video clip continue to provide useful relief against which to track the conversation especially as impasses emerge which seem impossible to overcome. Often the issue is precisely this code clash.

Hlabangani Mtshali's response to the video clip gives a way through the impasse. In a short article called 'How you probably misunderstood Science Must Fall' (Mtshali, 2016), he describes Science as 'the system of humans trying to explain and prove and predict natural occurring phenomena to themselves in a way that is as up to date as possible, can't have geography', a position that has stronger epistemic relations (ER+). He continues to explain that 'textbooks from primary school up to university, use the theory of 'heroic invention and discovery' – which gives props to one dude for observing and noting down something science-y, i.e. Isaac Newton and gravity – and not 'multiple discovery' – which suggests that that one dude probably wasn't the only guy who's ever had that observation', which has stronger social relations (SR+). His position could thus be characterized as an *élite code*, where both epistemic relations and social relations are relatively strong. If we are looking to mediate the often-emotive conversation about decolonization on science, we might do well to find a way to strengthen both epistemic relations and social relations.

The kind of social relations valorized in this conversation is best understood by turning our attention to the concept of gazes. As suggested earlier, legitimate knowers in science exhibit a trained gaze, acquired through mastering the appropriate knowledge. Knowers in science are created through learning the set of hierarchical theories, axioms, the scientific method, etc., in the knowledge framework. In science, the knower is just a means to the knowledge end. In contrast, knowledge acts merely as the means to the 'knower-creation' end in knower code fields (Maton, 2014). From this perspective, it makes sense that knowledge could be seen as dispensable, as suggested by the student in her comment about 'scrap[ping] the whole thing'.

Most evident in the student's comments, though, seems to be a social gaze, implying that legitimate knowers in her opinion are not those who have acquired certain knowledge (the trained gaze of science) or those who have shifted towards certain dispositions (cultivated gazes). As evidenced in her calls that science be restarted from an African perspective, it seems that legitimate knowers are those belonging to a certain social group – non-Westerners i.e. a social gaze.

> So Western identity is the problem that decolonization directly deals with, to say that we are going to decolonize by having knowledge that is produced by us, that speaks to us, and that is able to accommodate knowledge from our perspective.
>
> *(UCT Scientist, 2016)*

Based on this, we would thus suggest that an appropriate mediator in the conversation would have to be a scientist who has the appropriate social gaze. In the absence of such a mediator it is hard to see how a meaningful conversation can happen. Nonetheless while this is necessary, it is probably not sufficient to take us to a place where a curriculum can be recognized as both true to science and as decolonized. There is yet another aspect to consider: power relations.

Where does the power lie?

Fortunately, the furore over the #SMF clip and the disruption of #FeesMustFall precipitated real conversation with respect to the decolonization of curricula. Clearly those discussions have happened across the university, but we continue to limit our focus on the physical and biological sciences. This is because within these disciplines the argument of the neutrality of knowledge continues to prevail. For the few lecturers who readily embraced the idea of the importance of decolonization, it became clear that some interrogation of what was actually in play would be helpful. In all cases some attempt was made to make use of either indigenous knowledge or student experience of the world, but the way in which this prior knowledge was used was widely variant and it was not clear that all approaches would be equally meaningful or seen as a real move towards decolonization. It quickly became evident that the use of the LCT dimension of Autonomy would help to distinguish between the major approaches. We will use three real examples of approaches which have been implemented. But, first, a little explanation of Autonomy.

The Autonomy dimension in LCT 'begins from the simple premise that any set of practices comprises constituents that are related together in particular ways' (Maton and Howard, 2018, p. 6). In other words, a set of practices comprises positions, whether these are actors or ideas or objects or whatever it might be, and principles or the ways those things are organized – their ways of working, their aims, their purposes and so on. This sets up two relations. First, *positional autonomy* (PA) are relations between constituents (the things within it: actors, ideas, objects, theories, practices, ways of doing) positioned within a context and those positioned in other contexts or categories. The variation here is in the degree of insulation. Second, *relational autonomy* (RA) are relations between the constituents of a context or category (ways things are arranged, what they are for) and relations among constituents of other contexts or categories (Figure 14.2). The variation here is from autonomous to heteronomous.

Both positional autonomy and relational autonomy can be independently stronger or weaker; where stronger implies greater insulation, greater strength of boundaries and control and weaker means less insulation, etc. So, if a practice says there should be stronger boundaries between what is in this context and what lies beyond, that is stronger positional autonomy (PA+) and if it effectively announces that there should be stronger boundaries between how we do things here and how they are done elsewhere that is stronger relational autonomy

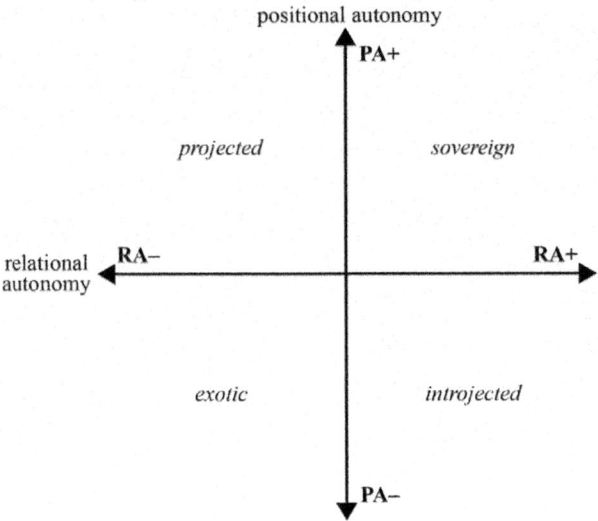

FIGURE 14.2 The autonomy plane

Source: Maton and Howard, 2018, p. 6

(RA+) (Maton and Howard, 2018, 2020). Simply put, we can ask 'where things come from and where the purpose to which they are being used for, comes from'. So, we can describe a continuum of strengths for positional autonomy, from weaker to stronger and a continuum of strengths for relational autonomy, from weaker to stronger on a Cartesian plane, and that will give us four principal autonomy codes.

In *sovereign codes* (PA+, RA+), there are strongly insulated positions and autonomous principles (Maton and Howard, 2020). In science curricula, this might translate to the scientists as well as the objects, ideas and theories of science being used to advance science and learning how to think and act like a scientist.

In *exotic codes* (PA−, RA−), there are weakly insulated positions and heteronomous principles (Maton and Howard, 2020). We might see this as science curricula using objects, ideas and theories from fields other than science for a purpose other than advancing science. For example, using content from social science to prepare students for group work projects.

In *introjected codes* (PA−, RA+), there are weakly insulated positions and autonomous principles (Maton and Howard, 2020). In science curricula, this might manifest as using the objects, theories and methods of science to dissuade students from their religious beliefs.

In *projected codes* (PA+, RA−), there are strongly insulated positions and heteronomous principles (Maton and Howard, 2020). In science curricula, we would see this in Indigenous Knowledge Systems (IKS) being used as examples for teaching scientific concepts.

What counts as decolonization of science curricula?

The Autonomy dimension was selected to explore this question since it speaks, to some degree, to power issues – whose content and whose purposes are valorized or advanced in this educational endeavour. In the translation device designed for this study, stronger positional autonomy (PA+) is defined as actors, ideas, theories, thoughts and objects that can be said to belong to science as a field of practice, and weaker positional autonomy (PA–) is weaker when science curricula draw on ideas, theories, actors, objects, methods from *outside* of science, e.g. IKS. Stronger relational autonomy (RA+) is defined as the purpose of advancing the learning or mastery of the ways of doing, knowing and thinking in science, and relational autonomy is weaker (RA–) when science curricula advances causes other than learning the ways of doing, knowing and thinking in science.

Since we are interested in decolonizing science, we will take science curricula as the starting point, looking at the things (actors, ideas, objects, theories, practices, ways of doing) and purposes (what things are for) within the curriculum space of science. It is useful to state again that this is about where the things and the purposes they are being used for comes from (Maton and Howard, 2018). The *sovereign code* would then become science content (scientists, theories, methods, etc.) used for the purpose of learning and advancing science. The *exotic code* would be things from outside science used for purposes other than learning or advancing science. The *introjected code* would have things from outside science used for the purpose of learning and advancing science (e.g. IKS), and conversely, in the *projected code* things from inside science would be used for purposes other than advancing or learning science (e.g. social justice) (see Table 14.1).

It is important to recognize that decolonization itself is a contested idea. That is to say that not all who are calling for decolonization are calling for the same changes. As a result it is vitally important that we have some way to analyse and critique any proposed change precisely so that we can answer the question of whether current decolonization activities in science can really be counted as decolonization. Thus,

TABLE 14.1 Translation device for decolonizing science

Concept		Manifested as	Example
PA	+	Actors, ideas, theories, thoughts and objects that can be said to belong to science as a field of practice	Science content
	–	Actors, ideas, theories, thoughts and objects from outside science as a field of practice	Content from elsewhere e.g. IKS
RA	+	Advancing the learning or mastery of the ways of doing, knowing and thinking in science	Teaching students scientific skills such as the scientific method
	–	Advancing the learning or mastery of things other than science	Content or topics that foster the development of graduate attributes

we will turn to look at a number of data sources in terms of where their content (who and what has power) and their purposes (what uses count as legitimate) originate from (inside or outside science). We will start in #SMF again, because while it is a caricature it does provide fairly clear illustration which can create the backdrop for the more subtle analysis of real practical examples. We will analyse each with the use of the Autonomy dimension, and finally consider the three scenarios suggested by Winberg and Winberg (2017).

#SMF and Autonomy

By our definition, science curricula are focused inwardly, on learning science and advancing the field of science through educating future scientists. Curricula might venture into using science for purposes other than advancing or learning science through projects or service learning components aimed at fostering a variety of graduate attributes, but these tend to be occasional. Science curricula in South Africa rarely draw on other disciplines, one notable exception being the inclusion of content on scientific writing and information literacy. Thus, science curricula tend to be situated mostly in the sovereign code. It is this very positioning which affords the strongly polarized positions over whether science is inherently neutral or profoundly, blindly colonizing. While many scientists would claim the philosophical neutrality of science, decolonization scholars have described science as both colonized and colonizing. Some critics, such as Heleta (2016a), have gone as far as saying that its epistemology, or colonial worldview, was 'designed to degrade, exploit and subjugate people in Africa, acting as an exploiter and gatekeeper'.

The Science Must Fall clip attracted a variety of responses, with those from the more virulent end of the spectrum giving it real traction in social media. Its significance in the current conversation is twofold. Firstly, despite dismissing the content as astoundingly ignorant, for many academic scientists this may have been the first real exposure to the thought that the science would not escape serious engagement in the decolonization conversation. Secondly, the clip is deeply polarizing. In the clip, a student leader gives her opinion of what decolonization in science might look like. She argues for 'restart[ing]' science from an African perspective and calls it a 'totalizing' product of Western modernity which, due to its colonized roots, is unable to respond to the worldview or experience of Africans. She explains the need for a science which is based on knowledge produced by non-Westerners, 'that speaks to us and that is able to accommodate knowledge from our perspective'. Her view of science is similar to that of decolonization scholars: it as product of the colonizers and is still colonizing, subduing all who differ from it. Her demand for a science that is able to accommodate the African experience (she gives the example of it being able to explain instances of witchcraft) would, as far as Western science goes, reside in the exotic code – using 'things' from outside science to advance a purpose that originates outside science. In essence she is calling for Indigenous Knowledge (IKS) to be equated with science.

According to our analysis, both IKS and the demands made in the Science Must Fall video clip reside in the exotic code while science occupies the sovereign code, making only occasional tours to the projected code and introjected code (see Figure 14.3). IKS and the #SMF demands must seem as foreign to science as science seems to the Indigenous way of knowing, doing and being. At this point the significance of the power dynamics comes into relief. Who is the gatekeeper to the knowledge?

The question becomes: can science be decolonized? If the definition requires equating IKS with scientific knowledge the answer must be no. To do so would be to completely eviscerate science. Is there an alternative? Can we take the call seriously and still retain the essence of essence? To answer this question, we will consider a few of these approaches through the lens of Autonomy, and we will do so by looking at the options in the various codes.

Introjected codes

In introjected codes (PA−, RA+), materials, actors and practices from outside (PA−) are used for inside purposes (RA+). These can comprise various forms, i.e. Science and Technology in Society (STS) (Winberg and Winberg, 2017) or IKS. Material on the history, philosophy and sociology of science is added to science curricula with the purpose of advancing science and helping students learn science, i.e. to better understand why one theory was selected over another, would qualify as a move into the introjected code. One of the most common responses to decolonization demands involves the inclusion of African or local illustrations in the curriculum content. For example, bringing a Gogo – an elderly Xhosa woman – into the teaching space to explain the way in which traditional beer is brewed, and then relating this to Microbiology concepts.

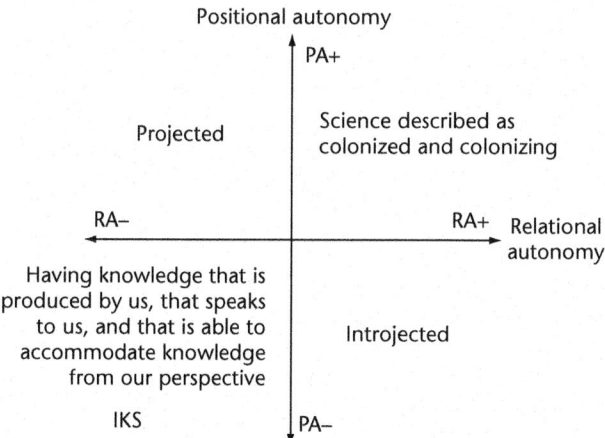

FIGURE 14.3 The autonomy plane: decolonizing science

Alas, this introjected approach is itself potentially problematic as a route to decolonization. Indeed it may be seen as a colonizing move in itself. Even if borne of good intentions, this might be considered, by those calling for the decolonization of science, as profaning that which is not Western (traditional beer brewing) to serve the purpose of advancing science, a product of 'Western modernity', and even of exploiting indigenous knowledge for the purpose of advancing Western science.

The issue at stake with venturing into the introjected code is the purpose to which something is used. As long as the purpose remains that of the colonizer, it cannot qualify as decolonization. We are reminded of Hammersmith's (2007) warning about just 'adding Indigenous content to the Western contexts' is not real transformation. One of the reasons put forward for this, is that 'Indigenous content is only meaningful within indigenous contexts and processes'. Here, the LCT dimension of Autonomy helps us to form a more nuanced understanding why this is so precisely because it reveals the power dynamic in play.

Projected codes

In projected codes (PA+, RA−), materials, actors and practices from inside science (PA+) are used for outside purposes (RA−), such as social justice. One of the most likely curricular approaches in this code is to have students do a project that serves an 'outside' purpose such as social justice, i.e. asking students to do projects related to their own context (applying science knowledge to their lived experience). In one such example in a science course, we saw a member of a specific rural community applying her science knowledge to a problem in her community, using her science knowledge to the benefit of her own community.

This is similar to the approach followed in the Nuffic and UNESCO/MOST's (2002) publication entitled 'Best Practices in IKS' (Boven and Morohashi, 2002). The lecturer allowed student groups to choose their own topics, and encouraged them to use examples from their lived experience, she also gave all teams the same budget, and required them to stay in it, not allowing wealthy students to top-up what they had been given. In addition to this, she opened her lab outside of the normal times scheduled for practical sessions. This complete overhaul of the practical portion of the course's curriculum, while staying true to the discipline, represents a break with how science is normally taught. Students were afforded the opportunity to determine what they were going to do and when they were going to do it. While the lecturer did not give up all her authority, she was no longer the only authority. Students were allowed to bring their indigenous knowledge into the curriculum, possible injustices were equalized by forcing all to stay in the same budget and the students were offered the opportunity to develop identities as co-producers of knowledge.

This example represents a start towards decolonization, because science is not the primary or only aim of these projects. Here the move towards decolonization is signalled by the awareness of power dynamics beyond the explicit curriculum which may be at play, and the attempt to level the playing field for all involved. However, other projects where students do research in communities or take solutions to them without partnering with the community for example, would not classify as decolonization. Such cases, even though they might look like moves into the projected code, are probably better described as sovereign acts since their purpose is still primarily the advance of science, whether in knowledge creation or knowledge dissemination.

In projected codes, the purpose is no longer advancing Western science. Authors such as Mbembe have pointed out that decolonization is not about doing away with all that is Western; it is about ending the dominance of Western knowledge systems and bringing Africa into the centre. Heleta (2016b), quoting Mamdani (1996) and McEwan (2009), refers to the undermining of indigenous people's identities, detailing how colonizers 'saw themselves as providers of supervision and guidance to the "weak" and "childlike" peoples in the colonies' and how Western academics and researchers 'often claim that Africa is nothing but misery, corruption, 'darkness' and irrationality' (quoting Mbembe, 2001) and cannot survive without a 'kind, white foreigner' (quoting Ngozi Adiche, 2009).

Here the Autonomy dimension highlights why this might be the case. Projected code activities might be more likely to be seen as decolonization attempts than introjected code activities.

Exotic codes

In exotic codes (PA–, RA–), materials, actors and practices from outside (PA–) are used for outside purposes (RA–), such as including STS content for the purpose of correcting historical accounts of the roots of science. In an example from Oenology, students are asked to research the effects of previous injustices related to this industry, such as the so-called 'dop-system' in which farm workers were 'paid' with a beaker of wine, usually downed, after each work day. The purpose of the project is to sensitize students to the social issues related to their field.

This initiative represents a move into exotic codes, since it uses content from outside the curriculum for a purpose other than learning or advancing science. Though a true example of decolonization, it is unlikely to qualify as science education in the eyes of academic scientists, and many academics might not be ready to sacrifice scarce teaching time towards this purpose. And frequently science students strongly resist these kinds of activities.

Traversing several codes

The last example involves asking students in a conservation science course to create a time-line, on the floor, depicting the discipline's history in the context of South Africa. This offers a valuable opportunity to correct students' view of the history of science, since their time lines often start in 1652 (with the arrival of Jan van Riebeeck). In this example the students move between various codes (see Figure 14.4).

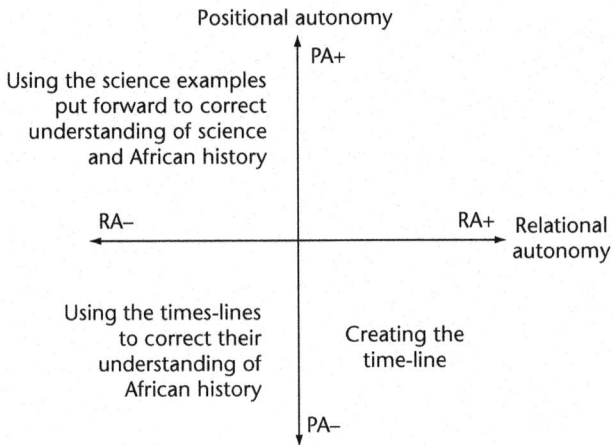

FIGURE 14.4 Additional autonomy codes in decolonizing science

This movement between codes is known as an 'autonomy tour' (Maton and Howard, 2018, 2020). In this case, the autonomy tour begins in the introjected code (having the students using content from history to depict their field of science) moves into the exotic code (using their depiction – e.g. the start date of the time-line – to correct their perspective on the history of science in Africa) and finally into the projected code (using the science examples students have put forward to correct their understanding of the history of the discipline in South Africa). This speaks directly to one of the themes identified by Winberg and Winberg (2017) and could be classified as an example of decolonization based on the fact that it aims to correct the history. This example does not sacrifice too much of the integrity of science and is more likely to be accepted by academics teaching science classes.

The Autonomy dimension has helped to make explicit why some, seemingly well-intended, decolonization attempts might be seen as further colonizing acts, especially if these acts involve IKS being used in the introjected code.

We will now turn to the suggestions of Winberg and Winberg (2017). Applied to science, the three scenarios might look as follows:

1. A specialized curriculum based on science content selected for its specific value in solving African needs.
2. A curriculum that focuses strongly on STS content to help students better understand science and its roots.
3. A curriculum based on science content, but including some STS and some content specific to the needs of Africa.

This first curriculum spans the sovereign code and projected code, using skills based on Western science to not only advance science but also to meet a social justice agenda.

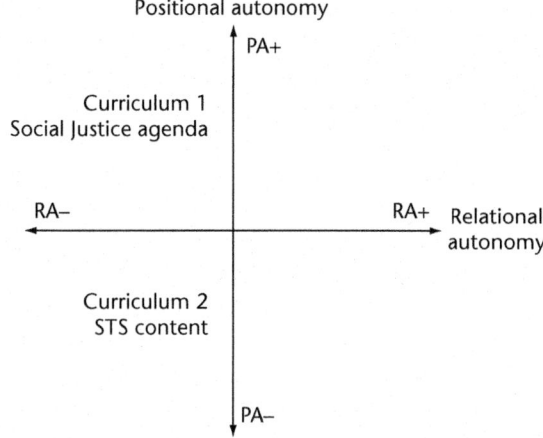

FIGURE 14.5 Winberg and Winberg's (2017) scenarios for decolonizing Engineering represented on the autonomy plane

The second curriculum, with its strong focus on STS, moves towards the exotic code, using positions from outside science (from the sociology of science knowledge, history and philosophy of science) to advance the purpose of social justice.

Lastly, the third curriculum, which includes elements from STS and adds social justice as a second purpose (alongside the purpose of advancing science), is still strongly based on the traditional curriculum. This scenario, though still in the sovereign code, includes some movement into the exotic code (drawing on STS for correcting science history) and projected code (applying science knowledge for social justice purposes).

It is worth noting that: (1) none of these scenarios involve the introjected code; and (2) that the participants in Winberg and Winberg's (2017) study chose scenario 3 as the best option. This scenario retains its sovereignty while adding deliberate tours into introjected codes and projected codes. It could be argued that it still has the feel of science, but a science that is starting to look beyond itself to some extent. Maton (2016) argues that the solution of wicked problems, such as those facing Africa, will require the ability to integrate knowledges by travelling across codes i.e. *autonomy tours* (Maton and Howard, 2018, 2020).

Where does this leave us in terms of what might count as decolonization and what will not?

Decolonization, in the words of Behari-Leak *et al.* (2017), is 'a nuanced, layered concept. Its meaning cannot be unlocked using a scientific formula, recipes or definitions. An understanding of the process of "decolonisation" lies more in its detail than its definition'. We have seen that it is not about discarding all that is European, but that it is about putting Africa in the centre (Mbembe, 2016). It is not about just adding local content, but about restoring the value-contribution of indigenous ways of knowing, doing and being (Hammersmith, 2007; Boiselle, 2016; Heleta,

2016a, 2016b). It is about derailing the perceived monopoly of Western science on producing sought after knowledge (Boiselle, 2016).

The examples listed here do not really address issues of epistemology. That will require a much deeper look at both the epistemology of science and that of indigenous knowledge systems, a process that Rip (2000) reminds us, will require relooking the assumptions of both knowledge systems. Garuba (2015), stating that it would 'not only be presumptuous, but impossible [for him] to describe in fine detail how this should be done in each discipline', offers the following advice on how to proceed:

> In your own discipline, you may, first, want to adopt a content-driven additive approach and expand the curriculum already in place. Or you may want to adopt the different approach of thinking how the object of study itself is constituted, what tools are used to study it and what concepts are used to frame it.

What we have shown here is not enough; and it is not going far enough. It is still not the decolonization that Garuba (2015) is speaking of the second approach (see above). But it does provide a starting point, similar to Garuba's (2015) first approach, for understanding why some actions might qualify as decolonization and others not. We have provided a language and framework for explaining these conclusions, and doing it in a way that can be heard and understood by scientists. It shows us that tinkering with the curriculum can be the start of a decolonizing process. But we need to avoid the tempting lure of the introjected code and venture rather into the projected code. Academic scientists will need to approach this from a willingness to learn, rather than the position of being the authority. As such, in some ways, the very conversation and exploration will begin to facilitate the shift in attitude which may be the unconscious driver of the symbolic violence which those calling for decolonization are perceiving.

Note

1. #RhodesMustFall began with protests at the University of Cape Town in March 2015 over the presence of a statue of Cecil John Rhodes in a prominent position on campus. The movement quickly spread across campuses in South Africa. #FeesMustFall followed in September 2015 and began over annual fee increases and the original promise of the incoming ANC government in 1994 to make higher education accessible for all. Both campaigns morphed into a much larger conversation around the nature of higher education.

References

Behari-Leak, K., Masehela, L., Marhaya, L., Tjabane, M. and Mercel, N. (2017) *Decolonising the curriculum: It's in the detail, not just in the definition.* 13 March. Retrieved from www.news.uct.ac.za/article/-2017-03-13-decolonising-the-curriculum-its-in-the-detail-not-just-in-the-definition.

Boisselle, L.N. (2016). Decolonizing science and science education in a postcolonial space (Trinidad, a Developing Caribbean Nation, Illustrates), *SAGE Open*, January–March, 1–11. doi:10.1177/2158244016635257.

Boven, K. and Morohashi, J. (2002). Best practices using indigenous knowledge. The Hague: Nuffic. Retrieved from https://unesdoc.unesco.org/ark:/48223/pf0000147859.

Bray, M. (1994). Decolonisation and education: New paradigms for the remnants of empire. *Compare, 24*(1), 37–51.

Cameron, J. (2016) Science decolonisers 'reprehensible', says top UCT scientist after watching THIS video. 18 October, *BizNews*. Retrieved from www.biznews.com/mailbox/2016/10/18/science-decolonisers-reprehensible-uct.

Garuba, H. (2015). What is an African curriculum? *Mail and Guardian*. Retrieved from https://mg.co.za/article/2015-04-17-what-is-an-african-curriculum/.

Hammersmith, J.A. (2007). *Converging indigenous and western knowledge systems: implications for tertiary education* (Unpublished doctoral thesis). University of South Africa (UNISA), South Africa.

Heleta, S. (2016a). Decolonisation: Academics must change what they teach, and how. *The Conversation*, November 2016. Retrieved from https://theconversation.com/decolonisation-academics-must-change-what-they-teach-and-how-68080.

Heleta, S. (2016b). Decolonisation of higher education: Dismantling epistemic violence and Eurocentrism in South Africa. *Transformation in Higher Education 1*(1), 1–8. http://doi.org/10.4102/the.v1i1.9.

Mamdani, M. (1996). *Citizen and subject: Contemporary Africa and the legacy of late colonialism*. Princeton, NJ. Princeton University Press.

McEwan, C. (2009). *Postcolonialism and development*. New York: Routledge.

Maton, K. (2014). *Knowledge and knowers: Towards a realist sociology of education*. London: Routledge.

Maton, K. (2016). Legitimation Code Theory: Building knowledge about knowledge-building. In K. Maton, S. Hood and S. Shay (Eds), *Knowledge-building: Educational studies in Legitimation Code Theory* (pp. 1–24). London: Routledge.

Maton, K. and Chen, R.T.-H. (2016). LCT in qualitative research: Creating a translation device for studying constructivist pedagogy. In K. Maton, S. Hood and S. Shay (Eds), *Knowledge-building: Educational studies in Legitimation Code Theory* (pp. 27–48). London: Routledge.

Maton, K. and Chen, R.T.-H. (2020). Specialization codes: Knowledge, knowers and student success. In J.R. Martin, K. Maton and Y.J. Doran (Eds), *Accessing academic discourse: Systemic functional linguistics and Legitimation Code Theory* (pp. 35–58). London: Routledge.

Maton, K. and Howard, S.K. (2016). LCT in mixed-methods research: Evolving an instrument for quantitative data. In K. Maton, S. Hood and S. Shay (Eds), *Knowledge-building: Educational studies in Legitimation Code Theory* (pp. 49–71). London: Routledge.

Maton, K. and Howard, S.K. (2018). Taking autonomy tours: A key to integrative knowledge-building. *LCT Centre Occasional Paper 1*, 1–35.

Maton, K. and Howard, S.K. (2020). Targeting science: Successfully integrating mathematics into science teaching. In K. Maton, J.R. Martin and Y.J. Doran (Eds), *Studying Science: Knowledge, language, pedagogy*. London: Routledge.

Mbembe, A. (2001). *On the postcolony*. Berkeley, CA: University of California Press.

Mbembe, A. (2016). Decolonising the university: New directions. *Arts and Humanities in Higher Education 15*(1), 29–45.

Mtshali, H. (2016). *How you probably misunderstood Science Must Fall*. Retrieved from http://connect.citizen.co.za/81832/probably-misunderstood-sciencemustfall/.

Ngozi Adiche, C. (2009). *The danger of a single story*, TED Global. Retrieved from www.ted.com/talks/chimamanda_adichie_the_danger_of_a_single_story

Rip, A. (2000). Indigenous knowledge and Western science – in practice. Cardiff conference, Demarcation Socialized, 25–27 August 2000.

UCT Scientist (2016). *Science Must Fall?* [Video]. 13 October. YouTube. Retrieved from www.youtube.com/watch?v=C9SiRNibD14

Winberg, S. and Winberg, C. (2017). Using a social justice approach to decolonize an engineering curriculum. *Proceedings of the IEEE Global Engineering Education Conference (EDUCON 2017)*, Athens, 25–26 April 2017, 248–254.

15
THE ROLE OF ASSESSMENT IN PREPARING ACADEMIC DEVELOPERS FOR PROFESSIONAL PRACTICE

Lynn Quinn

Introduction

Globally the field of academic development (AD),[1] despite being in existence for more than 40 years, remains a contested and complex space. In many contexts AD is in a precarious position, subject to changes in leadership and constant restructuring (Gosling, 2009; Fraser and Ryan, 2012). Some AD units are shut down whereas others are 'unmade and remade anew' (Brew and Peseta, 2008, p. 83). These 'zones marked by uncertainty and ambiguity' (Grant, 2007, p. 35) are difficult contexts for academic developers to work in. To undertake meaningful AD work which can contribute to solving some of the seemingly intractable problems in higher education (HE), there is a need for knowledgeable and competent academic developers (Quinn and Vorster, 2014). Historically there has been no formal route specifically designed to prepare academic developers to undertake the complex and varied work they are required to do.

The Centre for Higher Education Research, Teaching and Learning at Rhodes University in South Africa is an AD unit that has not been subject to the vagaries of the field as is the case with many of our counterparts in South Africa and beyond. My colleagues and I have built expertise in, and have experience of, AD work at a range of South African universities. Using hard earned knowledge from this experience and drawing on HE research, in 2011 we began to offer a postgraduate diploma in higher education[2] *for academic developers* that provides participants with theoretical and conceptual tools to analyse their contexts, and devise appropriate AD practices and approaches appropriate to their specific contexts. This we hope is contributing to strengthening the field of AD in South Africa, and making it less precarious.

However, despite positive course evaluations and external examiner reports, over time we have become more concerned with the range of marks awarded to summative portfolios in each cohort. It was clear that not everyone was able to access what Bernstein (2000) calls the realization rules, that is, they were not all able to produce what counts as legitimate texts to demonstrate their learning on the course equally well. Using some of the tools offered by Legitimation Code Theory (LCT) to analyse two summative assessment portfolios we have enhanced our understanding of exactly how, in their writing, some participants were able to provide evidence of cumulative learning and knowledge-building. The point of the analysis was to make explicit the often tacit 'rules' for success on the course to inform our pedagogic and assessment practices.

Context

The postgraduate diploma in higher education (PGDip) is offered to practising academic developers (in various roles) from across the diverse Southern African higher education landscape. Its stated purpose is

> to advance academic developers' *knowledge* of higher education as a *field of study* and to enable them to conceptualize, design and *implement* formal and informal *academic development initiatives appropriate to their contexts* and the challenges facing contemporary Southern African higher education.
> *(PGDip (HE) Course Guide, 2017–2018, emphasis added)*

The course consists of six compulsory modules: The higher education context; Teaching and learning in higher education; Curriculum development; Assessment of student learning; Development, enhancement and assurance of quality teaching and learning; and Conceptualising and designing contextually appropriate academic development initiatives. It is offered over two years with six one-week teaching-intensive contact sessions and online support between sessions.

Unlike most higher education courses, there is no summative assessment during the course. This was a conscious decision on our part to ensure that assessment *for* rather than *of* learning was the focus until the very end of the course when summative assessment is required to award the qualification.

For each module formative assessment consists of a pre-module task (which requires participants to explore their current contexts in relation to the topic of the module) and four or five tasks which provide scaffolding for the integrated, authentic module assignment. The group is divided into smaller tutorial groups and each group is assigned a tutor. The tutors provide feedback on all the smaller tasks and also affective encouragement and support to their group of students. The two course facilitators provide feedback on all the module assignments. No marks are awarded for the tasks or assignments. Explicit assignment instructions and assessment criteria are provided and discussed with participants.

Towards the end of the second year of the course, the participants use all the module assignments and the constructive and developmental feedback they have received to construct a coherent and integrated portfolio in which they demonstrate how they have achieved the purpose and outcomes of the course. They are offered further feedback on the completed draft of their portfolios. The only time they receive a summative mark for the course is when they submit their final portfolios.

Theorizing assessment practices

In professional and vocational education students need to demonstrate two distinct ways of knowing: 'knowing how' and 'knowing that' (Winch, 2009, drawing on Ryle, 1946, 1949). For Winch, theoretical or propositional knowledge ('knowing that') is an important part of practical knowing ('knowing how'). Thus for an assessor in a course to make a judgement of overall professional competence, both ways of knowing need to be assessed. Through our assessment methods we try to ascertain whether our participants have acquired and are able to articulate both ways of knowing and whether the theoretical tools we have offered them in the course enable them to critique current practices and to conceptualize new practices in their contexts.

As is the case in most professional courses, our pedagogic and assessment practices are designed with the intention of enabling cumulative learning and knowledge-building. According to Maton (2014a) cumulative learning enables students to integrate and build on their prior knowledge and experiences and apply these new understandings in novel contexts. Cumulative learning is enabled not only through pedagogic practices but also through the forms of knowledge that are taught (Wheelahan, 2010). Cumulative knowledge-building is used, in this context, to mean 'knowledge that builds on previous knowledge; knowledge that is coherent, that lays a strong foundation for further knowledge-building and that can be applied in innovative ways in a range of contexts' (Vorster and Quinn, 2016, p. 1033). Cumulative knowledge-building is particularly important for academic developers due to the diversity of the institutional contexts in which they work, the different conceptualizations of academic development that exist and the range of practices in which they engage.

Our participants from a range of disciplinary backgrounds and most have not been exposed to, or inducted into, how to produce the kinds of texts required to demonstrate their learning on a course for professional learning in the field of higher education studies (HES). The challenge is that a course of this nature has to 'face both ways' (Barnett, 2006), that is towards the field of practice and the theoretical disciplines that have contributed concepts and theoretical frameworks to better understand the field.

Using Stierer's concepts of reflectivity, criticality and praxis (2008) we have attempted, through the pedagogy and formative assessment methods employed, to make explicit to participants how, in their writing, they need to use concepts and theories to understand all levels of context that impact on their practices as academic developers, in order for them to devise interventions to contribute to improving teaching and learning in their specific contexts.

We implemented assessment in this way because we believe that being required, over the two-year period, to grapple with theories and concepts from the field of HES to solve complex problems in their contexts should lead to cumulative learning. Both the feedback and the long-term immersion in the course processes and knowledge contribute to making explicit the realization rules and evaluative criteria for the course.

Despite our being able to articulate these understandings of our pedagogic and assessment practices, it became increasingly clear to us that we needed to understand why some participants seem to thrive and are able to articulate their learning while others struggle to do so. LCT Semantics was used as a conceptual and analytical framework for undertaking the small-scale research project reported on in this chapter.

Enacting the LCT dimension of Semantics

LCT is 'a multidimensional conceptual toolkit for exploring the organising principles of practices' (Maton, 2014b, p. 36). For this project the LCT dimension of Semantics (Maton 2013, 2014a, 2016, 2020) was used to explore the bases for cumulative learning as evidenced in summative assessment portfolios. Two key organizing principles identified by Semantics are *semantic gravity* (SG) and *semantic density* (SD). Semantic gravity is the degree to which meaning is dependent on a specific context. The stronger the semantic gravity (SG+), the more a concept or idea is linked to a particular context. Semantic density concerns the complexity or degree of condensation of meaning contained in a concept or idea. A concept that condenses many meanings has stronger semantic density (SD+) whereas a concept that is associated with relatively fewer meanings has weaker semantic density (SD–).

Semantic gravity and semantic density can be used separately or together. When used together they can be used to conceptualize *semantic profiles*. If the writing (in this case) being analysed only deals with abstract, decontextualized theories and concepts then it exhibits a *high semantic flatline* ('A' in Figure 15.1); 'knowledge would therefore be freely floating and never *re*contextualized' (Maton, 2014b,

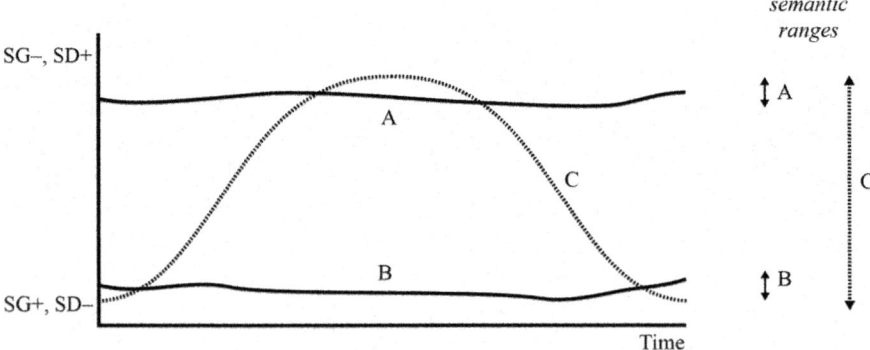

FIGURE 15.1 Illustrative semantic profiles and semantic ranges

Source: Maton, 2013, p. 13

p. 123). If the writing only describes contextual conditions without any reference to theoretical concepts, then it exhibits a *low semantic flatline* ('B' in Figure 15.1). The kind of semantic profile that should lead to or indicate cumulative knowledge-building or learning is what Maton (2013, 2020) calls a *semantic wave* ('C' in Figure 15.1). A semantic wave indicates movement between SG−, SD+ and SG+, SD−, and vice versa. Central to academic achievement and cumulative learning is the ability to extend the *semantic range* of movements between them, strengthening and weakening both semantic density and semantic gravity. This enables decontextualizing and recontextualizing of knowledge, increasing the possibility of knowledge-building across a range of contexts and over time.

This study

I purposively selected two research participants from among the 11 who were awarded distinctions for their summative portfolios at the end of 2016. Institutional ethical approval as well as informed consent from research participants was obtained. The two research participants, whom I have called Ntosh and Anna, have both worked in their institutions for a number of years but undertaken no formal qualification for their roles. Ntosh works in the quality unit of her institution and Anna is an academic staff developer with a specific focus on curriculum development. Neither of them speaks English as their first language. They both struggled to demonstrate their learning initially in the course but by the end of their two-year engagement they both produced what were judged as excellent portfolios. Their portfolios were each marked by two internal assessors and an external examiner. The final marks for both portfolios were high distinctions.

An analysis of the two portfolios – in terms of: (1) profiles of semantic gravity; (2) profiles of semantic density; and (3) semantic waves was – undertaken to see whether the mode of summative assessment of the course has enabled some participants to demonstrate that they have moved beyond common sense ways of enacting their roles to being able to transfer knowledge and knowledge practices across a range of contexts and over time.

Because AD practice, like most professional practice, is varied, complex and context-dependent, there is no 'one size fits all' way of practicing academic development. In order for academic developers to devise appropriate academic development practices for their contexts, analyses of the various levels of contexts in which they work is essential. To investigate how participants demonstrated their ability to do this in their portfolios I conceptualized semantic gravity at five different levels with semantic gravity strengthening from level 1 to level 5 (strong to stronger):

- level 1: global higher education context;
- level 2: national higher education context;
- level 3: institutional context;
- level 4: AD at institutional level; and
- level 5: individual academic developer's context (Figure 15.2).

SG–		
↑	Level 1	Global (higher education) context
	Level 2	National (higher education) context
	Level 3	Institutional context
↓	Level 4	AD at institutional level
SG+	Level 5	Individual academic developer

FIGURE 15.2 Semantic gravity scale for assessments

In my analysis I identified engagement with all these levels, that is, movement up and down the semantic gravity scale with explicit reference to how one level of context impacts on other levels of context.

Common-sense understandings of these contexts are insufficient; academic developers need in-depth and critical understandings. This is unlikely to occur unless they are using a strong analytical framework.

During the course we offer participants Margaret Archer's 'social realism' (1995) as an analytical framework through which to view HE as a social field. Archer's concepts of structure, culture and agency were suggested as useful tools to explore the HE context in general and their own institutional contexts in particular. In each module a range of concepts of varying semantic strengths and from different knowledge domains were introduced as 'thinking tools' for participants. My analysis was informed by the findings of a previous study in which the knowledge domains and key concepts used in the course were identified (Vorster and Quinn, 2015). In analysing the portfolios I traced how successfully participants were able to articulate their understandings of these concepts of varying semantic density and then how they were able to apply them to understanding their contextual realities and imagine different practices.

Findings and discussion

The most significant finding to emerge from the analysis is that semantic waves are a key characteristic of success for the participants that undertake our course. However, before focusing on semantic waves and why it is through semantic waves that cumulative learning and knowledge-building happens on the course, I briefly discuss the analysis of movement on the semantic gravity scale and movement on the semantic density scale.

Contextual understandings

In-depth understanding of a range of levels of context (Figure 15.2), both in relation to HE generally and AD specifically, is crucial for enabling academic developers to conceptualize appropriate practices for their specific contexts.

In both portfolios, there is evidence of movement up and down the semantic scale (between levels 1 and 5). They also both demonstrate that understanding context at macro and meso levels (levels 1 and 2) is crucial for making decisions about their practices (levels 4 and 5). Starting points for moving up and down the semantic gravity scale vary across and within portfolios. In the following excerpt, Anna chose to start with her institution (level 3) and then link it with macro contexts (levels 1 and 2):

> As an institution we are aligned with national priorities and are trying to find innovative solutions to challenges faced by other higher education institutions, South Africa, Africa and the world.

Ntosh, using her reading about quality in higher education globally (level 1), used it to think about her context (level 3):

> Some of the claims against the current quality management systems in higher education [globally] as identified by ... include: overemphasis on documentation to the detriment of teaching and research; and little evidence to show how the QA [quality assurance] systems bring about any fundamental change that can improve the educational experience of students.... These views voiced by ... further support XXX's[3] rationale for establishing a quality framework that will integrate elements of assurance and enhancement in order for the university to derive maximum value from program reviews.

For Anna, understanding the historical trajectory of her institution (level 3) generally, but particularly of AD (level 2) at her institution, is important: 'In order to critique the current culture and practices of academic development at the XXX Campus, it is important to understand the history of academic development at the XXX'. Candidates that are able to move the discussion up and down the various levels of context and are able to show how the different levels enable or constrain academic development and their specific practices have acquired the evaluative criteria related to the importance in a professional course of critically engaging with semantic gravity (SG+). Academic developers with a more nuanced understanding of these levels of context are more likely to be able to contribute to strengthening AD in their institutions and of contributing to the field more broadly.

If a portfolio evidences predominantly relatively weak semantic gravity it means the work is too abstract and disconnected from the writer's context of practice. However, if the engagement is mostly personal, subjective and rooted to their contexts, then they have not understood the evaluative criteria related to 'knowledge' in the course and are unlikely to have achieved cumulative knowledge-building.

Moving from common sense to theoretically informed understandings

It is clearly stated in all course documents that participants are required to engage with theories, concepts and ideas from the literature on HE. The analysis of the two portfolios showed engagement with semantically dense concepts of varying strengths and for a range of purposes throughout the portfolios.

A semantically dense concept that both Anna and Ntosh used in their portfolios in more sophisticated ways than most other candidates is that of 'globalization' which they used to better understand the HE landscape at all levels. In the extract below, Anna signals her understanding of the semantic density of the concept:

> This chapter explores the influence of globalisation on HE and how the various trends associated with globalisation have unmistakably transformed the core business of HEIs as well as created disruptive spaces for academic developers to work as catalysts of change. Altbach, Reisberg and Rumbley (2009, p. 171) refer to the complexity of globalisation as a 'knotted ball of string and trying to examine each of these trends separately is similar to trying to pull an individual string from a knotted mass-tugging one brings along several others'.

There was also evidence of some concepts being used in more semantically dense ways over time as cumulative knowledge-building was progressing. For example, at the start of Anna's portfolio she has a small glossary of terms which she defines. They are: transformation, responsiveness, third space, colonization, disruptive spaces. I asked in an email, why she had selected these terms specifically.

> In the beginning of the PGDip I have heard about these concepts but never really engaged in unpacking them. I had a limited understanding of these concepts but as we did the different modules I was continuously exposed to these concepts my knowing, being and doing was disrupted and I was challenged to think differently and deeper about these concepts and what they mean to me. As we returned to these concepts my understanding grew and reflecting on why I selected these concepts to unpack in my glossary I now realize that they scaffold onto each other. Understanding transformation and responsiveness in the HE context (module 1) made it easier to understand that teaching and learning, curriculum and assessment in HE (module 2,3 and 4) need to be responsive and that for education to be fair, we should engage in the decolonisation debate
>
> *(Personal communication 18 July 2017)*

Another example is the concept of 'diversity' which Ntosh initially uses in a common sense way. However, later in the portfolio she uses socio-cultural theories of learning to explore it in more depth:

> Northedge (2003a) argues that socio-cultural theories of learning offer an alternative theoretical underpinning to traditional theories for teaching in a diverse context. It is important for AD in my institution to advise and support

academics in applying these theories in their teaching context as XXX is also faced with the challenge of teaching large and diverse classes.... Northedge (2003a) refers to how teachers can design 'discursive environments' that will allow students to participate at different levels.

In Anna's portfolio other examples of the ability to use concepts in increasingly sophisticated ways over time are concepts of 'academic literacy' and 'epistemological access', 'responsiveness' and 'knowledge', which are used quite 'lightly' until the curriculum chapter where they are used in semantically dense ways to conceptualize her curriculum work.

Semantically dense concepts are used here by Anna to critique her institutional context:

> In an institutional report on transformation at the XXX, Van Vught et al. (2014, p. 25) state that the XXX's transformational goal of access and diversity targets are in line with national objectives of the Department of Higher Education and Training (DHET). My thought is that the current structures do allow for increased access, but an investigation into the throughput rate of distance students at the XXX shows a troubling pattern of access without success.

Without the semantically dense concepts introduced on the course, she would not have been able to offer this kind of critique of her institutional context.

From the analysis of semantic density it seems that we recognize the importance of knowledge in our course; we try to be explicit that claims cannot be made on the basis of personal experience only. However, we also discourage high semantic flat lines where ideas and arguments are presented from the literature without any explicit connection to contexts of practice. As will be seen below, of most interest is seeing how candidates have ridden the semantic wave – how they have used the knowledge gained to interrogate their contextual circumstances. In 'good' portfolios all the knowledge domains are woven together within and across chapters and there are 'waves within waves that aim to progressively move higher as they build upon previously waved knowledge ... [and there is] ... revisiting [of] knowledge to heighten or deepen past waves' (Maton, 2013, p. 17).

Moving between context and theory

For analytical purposes I separated semantic density and semantic gravity in the discussion above. In this section I describe examples of *semantic waves*, that is, movements between SG−, SD+ and SG+, SD− and vice versa (C in Figure 15.1).

Signposting movement between context and theory

Both candidates, through using explicit signposting in their writing, signal their understanding that the evaluative criteria for this course (and for their practice) require them to demonstrate semantic waves:

> A quality practitioner is required to have strong theoretical foundation and understanding of the higher education context, teaching and learning, curriculum development and quality management.
>
> *(Ntosh)*

In Anna's introduction she shows that she has clearly understood the 'rules' of what she was required to do and articulates the nature of the waves she has to provide evidence of.

In this portfolio I:

- analyse the higher education context at various levels in order to develop an understanding of ...
- investigate the conceptual domain of enhancement and assurance of quality teaching and learning in higher education. I explore theories of knowledge, the curriculum development process, theories of learning and teaching, assessment of student learning and academic literacy
- reflect on the development of my own personal capabilities as an academic developer.

Different starting points

Semantic waves start at different places on the vertical axis and take different forms. The most common wave I identified starts at SG−, SD+ and shifts to SG+, SD− (see Figure 15.1). For example, after using the literature to explore what sociocultural theories of learning are, Ntosh goes on to talk about her institution:

> One can trace the elements of the sociocultural theories in the pedagogies that XXX has adopted in the TandL strategy. One of the key pillars of the XXX TandL strategy is the use of transformational teaching which refers to teaching methods such as collaborative learning, experiential learning and problem-based learning. Transformational teaching has its roots in constructivism and social constructivism as discussed above. According to sociocultural theories, enhancement of learning is driven by the collaborative activities of the group where the more academically capable would assist the less capable students (Wang, 2007 as cited in XXX, 2014). There are academic departments in XXX (e.g. Pharmaceutical Sciences) that have implemented problem-based learning as a TandL strategy, to ensure that students are actively engaged in their own learning process.

In the next example, Anna starts with stronger semantic density (SD+) and then exhibits a number of smaller waves:

> Bernstein's 'pedagogic device' that operates on three distinct fields of practice, that is, the field of production (where knowledge is produced and positioned),

the field of re-contextualization (where knowledge is transformed into curriculum knowledge) and the field of reproduction (where the actual teaching and learning takes place) (Bernstein, 1964; Luckett, 2010a), I get the opportunity to work with the development team on curriculum development principles like scope, sequencing, integration, continuity, articulation, and balance in the curriculum. During the session we discuss the importance of constructive alignment and how to align the purpose, intended outcomes, learning activities, the teaching methods used and the assessment with assessment criteria, with each other. I found the knowledge typology framework devised by Shay, Oosthuizen, Paxton and Van der Merwe (2011) to be very valuable when analysing the level of cognitive demand or complexity, selection and sequencing of the curriculum. The framework made it possible to analyse the cognitive complexity by distinguishing between a conceptually oriented program that simply required recall....

Using the analytical framework to understand context

As alluded to earlier, in the course we offer participants Archer's (1995) social realist concepts of structure, culture and agency as an analytical framework to help them to better understand contexts at all levels. For example, early on in her portfolio Ntosh demonstrates how she moves between different levels of context and uses the analytical framework (SD+) to make sense of these contexts and to conceptualize practices:

> Chapter 2 ... Focuses on critically analysing the relationship between the higher education (HE) context and AD and how the HE context has influenced the conceptualisation of AD at XXX. I analyse the HE context at international, national and institutional levels. The analysis is done using Margaret Archer's Social Realism concepts of structure, culture and agency and the interplay between them. Drawing from the analysis of the XXX context, I conclude the chapter by identifying a possible trajectory for how QA approaches may evolve at XXX.

In her concluding chapter she describes how using the semantically dense concepts of the analytical framework enabled her conceptualize and ideal structure for combining quality assurance QA and AD in her institutional context.

In her conclusion Anna reflects on how the analytical framework contributed to her learning and her practice:

> The PGDip challenged me to critically reflect on my environment, my role as an academic developer and my practices. It was a turning point in my intellectual life. As a novice I didn't take time to reflect on structural, cultural or agential forces that could influence the situation. In fact, I didn't even know or think about using a framework to analyse work in teaching and

learning.... As I grew through newly acquired and applied knowledge, I started to be attentive to the discourse and tried to identify the sometimes hidden values, assumptions and ideologies. I now try to analyse a situation, identifying structural, cultural and agential forces influencing the situation and by listening to the discourse, identify the underpinning beliefs. To gain more insight I focus on asking the right questions and by understanding the context better....

It is unlikely that Anna would have been able to offer these insights if she had not been able to internalize and use these semantically dense concepts to analyse her context.

Using substantive theory to understand context

There was also evidence of semantic waves using the substantive theory related to all aspects of teaching and learning, which was offered to course participants. For example, in grappling with conceptualizing how AD can contribute to the quality of teaching and learning at a range of contextual levels Anna uses a relatively semantically dense conceptual framework:

> Luckett's conceptual framework (2006) ... enables me to classify and explain the different conceptualisations of quality and the different approaches and methods to the QA of teaching and learning on national, institutional as well as program level.... Reflecting on Luckett's QA and QE framework (2006), I think that academic development falls strongly in the quadrant 1: Collegial Rationality. As academic developers we aim to assist academics as well as role-players on management level to enhance the quality of teaching and learning.

Using Luckett's model of an epistemically diverse curriculum helps Anna to rethink how she can work with academics on curriculum development in her AD role:

> I find using Luckett's model (2001) very useful to disturb traditional ways of thinking about knowledge. Asking academics to plot the ways of knowing in their discipline and relating the types of knowing to exit level outcomes or graduate attributes, requires developers to critically examine the why, what and how of their curriculum decisions. I find that during this dialogical space there usually is a shift in thinking and developers start questioning if the reproduction of well-tried methods is responsive to 21st century needs.

Demonstrating praxis

Given the stated purpose of the course as described above, I was interested in semantic waves that entailed combining criticality (SD+) and reflectivity (SG+) to demonstrate praxis[4] (SG at level 5), that is the practical application of learning in any context. In both portfolios the writers describe being able to demonstrate praxis:

> I am able to add more value to the strategic debates on quality and academic development and also influence what should shape the agenda for quality at XXX …. I am now able to use theoretical and scholarly arguments to defend the positions that I am recommending.
>
> *(Ntosh)*

> By having an in-depth understanding of what curriculum is, what the purpose of the curriculum in higher education is and engaging in the 'scholarship of curriculum', I believe that I can change the current discourse and dominant culture about curriculum on our campus.
>
> *(Anna)*

For this project I chose to analyse portfolios of participants who were able to demonstrate semantic waves sufficiently to be awarded distinctions. However, I am well aware that there is a substantial number of academic developers who attend our course for whom cumulative learning does not occur and/or who struggle to demonstrate their learning in their written work despite the scaffolding and feedback that they receive over the two-year period.

Implications for pedagogy

According to Bernstein (2004) there are two generic types of pedagogy: visible and invisible. In visible pedagogy the 'rules' for success are explicitly communicated to students, whereas in invisible pedagogy the rules are largely implicit. The extent to which students are able to 'see' the evaluative rules in a learning context is closely related to the whether they bring the requisite 'cultural capital' (Bourdieu, 1986) with them into the classroom. The academic developers who attend our course come from a range of disciplinary backgrounds and some struggle with the kinds of literacy practices required for the Diploma. This, along with a history in South Africa of grossly unequal educational provision for the majority of people, has led me to realize that we have to continue to strive to make more visible the realization rules and evaluative criteria of our course if we want to level the playing fields. Following this analysis of portfolios written by candidates who successfully demonstrated that they have acquired the rules, I suggest three pedagogic strategies below.

Using exemplars to teach waves

As Morais says, 'explicating the evaluative criteria is the most crucial aspect of a pedagogic practice to promote higher levels of learning of all students' (2002, p. 568). This is, however, easier said than done. As mentioned earlier, we provide detailed assessment criteria for module assignments as well as for the integrated portfolio. These are discussed and explained in the contact sessions. This has not been enough for all our participants. Following Kirk (2017) I plan to develop a shared metalanguage with the participants which I will use, along with examples of participants' text, to demonstrate how they need to show in their writing:

1. exploration of the five different levels of context (in particular their own practice);
2. engagement with different levels of theory;
3. movement between context and theory in order to conceptualize their practice differently.

Particularly as the course proceeds, the emphasis will be on semantic waves (point 3 above). From the analysis I now have the 'data' to show them examples of: how to signpost semantic waves in their writing; how they can start a wave at different points on the SG−, SD+ and SG+, SD− axis and the different kinds of waves they can use; how they can use the social realist analytical framework as well as substantive theory in their waves; and finally how they can demonstrate praxis in their waves. Using the examples of texts of past participants along with a simplified explanation of semantic waves, will, I believe, give more participants access to the realization rules and evaluative criteria of the course.

Using the metaphor of a journey

Many of our participants use the metaphor of a journey to describe their two-year engagement with the course content and processes. For example, the way the journey is described by Anna below indicates how she used semantically dense concepts to make sense of her experience of the course, and also how her understanding of these concepts increased over time and allowed her to build frameworks showing the connections between the meanings:

> My learning journey during the PGDip was one like no other I had ever undertaken before. This unique learning and life changing experience challenged me on intellectual, personal and emotional levels. The PGDip enhanced my knowledge of higher education … I found certain topics to be particularly challenging and encountered various – what Mezirow (2000, p. 22) calls – 'disorienting dilemmas' … I entered conceptual spaces where I got stuck and struggled to grasp the threshold concepts like structure, culture, agency, ontology, epistemological access and Bernstein's pedagogic device to name a few. During my grappling I experienced confusion and in some cases instead of grappling with not-knowing, I would instead just not mention it in my assignment rather than trying to really understanding the essence of the concept. I only realised when studying other modules, that I needed to understand the concept in order to see the whole picture.

In her conclusion she articulates increasing understanding of semantically dense concepts over time.

> Through transformational mentoring in the form of rigorous learning conversations, facilitation and feedback into the discourse and practice of us as academic developers, the facilitators and mentors encouraged me to revisit the concepts I grappled with. By revisiting the thresholds in each module allowed for a deeper engagement and I can concur with Land *et al.* (2006) that once I understood these concepts, it contributed to a significant shift in my thinking and an extended use of discourse. Through the process of mentoring I moved from being a knower to being more knowledgeable, finding my own voice and identity as academic developer and part of a national and international community of us as academic developers.

Using excerpts such as these, I am planning in future to use the metaphor (and language) of a journey to explain to our participants that we are aiming for cumulative learning and knowledge-building. By doing this, I hope they will develop metacognition, that is, they will more consciously think about their own learning as the course proceeds.

How feedback can work

As explained earlier, feedback on written work has been an important part of the pedagogy of the course since its inception. What has become clear though is that not all participants are able to understand feedback as a form of pedagogy and are unclear of how to use the feedback they are given. Through using the voices of participants who understood the pedagogy, I hope to make more visible this aspect of our pedagogy using Anna's articulation of it:

> From our first assignment we received feedback from our mentors on our thinking, arguments and academic writing. Coming from a 'marks driven' background, I really struggled because I wanted to have marks ... I wanted to know how I was doing and at that time I believed by giving me a mark was the only way. I soon realised that the formative feedback was much more valuable and looking back I am so glad that we did not get marks for the assignments. I grew so much throughout the duration of the course. Looking back at my first assignment I even feel ashamed to say it was mine.
> The formative feedback in the form of questioning (I think it is more a case of disrupting) my thinking, challenging me to reflect on my thinking and doing, asking of me to be critical and question things, allowed me to grow, transform my thinking and it contributed tremendously to my learning. I believed that the specific and constructive feedback ... had such a powerful influence on my transformation. I had the opportunity to learn from the feedback and the mistakes I made. The positive feedback motivated

me to grapple with the things I did not understand, it inducted me into our AD 'discipline'/field and I used the feedback from the assignment to outline what I need to do in my next assignment. I believe the feedback was extremely helpful and it gave me the opportunity to learn, re-learn and practice the knowledge and skills I have gained. The way in which the formative assessment was done gave me the confidence to compile an integrated portfolio which I submitted as part of our summative assessment. Reflecting on the assessment used, I cannot see any other method of assessment being so effective

(Personal communication with Anna: 18 June 2017)

Conclusion

Using LCT Semantics, with the translation device of the levels of context and some of the key knowledge domains and concepts introduced in the Diploma, to analyse two portfolios has demonstrated that semantic waves, where knowledge is transformed between relatively decontextualized, condensed meanings and context-dependent, simplified meanings, are a key characteristic of the kind of cumulative learning that is required for professional learning. By making explicit the often tacit 'rules' for success on the course, it is now possible to envisage different pedagogies to ensure that more participants are able to show that they can move up and down the semantic gravity scale and to engage with concepts of stronger semantic density to formulate possible solutions for challenges they confront in their everyday practices as academic developers. It is hoped that this formal route into AD which offers opportunities for cumulative learning and knowledge-building for individual academic developers will contribute to a generation of scholarly academic developers better able to claim more credible spaces in their institutions and contribute to the growth and development of the field of AD.

Notes

1. Also frequently referred to as educational development.
2. This is different to the postgraduate certificates or diplomas offered by institutions for academics. As far as we knew, our course was the only course of its kind when we began offering it.
3. XXX denotes name of institution.
4. See Quinn and Vorster (2016) for more on using Stierer's (2008) concepts of criticality, reflectivity and praxis to theorize a pedagogy for a course for professional learning.

References

Archer, M. (1995). *Realist social theory: The morphogenetic approach*. Cambridge, UK: Cambridge University Press.

Barnett, M. (2006). Vocational knowledge and vocational pedagogy. In M. Young and J. Gamble (Eds), *Knowledge, curriculum and qualifications for South African further education* (pp. 143–157). Cape Town: HSRC Press.

Bernstein, B. (2000). *Pedagogy, symbolic control and identity: Theory, research, critique.* (Revised ed.). London: Rowman and Littlefield.

Bernstein, B. (2004). Social class and pedagogic practice. In J. Ball (Ed.), *RoutledgeFalmer reader in sociology of education* (pp. 216–218). London: RoutledgeFalmer.

Brew, A. and Peseta, T. (2008). The precarious existence of the academic development unit. *International Journal for Academic Development, 13*(2), 83–85.

Bourdieu, P. (1986). The forms of capital. In J.G. Richardson (Ed.), *Handbook of theory and research for the sociology of education* (pp. 241–258). New York: Greenwordpress.

Fraser, K. and Ryan, Y. (2012). Director turnover: An Australian academic development study. *International Journal for Academic Development, 17*(2), 135–147.

Gosling, D. (2009). Educational development in the UK: A complex and contradictory reality. *International Journal for Academic Development, 14*(1), 5–18.

Grant, B.M. (2007). The mourning after: Academic development in a time of doubt. *International Journal for Academic Development, 12*(1), 35–43.

Kirk, S. (2017). Waves of reflection: Seeing knowledges in academic writing. In J. Kemp (Ed.), *EAP in a rapidly changing landscape: Issues, challenges and solutions* (pp. 109–118). Proceedings of the 2015 BALEAP Conference. Reading: Garnet Publishing.

Maton, K. (2013). Making semantic waves: A key to cumulative knowledge-building. *Linguistics and Education, 24*(1), 8–22.

Maton, K. (2014a). *Knowledge and knowers: Towards a realist sociology of education*, London: Routledge.

Maton, K. (2014b). A TALL order? Legitimation Code Theory for academic language and learning. *Journal of Academic Language and Learning, 8*(3), A34–A38.

Maton, K. (2016). Legitimation Code Theory: Building knowledge about knowledge-building. In K. Maton, S. Hood and S. Shay (Eds), *Knowledge-building: Educational studies in Legitimation Code Theory* (pp. 1–24). London: Routledge.

Maton, K. (2020). Semantic waves: Context, complexity and academic discourse. In J.R. Martin, K. Maton and Y.J. Doran (Eds), *Accessing academic discourse: Systemic functional linguistics and Legitimation Code Theory* (pp. 59–85). London: Routledge.

Morais, A. (2002). Basil Bernstein at the micro level of the classroom. *British Journal of Sociology of Education, 23*(4), 559–569.

PGDip (HE) Course Guide. (2017–2018). Centre for Higher Education Research, Teaching and Learning, Rhodes University.

Quinn, L. and Vorster, L. (2014). Isn't it time to start thinking about 'developing' academic developers in a more systematic way? *International Journal for Academic Development, 19*(3), 255–258.

Quinn, L. and Vorster, J-A. (2016). Pedagogy for fostering criticality, reflectivity and praxis in a course on teaching for lecturers, *Assessment & Evaluation in Higher Education, 41*(7), 1100–1113.

Stierer, B. (2008). Learning to write about teaching: Understanding the writing demands of lecturer development programmes in higher education. In R. Murray (Ed.), *The scholarship of teaching and learning in higher education* (pp. 34–45). Maidenhead: Open University Press.

Vorster, J. and Quinn, L. (2015). Towards shaping the field: Theorising the knowledge in a formal course for academic developers in Higher Education. *Higher Education Research and Development, 34*(5), 1031–1044.

Wheelahan, L. (2010). *Why knowledge matters in curriculum. A social realist argument*. London: Routledge.

Winch, C. (2009). Ryle on knowing how and the possibility of vocational education. *Journal of Applied Philosophy 26*(1), 88–101.

16

ACADEMIC DEVELOPMENT

Autonomy pathways towards gaining legitimacy

Jo-Anne Vorster

Introduction

Internationally, higher education institutions are under pressure to respond to the demands of a rapidly changing world in which access to knowledge and patterns of knowledge production and dissemination have significantly changed the nature of teaching and learning. Universities and academics are in the process of reconceptualizing their roles as expectations from students, funders, employers and the state seem to demand greater levels of responsiveness from them (Barnett, 2000; Moll, 2004; Leibowitz *et al.*, 2017). Most universities now have teaching and learning centres staffed by academic developers whose role it is to contribute to the enhancement of teaching and learning. One of the ways in which this is being done in many countries is through professional development programmes focusing on academics' roles as teachers in higher education.

Volbrecht and Boughey (2004, p. 58) define academic development as 'an open set of practices concerned with improving the quality of teaching and learning in Higher Education and Training through integrating student, staff, curriculum, institutional and research development', while Taylor (2005, p. 33) notes that academic developers have 'diverse teaching, learning, research, leadership and service roles'. Clegg (2009) has argued that academic development 'is now a definable set of practices with its own distinctive values and professional organization'. Others, however, contend that its broad remit makes it difficult to 'pin down' the focus of the field (Leibowitz, 2014, p. 358) and, as is the case elsewhere in the world, academic development in South Africa remains 'a relatively blurred concept/field' (Sugrue *et al.* 2017, p. 2). The focus in this chapter is on academic staff developers (hereafter, developers) and their practice. (Hereafter, for the sake of brevity, I shall mainly use the term 'developers' when referring to academic staff developers.)

Even though the field of academic development has been in existence in British, American, Australian and European universities since the 1960s and in South African universities since the mid-1980s there are still somewhat divergent understandings of the field and the role it plays in higher education. In different parts of the world the field is known by different names, including academic development, educational development and faculty development (Leibowitz, 2014) and in South Africa, there is not one single nomenclature for the centres in which academic developers work. Some of the names of teaching and learning centres in South Africa include: Centre for Higher Education Research, Teaching and Learning; Centre for Innovation in Teaching and Learning; Centre for Academic Excellence, Centre for Academic Development, Centre for Teaching, Learning and Media, and a number of others. Globally, there is no formal route into the field and most developers are appointed based on their experience of and expertise as teachers of those disciplines. It could be argued that the number of developers who could be said to be 'qualified' for their positions is small. As such developers struggle to establish 'stable and authoritative – respected' identities (Grant, 2007, p. 38).

Academic development in South Africa

In South Africa, academic development emerged in the 1980s – initially for the purpose of assisting small numbers of black students to meet the demands of academic study at historically white institutions. However, this narrow view was later replaced by the recognition that universities and academics were not prepared to work with the ever-growing number of students for whom the articulation gap between high school and university and between the culture of home and that of the university was too big (Vilakazi and Tema, 1985; Scott, 2009). As was the case in universities elsewhere in the world, when the South African higher education system massified and the student body in all institutions became increasingly diverse, it was recognized that if the majority of students were to be offered the kind of tuition they needed and deserved then there would need to be a focus on the curriculum (Trow, 1973; Moll, 2004). In many universities it is academic developers who work with discipline experts to explore ways in which their curricula can best meet the learning needs of a diverse student body (O'Neill, 2009).

Although a few South African universities have been offering workshops on teaching to staff since about the 1970s, it was only from about the mid-1990s that more institutions started offering staff development programmes in the form of workshops and short courses (Quinn, 2007). From around 2000 a small number of universities initiated formally accredited and informal programmes in higher education studies with a focus on enhancing academics' knowledge of and practices related to teaching and learning, curriculum development, assessment of student learning and the evaluation of teaching and courses.

As noted by Volbrecht and Boughey (2004) academic development brings together diverse knowledge practices, and it could be argued that successful academic development practice depends on what Maton and Howard (2018) term *integrative knowledge-building*. Successful academic development practice needs to integrate knowledge about teaching and learning, curriculum and assessment with knowledge about the higher education context more broadly, knowledge of institutional contexts and requirements, as well as requirements from external stakeholders (Vorster and Quinn, 2015, Sugrue *et al.*, 2017). Furthermore, academic developers need to be able to use this knowledge to devise strategies to address the teaching and learning challenges experienced by the institution, departments and individual academics (Vorster and Quinn, 2015). Staff developers also have to enable the lecturers they work with to develop *cumulative knowledge* related to their teaching roles, that is, the ability to use knowledge from the field of HE in their own disciplinary contexts – also when confronted with novel teaching and learning challenges (see Quinn, this volume). Building integrative and cumulative knowledge requires developers to traverse the boundaries between their own field and those of the multiple disciplines of the academics they work with.

Even though many academics who participate in staff development programmes benefit from them (Cilliers and Herman, 2010; Sutherland and Hall, 2018), the uptake of these programmes varies across institutions, and where participation is voluntary, it remains limited. Furthermore, participation is often resisted (Quinn, 2012). The dimension of Autonomy from Legitimation Code Theory (LCT) is an analytical tool that makes it possible to explain the poor uptake of and resistance to professional development opportunities. In this chapter, I examine the status of the field of academic staff development and that of developers and their work in eight South African public universities using LCT's Autonomy dimension as the analytical lens. I argue that the differences in status experienced by developers in their institutions are the results of the different expectations held by different categories of people in the universities about the professional development of academics. Through an autonomy code analysis, this chapter examines how the roles developers are understood in the eight institutions.

In the next section, I provide an explanation of Autonomy as I have used it in my analysis. Thereafter I will show how Autonomy makes it possible to understand and explain the range of different understandings of the role of developers: among members of the field, senior managers in universities as well as academics who participate in staff development programmes.

Autonomy

Autonomy is one of several dimensions of LCT that offers the means for 'exploring the organising principles underlying actors' beliefs, dispositions and practices' (Locke and Maton, 2019, p. 4). Autonomy is based on the idea that every social practice is made up of constituents that are organized in particular ways. These constituents can be actors, ideas, objects, and so on, that are organized according to particular principles, including aims, purposes and ways of organizing/working. In this chapter the social practice that comes under the spotlight is that of academic staff development. The actors are the developers themselves, as well as their roles and the purposes of their practices. The roles and practices of developers are different from the roles and practices of academics and from those of senior managers in universities. There are thus boundaries between the roles of these different categories of actors in the university. What Autonomy makes possible is an analysis of the strength of the boundaries between developers as a group of professionals who play a particular role in universities, and academics whose role is to teach students and research their disciplines, and senior managers, whose role is the administration of the institution. The roles and practices of academic staff developers are thus examined and juxtaposed with those of academics and of senior managers such as vice chancellors, deputy vice chancellors and deans of faculties.

Maton and Howard (2018) distinguish between *positional autonomy* and *relational autonomy*. *Positional autonomy* (PA) is about the relations between positions in a context or category and positions from elsewhere. In this chapter, the focus of the analysis is the position or roles of developers in different university contexts. I argue that the position of academic developers is different from that occupied by academics and from that of senior managers. The roles of the latter two categories of actors fall outside the 'target' of the analysis I report on in this chapter. *Relational autonomy* (RA) is about relations between principles, aims or ways of working from within a context or category and principles from outside that category. Positional autonomy and relational autonomy can be stronger (+) or weaker (−) along a continuum of strengths that can be plotted on the *autonomy plane*.

Stronger positional autonomy (PA+) means that the constituents of a practice are strongly bounded or defined in relation to those of another practice and weaker

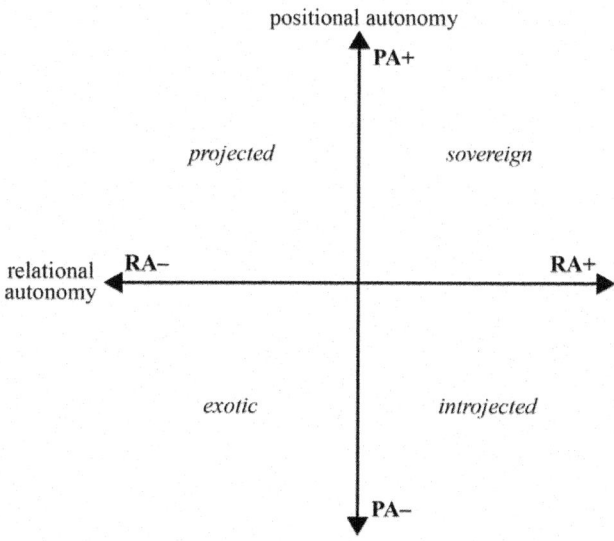

FIGURE 16.1 The autonomy plane

Source: Maton and Howard, 2018, p. 6

positional autonomy (PA−) means that they are weakly bounded. In the case of academic developers, stronger positional autonomy would mean that they are recognized as a group of professionals in the university whose role is different from that of discipline-based academics and also from the role of senior managers. For example, developers work differently from academics in that they do not work directly with students, their practices are concerned with the development of academics as teachers. In this way their positional autonomy is fairly distinctly bounded (PA+). Even though their focus is ultimately to enable success for the diverse student bodies of their institutions (Amundsen and Wilson, 2012), working with students is not their primary site of practice.

Stronger relational autonomy (RA+) points to well-defined distinctions between the principles, aims, and ways of working of a practice in relation to the principles, aims, and ways of working from another practice. Weaker relational autonomy (RA−) means that ways of working and purposes are shared with or emerge from other practices. For academic developers, the principles, aims and ways of working entail using the ideas, theories and concepts from the field of higher education studies and the field of academic development itself to shape their work with and for academics (Shay, 2012). This field is concerned with teaching, learning, curriculum, assessment of student learning and the evaluation of teaching and courses, among other matters. This field is thus distinct from the fields that form the main focus of academics in the disciplines. (Hereafter, I shall use the term 'academics' to refer to academics in the disciplines.) Relational autonomy is this case is thus stronger (RA+).

Generally, the practice of academic staff development has stronger relational autonomy in a shared set of values such as collegiality and respect for the disciplinary expertise of academics (Quinn, 2012), the principles of scholarly engagement to facilitate reflection of practice, and so on. If developers share these principles (which are different from the principles that inform the practice of academics) then this could be called stronger relational autonomy. Academics, for example, generally have a stronger focus on research productivity than is the case with developers. In cases where academic staff developers work according heteronomous principles and have diverse ways of working then relational autonomy is weaker.

As noted above, positional autonomy and relational autonomy can be stronger (+) or weaker (−) along a continuum of strengths that can be plotted on a Cartesian plane. If both positional autonomy and relational autonomy are stronger, a *sovereign code* is generated (PA+, RA+). This means that the positions of the developers are strongly bounded, and the principles of the practice are autonomous. In such a case what is valued or legitimated is from within the field of academic development, that is, ideas, concepts, theories and approaches that are different from those used elsewhere in the academy and they are used for purposes aligned with the raison d'être of the field of academic development.

When positional autonomy is weaker but relational autonomy is stronger, an *introjected code* is generated (PA−, RA+). In such a case the role of academic developers would be to integrate the external requirements from outside of the field such as senior managers, professional bodies or the state. This could, for example, include assisting academics to complete accreditation procedures for new programmes to comply with national quality assurance requirements (PA−). But if the academic developers can undertake such processes using their preferred ways of working by, for example, focusing on issues of social inclusion and student engagement in the completion of such processes, then this would suggest stronger relational autonomy (RA+). Here academic development practice weakens what is normally a stronger boundary with another set of practices, but the principles according to which they operate are autonomous (PA−, RA+).

If the position of developers in the institution is clearly defined, perhaps with a fair amount of autonomy (PA+), but they are then asked to engage in ways of working that emerge from elsewhere, such as implementing performance management processes in ways that are at odds with core academic development values, then relational autonomy is weaker (RA−). An example would be being asked to conduct and evaluation of teaching and courses (a task that developers would ordinarily engage in for developmental purposes) by a head of department for the purposes of judging the quality of an academic's work in a performance management process. In this case positional autonomy is stronger and relational autonomy weaker, and a *projected code* is evinced (PA+, RA−).

Where both positional autonomy and relational autonomy are weaker, an *exotic code* is evinced (PA−, RA−). An example would be if an academic developer is asked to serve on a personal promotions committee where in making decisions about an academic's promotability s/he is required to apply university policies, criteria, etc. rather than the principles and values associated with the field of academic development. Judging a promotions portfolio on a metric as one of a large team of members of the promotions committee may mean that weakly bounded constituents and ways of working emerging from elsewhere are legitimated in this instance.

In the next section I shall draw on the data from a study on the professional development of academics to demonstrate how Autonomy can be used to understand the underlying principles that shape the position and status of developers in different institutions.

The study

In the analysis below, I use data from a study on the influences of institutional context on the professional development of academics in eight South African universities. I use the data to show how academic development, developers in Teaching and Learning Centres, and their practices are understood and valued in different universities. Since all universities in South Africa still evince the influences of privilege or disadvantage emerging, inter alia, from the unequal resourcing of institutions in the past, the study included historically black and historically white universities. Four historically white institutions (HWU1 – HWU4) and four historically black institutions (HBU1 – HBU4) participated in the study. During the

Apartheid era universities were differentiated along the lines of race and in the case of HWUs, also along language lines, with institutions designated for English and Afrikaans-speaking whites. Among the eight institutions were universities representing each of the three institutional types that form part of the South African higher education system, that is, traditional universities, universities of technology as well as comprehensive universities (these institutions offer a mix of traditional and professional and vocational qualifications).

The purpose of the interviews was to inquire about participants' views on the professional development of academics as teachers and included questions about the roles and purposes of Teaching and Learning Centres. Semi-structured interviews were conducted with lecturers (of various levels of seniority) and senior managers (including vice-chancellors, deputy vice-chancellors and deans of faculties). Senior managers of the universities were asked about their views on the roles and purposes of Teaching and Learning Centres while the lecturers were asked about their views on professional development opportunities in their institutions. In each case, the interviewees also expressed their views on academic developers in their institutions. Interviews were also conducted with members of the Teaching and Learning Centres in these institutions, and with heads of such centres. The position of academic developers and the range of practices that they are involved in are highly dependent on and influenced by complex institutional contexts.

Autonomy in this analysis – relating data to theory

I developed what Bernstein (2000) originally termed an 'external language of description' and has been elaborated in LCT as a 'translation device' to facilitate the data analysis process (see Maton and Chen 2016; Maton and Howard 2016). A translation device makes it possible for the researcher to recognize instances in the data that relate to theoretical constructs that frame the study (Maton and Chen, 2016) and to move iteratively between the data and theory to understand what the data reveals about the context. The translation device is loosely based on guidelines for such a tool from Maton and Chen (2016) (see Table 16.1).

Positioning and valuing of academic development, developers and their practices

In this section, I draw from the data to illuminate how academic developers are positioned by both senior managers in their institutions and by the academics with whom they work. The data therefore offer insights into how academic developers are legitimated in institutions. There are also some examples of the kinds of beliefs about academic development as a field, and about academic developers and their practices that tend to de-legitimate the field. It can be argued that the purpose of having academic developers in an institution is to enhance teaching and learning. As such they use their expertise in the service of a bigger project – that of the enhancement of the expertise of academics as teachers so that the latter can acquire

Academic development 279

TABLE 16.1 Translation device that guided analysis of data

Strengths of PA/RA	Description of element in this study	Explanation of the element in relation to the field of academic development	Examples from the data
Stronger positional autonomy (PA+)	Position/roles/theoretical orientations of developers are clearly defined/articulated in relation to other entities in the institution.	The focus of the role of developers is the professional development of academics as scholarly teachers through workshops, short courses, formal accredited programmes and individual and departmental consultations. Developers draw on ideas, concepts and theories from the fields of higher education studies and academic development. They engage in research about teaching and learning, the field of academic development and about their practices.	The function of the [Teaching and Learning Centre] is twofold … one is really to try and understand how we can support students who are struggling, and finding interventions which will work for students. The second, of course, is to try and understand how to improve the quality of learning and teaching, and assessment and all of that jazz.
Weaker positional autonomy (PA−)	Position/roles/theoretical orientations of academic developers are weakly defined/articulated in relation to those of others in the institution.	The focus of the practice of academic developers is from outside the field of academic development. For example, when they assist academics or the institution to meet the requirements of external quality assurance requirements. Developers do not use the theoretical tools and ways of working valued by the field.	The [Teaching and Learning Centre], particularly their role in implementing our action plan, which is some eight-page something document.
Stronger relational autonomy (RA+)	Relatively strong articulation of the principles, i.e. ways of working, aims, purposes of academic developers in relation to other entities in the university.	Developers work according to the principles of scholarly engagement in relation to teaching and learning, respect for the disciplinary expertise of academics, taking cognisance of the influence of context on academics' practices, value the principles of reflective practice, and so on.	Our teaching and learning must pay attention to a number of issues and factors … the challenges of this context … of the discipline and what it means for how we structure the curriculum … structure teaching and learning. We have to be aware of a changing world and what different technologies … mean for the process of teaching or pedagogy.
Weaker relational autonomy (RA−)	Relatively weak articulation of the principles, i.e. ways of working, aims, purposes, of academic developers in relation to other entities in the university.	Academic developers participate in work that is not related to staff development work and working according to principles that are not integral to the field.	(T)he people in the faculties, the deans and also some of the staff have started to look at the [Teaching and Learning Centre] as bureaucracy … as if it was academic planning.

the knowledge and know-how to work more successfully with the students they teach. As the data will show, if academic developers are to play their roles well, they cannot only operate in the *sovereign code* (PA+, RA+) of their field; they have to, at times, weaken either relational autonomy to work with academics, or weaken positional autonomy to serve some of the purposes of university management.

Views on the roles and the structural positioning of academic developers

The literature shows that there is general consensus across the higher education landscape that developers contribute to improving student learning; in the case of staff developers, this happens indirectly through work with academics in the disciplines. Developers in some institutions also engage in research on how to improve teaching and learning. The excerpt below from an interview with a senior manager shows that his institution values the research academic developers do into teaching and learning and their role of devising teaching and learning practices that academics can use to enhance student learning.

> The function of the [Teaching and Learning Centre] is twofold ... one is really to try and understand how we can support students who are struggling, and finding interventions which will work for students. The second, of course, is to try and understand how to improve the quality of learning and teaching, and assessment and all of that jazz. [PA+].
>
> *(Senior Manager, HBU1)*

Here developers are seen as having a role in conducting research in order to understand how the institution can support struggling students more effectively, and doing research into improving various aspects of teaching and learning. This is an indication of stronger positional autonomy (PA+) as developers do research into aspects of their area of expertise – teaching and learning. This view is reiterated by the Director of the institution's Teaching and Learning Centre:

> The academic development people in ... [the Teaching and Learning Centre) would focus on research ... they would track student performance, and they would provide an intellectual home for academic development. [PA+].
>
> *(Director, Teaching and Learning Centre HBU1)*

This Teaching and Learning Centre Director recognizes that the field of academic requires what he calls 'an intellectual home' that is distinct from other areas in the university. Positional autonomy is therefore stronger (PA+).

The views expressed below by the senior managers in two very different kinds of institutions, HBU1 and HWU1, are indicative of some of the challenges in arriving at a shared understanding of the most appropriate structural location in the institution for developers. Where developers are located in the institution is also indicative of the degree of distinction that is made between their roles and the roles of disciplinary academics, for example.

> And, there's another debate about the structure, the organizational structure of AD. There are people who are suggesting that AD practitioners should be located in the faculties, they shouldn't be here, they shouldn't be in a central unit. We have had to give away six posts to faculties, we have six faculties. So, when I took over the directorship of the unit, I was instructed to give each faculty a post, if someone resigned or retired, I had to give the post to a particular faculty. [PA−].
>
> *(Director, Teaching and Learning Centre HBU1)*

I would argue that in the context of HBU1, where the Teaching and Learning Centre director noted the importance of academic development having 'an intellectual' home, having to 'give away [academic development] posts to faculties', signifies a potential weakening of positional autonomy (PA−). Where academic developers are placed, physically, in the institution, has in some institutions, contributed to developers not maintaining or developing a distinct identity as members of the field, and they have in many instances not kept abreast with the development of knowledge in an ways of working of the field (Harland and Staniforth, 2003). Being physically situated in a faculty or an academic department potentially means that academic developers are seen as belonging to the academic discipline and not to the field of academic development (PA−); it could also lead to developers being absorbed into disciplinary ways of working that are not necessarily aligned to the ways of working of the field of academic development.

In the second university (HWU1) where there was a debate about where academic developers should be placed, a senior manager said the following:

> Now we are going through a very difficult moment with the people from the [Teaching and Learning Centre], and that is to place themselves within those faculties, closer to the academic environment to where the scholarship actually takes place. [PA−, RA−].
>
> *(Senior Manager, HWU 1)*

As noted above, being placed in a faculty (or a specific department) is not an easy decision and is likely to blur the boundaries between the roles of academic developers and those of disciplinary academics (PA−). This quote seems to indicate that the senior manager does not recognize academic developers as engaging in their own scholarship (PA−).

Where the location of developers has not been settled it is likely that there will be confusion or misrecognition about the role of academic development (Harland and Staniforth, 2003). The view that developers may be better placed in faculties rather than in a central unit may arise from the view that in order to understand the needs of academics, how they think and how they practice in the disciplines, it is necessary to work in close proximity to them (PA−). The same argument applies to adopting an identity as and the ways of working of an academic developer. I would argue that the likelihood of cultivating a stronger sense of identity as a developer (PA+) and of building a coherent conceptualization of the principles that shape field as well as the ways of working in the field (RA+) are more likely when developers work in the same physical space such as a Teaching and Learning Centre.

Some senior managers in some of the eight universities recognized that academic development work is not necessarily discipline-specific and that developers have a role in exploring ways of enhancing teaching and learning that may be applied across the disciplinary spectrum, 'The [Teaching and Learning Centre] identifies certain themes, higher level issues … that cut across …' (Senior Manager, HWU 2). The senior manager recognized that the ways of working of academic developers is often meta-level work where general issues are identified, such as poor performance by students from particular kinds of schools (RA+). However, these general issues need to be addressed in discipline-specific ways (Boughey and McKenna, 2016). Academic developers have knowledge that enables them to analyse the higher education context as well as their institutional contexts to establish staff development needs. According to Vorster and Quinn (2015, p. 1033), developers need to cultivate four knowledge domains: a meta-level analytical framework that enables sophisticated analyses of contextual dynamics; knowledge of the field of AD; knowledge of the HE context; and substantive knowledge related to teaching and learning. Sugrue *et al.* (2017) argue that these knowledges are necessary for academic developers to 'continue to "broker" their authority and autonomy' (p. 9). Integral to the ways of working of academic developers, is the ability to move between and where necessary, integrate their different knowledge domains and in the process traverse the different quadrants of the autonomy plane.

AD serves several constituents at once

The role of Teaching and Learning Centres and of developers is to serve the institution by contributing to the development of teaching expertise. This role has been recognized by the Department of Higher Education (South African Department of Higher Education, 1997) and the Higher Education Quality Committee of the Council on Higher Education in South Africa (Department of Higher Education and Training (DHET), 2018). According to a senior manager from one institution, they were mandated to establish a Teaching and Learning Centre as a mechanism to improve student success.

> So our centre … was formed … because of a concern that was raised by the Minister of Higher Education and Training concerning the low throughput rates.… The university was urged to put in place a centre that would assist in developing both staff and students so that we could improve throughput rates.… Our DVC is also a key agent in this regard; she has a passion for developing the quality of teaching and learning. [PA+, RA−].
>
> *(Senior Manager, HBU3)*

Even though the outcome of the work done by academic developers may result in the improvement of the institution's throughput rate (both an institutional and national imperative), developers generally see their remit much more broadly, i.e. as working to improve teaching to improve student learning (PA+). In fact, developers would resist this framing of their work in narrow efficiency terms (McKenna, 2012; Quinn, 2012). This quotation therefore indicates weaker relational autonomy (RA–). However, the senior manager does recognize the Teaching and Learning Centre as having a separate and significant identity (PA+). This is therefore is an example of the *projected code* (PA+, RA–).

In most institutions a probation requirement for new academics is that they attend some form of professional development, be it completing a course on assessment, curriculum development or a formal programme on teaching and learning or another form of introduction to teaching or academic practice. The fact that this is a mandate from the institutional management sends a strong message that academic developers serve the needs of the institution (PA–). Given the growing divide between academics and institutional management in the managerialist university (McKenna, 2012), it is necessary that developers gain the trust of academics by shaping the work they do on behalf of management, in ways that are educationally sound and congruent with academics' sense of their own autonomy. An example would be institutional requirements to evaluate teaching and courses. Framing this work as developmental rather than as policing (Boughey, 2003), and providing the necessary support to enhance pedagogic practices by taking account of feedback data from students is one way for developers to maintain the integrity of their staff development role.

> So, there is a whole governing system that is very important in supporting teaching and learning and making sure that there is synergy between what is going on at the faculty level and centrally within the teaching and learning committee. (PA+) So, fleshing that out and also in the process getting buy-in from, not only faculties … but from the [Teaching and Learning Centre], particularly their role in implementing our action plan, which is some eight-page something document. [PA–].
>
> *(Senior Manager, HWU 3)*

This quotation shows the complexity of the relationships and roles of developers. One the one hand there is recognition of their stronger positional autonomy in the role of supporting teaching and learning. On the other hand, positional autonomy is weaker when the work of developers is seen as implementing the plans of the university management. The ambiguity in terms of the kind of power that developers wield in the institution can result in instances of resistance (Quinn, 2012) as is seen in the next quote:

> (T)he people in the faculties, the deans and also some of the staff have started to look at the [Teaching and Learning Centre] as bureaucracy … as if it was academic planning. [RA–].
>
> *(Senior Manager, HWU1)*

Being an institutionally recognized centre can at times lead to interaction with developers being seen as an institutional requirement where developers are expected to engage with particular practices around, for example, quality assurance and 'staff training' which is oppositional to the values of many academic developers. Such a view of their work denotes weaker relational autonomy (RA−) and could result in developers as being complicit in a managerial project, a conception of their work that they would resist (McKenna, 2012).

If the work of developers is to be experienced as legitimate by the academics they work with, it is crucial that it be useful for the academic projects of those academics and not, in the first instance, useful only to the academic development project (RA−). Put differently, it is a necessary strategy for academic developers to weaken relational autonomy by relating their ideas to the disciplinary and perhaps departmental contexts of the disciplinary academics (RA−).

The educational purpose of the work of the academic developers needs to be clearly articulated in terms that seem useful for the academic as teacher. Relational autonomy needs to be weaker (RA−); it is possible to do so, if developers have a strong sense of the academic development project (RA+). To do this successfully, it helps if it is negotiated via the *sovereign code* of academic developers so that they use their educational knowledge and specialized staff development practices to mediate the educational relevance of institutional requirements.

Addressing contextual demands

Developers gain legitimacy when offering the conceptual and practical means for lecturers (and the institution more broadly) to meet contemporary contextual and educational demands. Below I quote from an interview with a senior manager from a traditional research university who articulated the need for the professional development of academics (and thus the role that developers have to play) to address to the contextual challenges that face higher education institutions in South Africa (and perhaps internationally).

> Our teaching and learning must pay attention to a number of issues and factors … the challenges of this context … of the discipline and what it means for how we structure the curriculum … structure teaching and learning [RA+]. We have to be aware of a changing world and what different technologies [RA−] … mean for the process of teaching or pedagogy [RA+].
>
> *(Senior Manager, HWU 4)*

For this senior manager the work of developers is strongly bounded by their work on curriculum, teaching and learning and, in particular, addressing how the changing context and also technologies influence curriculum and teaching and learning. Positional autonomy is therefore stronger (PA+). One of the focus areas in the field of academic staff development is the role of technologies in the curriculum and in relation to pedagogy and learning (PA+). Making the links between contextual challenges emerging from a rapidly changing world, including technological innovation (RA–) with the needs of the curriculum, and in particular, with teaching and learning (RA+) will contribute to the legitimacy of developers. The senior manager points to how developers have to focus their staff development initiatives to address challenges that emerge from inside and from beyond the institution. Curriculum, teaching and learning are part of the concern of the field of academic development, as is the challenge of understanding what it means to teach a diverse student body.

This senior manager also noted the following:

> (We are not) fully aware and fully equipped to deal with the changing student body. Rather than just blaming the student, perhaps we need to be better equipped as universities and as academics.... About how we work with the diversity that is our university.
>
> *(Senior Manager, HWU4)*

One of the focus areas for developers is sharing robust knowledge with academics about how to work with a diverse student body. As this focus is integral to developers' practice and sets them apart from academics in the disciplines and from the work of senior managers, positional autonomy is stronger (PA+). Developers also need to enable a better understanding of the needs of the changing student body through their research role. What is called for are 'more rigorous research designs, more qualitative research, better theoretical and conceptual grounding of education development practice, and a more detailed description of practice so that each new study can build more explicitly on previous ones' (Amundsen and Wilson, 2012, p. 91). I would argue that developers who have in-depth knowledge of the academic project and the challenges that face academics, will be able to meet the needs of academics more effectively.

The importance of meeting the real teaching and learning needs of academics

The biggest challenge for the legitimacy of developers is to ensure that they offer programmes and services that meet the needs of academics. One senior manager noted the following about the [Teaching and Learning Centre] in his institution:

> I think there's still a feeling among faculties that this Teaching and Learning Centre, this central institutional support service for them, isn't tuned in finely enough to their needs. (They say) '[TLC] does their own research, but it's not necessarily what we want [PA+]. They don't know what our needs and challenges are. We want them to hear us better; to focus more on what we want to do, on what we need' [RA–].
>
> *(Senior Manager, HWU1)*

Here it seems that the developers are perceived to have stronger relational autonomy than is considered legitimate in this context. It can thus be argued that developers need to be more attuned to what academics need from them and that it is necessary to weaken relational autonomy so that they can serve the needs of the academics they work with, better (RA−). I would furthermore suggest that developers, when working with disciplinary academics, should work in an *introjected code* (PA+, RA−). The role of the developers is that of working to enhance teaching and learning (PA+), however, they need to do it in ways that are congruent with the disciplinary perspectives of academics (RA−). It is important to balance between operating in the *sovereign code* of the field of academic development (PA+, RA+) and serving the needs of academics by working in the *introjected code*.

One of the academics interviewed, articulated what many of his/her colleagues ask themselves before committing to spending valuable time on a professional development course offered by developers:

> The question would be, would I as an academic see value in that professional development course? Would I believe that it would genuinely improve my practice or would I see it as something that would take up a lot of my time, involve a lot of work on my behalf and not genuinely improve my practice?
> *(Lecturer, HWU4)*

This lecturer wants the developer to contribute to the improvement of his/her practice as a teacher; the academic developers would therefore need to weaken relational autonomy so that their ways of working are in line with the needs of the academic (RA−).

A different sentiment from the one above, was expressed by another lecturer from the same university:

> When you're dealing with philosophers and photographers ... it's not the same thing, some things are different. But even that, I've sat in on two sets of scheduled courses now, and I've felt that there's been a general tendency. It's worked for everybody involved and in fact, the engagement, cross disciplines in those courses, is one of the strengths of it. [RA].
> *(Lecturer, HWU4)*

Even though academic developers, for the most part, do not share the disciplinary backgrounds and expertise of the people they work with, it is their responsibility to make their offerings relevant to academics from all disciplines (RA−).

What is, however, less useful is to offer generic tips that do not emerge either from the field of higher education studies nor from the disciplines of the lecturers who participate. Some generic information might be useful, but more often than not it runs the risk of alienating academics. The following example, which is probably somewhat extreme, exemplifies a possible effect when academic developers tend to operate in the *exotic code:*

I did a course at Uni X once ... that was when I was a new member of staff there, and it was supposed to tell us how to teach, and I think that, I think it helped a bit. I remember that when **we were discussing discipline**, they told me ... because I looked really young and I had these big classes of engineers.... **They told me that I should wear make-up** and they would take me more seriously **and power-dress. So I was like, 'hmmm, okay, I don't really want to take these people seriously anymore'.**

(Lecturer, HWU3 – relating an experience at another institution)

Here the academic developer did not offer solutions that derived from the field of academic development and positional autonomy was thus weaker (PA–). This kind of advice is not congruent with the scholarly approach or ways of working that many academic developers subscribe to – relational autonomy was therefore also weaker (RA–). The example shows that working in the *exotic code* is likely to detract from the legitimacy that academic developers need and seek (PA–, RA–).

Conclusion: insights gained from Autonomy

In this chapter I have shown how using Autonomy as an analytical lens to examine how academic developers and academic development practice are understood and legitimated or not by academics and also by institutional managers. I examined the implications of the structural positioning of developers and argued that it has implications for the both positional and relational autonomy of developers. It is ironic that South African developers have been and continue to make significant contributions to knowledge of the field and of teaching and learning, assessment and curriculum practices that are responsive the national and institutional contexts and have received international recognition for this work (Clegg, 2009; Sutherland and Hall, 2018). Despite this fact, the roles and identities of developers remain constantly '"under construction" in conditions of indeterminacy and complexity' (Land, 2008, p. 135). Understanding why this is the case is a step in the direction of changing this state of affairs.

I noted the importance of developers sharing a conception of the roles and of the ways of working in the field. It is especially necessary because the positioning of developer, whether in a relatively autonomous central unit or integrated into departments and faculties, is still a matter of debate in some institutions. Furthermore, developers serve academics in the disciplines and the institutional management at the same time. They therefore have to have a clear sense of their main role which is to serve the real learning needs of academics in the latter's pursuit of facilitating epistemic access for their own students.

I believe that developers will be in a better place to claim their voice and the right to speak and be heard in their institutions and beyond, if they understand the possibilities and also the limits of how they can position themselves and the ways they relate to their senior management as well as their academic colleagues. Developers are more likely to gain legitimacy among academics if they understand the nature and implications of their own positional and relational autonomy vis-à-vis those of academics and senior managers.

I believe that a strong academic developer identity is good for academic development work. This means that academic developers need to have a strong sense of who they are, what they do, in what ways and for what purposes. When these conditions are met, academic developers are better able to do strongly theorized work with credibility.

References

Amundsen, C. and Wilson, M. (2012). Are we asking the right questions? A review of the educational development literature in higher education, *Review of Educational Research*, *82*(1), 90–126.

Barnett, R. (2000). University knowledge in an age of supercomplexity. *Higher Education*, *40*(4), 409–422.

Bernstein, B. (2000). *Pedagogy, symbolic control and identity. Theory, research and critique*. London: Rowman and Littlefield.

Boughey, C. (2003). From equity to efficiency: Access to higher education in South Africa. *Arts and Humanities in Higher Education*, *2*(1), 65–71.

Boughey, C. and McKenna, S. (2016). Academic literacy and the decontextualized learner. *Critical Studies in Teaching and Learning*, *4*(2), 1–9.

Cilliers, F. and Herman, N. (2010). Impact of an educational development programme on teaching practice of academics at a research-intensive university. *International Journal for Academic Development*, *15*(3), 253–267.

Clegg, S. (2009). Forms of knowing and academic practice. *Studies in Higher Education*, *34*(4), 403–416.

Department of Higher Education and Training (DHET). (2018). *A National Framework for Enhancing Academic as University Teachers*. Pretoria, South Africa: Department of Higher Education and Training.

Grant, B.M. (2007). The mourning after: Academic development in a time of doubt. *International Journal for Academic Development*, *12*(1), 35–43.

Harland, T. and Staniforth, D. (2003). Academic development as academic work. *International Journal for Academic Development*, *8*(1/2), 25–35.

Land, R. (2008). Academic development. Identity and paradox. In R. Barnett and R. Di Napoli (Eds), *Changing identities in higher education. Voicing perspectives* (pp. 134–144). London and New York: Routledge.

Leibowitz, B. (2014). Reflections on academic development: What's in a name? *International Journal for Academic Development*, *19*(4), 357–360.

Leibowitz, B., Bozalek, V., Garraway, J., Herman, N., Jawitz, J., Muhuro, P., Ndebele, C., Quinn, L., van Schalkwyk, S., Vorster, J-A. and Winberg, C. 2017. Learning to teach in Higher Education in South Africa: An investigation into the influences of institutional context on the professional learning of academics in their roles as teachers. *HE Monitor No. 14*, April 2017. Pretoria: South Africa: South African Council on Higher Education.

Locke, P. and Maton, K. (2019). Serving two masters: How vocational educators experience marketisation reforms. *Journal of Vocational Education and Training*, *71*(1), 1–20.

Maton, K. and Chen, R.T-H. (2016). LCT in qualitative research: Creating a translation device for studying constructivist pedagogy. In K. Maton, S. Hood and S. Shay (Eds), *Knowledge-building: Educational studies in Legitimation Code Theory* (pp. 27–48). London: Routledge.

Maton, K. and Howard, S.K. (2016). LCT in mixed-methods research: Evolving an instrument for quantitative data. In K. Maton, S. Hood and S. Shay (Eds), *Knowledge-building: Educational studies in Legitimation Code Theory* (pp. 49–71). London: Routledge.

Maton, K. and Howard, S.K. (2018). Taking autonomy tours: A key to integrative knowledge-building. *LCT Centre Occasional Paper 1*: 1–35.

McKenna, S. (2012). The context of access and foundation provisioning in South Africa. In Dhunpath, R. and Vithal, R. (Eds), *Alternative access to higher education: Underprepared students or underprepared institutions* (pp. 51–61). Cape Town, South Africa: Pearson Education South Africa.

Moll, I. (2004). Curriculum responsiveness. The anatomy of a concept. In H. Griesel (Ed.), *Curriculum responsiveness. Case Studies in higher education* (pp. 1–19). Pretoria: SAUVA.

O'Neill, M. (2009). Forty years on: Education for a culturally diverse Australia. *SA-eDUC Journal Special Edition on Education and Ethnicity, 6*(2), 81–99.

Quinn, L. (2007). *A social realist account of the emergence of a formal academic staff development programme at a small South African university*. Unpublished PhD thesis. Grahamstown: Rhodes University.

Quinn, L. (2012). Understanding resistance: An analysis of discourses in academic staff development. *Studies in Higher Education, 37*(1), 69–83.

Shay, S. (2012). Educational development as a field: Are we there yet? *Higher Education Research and Development, 31*(3), 311–323.

Scott, I. (2009). First year experience as terrain of failure or platform for development. In B. Leibowitz, A. van der Merwe and S. van Schalkwyk (Eds), *Focus on First-Year Success. Perspectives emerging from South Africa and Beyond* (pp. 17–35). Stellenbosch: SUN Press.

South African Department of Education. (1997). *Education White Paper 3: A Programme for the Transformation of Higher Education*. Pretoria, South Africa: South African Department of Education, 24 July.

Sugrue, C., Englund, T., Solbrekke, T.D. and Fossland, T. (2017). Trends in the practices of academic developers: Trajectories of higher education? *Studies in Higher Education, 43*(12), 2336–2353.

Sutherland, K. and Hall, M. (2018). The impact of academic development. *International Journal for Academic Development, 23*(2), 69–71.

Taylor, L.K. (2005). Academic development as institutional leadership: An interplay of person, role, strategy and institution. *International Journal for Academic Development, 10*(1), 31–46.

Trow, M. (1973). *Problems in the transition from elite to mass higher education*. Berkeley, CA: Carnegie Commission on Higher Education.

Vilakazi, H. and Tema, B. (1985). White universities and the black revolution. *ASPects: Journal of the Academic Support Programmes at the University of Cape Town, the University of Natal, Rhodes University and the University of the Witwatersrand, 6*, 18–40.

Volbrecht, T. and Boughey, C. (2004). Curriculum responsiveness from the margins? A reappraisal of Academic Development in South Africa. In H. Griesel (Ed.), *Curriculum responsiveness. Case Studies in higher education* (pp. 57–79). Pretoria: SAUVA.

Vorster, J. and Quinn, L. (2015). Towards shaping the field: Theorising the knowledge in a formal course for academic developers in Higher Education. *Higher Education Research and Development, 34*(5), 1031–1044.

INDEX

Page numbers in **bold** denote tables, those in *italics* denote figures.

4-K model 235; *see also* discursive relations; ontic relations

academic development (AD), and programme renewal 4, 13, 220–36; staff development 145–61
Adendorff, H. 13, 237–54
Airey, J. 56–7
Archer, M. 260, 265
assessment: and academic developers 255–71; assessment forms 55–75; misalignments in chemistry 76–89
Autonomy 7–9, *8*, 245, 246, 247, 248, 249, 250, 274–5, 277, 278, 282, 287
autonomy codes 7, 7–9, *8*, *8*, 244, *244*, 245, 247, *250*, 274, 276–7; *see also* exotic codes; introjected codes; projected codes; sovereign codes
autonomy pathways 9, 272–89; *see also* autonomy tours
autonomy plane 275–6, *275*; *see also* one-way trips
autonomy tours 250, *251*; *see also* autonomy pathways

Behari-Leak, K. 251
Bernstein, B. 2, 181, 256, 267, 278
Bitzer, E. 221, 229
Blackie, M. 10–11, 13, 76–89, 176, 237–54
born gazes 224, 240
Bosman, J.P. 12–13, 198–219

Boughey, C. 146, 272, 273
Bourdieu, P. 2
Bruner, J. 23
business studies 21, 105–25, *113*

Calderhead, J. 20
Carvalho, L. 217
Case, J. 12, 162–79
Challis, D. 220
chemistry 76–89; context of the study 80–1; discussion of findings 87–8; results of the study 84, *84*, 86–7, *86*; translation devices: semantic density 82, 84, **85**; translation devices: semantic gravity 81–2, **83**
Chen, R.T.-H. 278
Christie, F. 52
Clarence, S. 12, 145–61
Clegg, S. 272
code clashes 4, 205, 242; blended learning 213, 214, 215–16; programme renewals 232–3; science curriculum decolonization 242
code matches 4; blended learning 205, **212**, 213; programme renewals 233
code shifting 186, 189, 190–1, *190*, 192, 193, *193*, 194–5, 214
communication: science communication 56–7; skills 55, 56, 70–1, **71**
complexity 1, 4, 40, 56, 57, 71–3, 78, 92; combining image and narration; results

and analysis 66–9, *66*, *67*, *68*, *69*; communication of complex ideas 70–1, **71**; results of the complexity analysis 65–6, *65*; sample and analysis 60–5, **61**, **62**, **63**, *64*, **65**; theorizing complexity 60–70

Conana, H. 12, 162–79

condensation 6–7, 60, 71, 78, 148, 166, 258; *see also* semantic density

constellations 11, 56; axiological constellations 112–13, *113*; constellation analysis 96–102, *98*, *101*, *102*; epistemological constellations 90, 91–4, *91*, *92*, *94*; *see also* cosmologies

context-dependence 4, 10, 20, *26*, 31, *32*, 40–1, 57, 78, 129, 166; *see also* semantic gravity

cosmologies 6–7; axiological cosmologies 11, 105, 107, 109–10, 114–15, 121; *see also* constellations

Costandius, E. 221, 229

Crowe, T. 241

cultivated gazes 119, 121, 224, 232, 240, 242

curriculum development 12, 13, 147, 199, 221, 233, 234, 259, 264, 265, 266

Czerniewicz, L. 215, 217

decolonized curricula, science curriculum decolonization 13, 237–54

deconstruction/reconstruction model 114–15

discursive relations 184, 186

doctoral writing 11, 126–41; analysis 132–8, **132**; discussion of findings 13–40; divorce of writing from research practices 126–7; draft text analysis 132–5, *134*; drafting process 127; feedback 127; final text analysis 135–8, *138*; pedagogy 126–7; semantic gravity analysis 129–31, *130*, 139, 140; semantic profile 131, *131*, 140; supervision 127, 128, 139; theoretical framework and methodology 128–32; theorizing process 127–8, 128–9, 136, 138, 139

doctrinal insight 185, *185*, 188–94; *see also* no/knower insight; purist insight; situational insight

Dong, A. 217

Doran, Y.J. 60, 63

Dwyer, P. 121

élite codes 4, 202, 205, **209**, **210**, 213, 214, 215, 227, 232, 239, 242

Elton, L.R.B. 77

engineering education 180–97

Entwistle, A. and N. 77

epistemic plane 184, *185*, 186, 186–7, *187*, 194

epistemic relations; *see also* specialization codes

epistemic relations (ER) 3, *3*, 12, 136–7, 184, 185–6, 202, 203, **204**, 205, **206–7**, 223–5, 225, **226**, *227*, 229, 230, 232; *see also* autonomy codes; exotic codes

epistemic transitions; *see also* social relations (SR)

exotic codes 249, 277, 286–7

explanatory power 158–9, 160, 166, 215, 240

Fang, Z. 57, 60

feedback 154–8, *157*, 269–70

Finkelstein, N.D. 172, 175

Fook, J. 107, 114

framing 25–6, *26*

Fredlund, T. 163

Garuba, H. 252

gazes 13, 90, 94, 99, 100, 101, 102; born gazes 224, 240; cultivated gazes 119, 121, 224, 232, 240, 242; social gazes 224, 230, 240, 242–3; trained gaze 224, 230, 240, 242

Gee, J. 147

Georgiou, H. 10, 55–75

Giltrow, J. 128

Gosling, D. 220

guided preparing 25, *26*

Halliday, M. 63

Hammersmith, J.A. 248

Hammond, M. 131

Heerden, M. van 12, 145–61

Heleta, S. 246, 249

history 99–102, *101*, *102*

Holt, D. 220

Hood, S. 52

Howard, S.K. 7, 9, 222–3, 273–4, 275

Humphrey, S. 31

Illeris, K. 37

insights 193, 194, 189–191; *see also* doctrinal insight; no/knower insight; purist insight; situational insight

introjected codes 247–8, 277, 286; *see also* autonomy codes

Jacobs, C. 13, 147, 220–36

jigsaw reading 43–5

Kamler, B. 139
Kirk, S. 48, 268
Klafki, W. 37
knower codes 4, 137, 202, 205, **209**, **210**, 213, 214, 215, 216, 225, 227, 232, 239, 240, 241, 242; *see also* specialization codes
knowledge codes 4, 202, 205, **209**, **210**, **212**, 213, 214, 215, 216, 225, 232, 233, 235, 239–40, 241
Kohl, P.B. 172, 175

language of description 203, 205, **206–7**, **208**, 209–10, 216, 278
Laurillard, D.M. 77, 201
Lee, A. 127, 139
Legitimation Code Theory (LCT) 1–15, 20, 33, 51, 57, 77–8, 105–6, 128, 140, 145, 163, 181, 184, 222, 223, 234–5, 238, 256, 274; higher education studies, introduction to 1–2; introduction to the theory 2–9; legitimation codes 2–3; *see also* Autonomy; cosmologies; Semantics; Specialization
legitimation codes 2–3; *see also* autonomy codes; semantic codes; specialization codes
Linder, C. 56–7
Luckett, K. 266

Macnaught, L. 10, 19–36, 31
Malcolm, J. 233
Marshall, D. 12, 162–79
Martin, J.R. 121
Maton, K. 2, 7, 9, 27, 30, 46, 60, 63, 78, 93, 108, 121, 122, 166, 202, 217, 222–3, 224, 232, 240, 257, 258, 273–4, 275, 278; *see also* the son and the heir of a shyness that is criminally vulgar
Matthieson, C. 63
Mazur, E. 77
Mbembe, A. 249
McKenna, S. 1–15, 146
modelling 25, *26*, 27–30; self-evaluating 30–1, *31*; sentence starters 29–30, *30*; text annotation 28–9, *29*; text profiling 27–8, *28*, *29*
Morais, A. 267
morality development theory 28
Mtshali, H. 242
Murray, R. 127, 139

Nielsen, W. 10, 55–75
no/knower insight 185, *185*; *see also* doctrinal insight; purist insight; situational insight

ontic relations 184, 186

Palmer, S. 220
Paré, A. 127, 128
praxis 146, 150, 159, 266–7
problem-solving *see* physics teaching, semantics analysis
profiling: semantics 5–6, *6*, 27, 40–2, 131, *131*, 167, 169–73, *169*, *170*, *171*, *172*, 173–5, *173*, *174*, 176–7; text profiling 27–8, *28*, *29*, 131, 138
programme renewals 4; academic developers 227–30; administrative procedures 228–9
projected codes 8, 9, 244, 245, 247, 248–9, 250, 251, 252, 277, 283
prosaic codes 5, 149–50, 156
psychosocial theory 28, *29*
purist insight 184, *185*, 188, 190, 192, 194; *see also* doctrinal insight; no/knower insight; situational insight

Quinn, L. 13, 217, 255–71, 282

rarefied codes 5, 149, 156; *see also* semantic codes
reflection 10, 11; axiological cosmology in business journals 109–10; axiological cosmology in social work essays 114–15; building a constellation of values 112–14, *113*; clusters of axiological meanings in reflective assignments 107–8, *108*; critical reflection 19, 105–25; critical reflection, discussion of findings 119–21; deconstruction/reconstruction model 114–15; distinction between personal and academic reflection 19–20; evaluation 108, 110–12, **111**, **112**, 115–19, 116, **116**, **117**, *117*, *118*, *119*, *120*; legitimation code theory and axiological cosmologies 107; power and powerlessness in social work: revealing disciplinary values 115–19, **116**, **117**, *117*, *118*, **119**, *120*; reasons for inappropriate behaviour: uncovering hidden values 110–12, **111**, **112**; research methods 107–9; review of literature on reflective writing 106–7; student resistance to critical reflection 121
reflective writing in teacher education 19–36; academic reflections in teacher education 20–1; embedded academic literacy 22; findings and discussion

25–32; framing 25–6, *26*; guided preparing 25, *26*, 31–2, *32*; methodology 24–5; modelling 25, *26*, 27–30, *28*, *29*, *30*; research context 21–2; self-evaluating 25, *26*, 30–1, *31*; sentence starters 29–30, *30*; text annotation 28–9, *29*; text profiling 27–8, *27*, *28*; theoretical frameworks 22–4

Reimann, N. 228

relativist codes 4, 202, 205, **209**, 210, **210**, 212, 213, 214, 215, 216, 225, 239; *see also* specialization codes

rhizomatic codes 5, 78, 149, 151, 156; *see also* semantic codes

Rip. A. 252

Rogers, R.R. 19

Rootman-le Grange, I. 10–11

Rootman-le Grange, Ilse 76–89

Ross, G. 23

Rusznyak, L. 11, 90–104

Salmon, G. 201

scaffolding 23, 25, *26*, 32–3, 37, 38, 42–3, 49, 52; framing 25–6, *26*; guided preparing 25, 31–2, *32*; modelling 25, 27–30, *28*, *29*, *30*; self-evaluating 25, 30–1, *31*

Schell, M.S. 109, 111, 114

science curriculum decolonization 13, 237–54; autonomy 243–4, *244*, 245, 246–7, *247*; codes 239–40, *239*; epistemic relations (ER) 240; epistemology 252; exotic codes 249; factors that count as science curricula decolonization 245–6, **245**; gazes 240, 241–3; introjected codes 247–8; knowledge-knower structures 240; legitimation code theory (LCT) 238; polarized discourse on 238–9, 246; projected codes 248–9; social relations (SR) 241; specialization 238, 239, *239*, 241–3; traversing several codes 249–52, *250*, 251

semantic codes 4, 4–5, 5, *5*; *see also* prosaic codes; rarefied codes; rhizomatic codes; worldly codes

semantic density 7, 10–11, 12, 13, 57, 60, 63–4, *64*, **65**, *65*, 66–8, *66*, 70, 71–3, 78–9, 81, 82, 84, **85**, 92–3, 95–6, 147, 148, 152–3, 155–6, 159, 166, 176, 257–8, *258*, 263; and translation devices 82, 84, **85**

semantic flatline 258, 259

semantic flow 30

semantic gravity 10–11, 12, 20, 22, 25, 26, 33, 40–2, 43–4, 45–7, 48, *48*, 51–2, 57, 78–80, 81–2, **83**, 128, 129–31, *130*, 139, 140, 147, 148, 152–3, 155, 159, 166, 176, 259–60, *260*

semantic plane 148–51, *150*, 156–8, *157*

semantic profile 5–6, 27, 40–2, 131, *131*, 140, 167, 169–73, *169*, *170*, *171*, *172*, 173–5, *173*, *174*, 176–7

semantic range 5, 87, 176, *258*, 259

semantic waves 27–8, *27*, *28*, 41–2, *41*, 44, 45, 46–7, *46*, *49*, 51, 147, 148, *149*, 153–4, *154*, 166–7, 173, 213, 260, 263–5, 268

Semantics 4–6, *5*, *6*, 21, 77–8, 78, 80, 147, 159, 160, 257–8, *258*

Shanahan, T. and C. 70

Shay, S. 217

Shum, S. 32

Sigsgaard, A. 10, 37–54

situational insight 185, *185*, 191–4; *see also* doctrinal insight; no/knower insight; purist insight

social gazes 224, 230, 240, 242–3

social relations (SR) 3, *3*, 4, 7, 136–7, 184, 185, 202, 203, **204**, 205, **206–7**, **208**, 223–5, 225, **226**, 227, *227*; gazes 224, 229–30, 232, 235, 240, 241–3; *see also* epistemic relations (ER); specialization codes

social work *see* reflection

sociology 90, 95, 96, 97–9, *98*, 103

Solomon, C.M. 109, 111, 114

sovereign codes 8, 244, 245, 246, 247, 250, 251, 276, 280, 284, 286; *see also* autonomy codes

Specialization 13, 215, 216, 222, 223; academic development (AD) units and programme renewal 222, 223, 225, *227*, 234–5; blended learning 201–3, *202*, 210–11, **210**, *211*, **212**, 213; science curriculum decolonization 238, 239, *239*, 241–3

specialization codes 3–4, *3*, 5, 202, 203, 205, **209**, 210, **210**, **212**, 213, 214, 215, 217, 225, 239–40, *239*

specialization plane 3–4, *3*, 202, *202*, 203, 205, 210–11, *211*, 225, *227*, *239*

STEM education 9, 10, 56, 79, 80, 88, 162, 180–1, 238

Steyn, D. 217

Stierer, B. 257

Strydom, S. 13, 198–219

substantive theory 266

Sugrue, C. 282

systemic functional linguistics (SFL) 23, 57, 60, 63, 108
Szenes, E. 11, 33, 46, 105–25, 108

Taylor, L.K. 272
teaching and learning cycle (TLC) 23, 25
Thomson, P 139
Tilakaratna, N. 11, 33, 46, 105–25
trained gaze 224, 230, 240, 242
translation devices 60, 80, **83**, 87, 139, 167–8; academic development (AD) units and programme renewal **226**; Autonomy 278, **279**; blended learning 203, 205–6, **209**; science curriculum decolonization 240, **245**; for semantic density 82, 84, **85**; for semantic gravity 81–2, 129–31, *130*, *131*
Trow, M. 1

Van Heuvelen, A. 163–4
Volbrecht, T. 272, 273
Vorster, Jo-Anne 13–14, 217, 272–89

Wilmot, K. 1–15, 126–41
Winberg, C. 1–15, 250–1
Winberg, S. 250–1
Winch, C. 257
Wolff, K. 12, 180–97
Wood, D. 23
worldly codes 5, 150, 151, 157; *see also* semantic codes

Young, G. 13, 220–36

Zappavigna, M. 121
Zukas, M. 233